SOUND SPEED MARKER

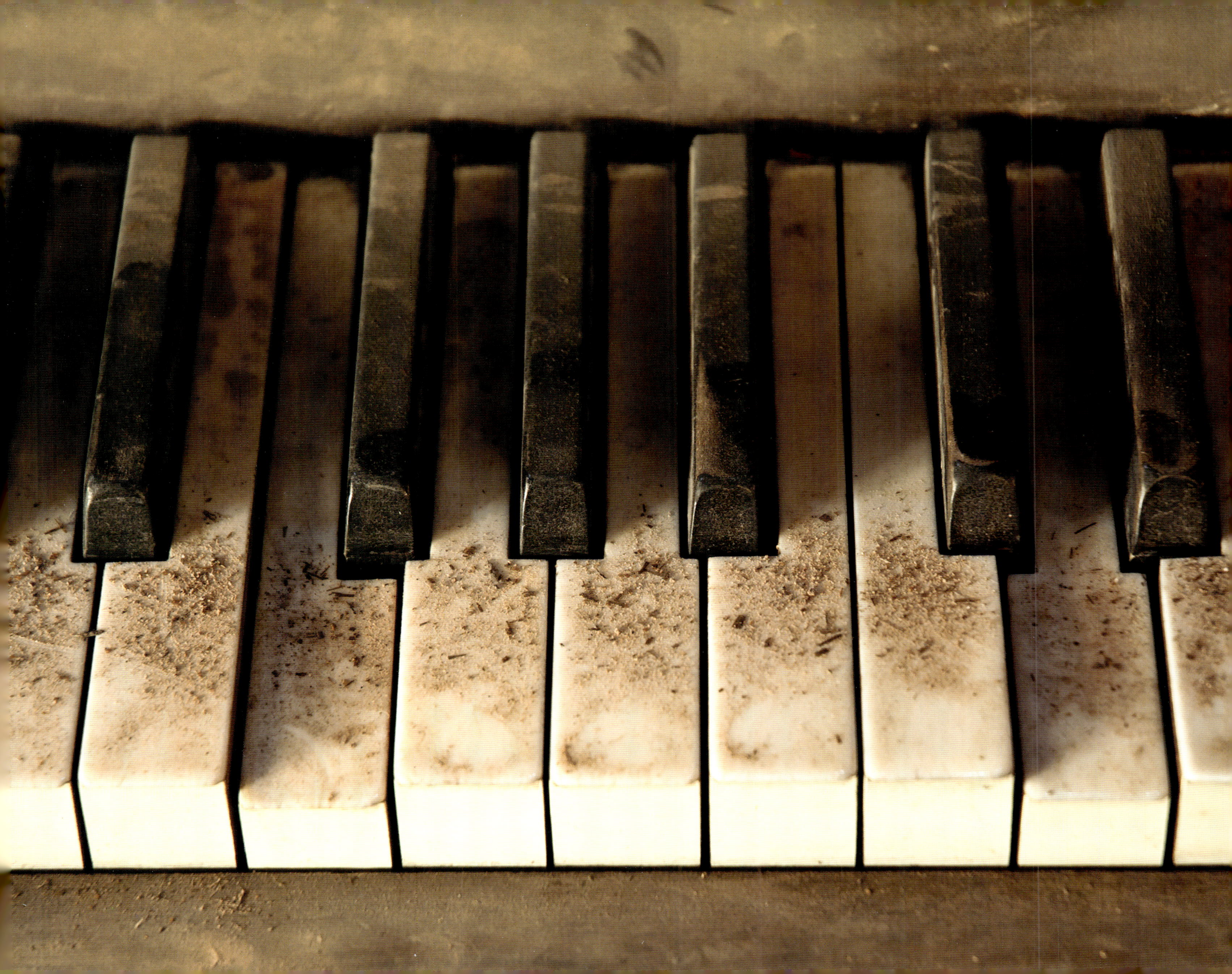

With Contributions by

Fairfax Dorn
Anne Ellegood
Inka Graeve Ingelmann
Jeffrey Kastner
Seán Kissane
Claudia Schmuckli

Edited by Andrea Codrington Lippke

TERESA HUBBARD / ALEXANDER BIRCHLER

SOUND SPEED MARKER

BALLROOM MARFA

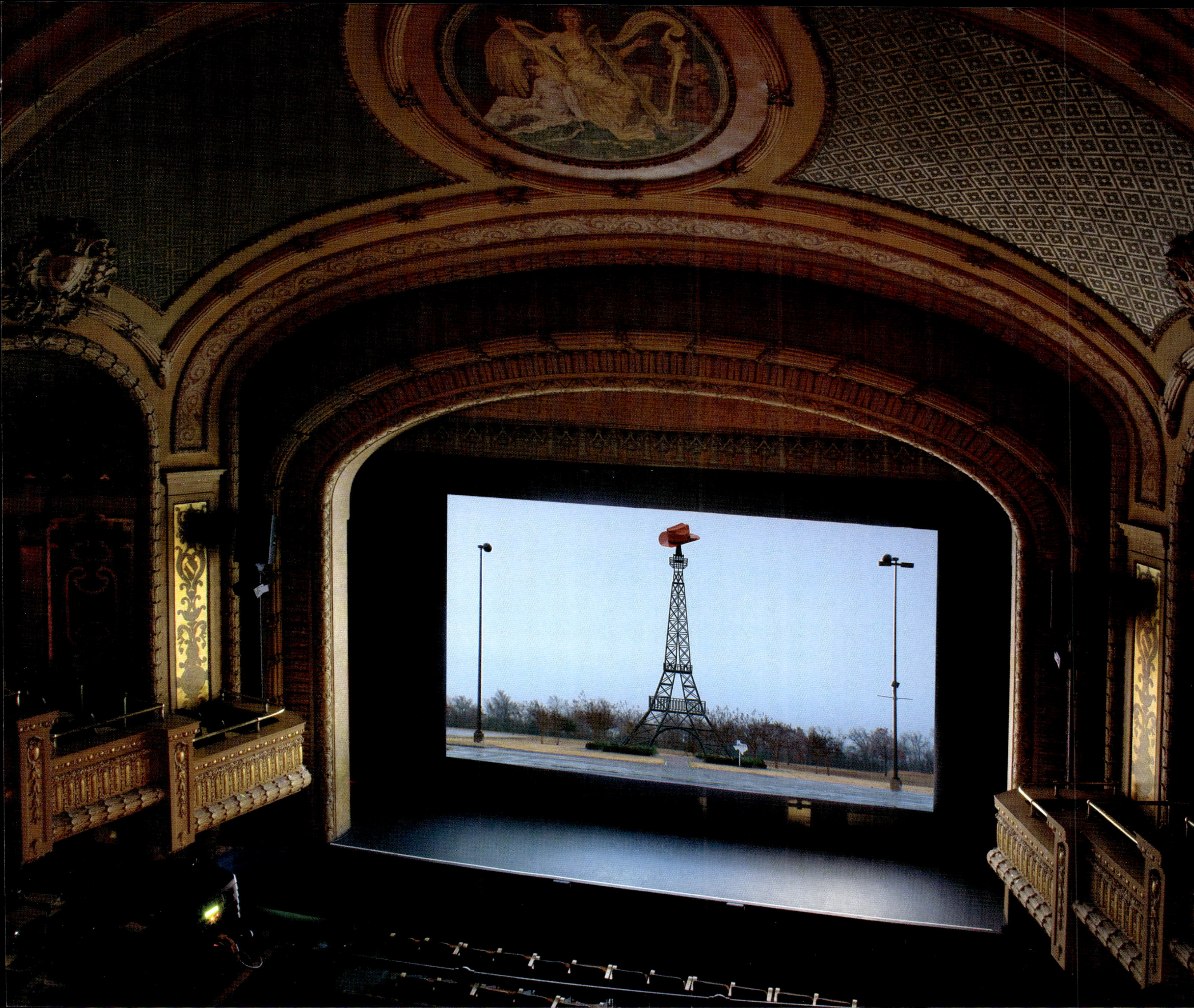

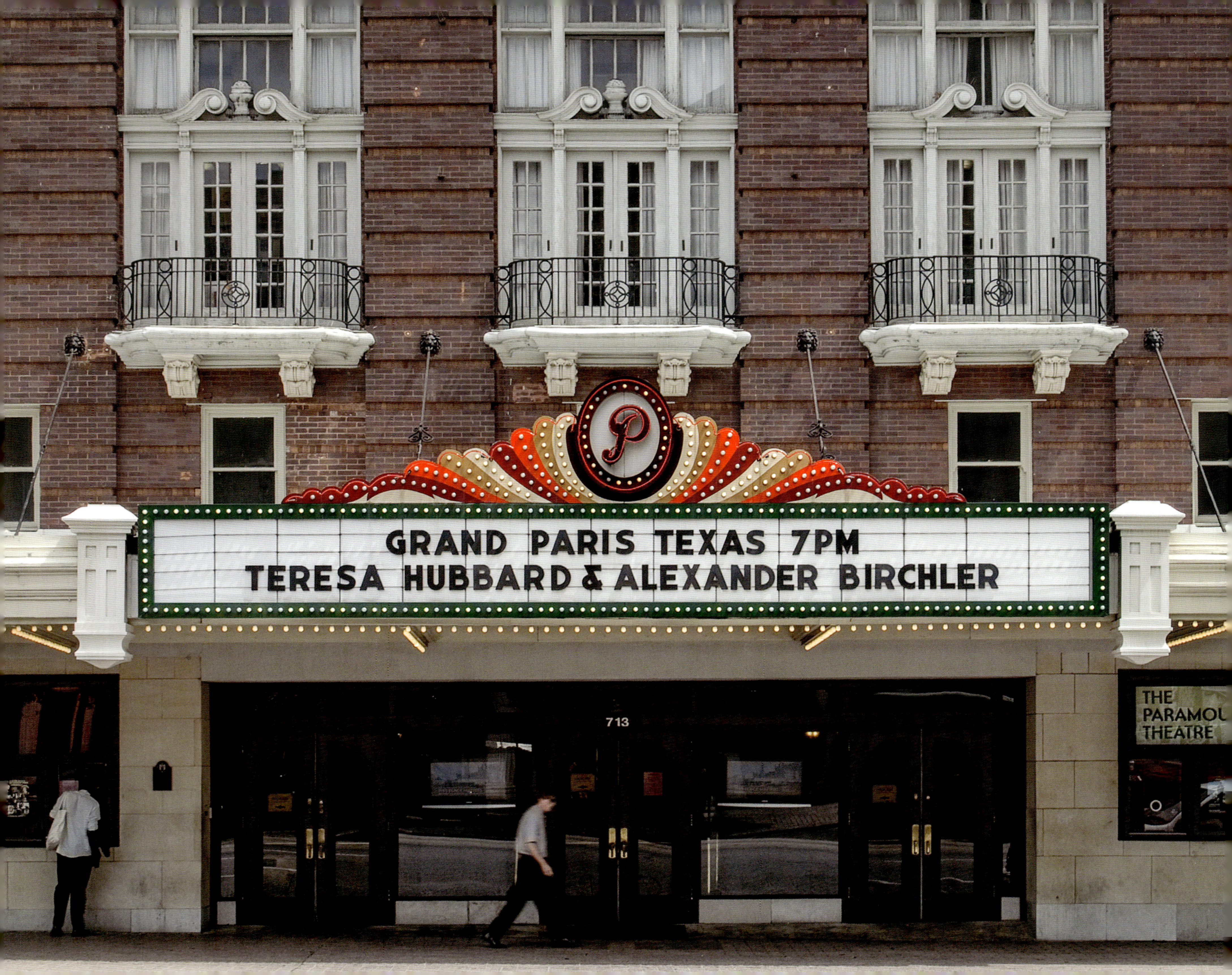
GRAND PARIS TEXAS 7PM
TERESA HUBBARD & ALEXANDER BIRCHLER
713
THE
PARAMOU
THEATRE

Table of Contents

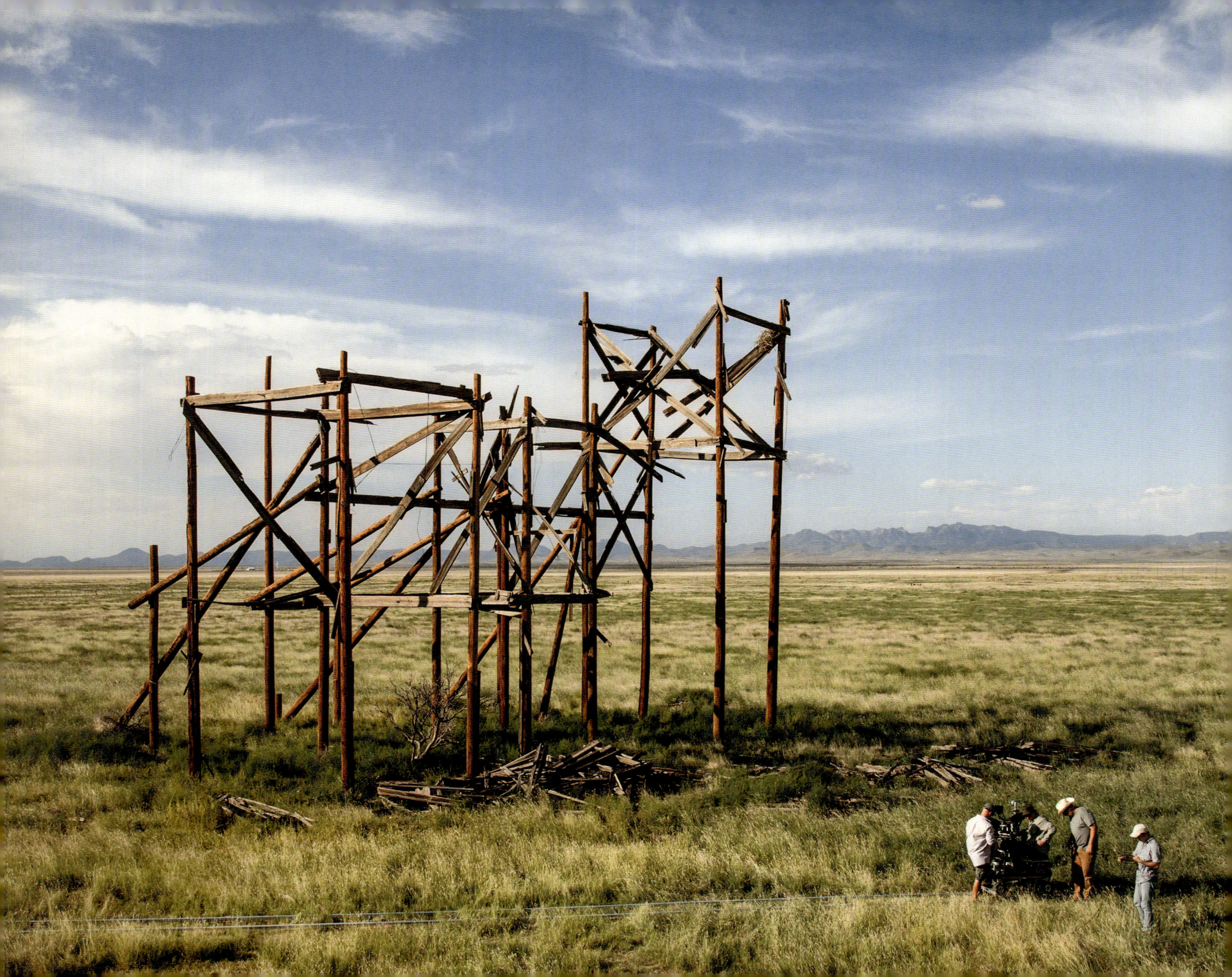

FAIRFAX DORN

Introduction

The 2009 film *Grand Paris Texas* was my introduction to the work of Teresa Hubbard and Alexander Birchler. I was intrigued by the artists' process of filmmaking, as well as their twisting of the documentary format. What begins as a narrative about the disconnect between the actual town of Paris, Texas, and its fictional counterpart in Wim Wenders's film of the same name soon becomes a story that unfolds into multiple threads, including the discovery of a mysterious, partially erased VHS tape of the film available for rent from the local video store.

Grand Paris Texas is the first component in a trilogy of films in which Hubbard/Birchler explore the physical, social and psychological traces that movies leave behind. The second part of the trilogy, *Movie Mountain (Méliès)*, is based on an actual geographic site named Movie Mountain near Sierra Blanca in a mountainous desert landscape close to the border of Texas and Mexico. For the third and final part of their trilogy, Hubbard/Birchler began filming on the site of the remains of the film set from the epic 1956 Warner Bros. film, *Giant*, located near Marfa. From the onset, I was convinced that the artists' method of discovery would reveal something profound in the Far West Texas landscape, unraveling the history of film as they investigated its internal rumors.

Support for the creation of new work has been an essential part of Ballroom Marfa's mission, and since our founding in 2003 we have assisted with more than 30 original new works, including Elmgreen & Dragset's *Prada Marfa* (2005). Hubbard/Birchler's ambitious plan for filming the skeletal remains of the film set on location over a period of more than two years represents the kind of artistic scope that Ballroom Marfa is committed to supporting. It was in the spirit of these prior projects that Ballroom Marfa decided to commission Hubbard/Birchler's *Giant* and to subsequently host the exhibition *Sound Speed Marker*, which served as the premiere of their completed trilogy.

In Hubbard/Birchler's *Giant*, the artists found a focal point in the dilapidated Reata mansion, the iconic Victorian ranch house at the center of the highly acclaimed and controversial 1956 movie. With the generous cooperation of the Evans family, Hubbard/Birchler spent two years visiting the location and filming the ruin in wind, rain, dust, sun and frost. The result is an astonishing montage of intricate field recordings of cycles of life and death; close-up observations of the ruin's creaking joints; panoramic vistas of the surrounding landscape; distant cargo trains and intermittent appearances of a film crew working on site. These scenes are contrasted with a reconstructed

Giant, 2014
Production still

scene in a Warner Bros. Burbank office, where on February 9, 1955, a secretary types up the location contract, four months before the filming of *Giant* begins.

Rather than focus on the highly publicized moment in which Hollywood celebrities Carroll Baker, James Dean, Dennis Hopper, Rock Hudson and Elizabeth Taylor stayed in Marfa during the filming of *Giant*—a story that has been retold many times—Hubbard/Birchler decided to imaginatively excavate the time leading up to the production. Through conversations with the Evans family and research visits to the Warner Bros. Archives at the University of Southern California and the Margaret Herrick Library at the Academy of Motion Picture Arts and Sciences in Los Angeles, Hubbard/Birchler uncovered a vast amount of pre-production documents, including handwritten weather reports, architectural sketches of the proposed set, notes on local flora and fauna and a location manager's notebook detailing a year of traveling throughout Texas searching for the ideal location to construct the film set.

Juxtaposing the moment of typing up the location contract—which outlined the shoot's legal conditions—with the site itself in its decrepit state almost 60 years later, Hubbard/Birchler have created a framing device that profoundly speaks to the obscurity of history and the harsh beauty of the Far West Texas landscape.

Hubbard/Birchler's trilogy serves as a milestone within their far-reaching, distinctive practice that grabbed my attention so emphatically when I first saw *Grand Paris Texas*. The title of the exhibition, *Sound Speed Marker,* on one hand refers to the mundane directions called out on set at the beginning of each take before shooting a scene in a movie. On the other, it breaks down the artists' process and interests into three essential ideas. *Sound* foregrounds the importance of attuned listening; *Speed* points to a meditation on time, a trenchant tracking of the erosion of human memory; and *Marker* simultaneously refers to the traces the artists are searching for and the traces their creative process leaves behind.

Ballroom Marfa's hosting of *Sound Speed Marker* included the premiere of *Giant* alongside the other two trilogy components, *Grand Paris Texas* and *Movie Mountain (Méliès),* as well as a group of related photographic works and *Missing Truffaut,* a new sculpture that was installed in our outdoor courtyard. We are excited that the exhibition is traveling to two partnering museums: the Irish Museum of Modern Art, Dublin, and the Blaffer Art Museum at the University of Houston. I would like to thank Claudia Schmuckli, Director and Chief Curator at the Blaffer Art Museum; Sarah Glennie, Director, and Seán Kissane, Curator, at the Irish Museum of Modern Art for their collaboration and shared institutional vision to host this important exhibition. I would also like to acknowledge our main exhibition lenders, the Museum of Fine Arts, Houston, and the Modern Art Museum of Fort Worth.

On the occasion of *Sound Speed Marker,* Hubbard/Birchler and Ballroom Marfa have collaborated on a publication documenting the creation of this trilogy. We are grateful to Anne Ellegood, Claudia Schmuckli, Seán Kissane and Jeffrey Kastner for their distinctive and highly insightful essays exploring Hubbard/Birchler's practice, and Inka Graeve Ingelmann for her engaging in-depth conversation with the artists. We are also thankful to Andrea Codrington Lippke for overseeing and managing the publication as editor. The artists have worked closely with Pentagram to design a publication that would best represent their work in print form and I would like to thank Julie Savasky and Barrett Fry specifically for their expertise and vision on the project.

We are extremely grateful for the generous exhibition support by the Andy Warhol Foundation for the Visual Arts; L & M Charitable Foundation, Inc.; National Endowment for the Arts; Texas Commission on the Arts; The Moody Foundation; the Aargauer Kuratorium, Switzerland; and The Brown Foundation, Inc., Houston.

I would like to thank Hubbard/Birchler for creating a special photographic edition, *Sunrise Filmset Sunset,* which helped raise additional funds for this ambitious exhibition and catalogue, with underwriting support by Charles Attal, Suzanne Deal Booth, J. Travis Capps, Jr., Molly Kemp, Jeanne and Michael Klein, John Thornton and Melba and Ted Whatley. This exhibition would not have been possible without the profound commitment of the Ballroom Marfa staff, the Evans family and Hubbard/Birchler's installation team, Skye Ashbrook and Bill Haddad. We are indebted to Lora Reynolds, her gallery and her staff for their assistance and support throughout the process of developing this exhibition. Additional support has been provided by Tanya Bonakdar Gallery, New York, and the William and Bettye Nowlin Research Fellowship in Photography at the University of Texas at Austin.

We extend enormous gratitude to Ballroom Marfa's board members for their support. They are the backbone of our organization, enabling the experimental and innovative realization of major works such as *Giant*. Lastly, I am particulary thankful to Teresa Hubbard and Alexander Birchler for their unwavering dedication to Ballroom Marfa and for the fierce curiosity and enthusiasm that went into the creation of this extraordinary exhibition.

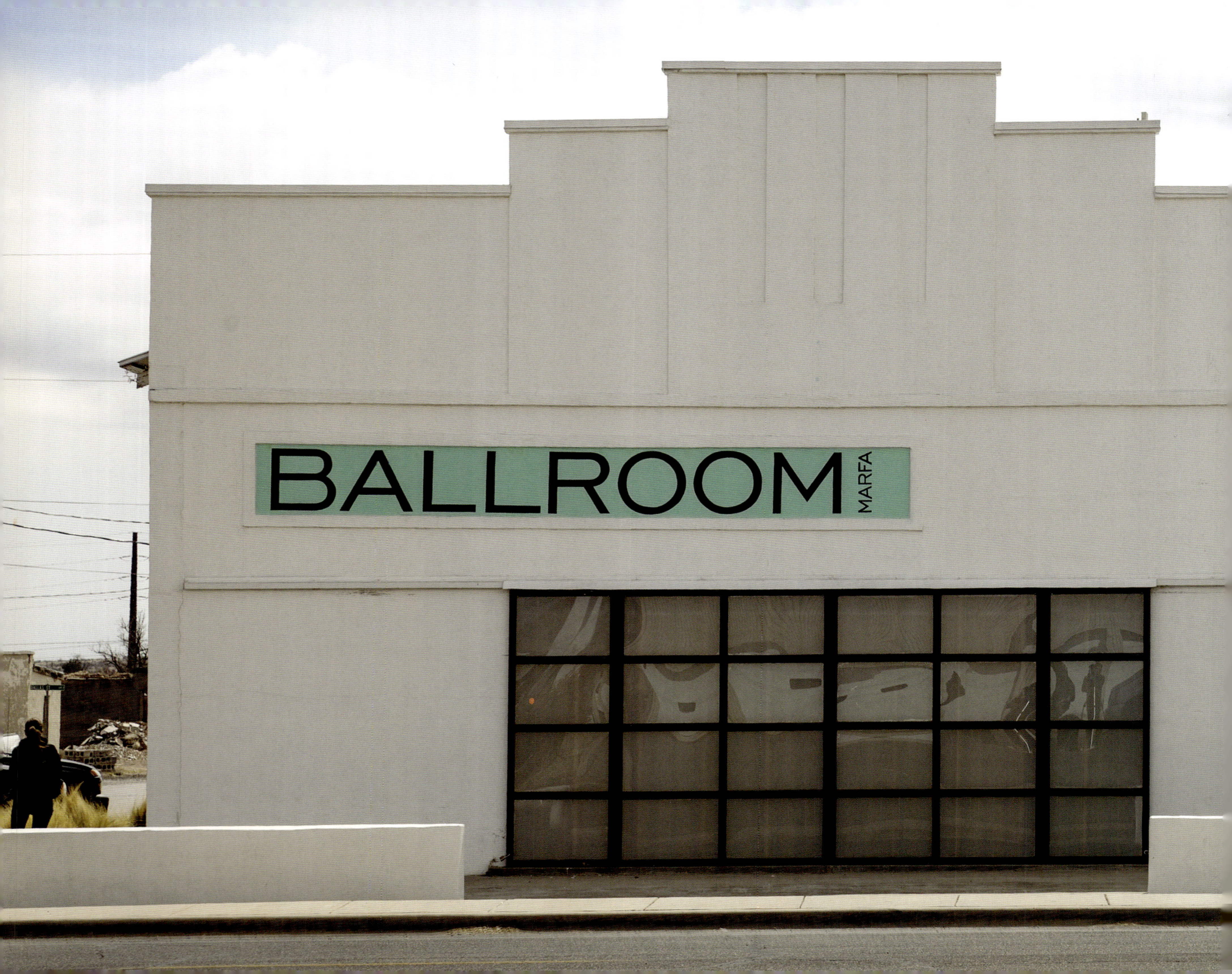
BALLROOM
MARFA

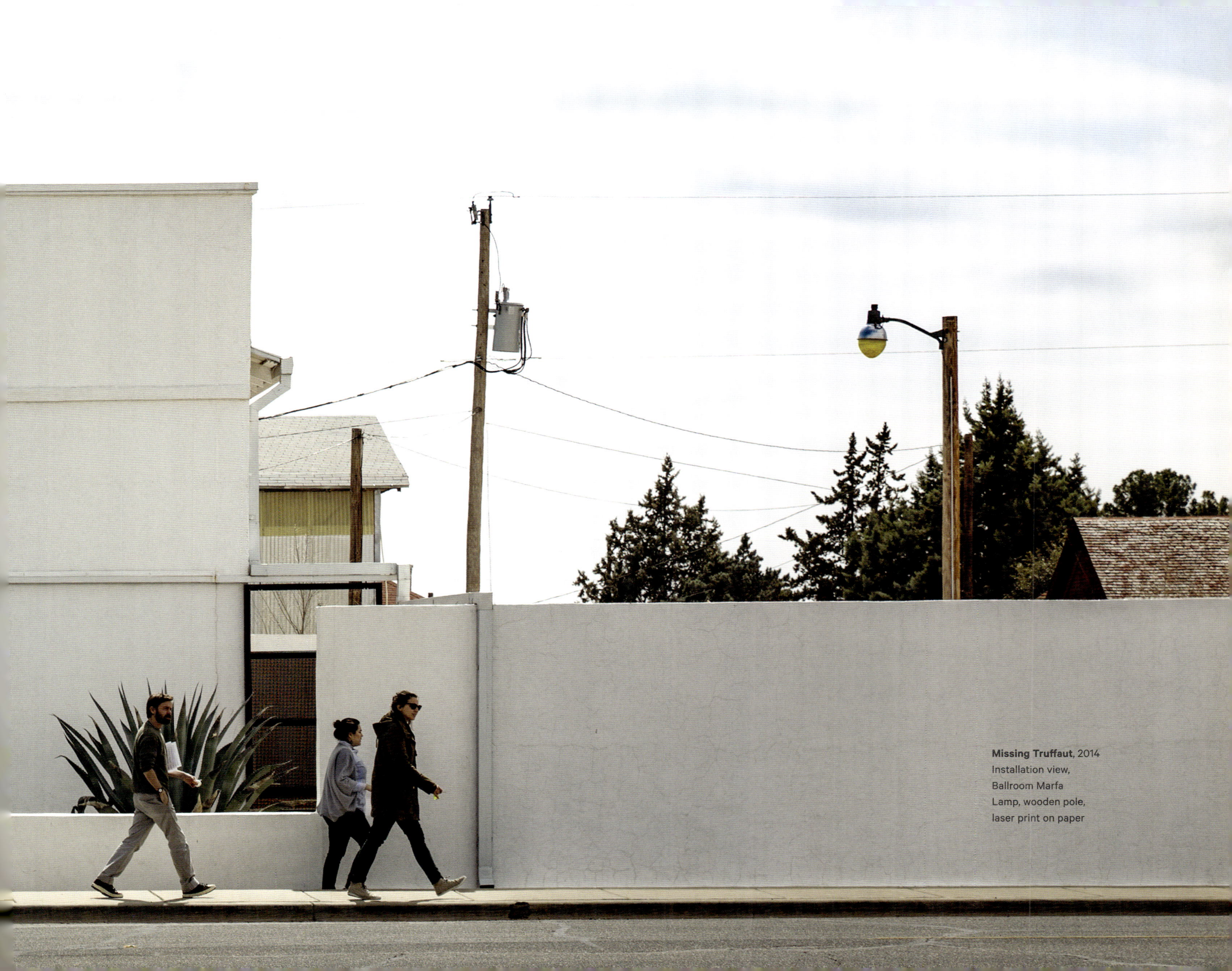

Missing Truffaut, 2014
Installation view,
Ballroom Marfa
Lamp, wooden pole,
laser print on paper

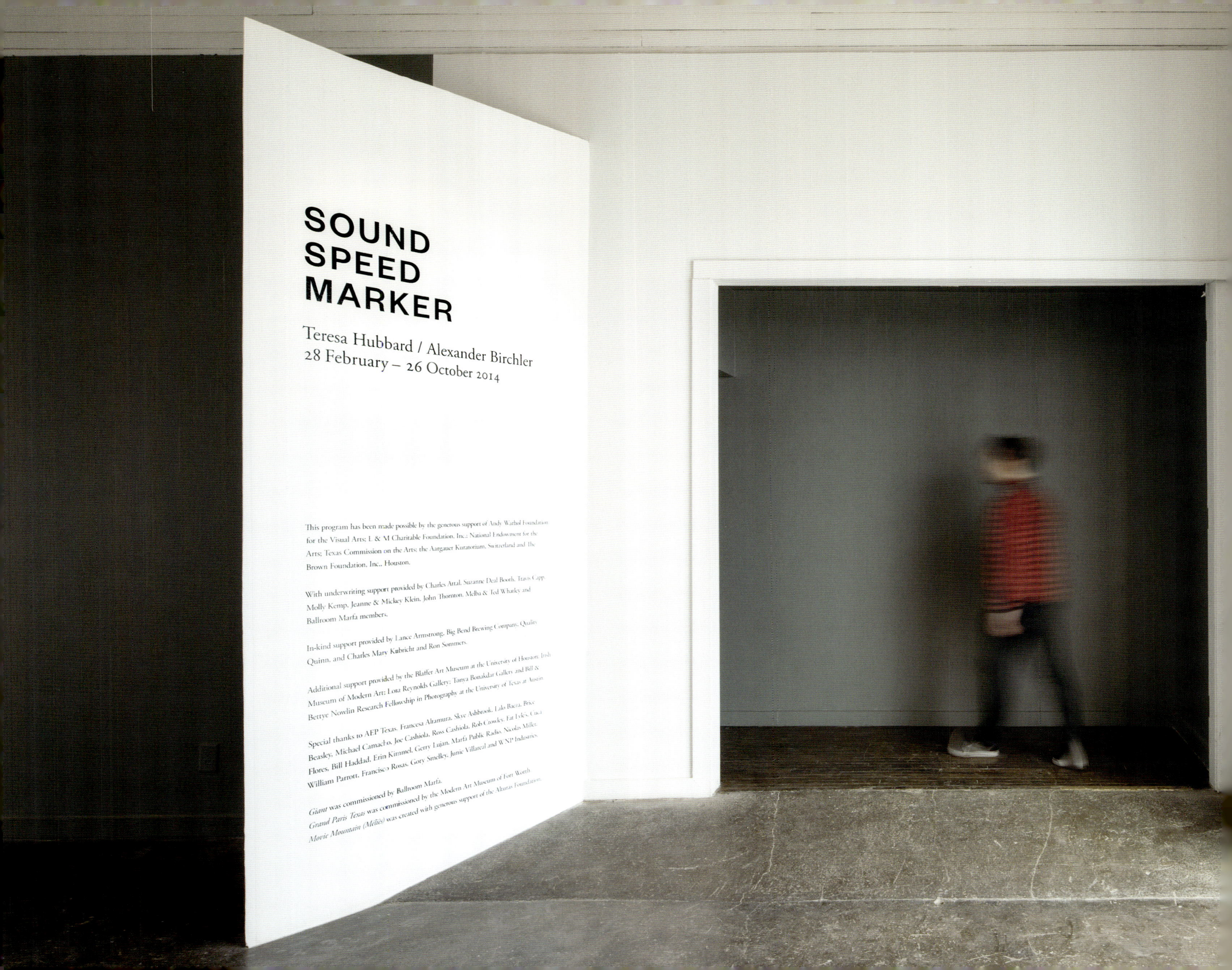
SOUND
SPEED
MARKER
Teresa Hubbard / Alexander Birchler
28 February – 26 October 2014
This program has been made possible by the generous support of Andy Warhol Foundation for the Visual Arts; L & M Charitable Foundation, Inc.; National Endowment for the Arts; Texas Commission on the Arts; the Aargauer Kuratorium, Switzerland and The Brown Foundation, Inc., Houston.
With underwriting support provided by Charles Attal, Suzanne Deal Booth, Travis Capp, Molly Kemp, Jeanne & Mickey Klein, John Thornton, Melba & Ted Whatley and Ballroom Marfa members.
In-kind support provided by Lance Armstrong, Big Bend Brewing Company, Quality Quinn, and Charles Mary Kubricht and Ron Sommers.
Additional support provided by the Blaffer Art Museum at the University of Houston; Irish Museum of Modern Art; Lora Reynolds Gallery; Tanya Bonakdar Gallery and Bill & Bettye Nowlin Research Fellowship in Photography at the University of Texas at Austin.
Special thanks to AEP Texas, Francesa Altamura, Skye Ashbrook, Lalo Baeza, Brice Beasley, Michael Camacho, Joe Cashiola, Ross Cashiola, Rob Crowley, Fat Lyle's, Cuca Flores, Bill Haddad, Erin Kimmel, Gerry Lujan, Marfa Public Radio, Nicolas Miller, William Parrott, Francisco Rosas, Gory Smelley, Junie Villareal and WNP Industries.
Giant was commissioned by Ballroom Marfa.
Grand Paris Texas was commissioned by the Modern Art Museum of Fort Worth.
Movie Mountain (Méliès) was created with generous support of the Alturas Foundation.

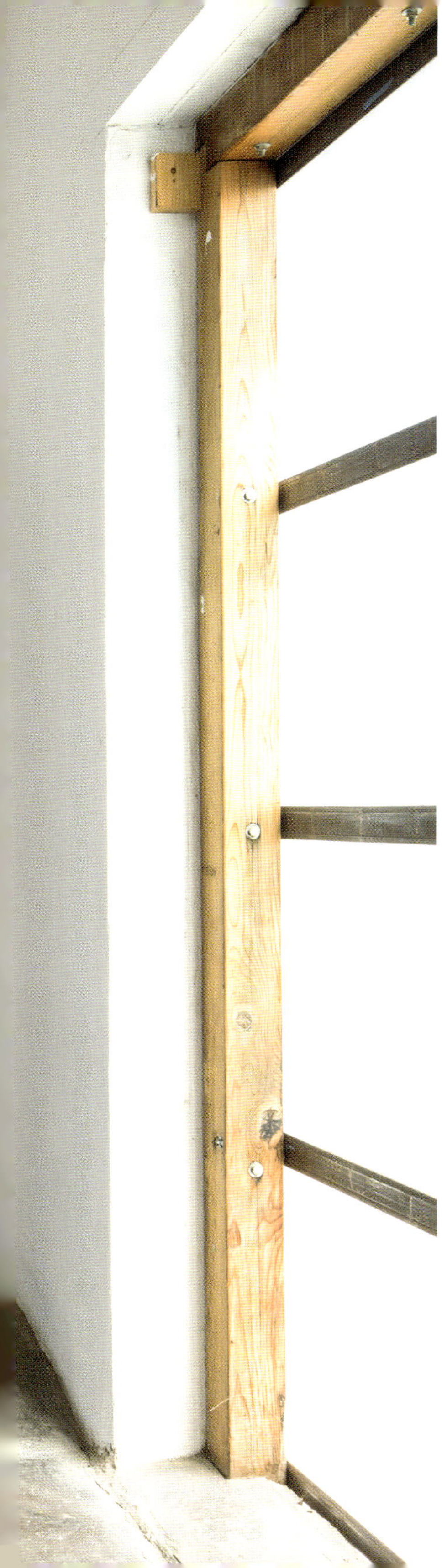

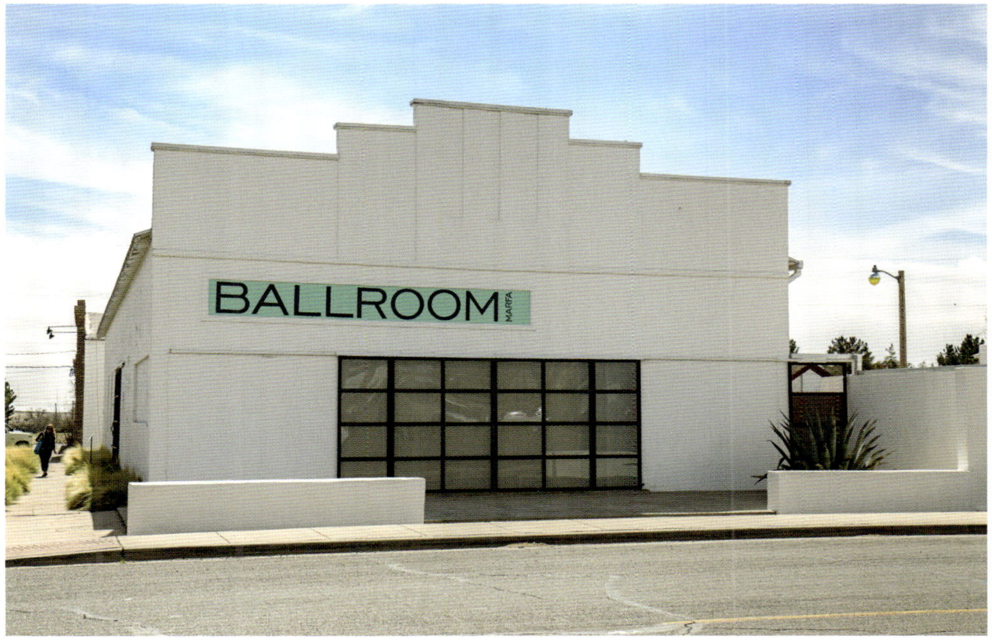

OPPOSITE:
Sound Speed Marker,
Exhibition view,
Ballroom Marfa

ABOVE:
Missing Truffaut, 2014
Installation view,
Ballroom Marfa
Lamp, wooden pole
laser print on paper

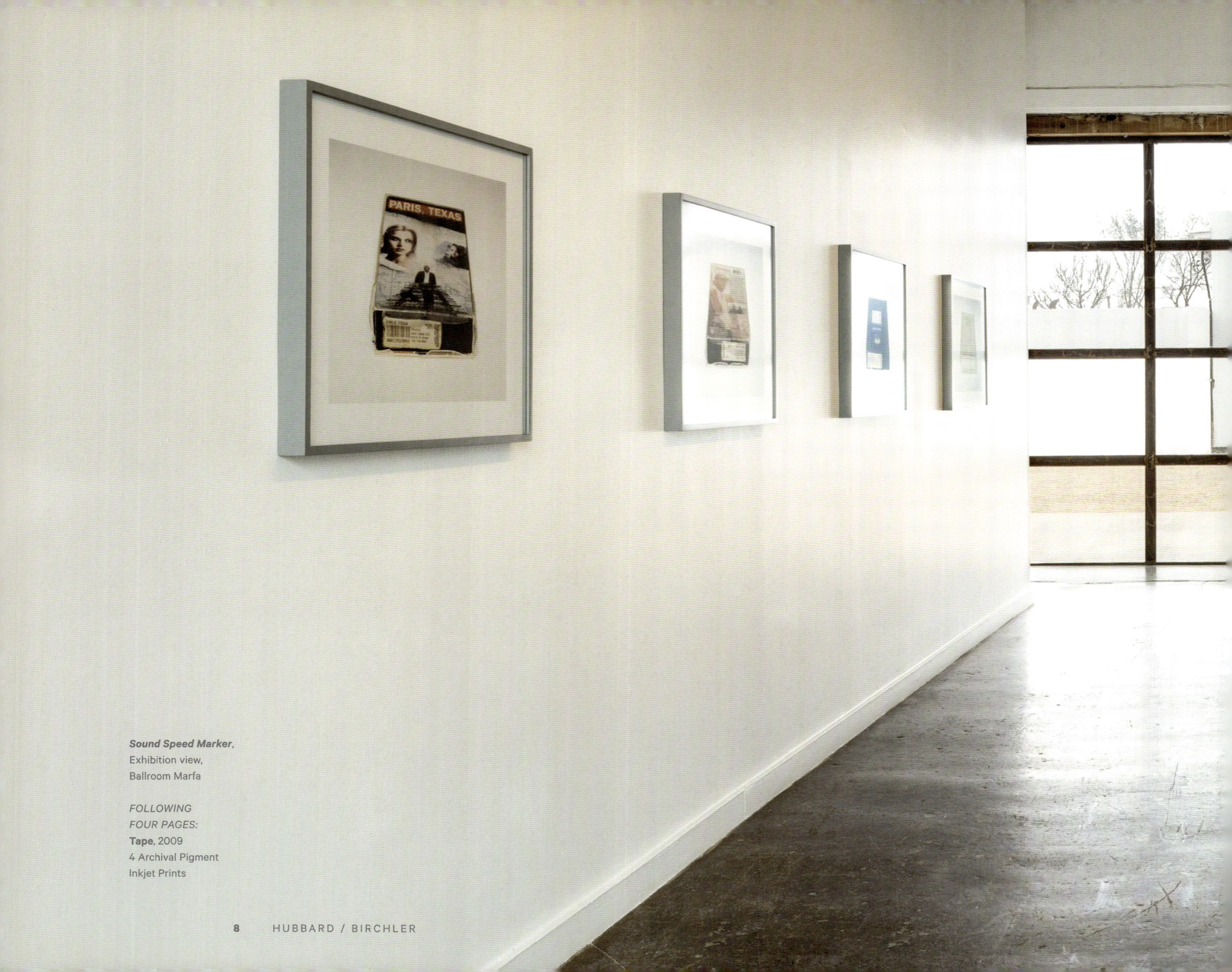

Sound Speed Marker,
Exhibition view,
Ballroom Marfa

FOLLOWING FOUR PAGES:
Tape, 2009
4 Archival Pigment Inkjet Prints

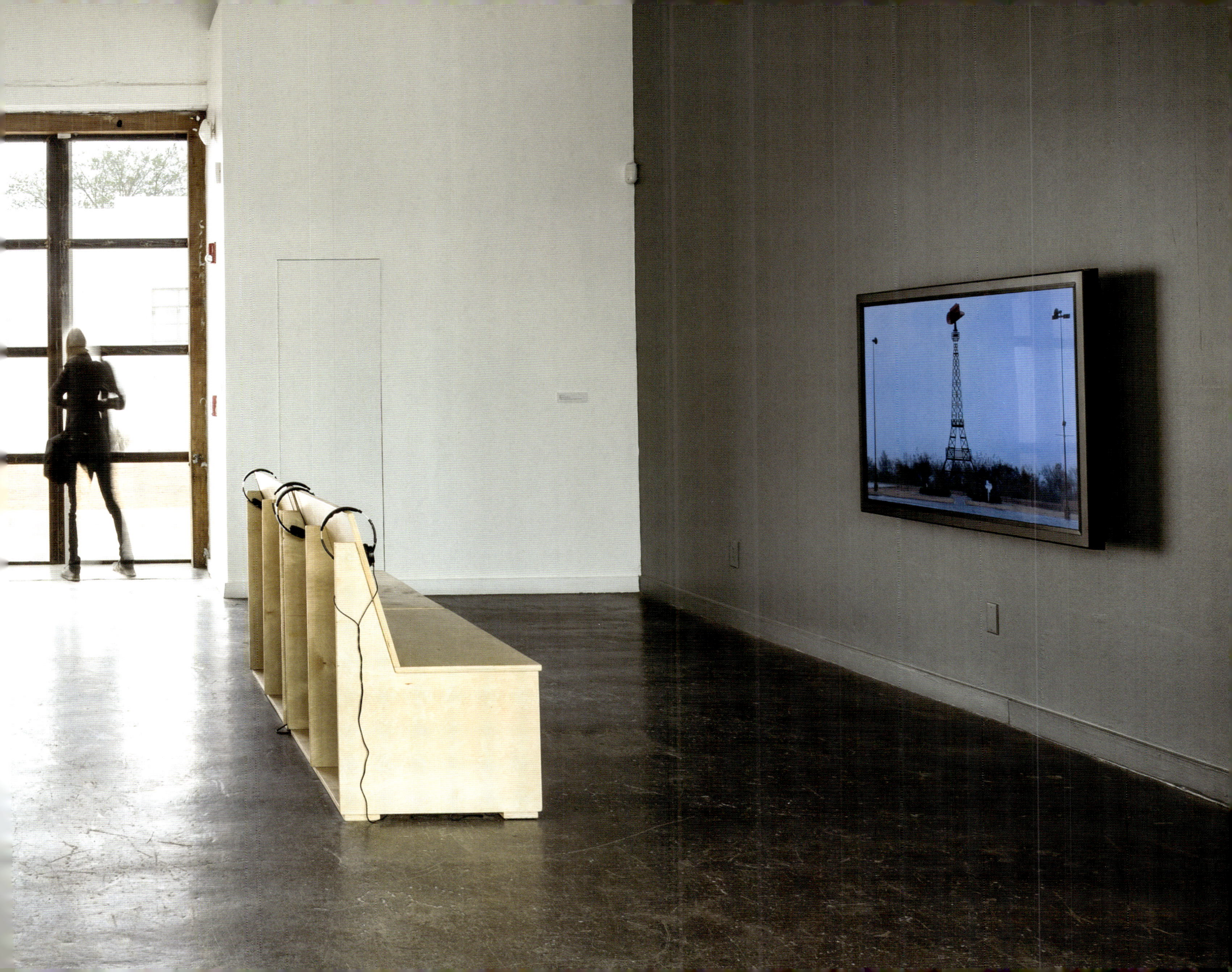

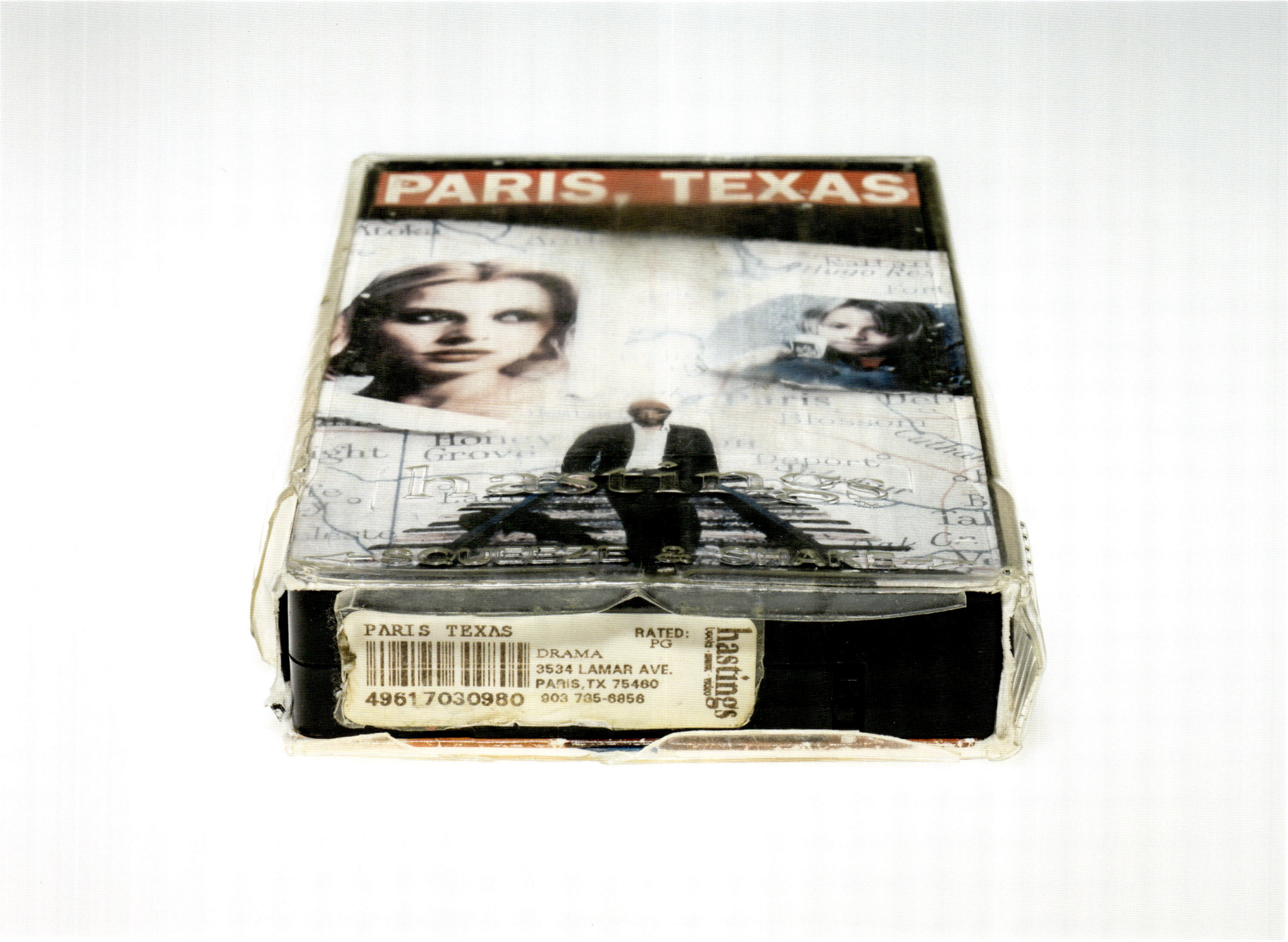
PARIS, TEXAS
hastings
SQUEEZE & SHAKE
PARIS TEXAS
RATED: PG
DRAMA
3534 LAMAR AVE.
PARIS,TX 75460
49617030980
903 785-6856
hastings

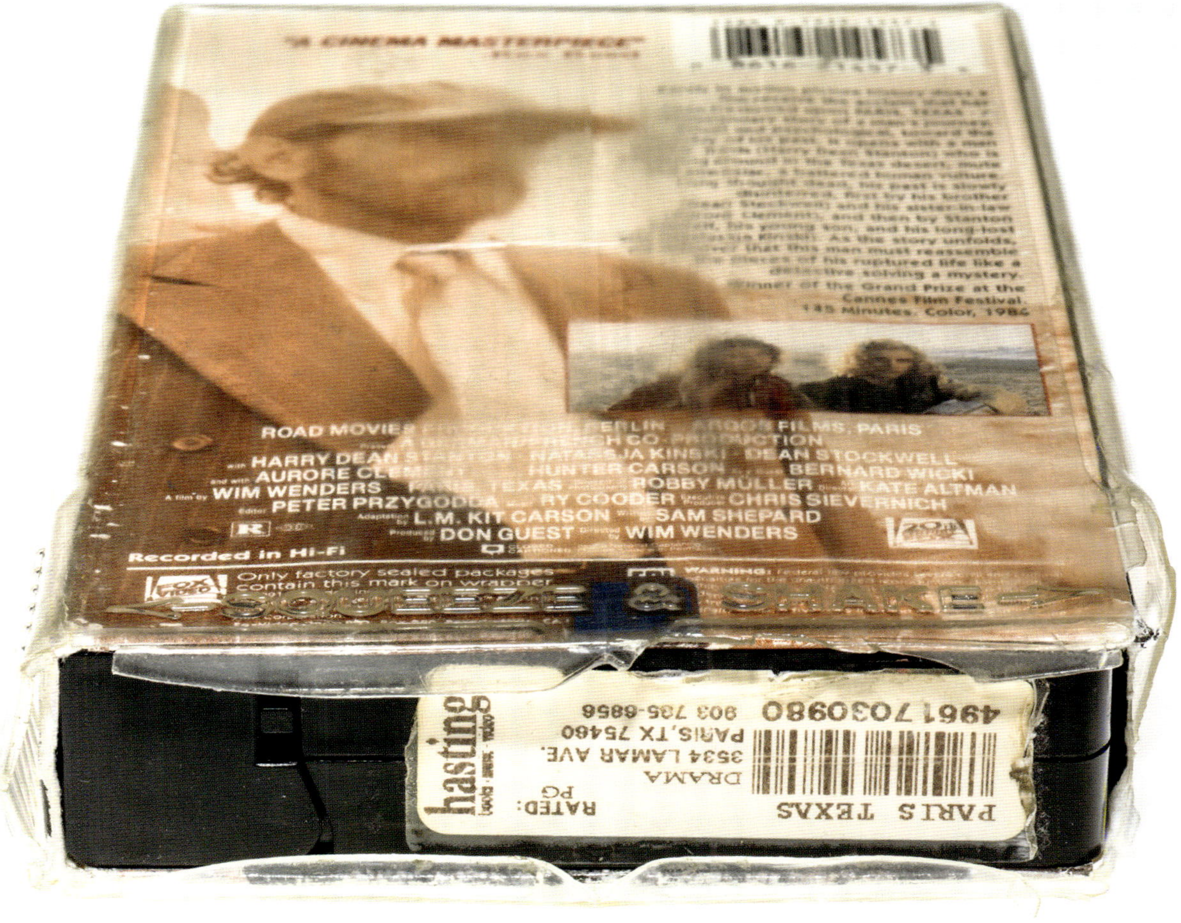
"A CINEMA MASTERPIECE"
Winner of the Grand Prize at the
Cannes Film Festival.
145 Minutes. Color, 1984
ROAD MOVIES
ARGOS FILMS, PARIS
HUNTER CARSON
BERNARD WICKI
DEAN STOCKWELL
WIM WENDERS
ROBBY MÜLLER
KATE ALTMAN
PETER PRZYGODDA
CHRIS SIEVERNICH
L.M. KIT CARSON
SAM SHEPARD
DON GUEST
WIM WENDERS
Recorded in Hi-Fi
Only factory sealed packages
contain this mark on wrapper
PARIS TEXAS
DRAMA
RATED: PG
3534 LAMAR AVE.
PARIS, TX 75460
903 785-6856
4961 7030980
hasting

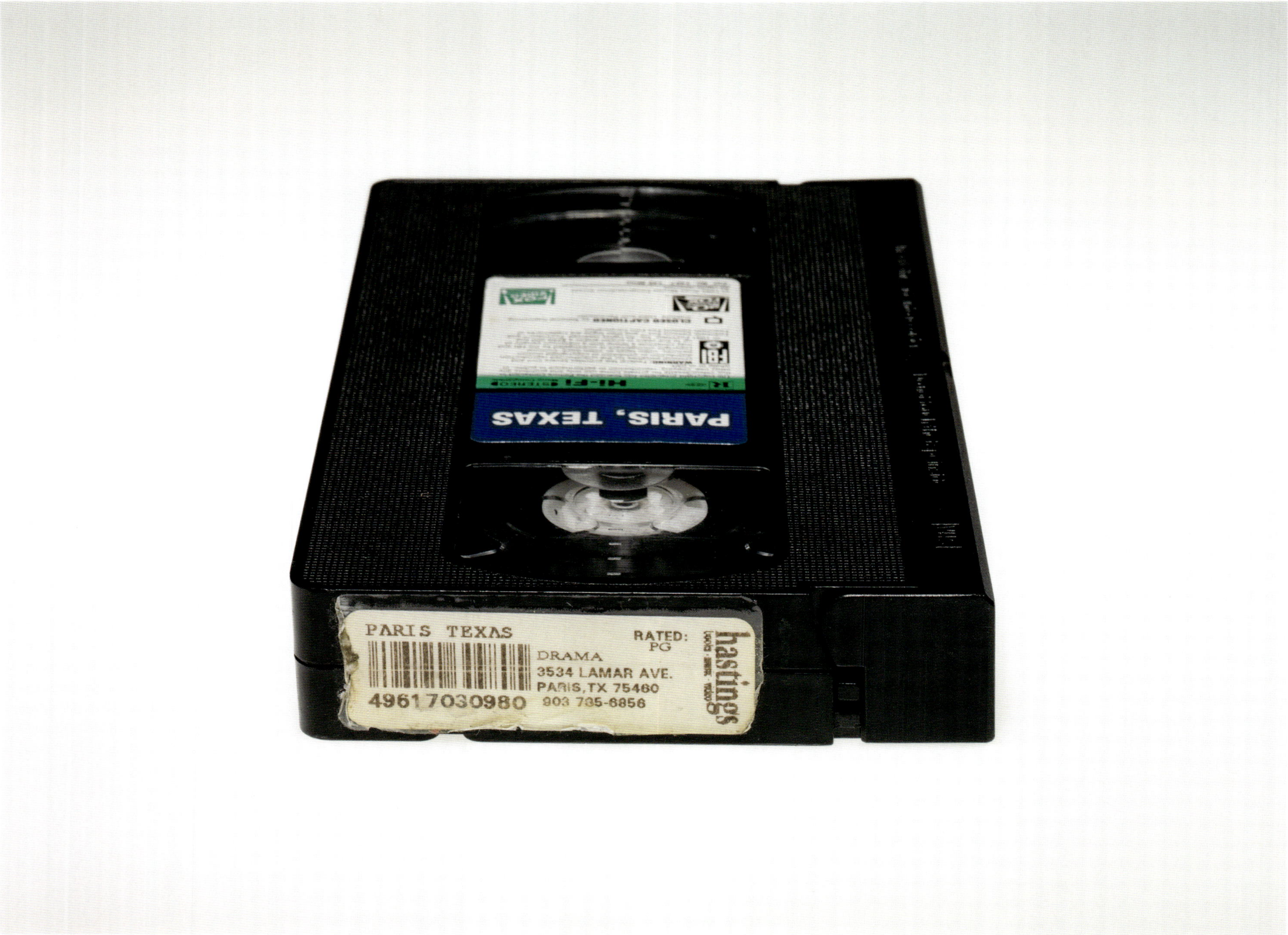
PARIS, TEXAS
PARIS TEXAS
RATED: PG
DRAMA
3534 LAMAR AVE.
PARIS,TX 75460
49617030980
hastings

hastings
SQUEEZE & SHAKE

CLAUDIA SCHMUCKLI

Reeling, Lassoing, Typewriting: Generative Tension and Conceptual Solidarity in Hubbard/Birchler's *Sound Speed Marker*

Sound Speed Marker is a trilogy of filmic works in which cinematically defined sites become the subject of excavation and re-imagination. In a reversal of fate from their passing association with a simple mention as locations in the closing credits, the towns and countrysides of Paris, Sierra Blanca and Ryan, Texas, take center stage in *Grand Paris Texas* (2009), *Movie Mountain (Méliès)* (2011) and *Giant* (2014) as the artists and their crew attentively look and listen to these places and the people who define them.

Grand Paris Texas, the first work in the triad, revolves around an abandoned theater called the Grand in the town of Paris, Texas, whose rise and fall serve as the anchor for residents to reflect on their personal histories with cinema, their remembrances of the Grand and their connections to the 1984 Wim Wenders film that borrowed the town's name as its title. Hubbard/Birchler carefully but insistently explore the bird-infested interior of the theater whose former grandeur, reestablished temporarily by a benefit premiere of the movie's release, is resuscitated by the camera from beneath layers of feathers and debris.

Eiffel Tower, Paris Texas, 2009
Archival Pigment Inkjet Print

With job opportunities mostly defined by the presence of three Fortune 100 Companies and the associated industries they engender, instances to dream in Paris, Texas, appear few and far between. Teenage entertainment is described by Kristy Riffle as a choice between Hastings video store and Wal-Mart or by the Hunt twins as a trip to the mainstream multiplex to see "what sells" or to the mall to rent "real movies." In *Grand Paris Texas,* having a meaningful relationship to cinema—Elric De La Peña is mindful to explain the difference between films and movies as an experience of transformation versus consumption—opens up a world and an imagination that is otherwise fairly limited. Both Toni Clem and Harold Wayne Adams came to their professions as movie critic and projectionist at the Grand through army life. Jack Norman recalls the days of his mother performing as part of the orchestra accompanying the silent films at the Grand and Dorothea Gillies speaks fondly of her days as a candy girl. Allan Hubbard (no relation to the artist) wistfully reminisces about being cast as a nine year old in the 1983 film *Tender Mercies* with Robert Duvall, which afforded him a short-lived career in film never to be repeated after years of unsuccessful auditioning. And lastly, Marcus Roden, director of a funeral home, only too happily draws parallels between orchestrating a funeral and cinematic direction.

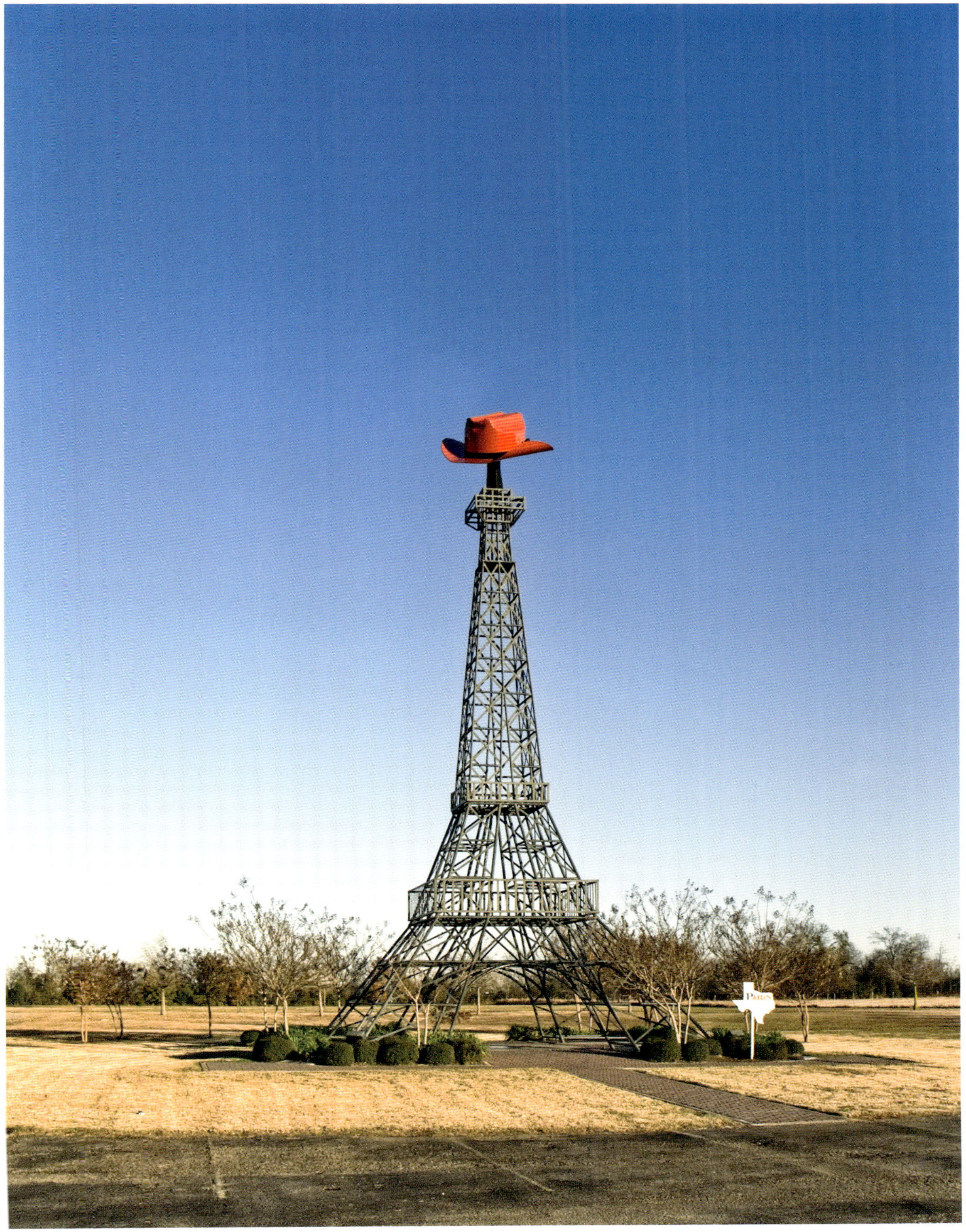
PARIS

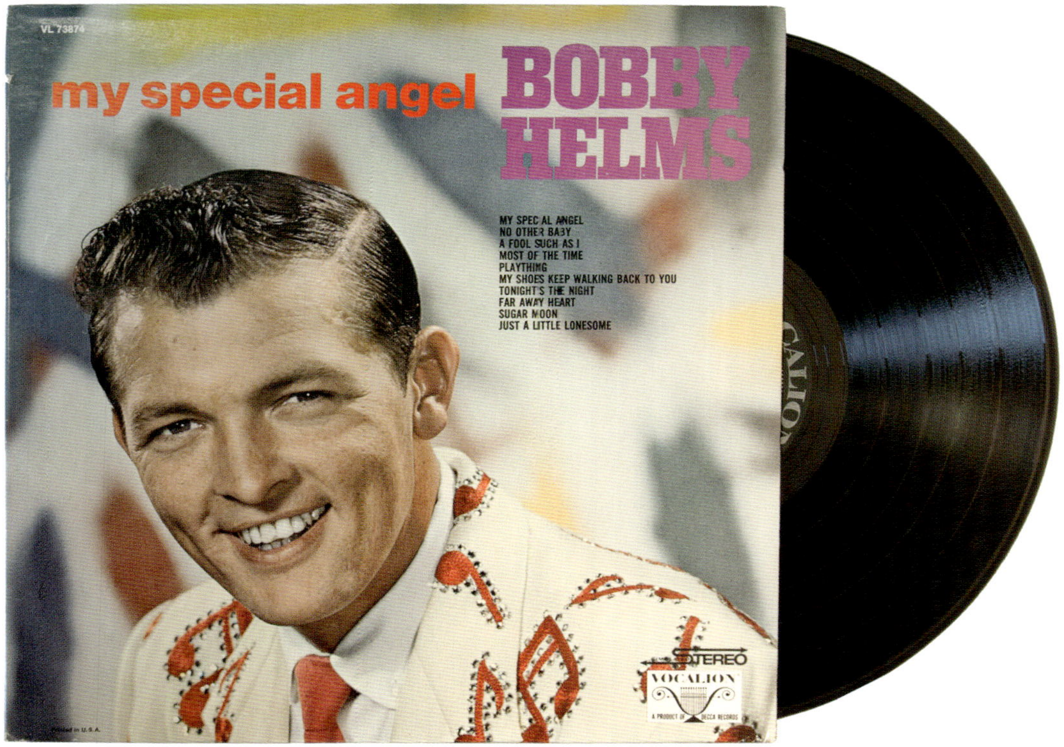

ABOVE:
Bobby Helms's 1969 record *My Special Angel* includes the Jimmy Duncan song of the same name, first released in 1957

OPPOSITE TOP:
Lobby card from the 1983 film *Tender Mercies* with Robert Duvall and Allan Hubbard

OPPOSITE BOTTOM:
Grand Paris Texas, 2009, Video still, Allan Hubbard playing guitar

In this context, the story of the Grand and the people in Paris whose lives have been affected by cinema emerges as an aspirational narrative. Beginning with the mention of *Superman* as the most successful movie ever played there, metaphors of flying abound: flocks of birds surging within and through the roof of the building, the construction of dollies and cranes that culminate in the exuberant flight of the camera up, down and alongside the theater's façade, and the tune "My Special Angel" by the Grand's onetime projectionist and owner Jimmy Duncan released in its heyday (1957) all signal that the story of the theater is far from over. As we learn in the closing credits, a capital campaign is under way to secure its renovation. The sense of uplift even extends to the town's landmark, a downsized copy of the Eiffel Tower capped with a metallic cowboy hat—lest anyone confuse Paris, Texas, with Paris, France, as Walt—Travis's brother in the Wenders movie—first does upon learning of his desired destination. Flying high and topping this iconic symbol of industrialization like a crown, the cowboy hat sculpture invokes the settlement of the town as a story of individual heroism that feeds off the idea of the cowboy as a romantic hero who makes his own rules.

This idea, of course, also applies to the lead character of the Wenders movie, to whom Paris, Texas, represents an ideal for a life yet to be realized. And so it never appears in the actual film to the great consternation of the many Paris, Texas, residents who saw it at the Grand in 1984 or rented it from Hastings up until 2007, when Hubbard/Birchler bought the only VHS copy available. The artists rushed to acquire it after learning that the ending had been recorded over. The sad irony of denying the Paris residents who rented the movie the satisfaction of knowing how the film ends is heightened by the specific nature of the recording, namely a silent Western that turned out to be King Baggot's 1925 classic *Tumbleweeds*. Apart from being a classic natural sight along West Texas roads, "tumbleweed" is also slang for a drifter, and thus this accident of the recording that was completely out of the artists' control accrues meaning not only by referring back to the drifting beginnings of Travis's character but also by effectively making him part of the landscape that embodies his hopes and dreams.

Even though the filmmakers had not yet stumbled upon the subject of their next film, *Movie Mountain (Méliès)*, the discovery of *Tumbleweeds* at the end of *Grand Paris Texas* has a prescient quality. Hubbard/Birchler's research in and around Sierra Blanca after they first followed rumors about a place nearby called Movie Mountain sent them straight back to the beginning of the twentieth century and the era of the silent Western, which was at its peak when Movie Mountain became the anonymous hero of Sierra Blanca and the stuff of now nearly forgotten lore.

From the outset it is clear that the details of the story behind Movie Mountain are shaky. As the film opens, interviewee Tom Ellison confesses, "I've been to Movie Mountain many a time, on top of it, all around it, but I never knew it was called Movie Mountain." This sets the tone for the staging of a circuitous oral history grounded in second- and third-generation recollection and speculation about events whose only lasting impact was an aggrandizing name given to an otherwise negligible bump in the landscape where an unknown or forgotten B-Western was filmed around 1911. The camera, when directed at the unspectacular peak, searchingly moves around it—first from afar, then drawing in tighter until a group of cattle herders on truck and horseback lead the eye closer.

The interview thread with residents of Sierra Blanca mimics the zooming logic of the camera work as people with different degrees of awareness and relations to the making of the movie gradually reveal their knowledge about the mountain's identity-defining event. Frequent sequences of long-distance trains serve as an additional framing device: shot close up, the passing cars read like the individual frames of actual film reel unfolding in front of the camera. As if to underline the ultimate insignificance of the site under discussion, the trains never stop in Sierra Blanca. Unlike in the 1910s, the town no longer has a station on the East-West passage at the core of the film that was supposedly shot there when it was still a borderline marker of a new frontier.

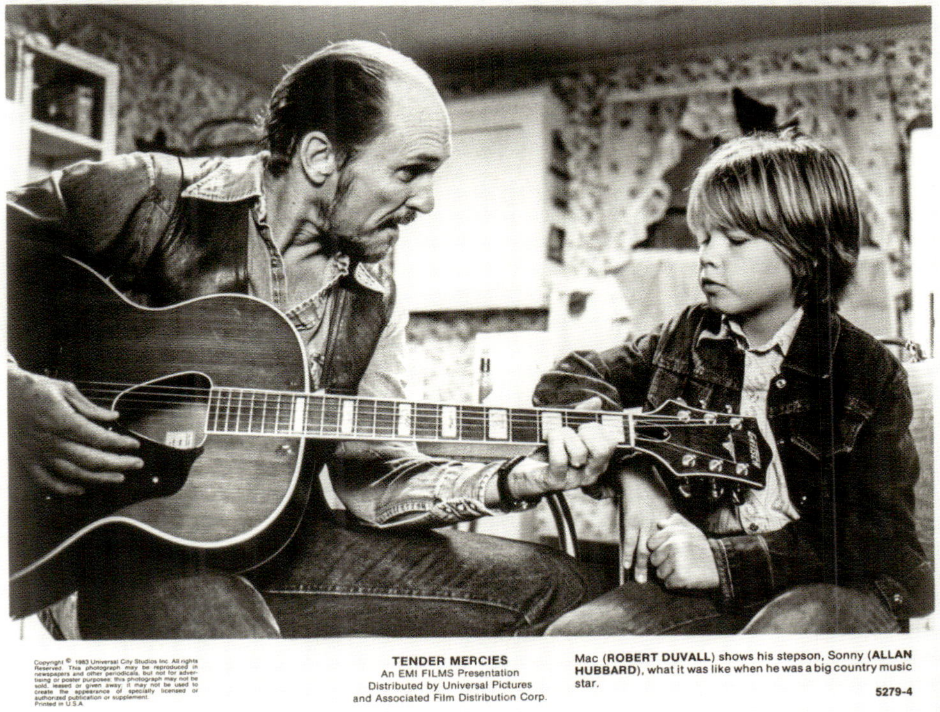

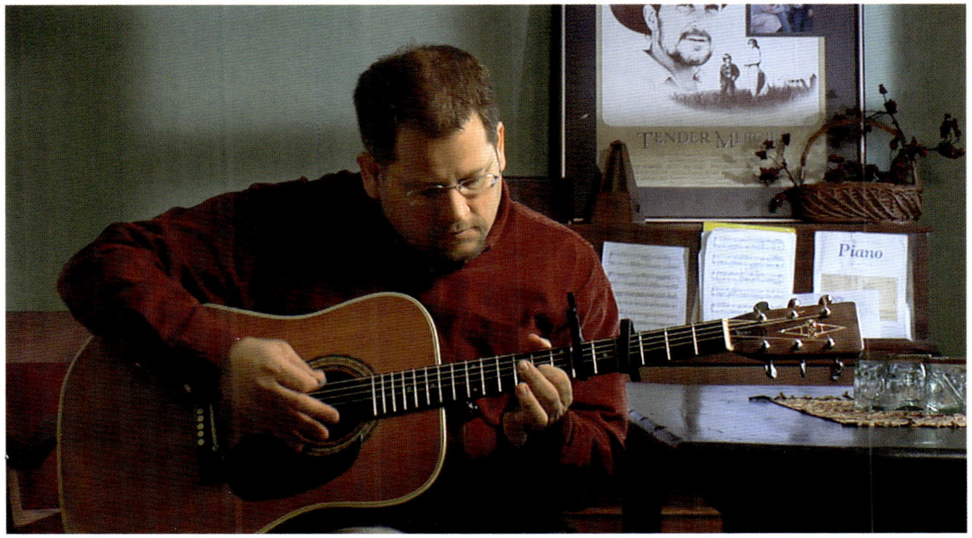

Hastings

HASTINGS ENTERTAINMENT # 9617
3518 LAMAR AVE.
PARIS, TX 75460
903-785-6856 12/03/2007 14:27
MICHAEL S. TRANS# 3127263 TERM# 2

1 98 PARIS TEXAS	2.99
SUBTOTAL	$2.99
TAX	$0.25
TOTAL	$3.24
CASH	$10.00
CHANGE DUE	$6.76

Receipt ID: 072842383743
ONE WEEK
Movie and Game Rentals
Up to $2 Movie Early Return Credits

SELL us your USED
Books, CDs, DVDs, Games and Systems

New and Used Entertainment at
gohastings.com

*** CUSTOMER COPY ***

Receipt from the purchase of *Paris, Texas*, VHS tape at the Hastings video store, in Paris, Texas, 2007

OPPOSITE:
No Room To Answer, Exhibition view, Aargauer Kunsthaus, Aarau, Production Archive in foreground; **Tape**, 2009, and **Eiffel Tower, Paris Texas**, 2009, in background

While Ellison tells a speculative and slightly dismissive story about the movie being the only reason for the mountain to have made it onto a map, Kit Bramblett actually learned of it as a young man wooing his future wife, whose father owned a ranch nearby. David Armstrong found out about Movie Mountain as a five year old and has dreamt about being in the movie business ever since. Tom Neely was completely unaware of the film until this interview but speculates on it having been a shoot-'em-up movie, which is subsequently confirmed by John Elder, whose grandfather witnessed the production and implies that someone famous was involved. Christina Ramirez, whose Apache ancestors came to Sierra Blanca across the Mexican Border to escape the 1910 revolution, recalls stories of her uncle José Sanchez and some of his friends being recruited as riders; since none of them spoke English at the time, details of the movie, especially its name, escape her. Gary Jennings recalls his grandfather Charlie Norton being in the movie as a roper because he was "a real cowboy, not the kind you see in the movies" and "a great roper and hard-working cattleman who loved his horses more than people."

In the absence of a concrete cinematic reference, the artists introduce a yet-to-be-made movie scripted by David Armstrong, a present-day cowboy with disappointed Hollywood ambitions. Unwilling to give up the right to act in his own film when presented with the opportunity to sell his script to a production company, he and his fictional alter ego, "Shot," remain eternally trapped in an existence they are trying to overcome. Ironically, it is through such reflections on his frustrated attempts to become a star that Armstrong finally assumes a lead role in a film, albeit not the kind that he imagined. Hubbard/Birchler are careful, however, to treat his broken dreams with delicacy and thus we respectfully follow

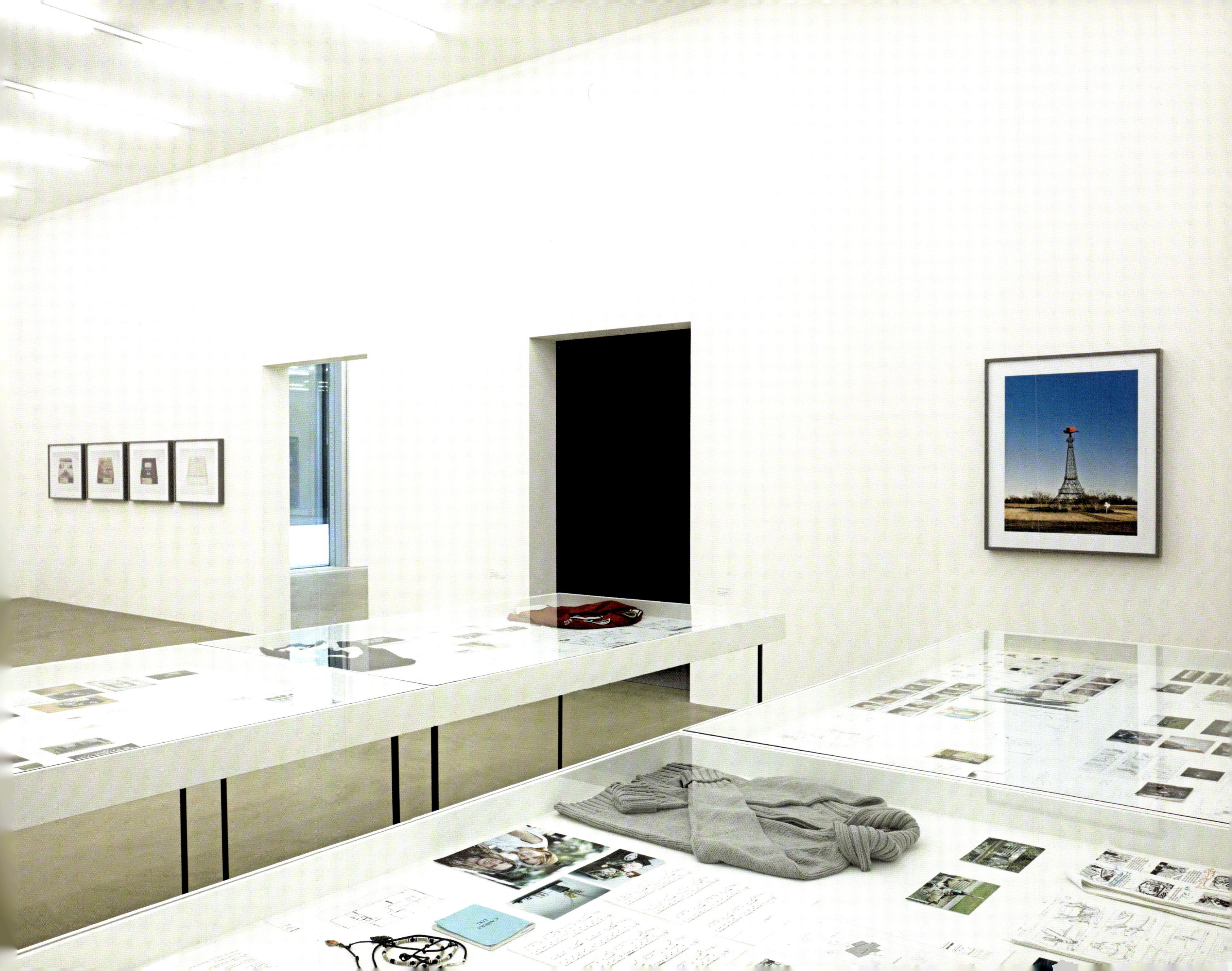

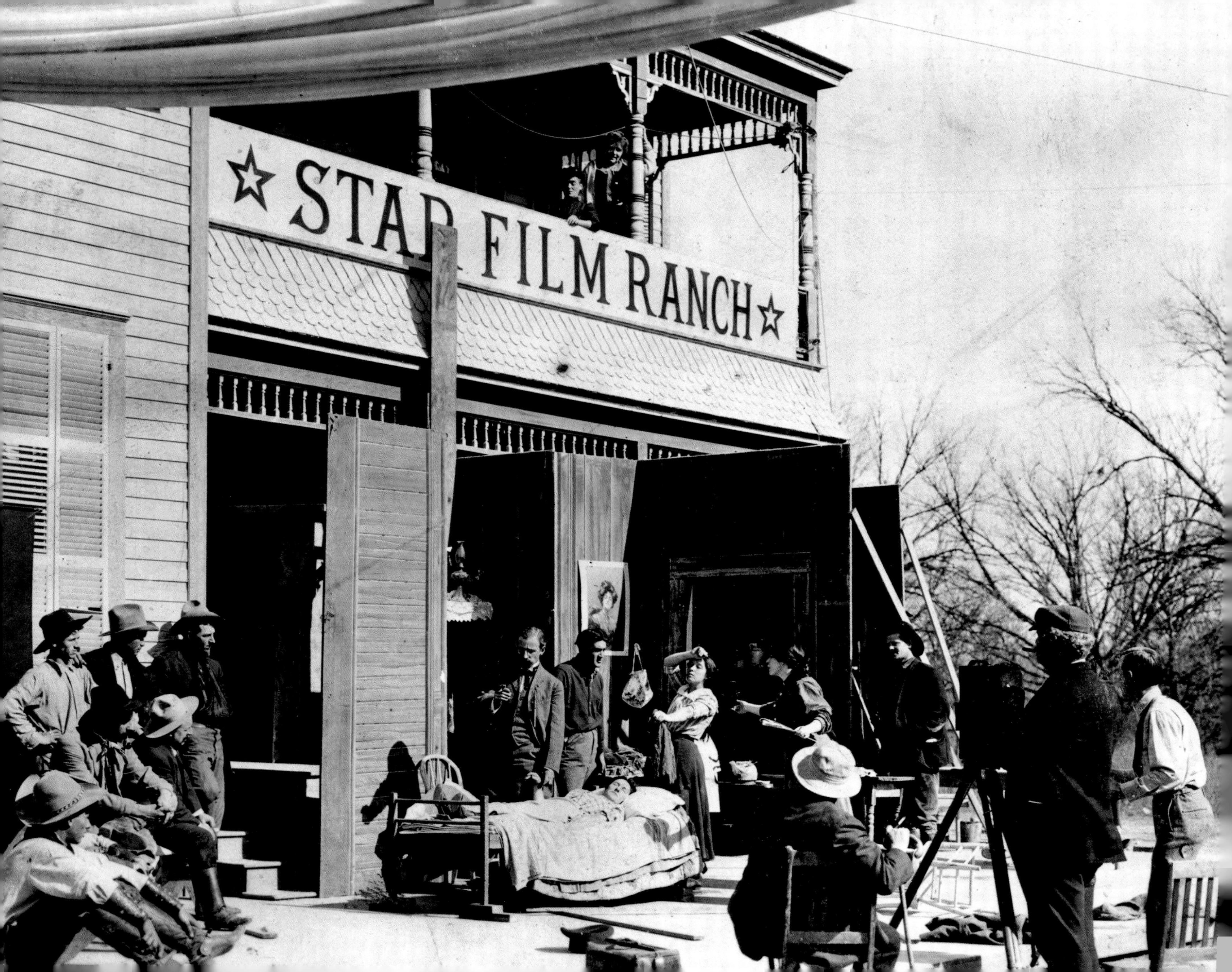
STAR FILM RANCH

him and his fellow cattlemen and -women toward the mountain whose name has inspired all this longing.

While Hubbard/Birchler's research suggests the possibility that Gaston Méliès—the lesser-known brother and business partner of the famous French filmmaker Georges Méliès—alit from the Sunset Express Train in Sierra Blanca in April 1911 en route to relocating his struggling movie company from San Antonio to California, this thesis remains unsubstantiated by the witnesses who attempt to piece together the mythos of Movie Mountain.

In *Giant*, Hubbard/Birchler break with the format of the interview that provides the fundamental structure and connective tissue for *Grand Paris Texas* and *Movie Mountain (Méliès)*. The spoken word, recalling events of the past and relating them to the present, is replaced by the representation of intent acts of listening and looking that serve as springboards for an imaginary invocation of the classic 1956 movie from points in time both past and present, before and after. *Giant* jumps back and forth between two narratives: the audio-visual exploration of the ruin and terrain of Reata, the iconic home of the film's Benedict family, and a fictional mise-en-scène of a 1950s Los Angeles clerical office where an attractive young woman types out stenographic notes on her nail-polish-chip-resistant Underwood, interrupted only by the occasional cigarette break or gaze out the window. Her insistent typing is of the 1955 contract between Warner Bros. and the Fort Davis, Texas, landowner whose property, horses and cattle became the backdrop for the epic picture featuring Elizabeth Taylor, Rock Hudson and James Dean.

The impassioned language of the document literally thumps and threads its way through the film as letter after letter hits

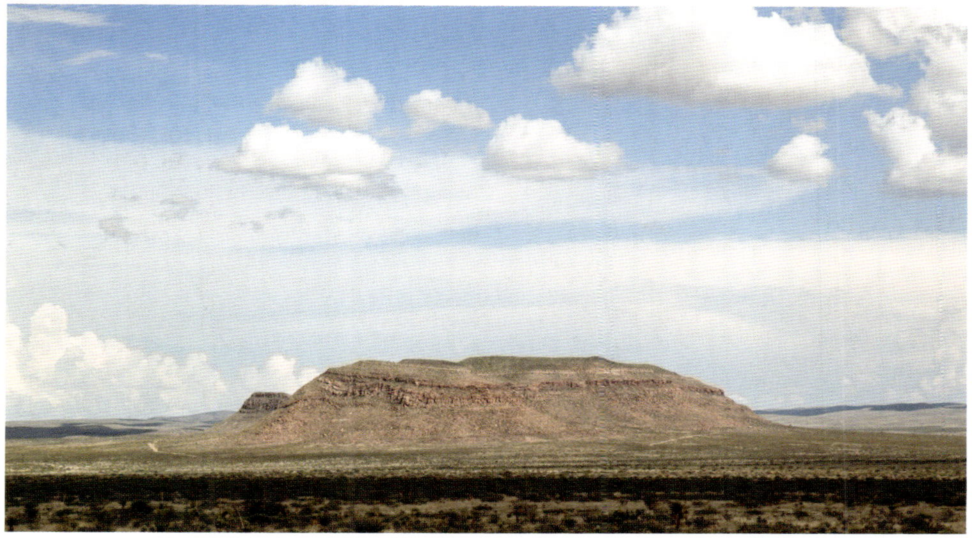

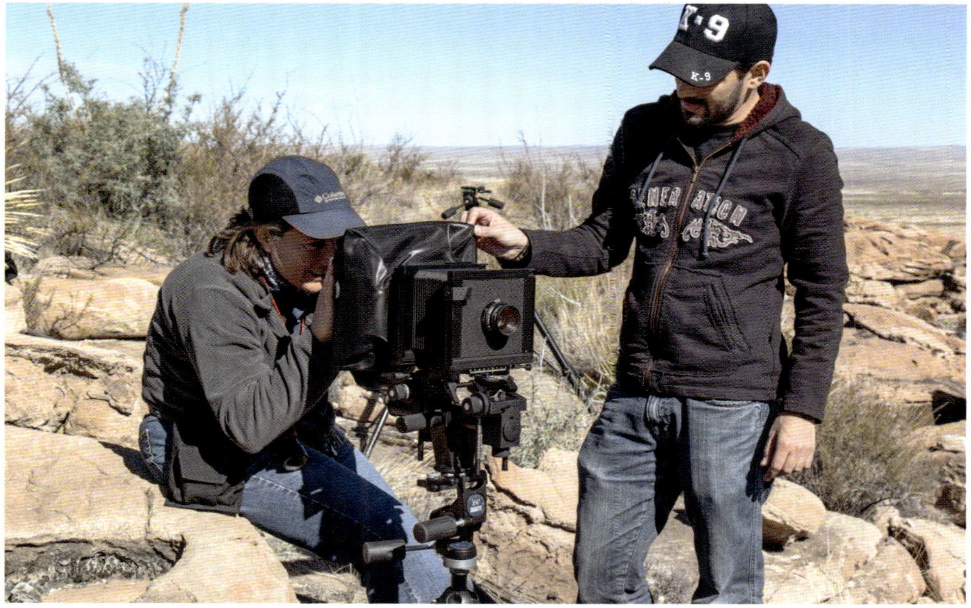

OPPOSITE:
Star Film Ranch, San Antonio, Texas, ca. 1911
Gaston Méliès seated in foreground

TOP:
Movie Mountain (Méliès), 2011
Production still, view from Movie Mountain

ABOVE:
Dead Cat on Movie Mountain, 2011
Production still

the ribbon. Limiting by the very nature of its purpose, the contract not only sets the condition for the projection of the typist's imagination but also serves as a contrasting foil for the limitlessness of the landscape whose use it aims to contain. When we see the young woman pensively look up and out the window, we imagine that she is conjuring up this movie whose parameters are being negotiated beneath her fingertips. If the notion of Hollywood as a dream factory comes alive in her looking and anticipating, the sound recordist—her female counterpart across time and place—invokes it through attentive listening and reimagining. Sound and vision alternately take turns as primary agents of recognition, whether in the form of an approaching train or a storm brewing in the distance. The first shot of the sound recordist shows her pressing her ear against one of the remaining poles of the Reata set whose soundscape of crackling wood and clanging metal she sets out to record. By now nearly 60 years old, the set's skeleton has become part of a natural cycle in which the life and death of birds, bugs, crickets and ants are as integral to the sounds of the site as those of the structure itself. With the set having become part of nature, it is the West Texas landscape that emerges as the true protagonist. Whether drenched in sun, battered by drought, swept by tornados or pounded by rain, it is the raison d'être for both the Warner Bros. and the Hubbard/Birchler versions of *Giant*. In the 1956 epic family saga people's lives evolve and change with their relationship to and ownership of land. Hubbard/Birchler's parallel narratives about the set's creation and its falling into ruin state ownership as a condition for the reality and the fiction of *Giant*.

BELOW LEFT: *Tumbleweeds*, 1925, Film still, William S. Hart starring in the role of Don Carver

BELOW RIGHT: Promotional movie poster for *Giant*, 1956

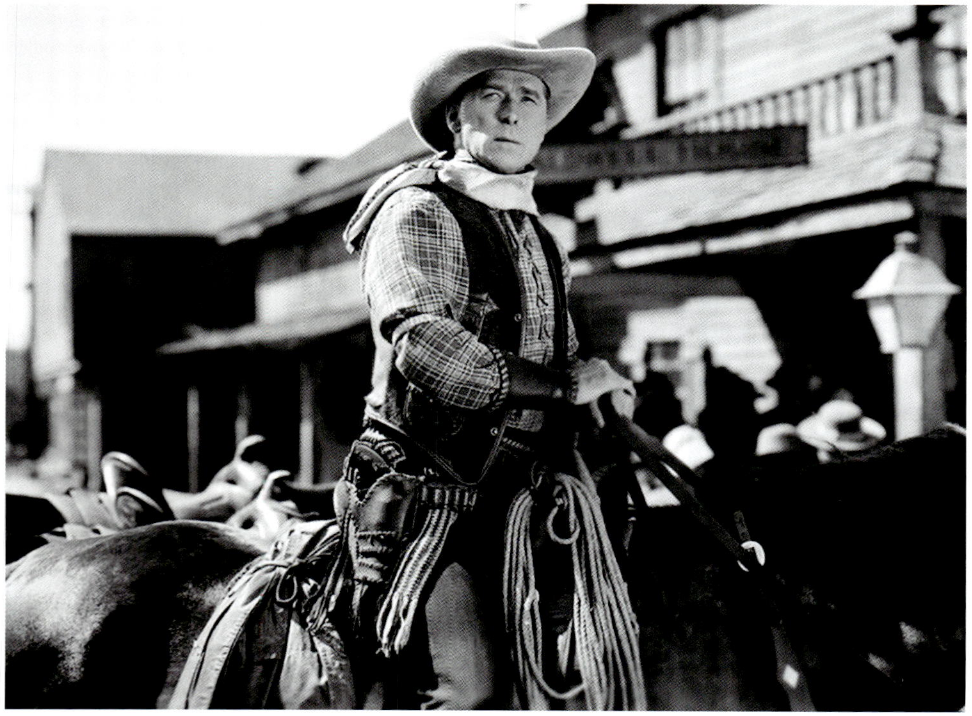

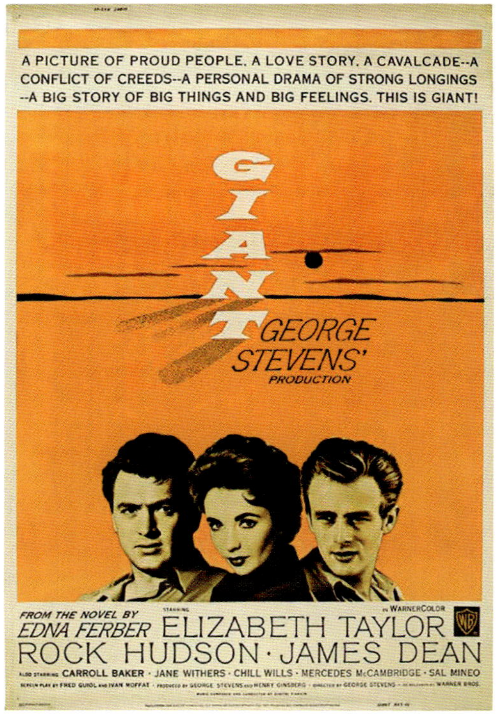

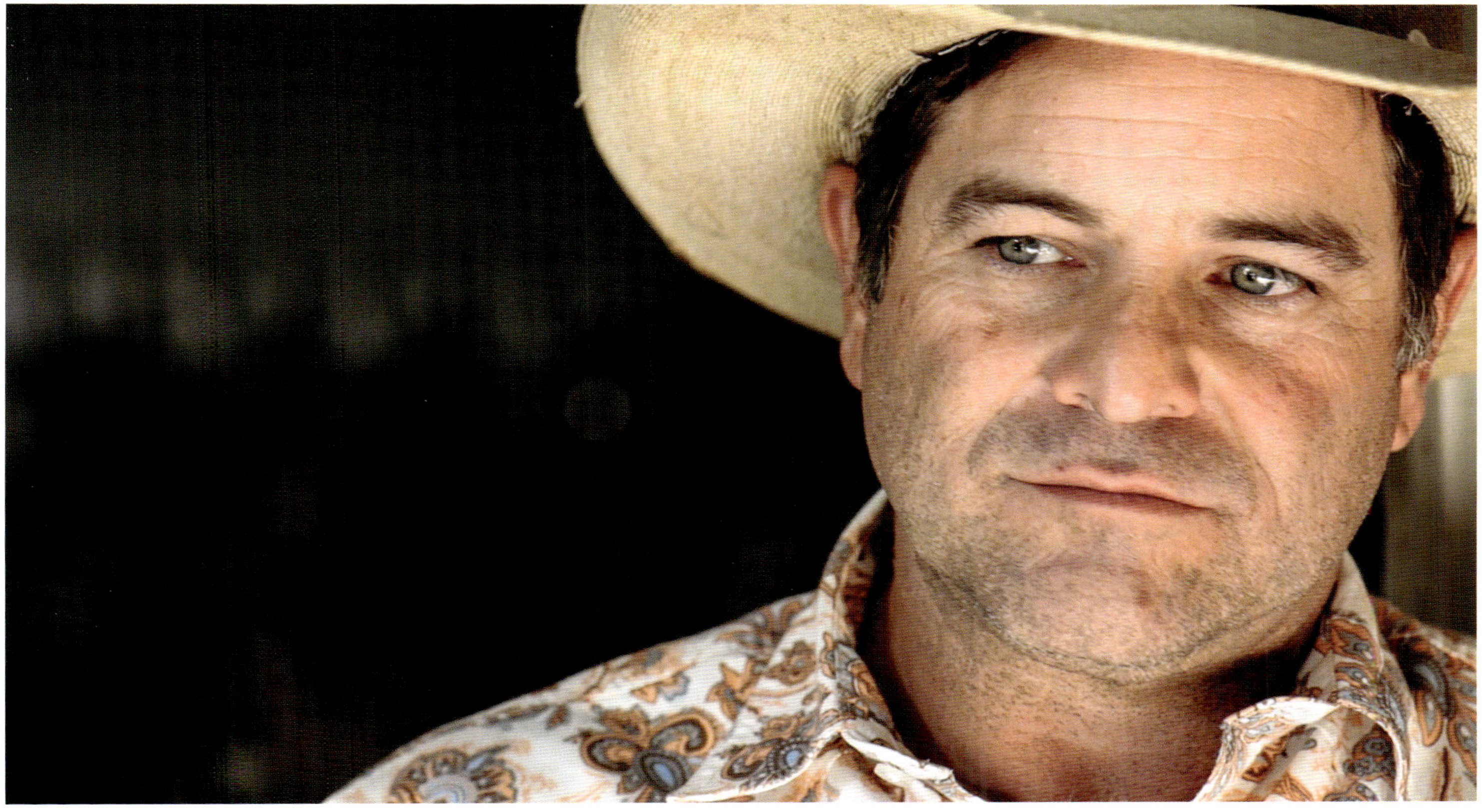

Together, the three ruins at the heart of each work in *Sound Speed Marker* represent three different aspects of cinema: the theater in *Grand Paris Texas* is the site of its experience, the locus of projection and immersion on the part of the viewer; *Movie Mountain (Méliès)* indicates the site of its making, the locus of action; and in *Giant*, the set represents the site of direction, the locus of ideas becoming form. The formal structure of each part—single-channel projection for *Grand Paris Texas*, dual-channel projection for *Movie Mountain (Méliès)* and triple-channel projection for *Giant*—reflects these different roles and speaks to the visual power of each site to itself command the large screen. It also speaks to the role that landscape plays in the films associated with each part: as an abstract ideal and goal in *Grand Paris, Texas*, as a generic location and backdrop for action in *Movie Mountain (Méliès)* and as a character of epic proportion in *Giant*.

More specifically, though, the trio of work that makes up *Sound Speed Marker* offers a meditation on the shaping of a visual lexicon of Texas throughout twentieth-century filmmaking that resonates to this day. *Movie Mountain (Méliès)* references the development of the Texan West's filmic mythos through references to the Silent Western and its classic themes of conflict and conquest between settlers and natives, farmers and

Movie Mountain (Méliès), 2011
Video still

ranchers, and men who make or break laws in the pursuit of new frontiers. However, the reality of the present-day "cowboy" and "indian" interviewed in *Movie Mountain (Méliès)* is quick to diffuse any notion of lingering romanticism attached to these tropes as they are stripped of their aspirational logic and become the portrayal of a specific way of life.

The 1956 Hollywood feature *Giant* delivered an enduring portrait of the American West catapulted into modernity through the discovery of oil, its rags-to-riches story and generational challenge to traditional conceptions of class, gender and race relations. Despite the film's firmly established association of modernization with industry, Hubbard/Birchler avoid images of a landscape covered in derricks and men slathered in black gold. Instead, the focus is on the skeleton of Reata, the home run by the willful Leslie Benedict as the true site of the film's progressiveness. By constructing a dual storyline with two self-aware and confident women protagonists around the physical structure of the house, the artists pay homage to Benedict's role as the arbiter of change and the ultimate embodiment of modernization in terms of ideology. The sight of Reata set against the wide Texas skies evokes the last scene of *Giant* in which Benedict, seated by the window against the same scenery as 60-odd years ago, declares her family to finally be a success. She does so not because of the greater wealth it accrued with Bick having reluctantly come around to mine their land for oil, but because of his hard-won

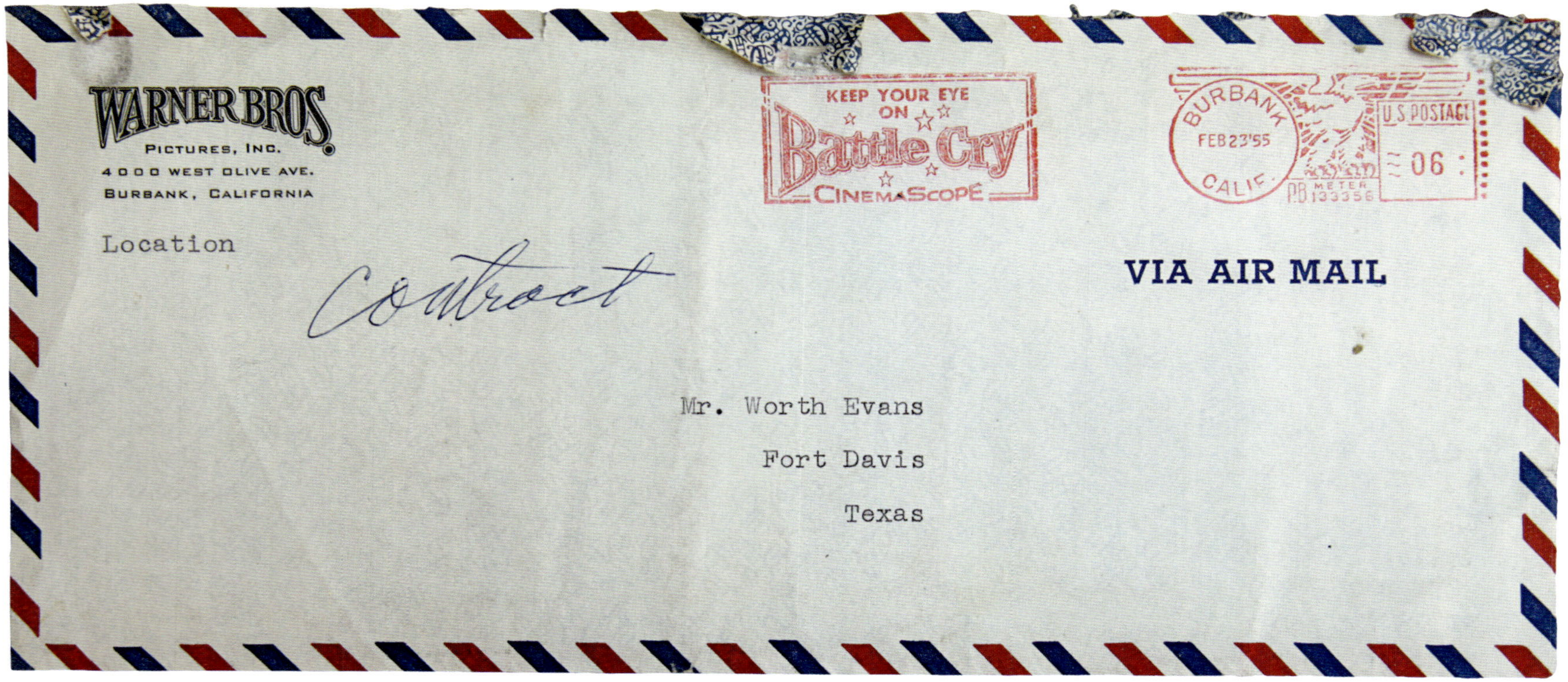

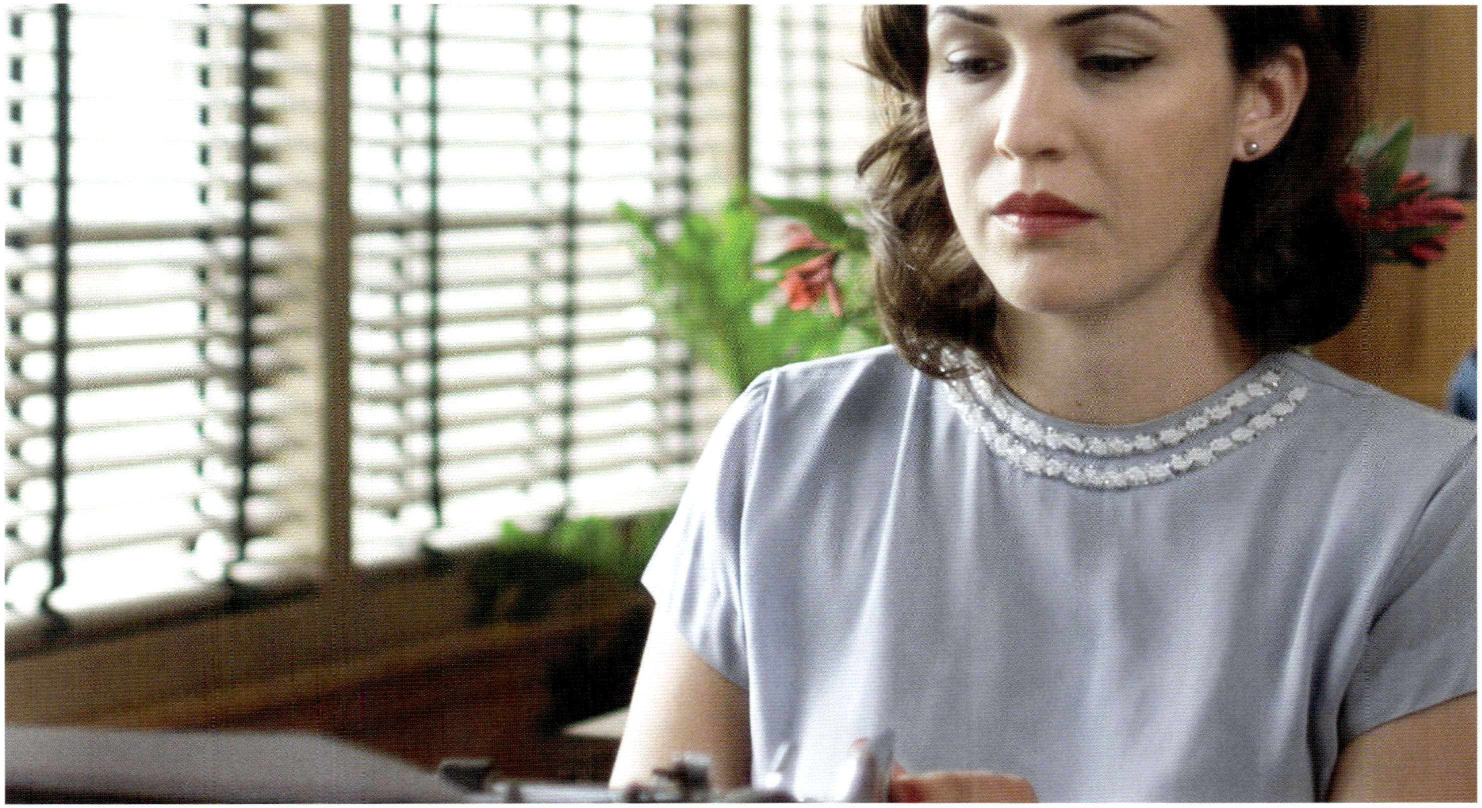

recognition and acceptance of the necessity for equal rights for people of different gender, class and race.

In the 1984 film *Paris, Texas,* the figure of the outlaw in moral conflict with a nascent society is recast as one in psychological conflict with existing societal structures. Travis is the lone drifter, the tumbleweed blown about life until his brother forces him to reconnect with reality, overcome the estrangement from his son Hunter and reunite with his ex-wife. The frontier is more emotional than territorial and the process of civilization is tied to questions of identity. While the plot of land shown at the very outset of the film as awaiting Travis at the end of his journey exists as a physical destination throughout, its importance lies in it marking a place of mental arrival. If Travis is reimagined as the outlaw, his son Hunter assumes the role of the cowboy. In a key scene of the film Hunter is seen wearing military fatigues and a NASA jacket, emblems of the modern-day explorers and defenders of new frontiers who long replaced the image of the gun-toting, lasso-wielding pioneering hero in the wake of the colonization of the North American continent. In the process of Travis's "civilization," both undergo a transformation, but while Hunter's quest comes to a conclusion that marks a new beginning, Travis's journey continues. While we are led to believe that he is finally en route to Paris, Texas, we never find

ABOVE:
Giant, 2014
Video still

OPPOSITE:
Envelope, postmarked February 23, 1955, containing the location contract for the Warner Bros. movie *Giant*, 1956

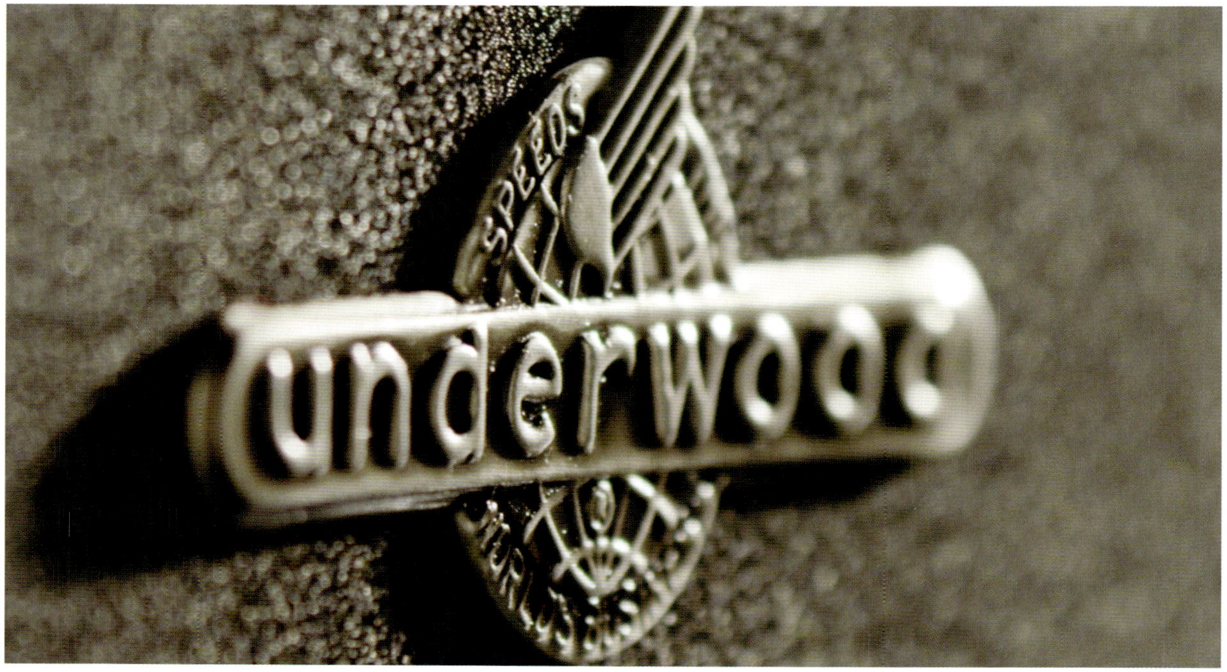

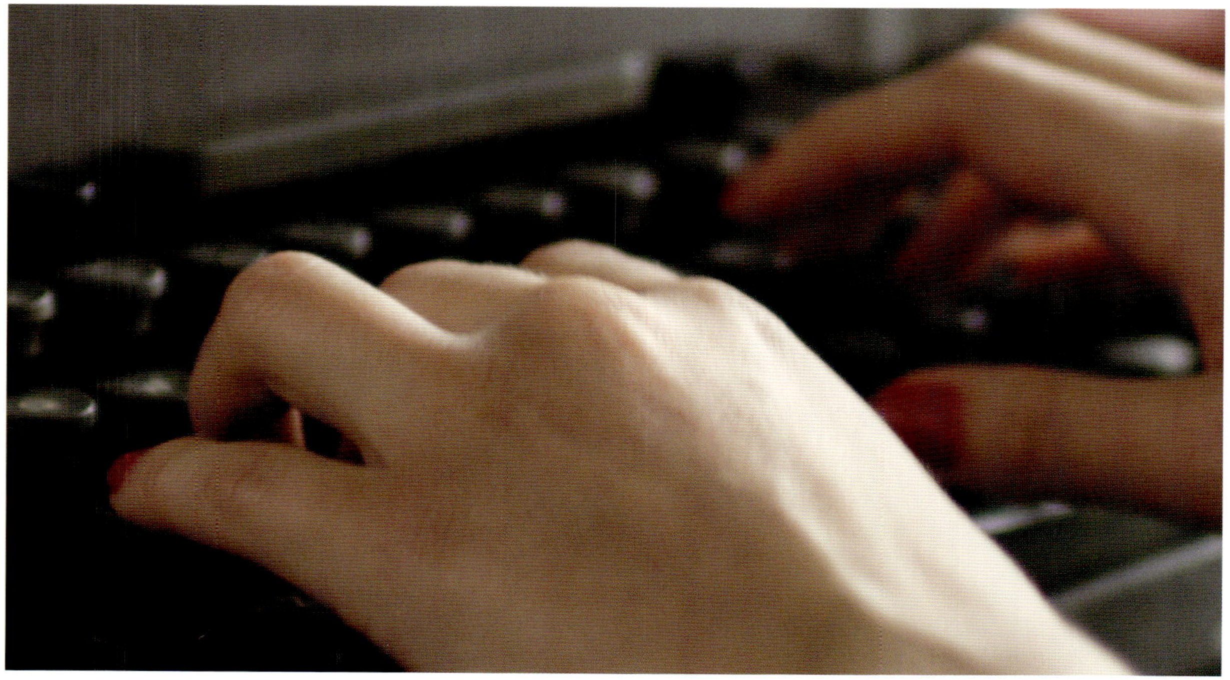

Giant 2014
Video stills

out whether he truly arrives. By giving faces and voices to the real residents of Paris—the elusive place of Travis's supposed destiny—*Grand Paris Texas* only reinforces the notion that his longing is one for an idealized ordinariness embodied by the image of a plot of land.

Sound Speed Marker addresses all the known clichés associated with Texas: its industries of cattle, oil and space, its heroes of cowboys, wild-catters and astronauts, its vast land and skies and extreme weather. But it removes them from their isolated existence of singular ideas and concepts and inflects them with real times, places and people who collectively deny their simple perpetuation. By reflecting on the representation of Texas throughout key moments in twentieth-century cinema, Hubbard/Birchler also take into account their own initial assumptions and preconceptions. Originally from Ireland and Switzerland, the artists' idea of Texas—like those of most Europeans growing up in the 1970s and 1980s—was dependent on the cinematic imagery of now-classic films of which Texas was either subject or site. With *Sound Speed Marker* Hubbard/Birchler have created both an homage to and a revision of this imagery by reflecting on the geography of Texas and its cinematic landscape as tropes of representation and presentation.

But the trilogy also functions on a meta level: In this context the site, subject and mystique of Texas and its associated cinematic imagery serve as a platform for reflection on filmmaking itself. There are the obvious indicators of the artists and the crew being filmed in the process of set-up and recording. Each work opens and closes with a sequence of one or several crew members at work, whether it is the set-up and tear-down of the flying camera rig in front of the theater in *Grand Paris Texas*, recording

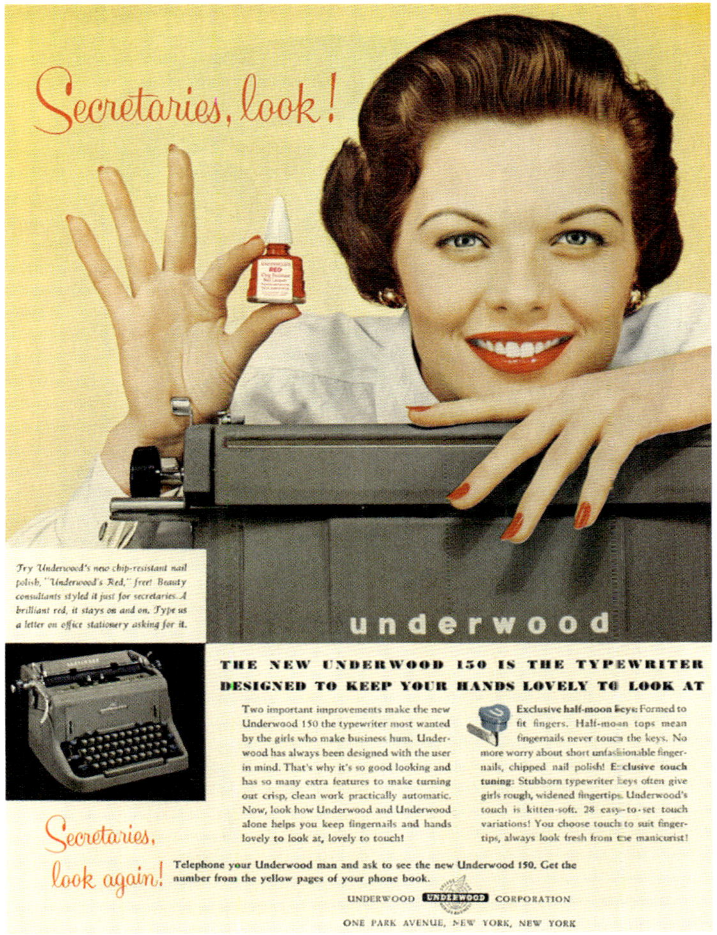

Advertisement, ca. 1955 for the *Underwood 150* typewriter, featuring exclusive nail chip-proof half-moon shaped keys. The typewriter was shipped together with a bottle of *Underwood Red* nail polish.

the sounds of the main road of Sierra Blanca and the "peak" of Movie Mountain or capturing the sonic atmosphere of sunrise and sunset around the Reata set in *Giant*. This mise-en-abîme of documenting the documentaries is complemented by a set of metaphorical allusions to conception, realization and reception of filmmaking through the choice and treatment of the three actual sites under investigation. While the Grand and Reata are physical ruins that carry within them the Romantic idea of the ephemerality of the man-made and the enduring

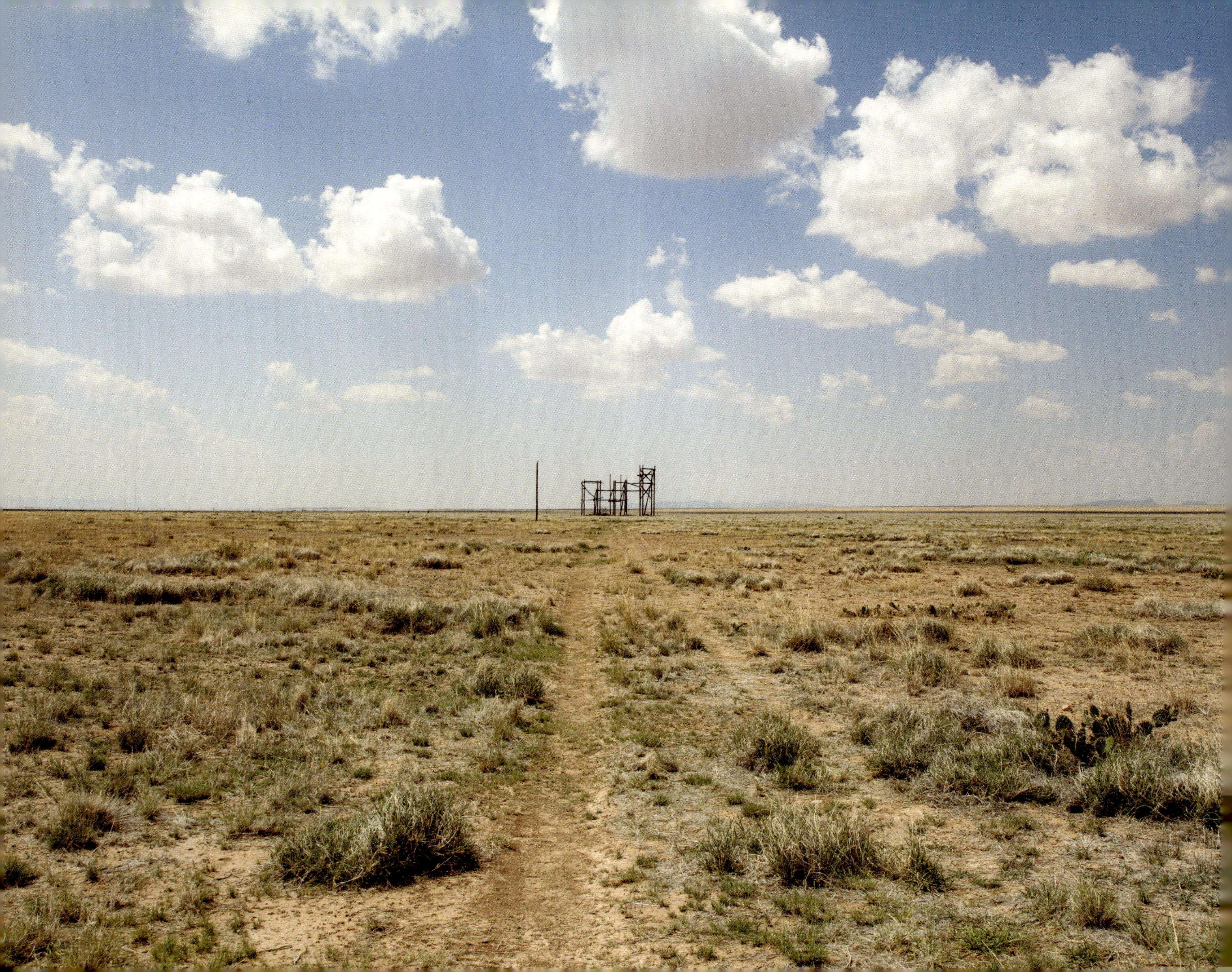

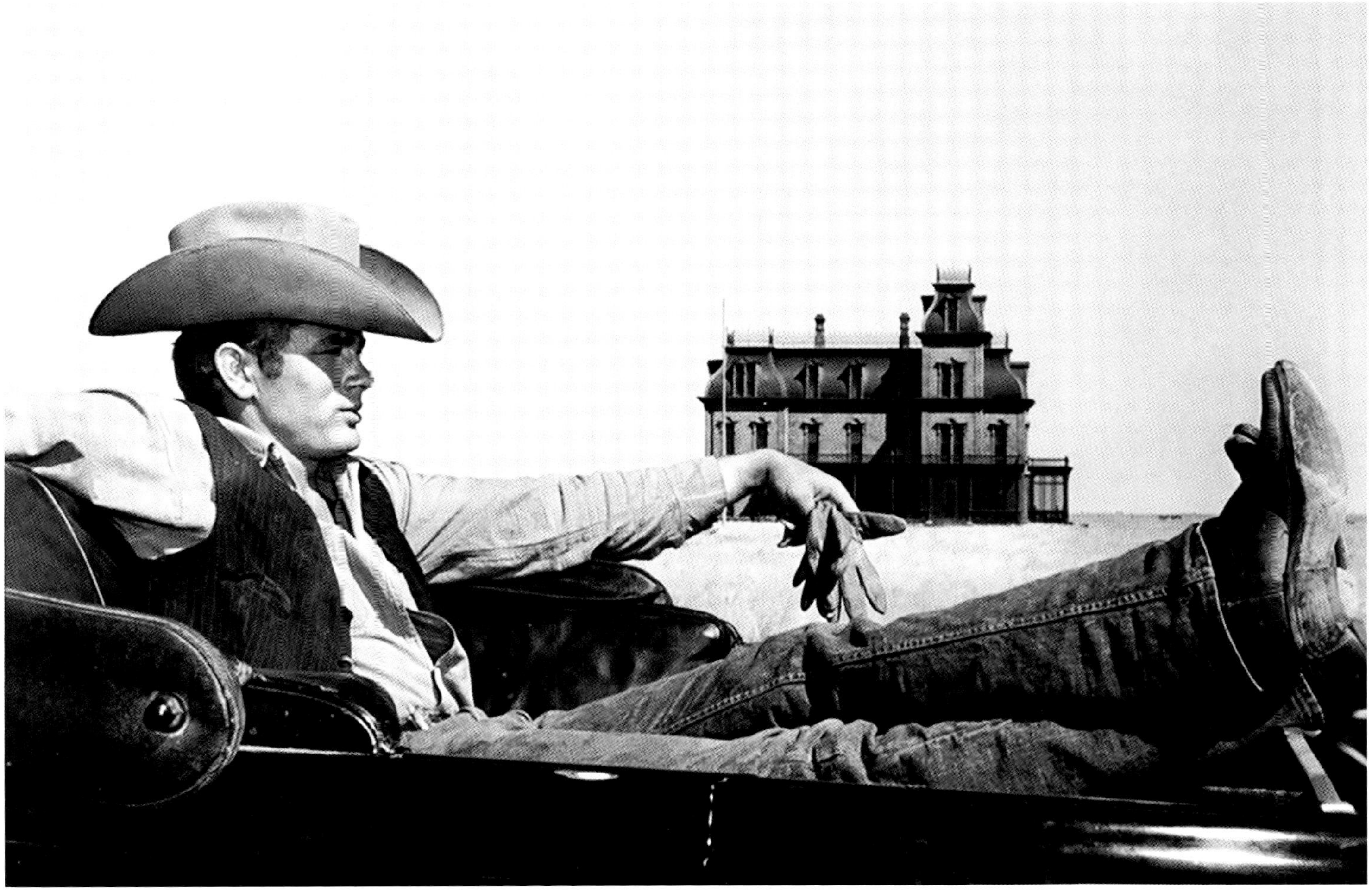

sublimity of nature, Movie Mountain is ruinous in the reduction of its name to a generic signifier whose specific raison d'être is on the brink of oblivion.

But rather than being a passive subject of contemplation, the ruins here give occasion for structural investigation and active reimagining of the possibilities of filmmaking in the service of both illusion and reality. Each film visualizes this productive dynamic through a recurring image that materializes its protagonist's modus operandi. Each consists of an object whose function is determined by two whirling wheels or circular motions holding the tension of a linear element: the 35mm film in *Grand Paris Texas,* the cowboy's lasso in *Movie Mountain (Méliès)* and the typewriter ribbon in *Giant.* The two-reel system is as fundamental to the projection of classic cinema as is the lasso to the work of the herding cowboy and the ribbon to the drafting of a contract on a manual typewriter. In an old-fashioned theater such as the Grand, a film's experience was dependent on the

ABOVE:
Publicity still from *Giant*, 1956, James Dean starring in the role of Jett Rink

OPPOSITE:
Giant, 2014
Production still

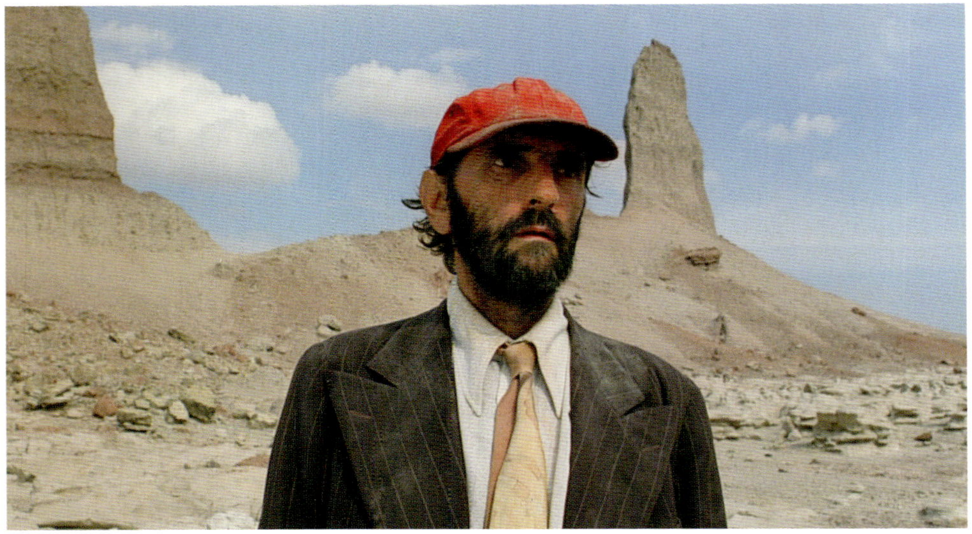

projectionist's skilled changeovers of reels to create a seamless transition between a film preserved and delivered in many pieces. The lasso embodies the cowboy's work as an effort of containment, with him on one end of a tight rope and the animal on the other end. No ink would imprint itself onto paper by a typewriter if the ribbon weren't stressed between the spools of the machine. Film, lasso, ribbon: each depends on the creation of tension for their operation. Together, they invoke the processual dynamic underlying the creation of imageries and metanarratives in *Sound Speed Marker*. It is precisely this type of generative tension and conceptual solidarity at the heart of Hubbard/Birchler's collaborative practice that makes the experience of their work so profoundly rewarding.

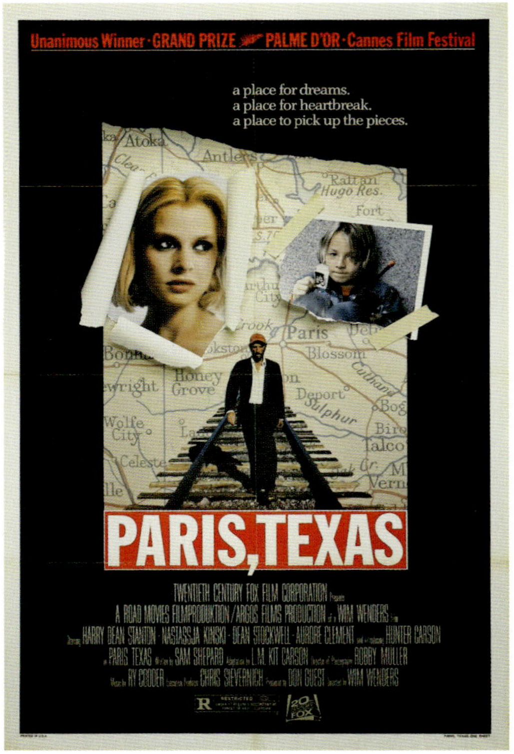

ABOVE:
Film still from *Paris, Texas*, 1984, Harry Dean Stanton starring in the role of Travis Henderson

RIGHT:
Promotional movie poster for *Paris, Texas*, 1984

OPPOSITE:
Reata film set from the Warners Bros. production *Giant* 1956, photographed in 1968

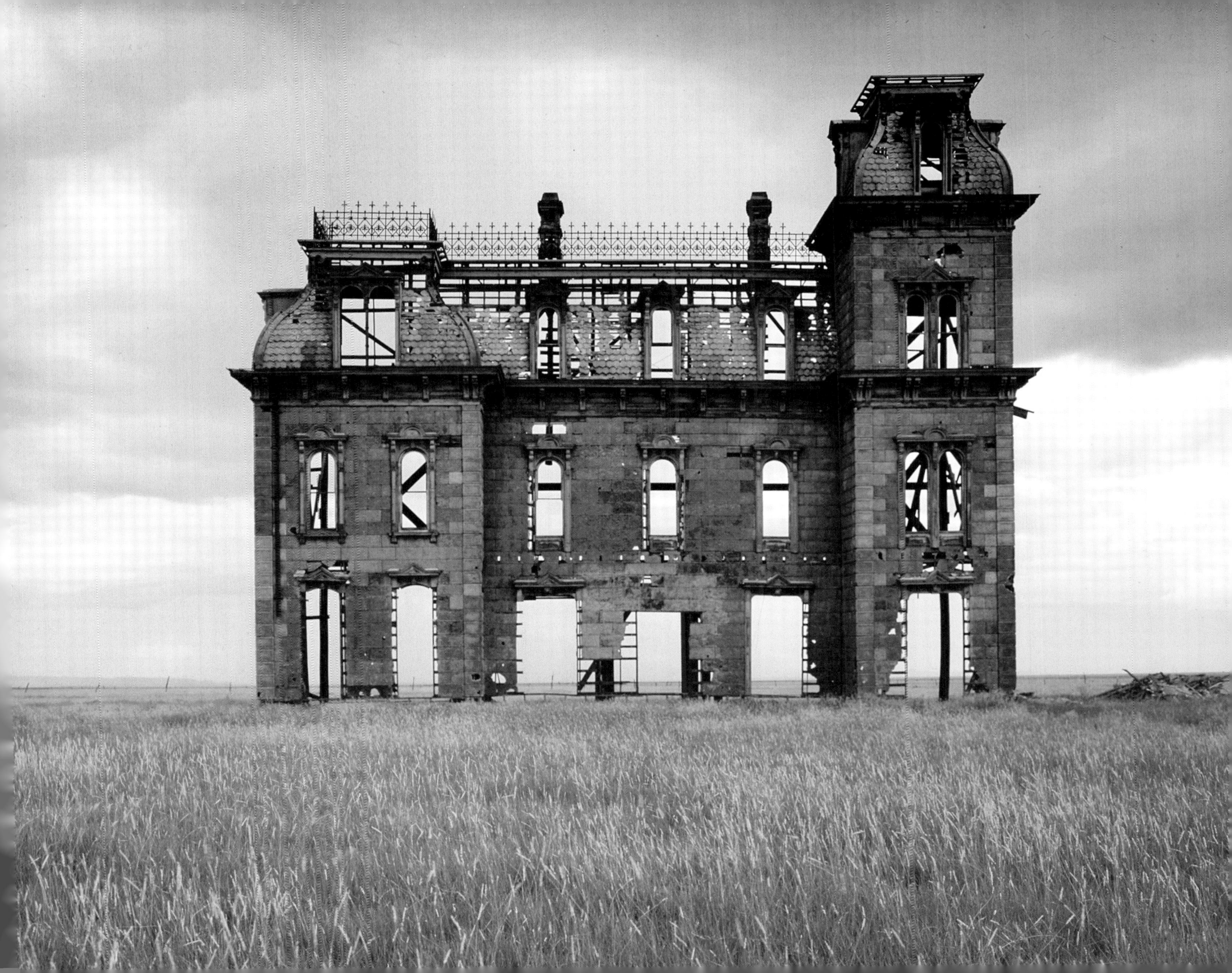

GRAND PARIS TEXAS, 2009
High-Definition Video with Sound
Single Channel, 54 minutes
Installation dimensions variable

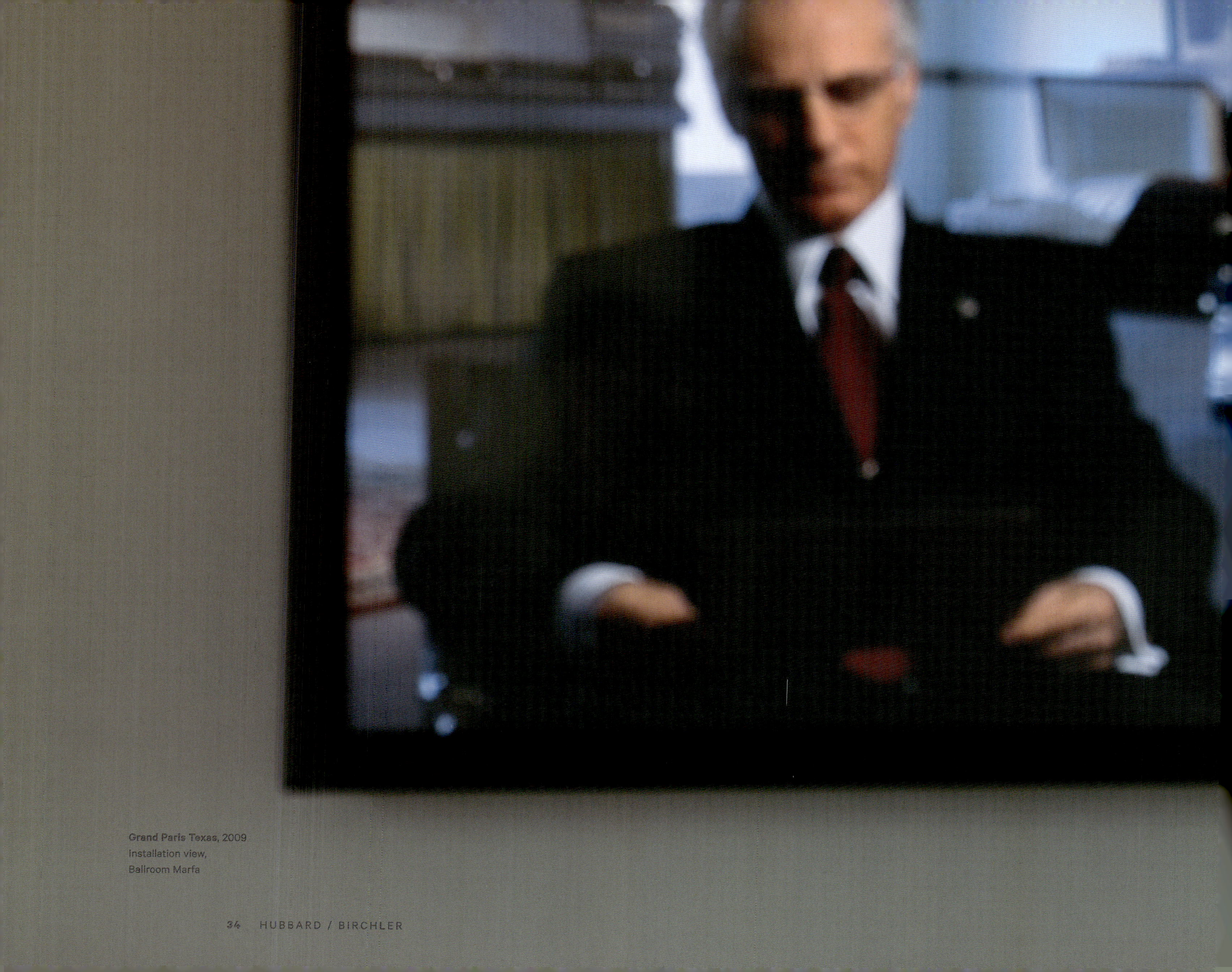

Grand Paris Texas, 2009
Installation view,
Ballroom Marfa

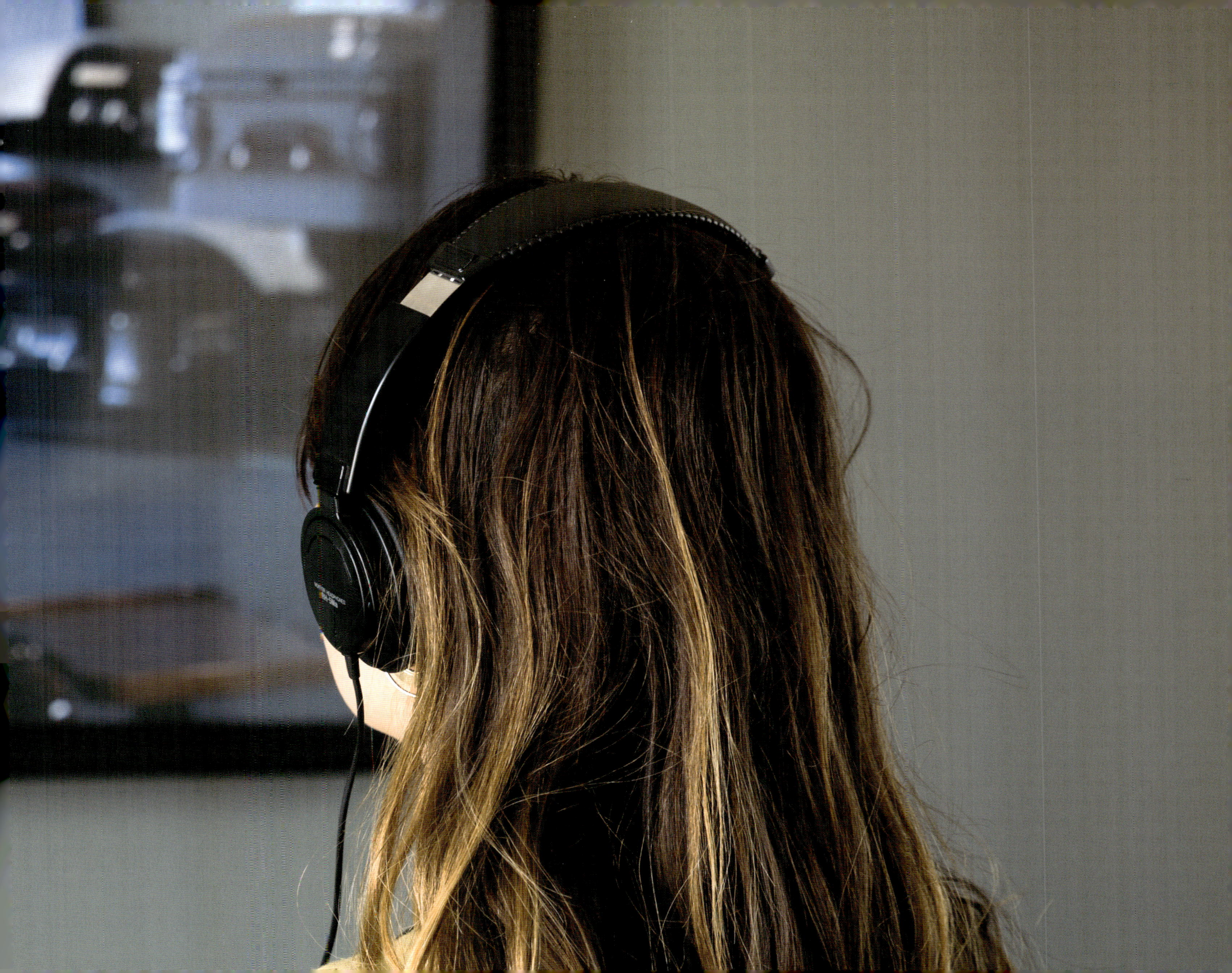

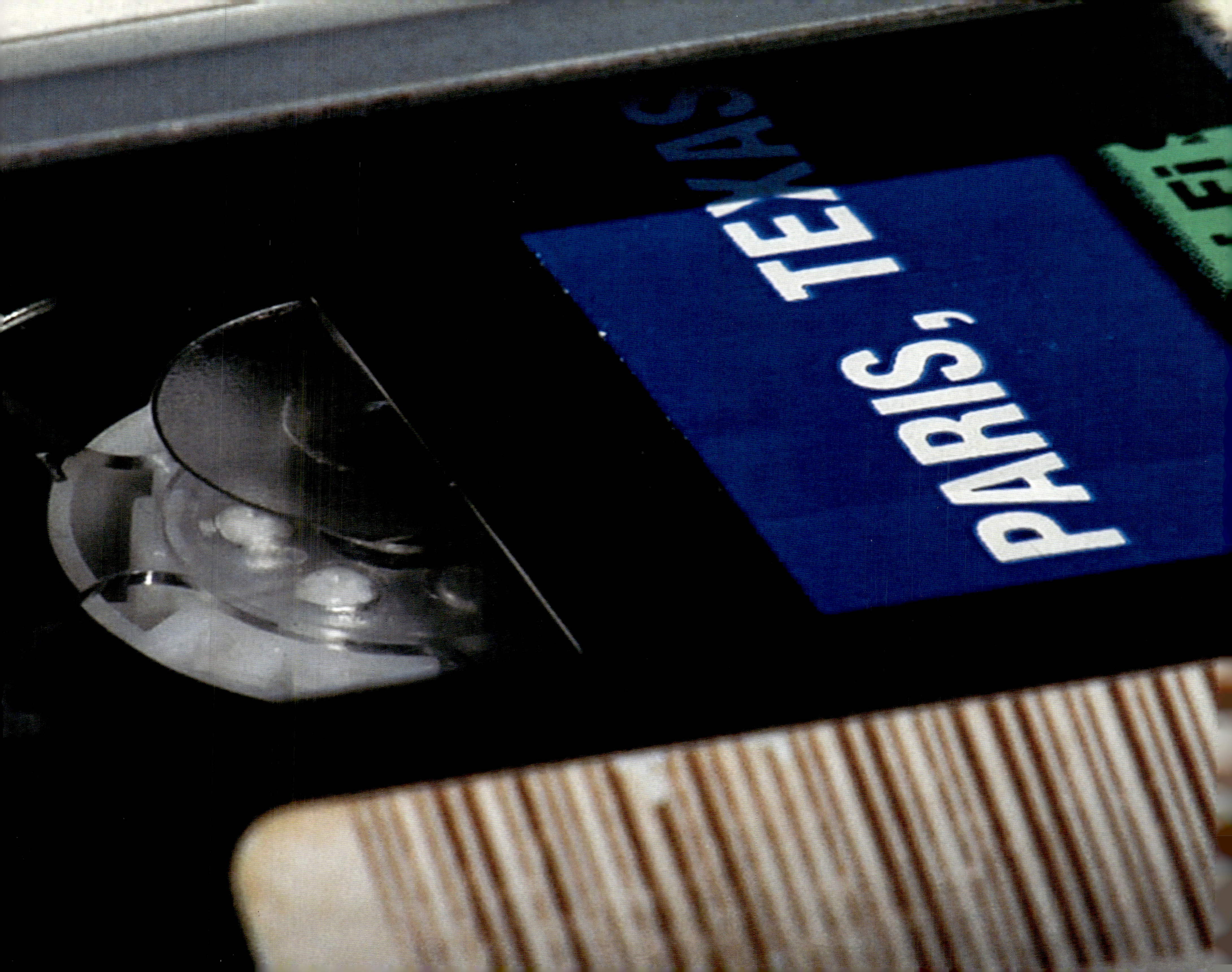
PARIS, TEXAS

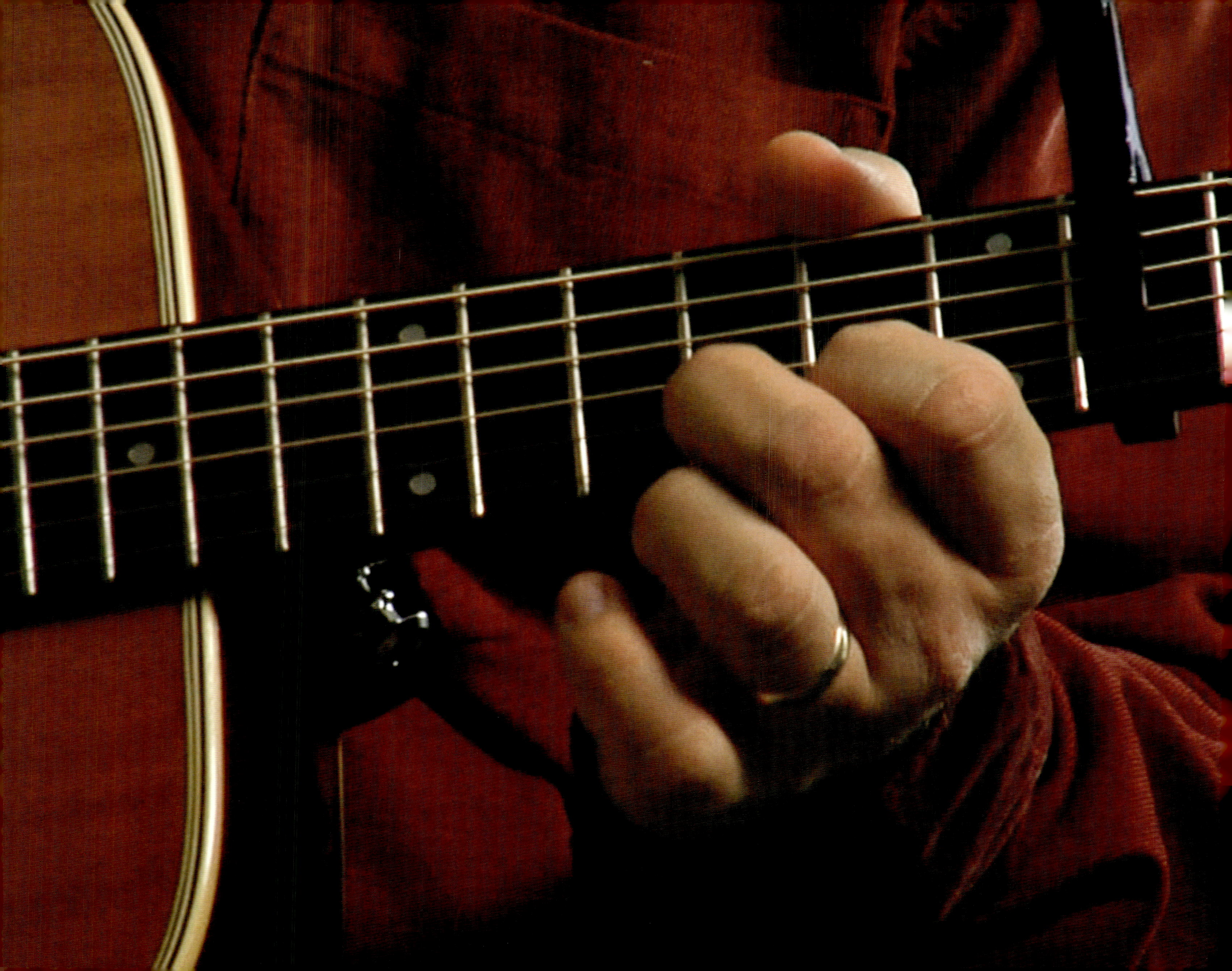

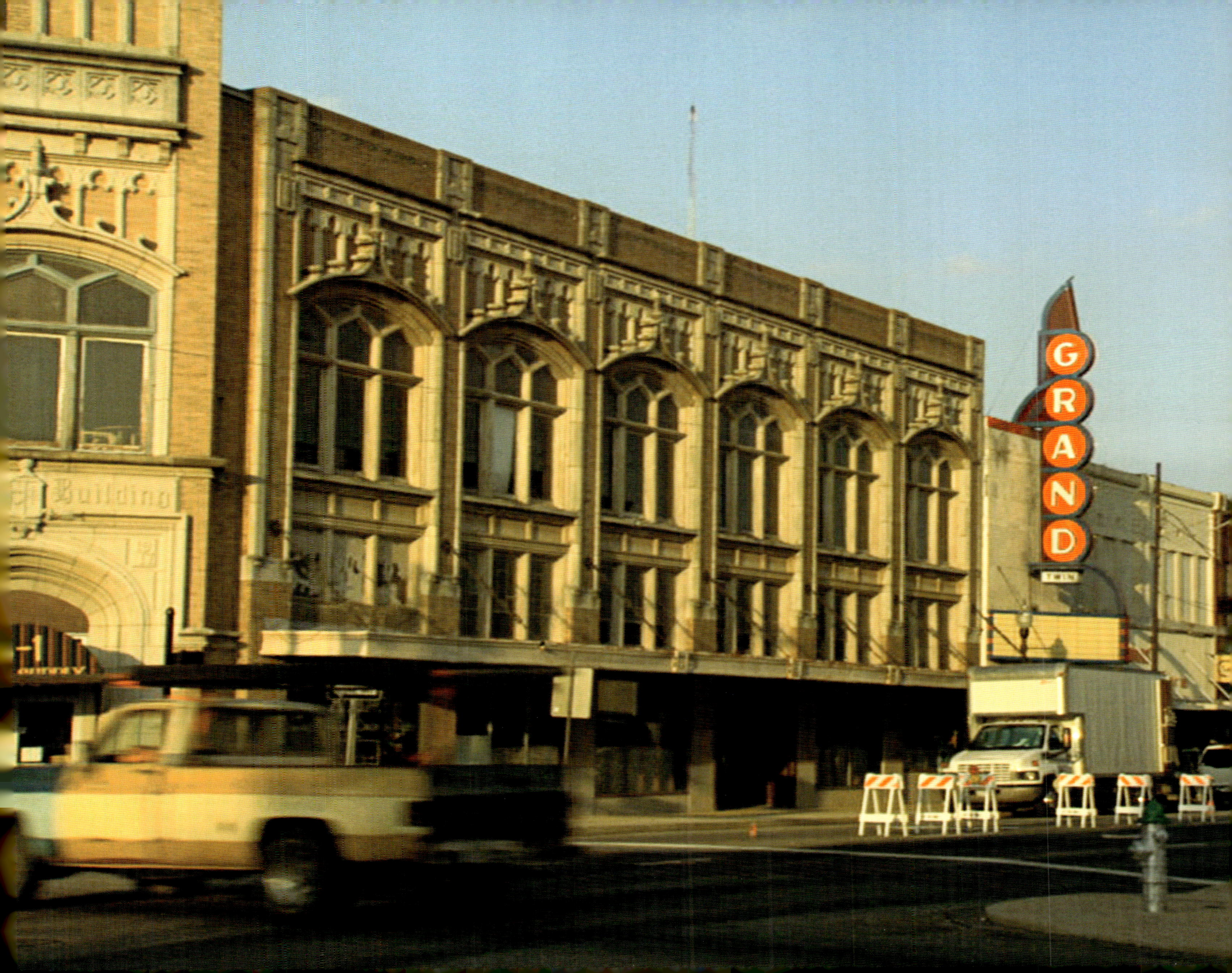
Building
GRAND

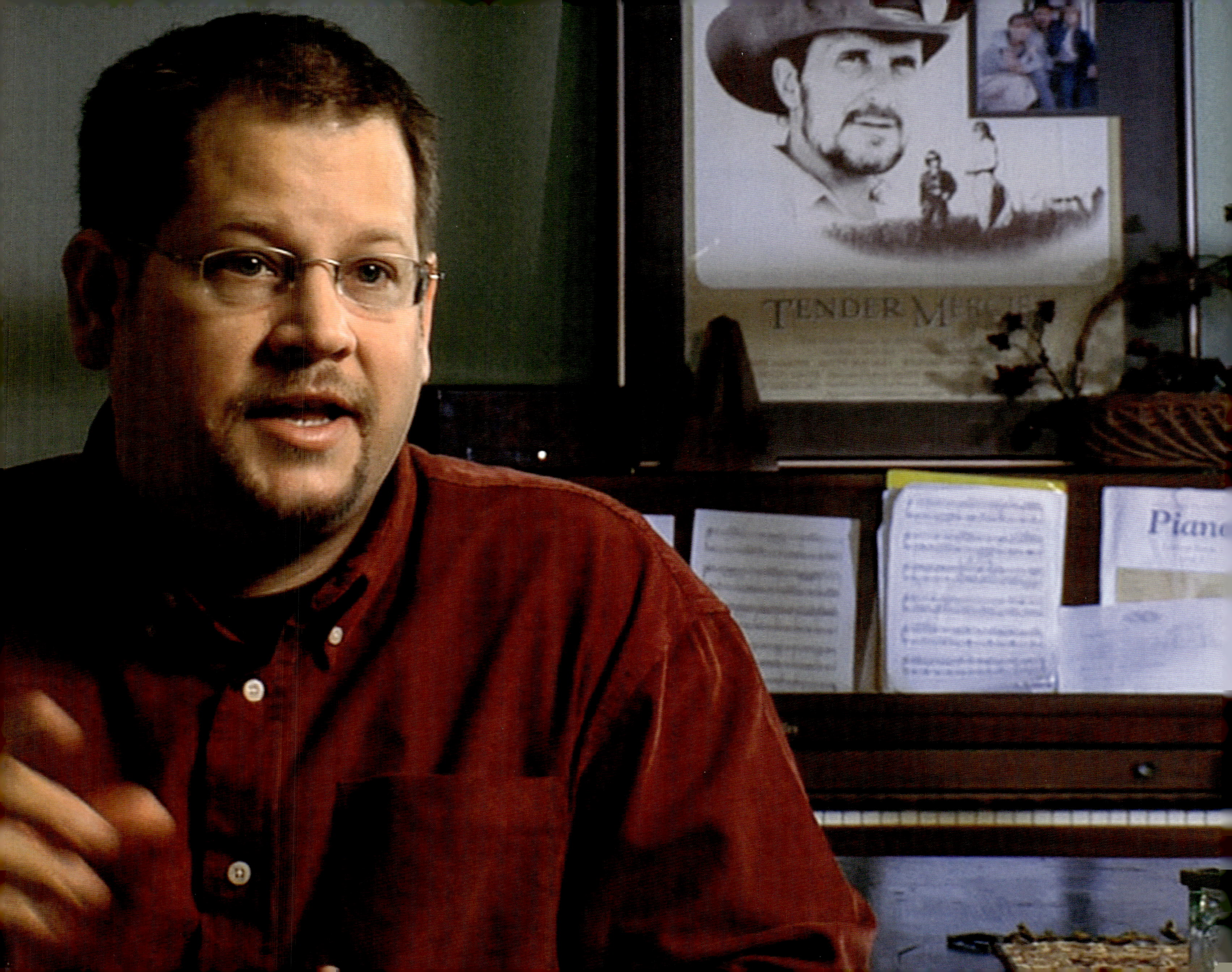
TENDER MERC

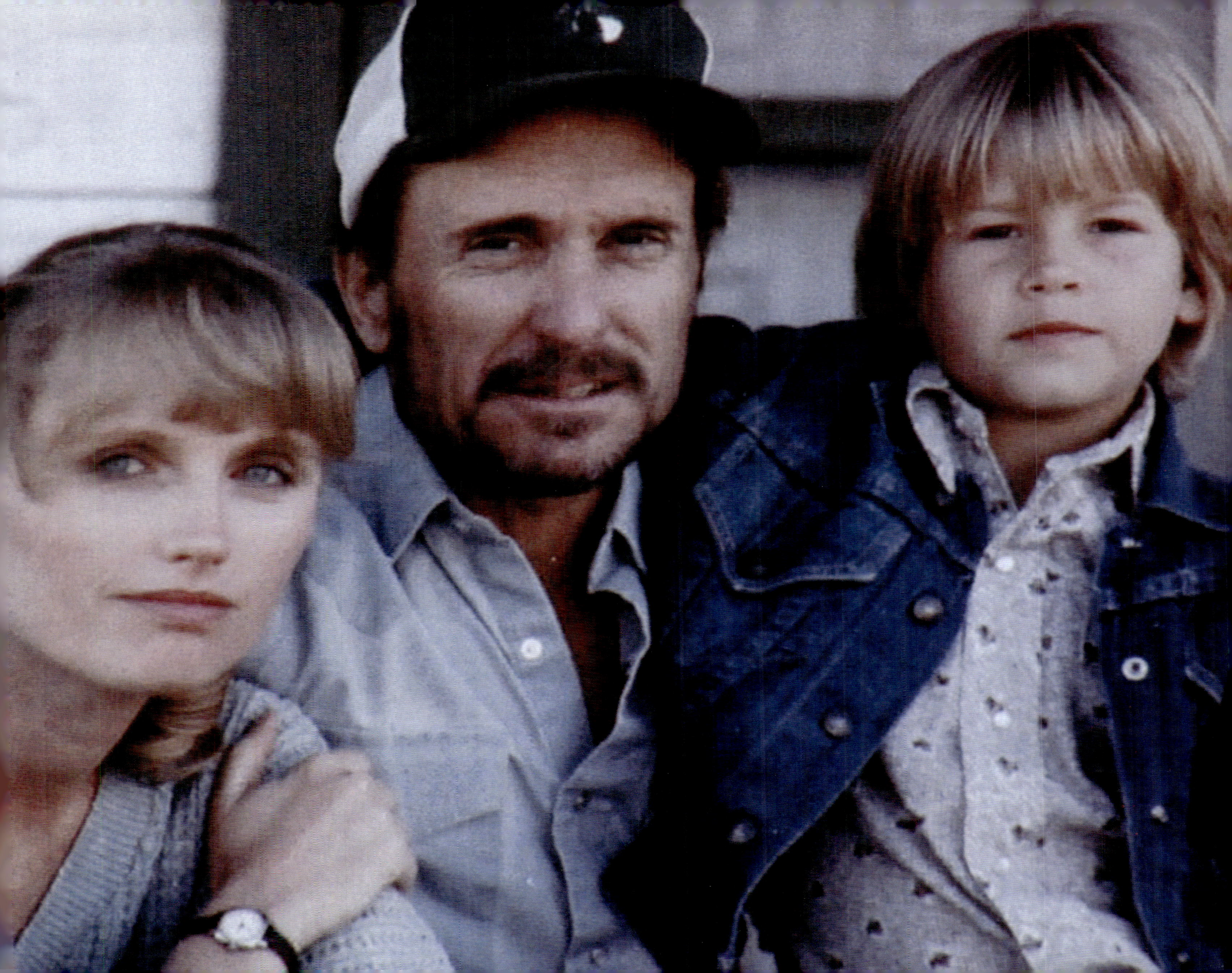

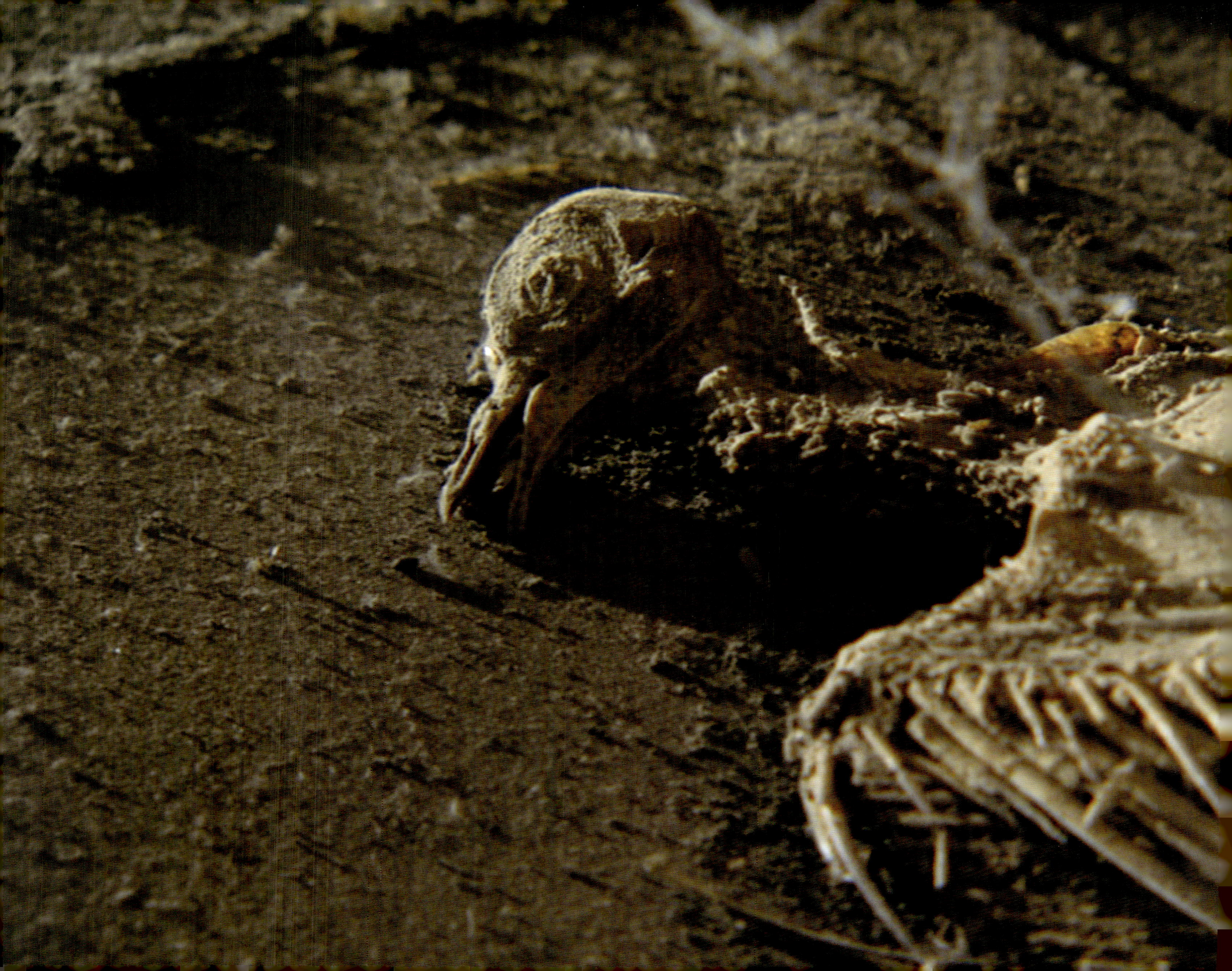

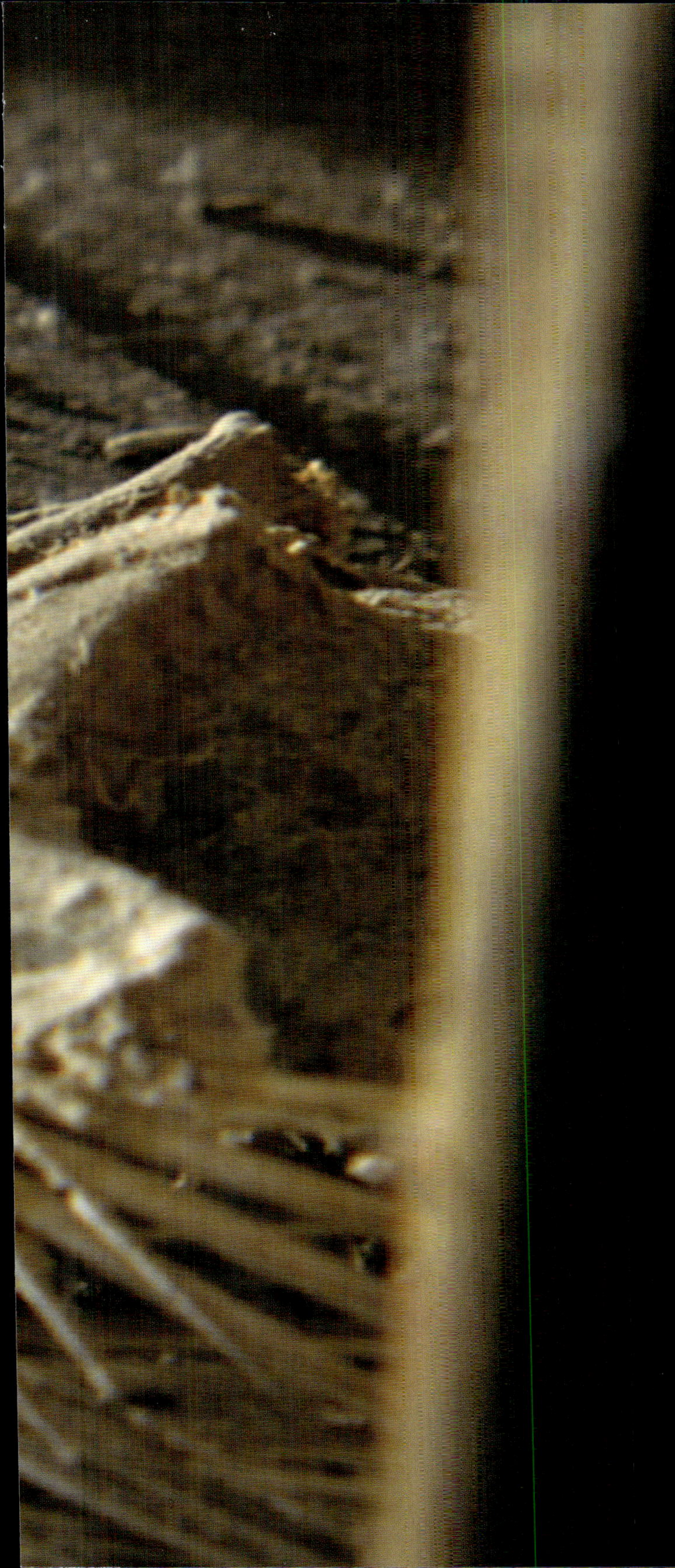

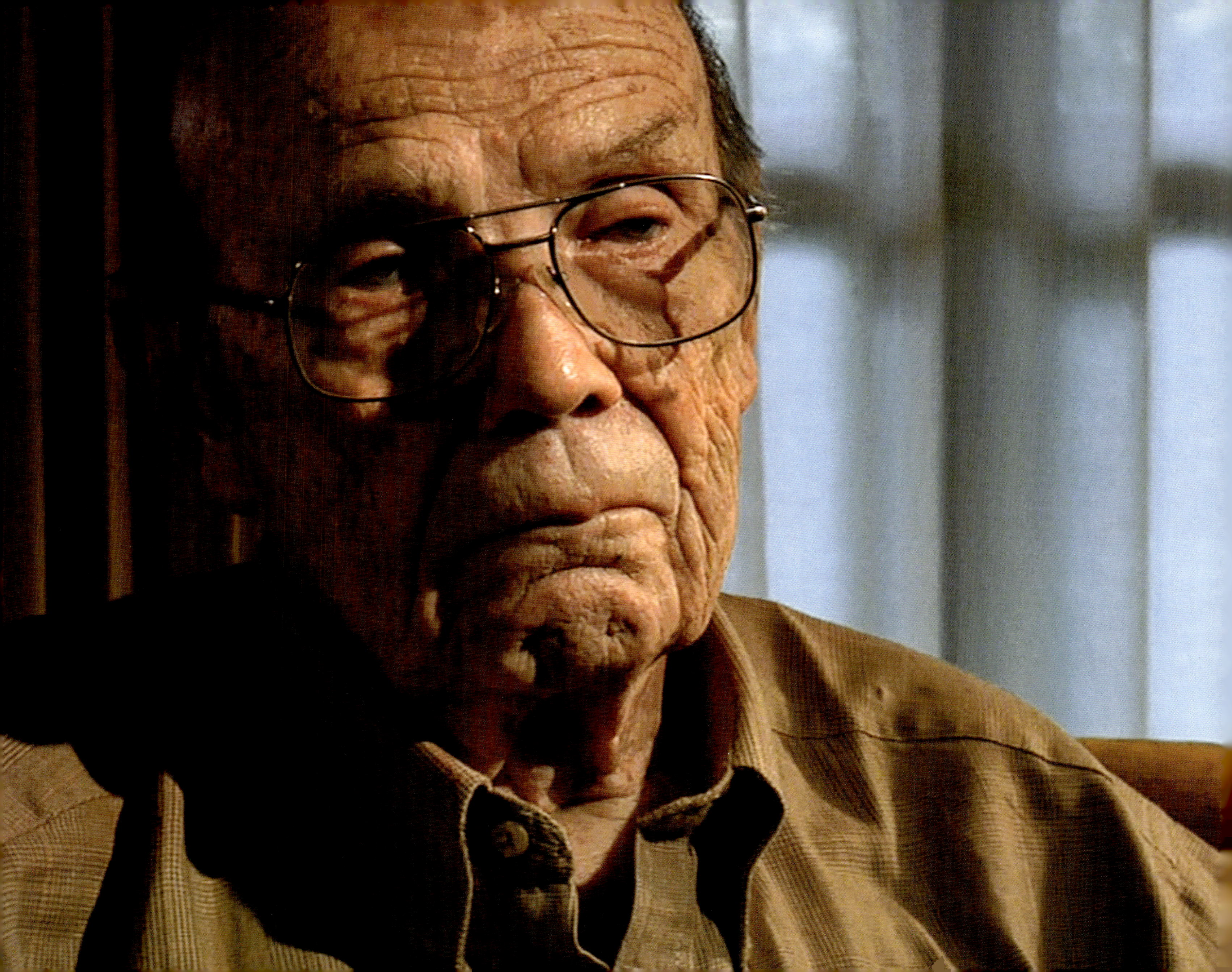

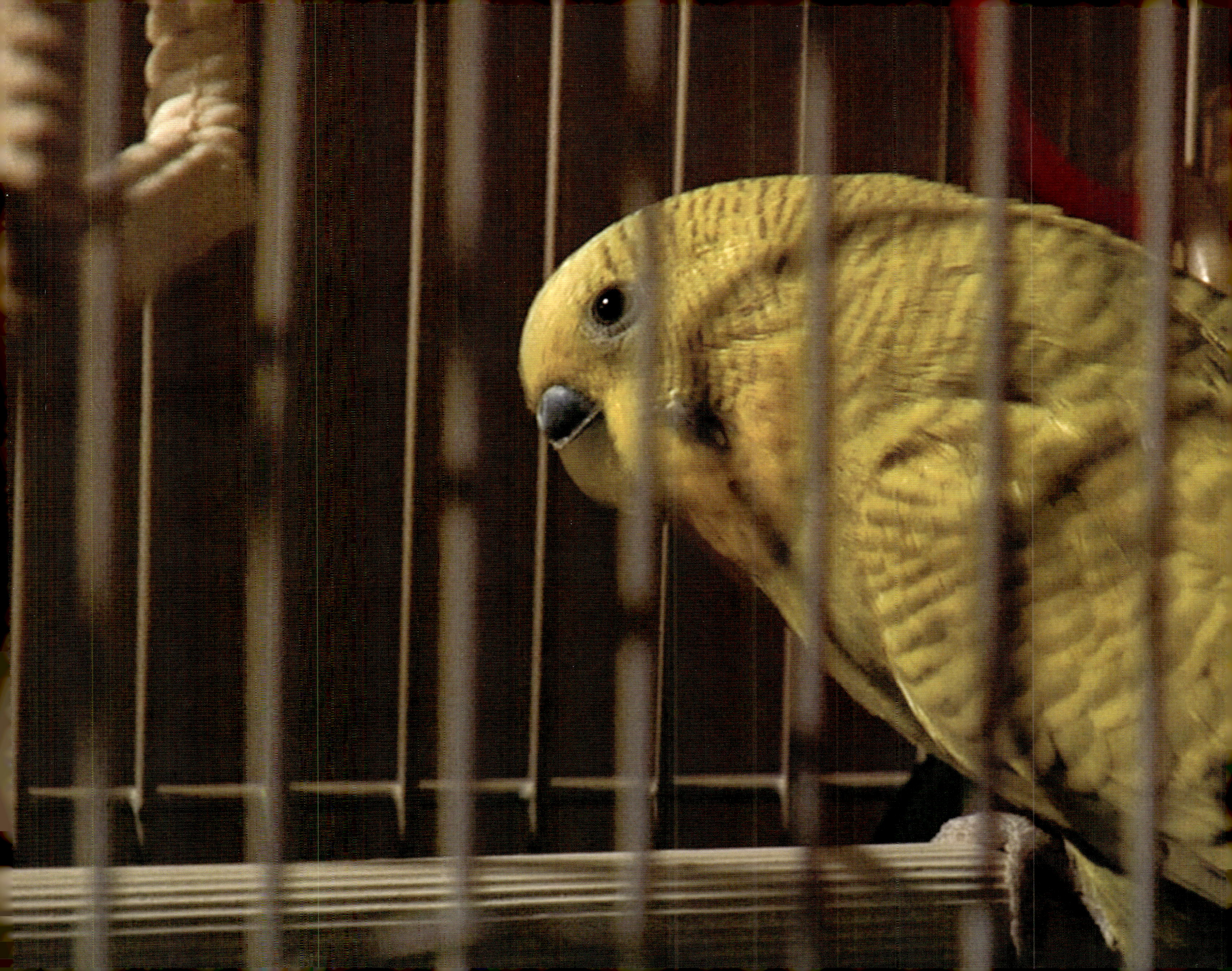

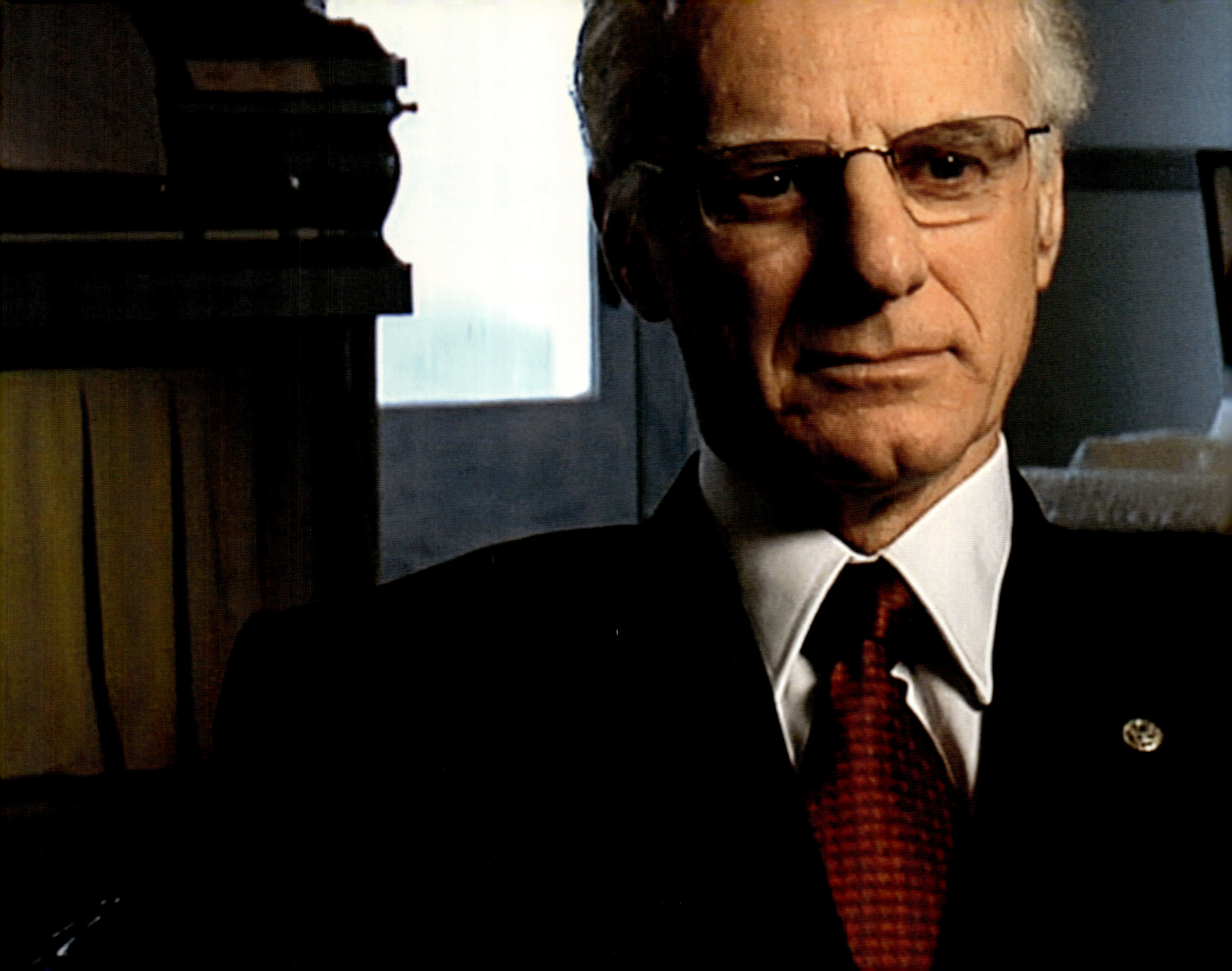

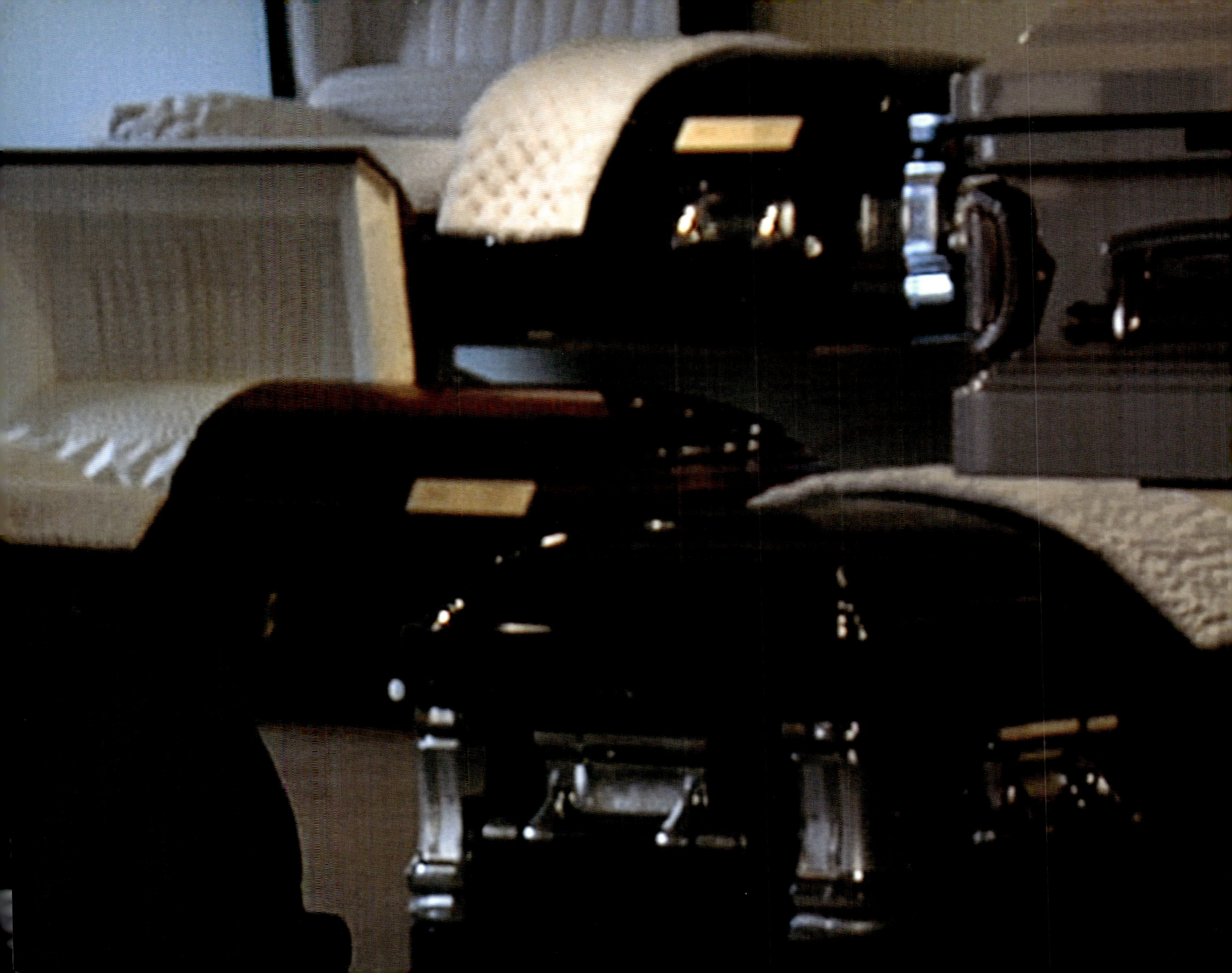

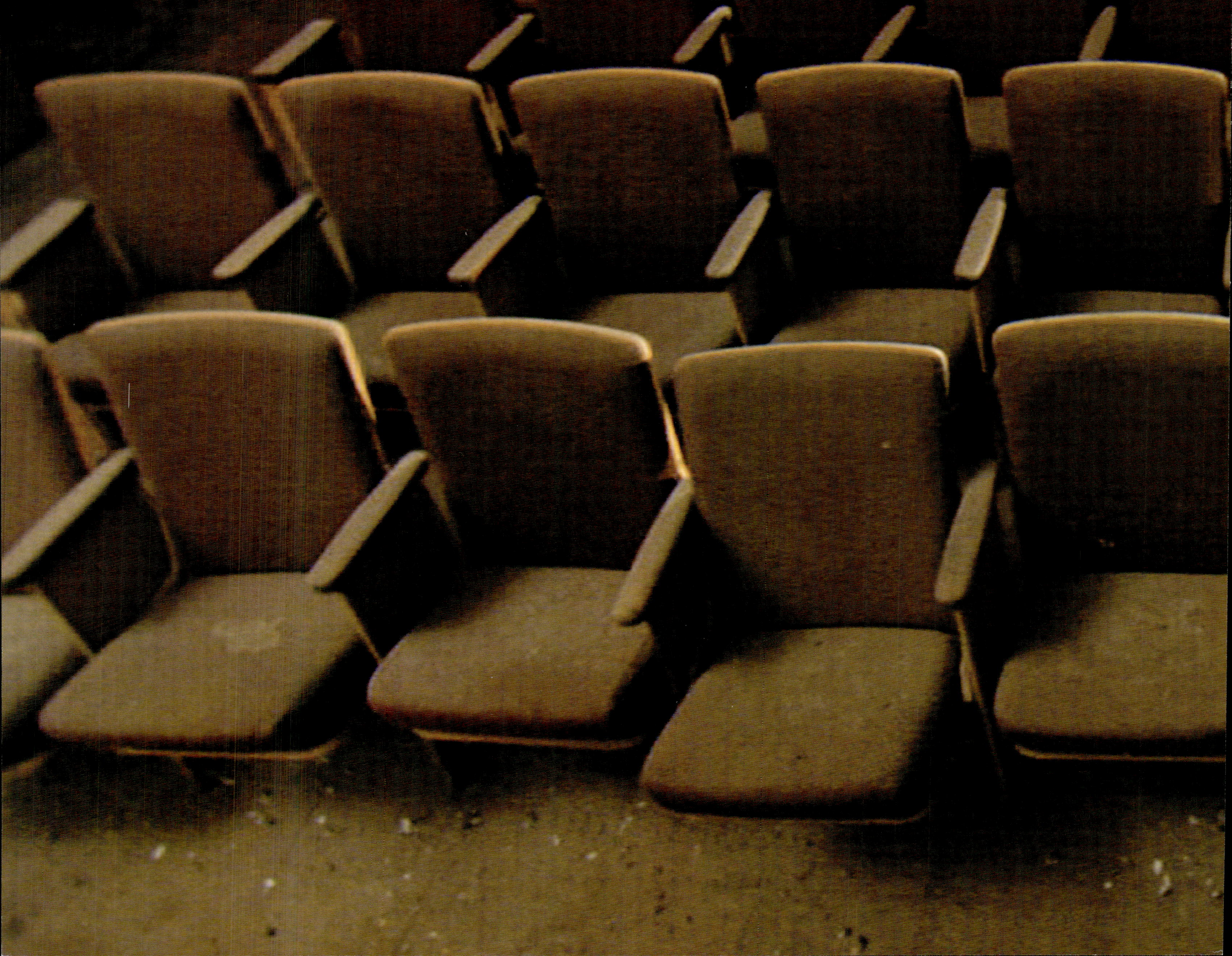

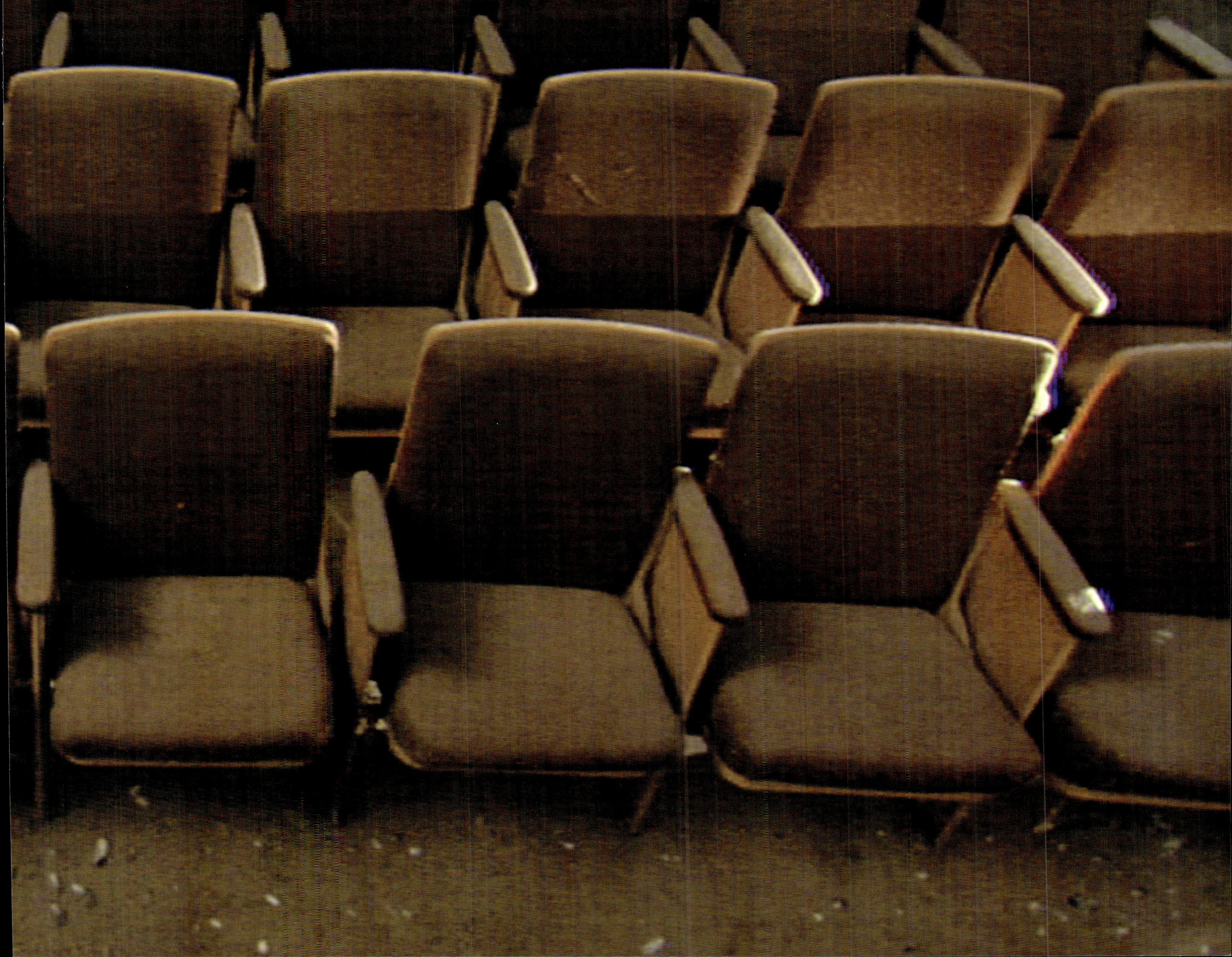

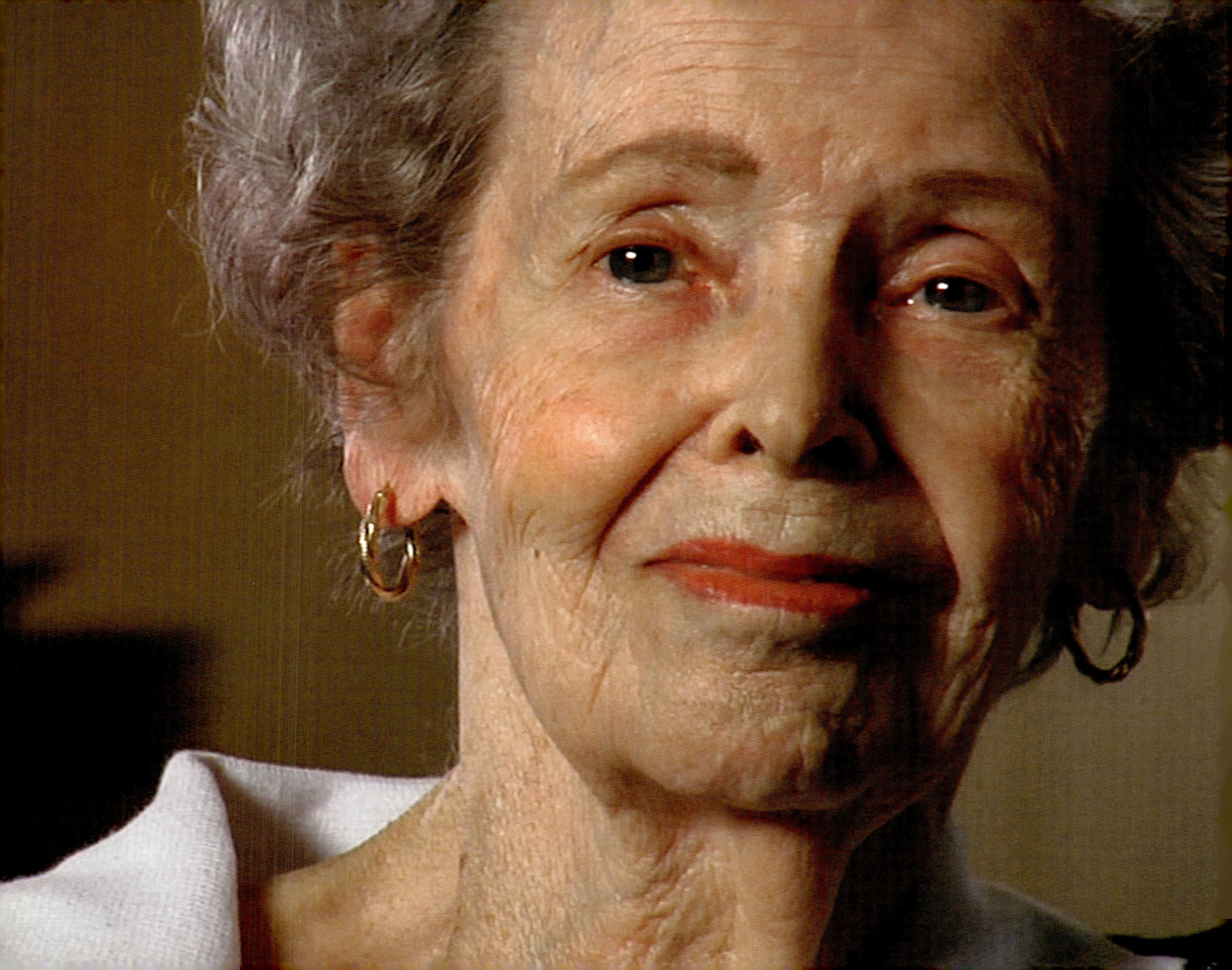

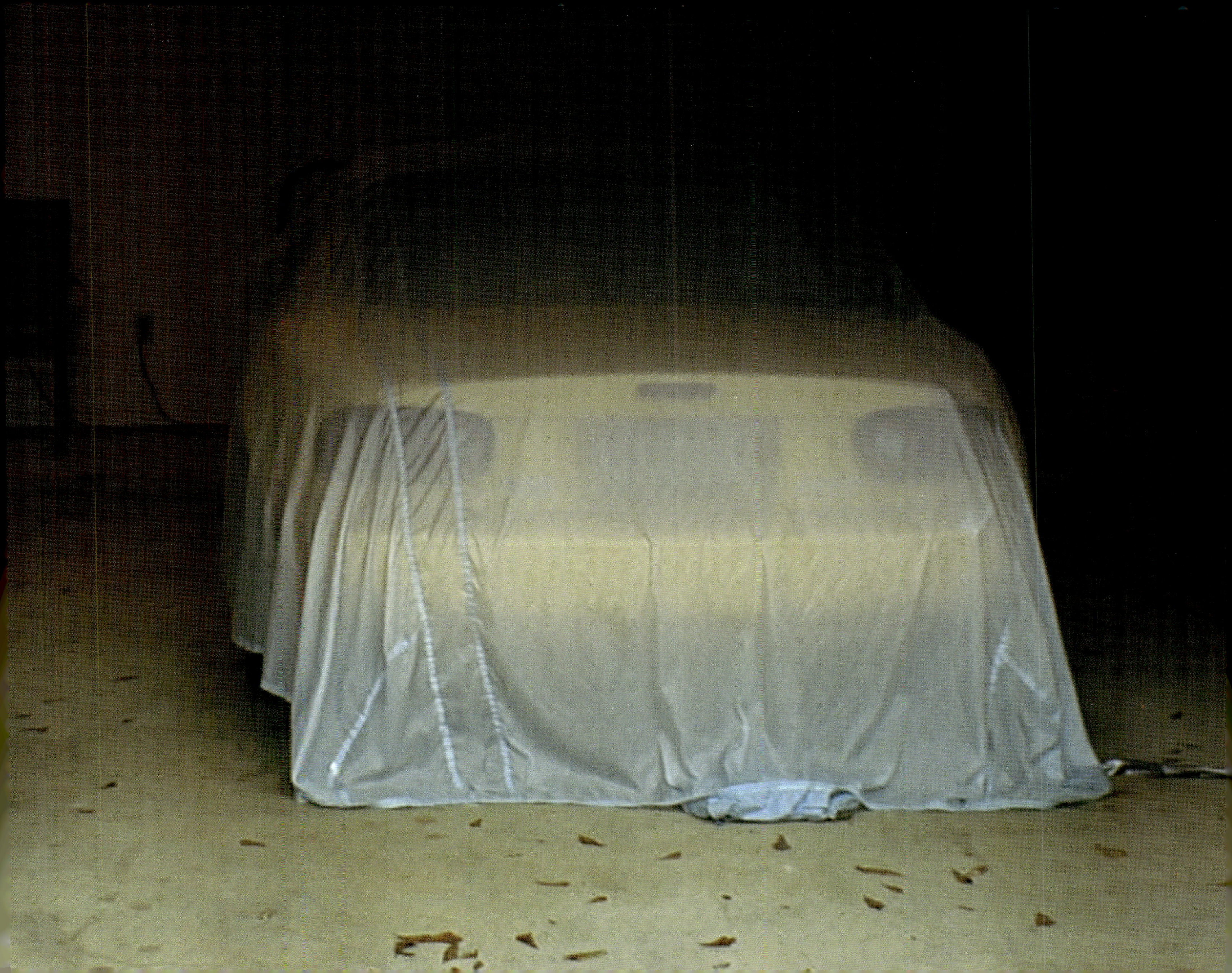

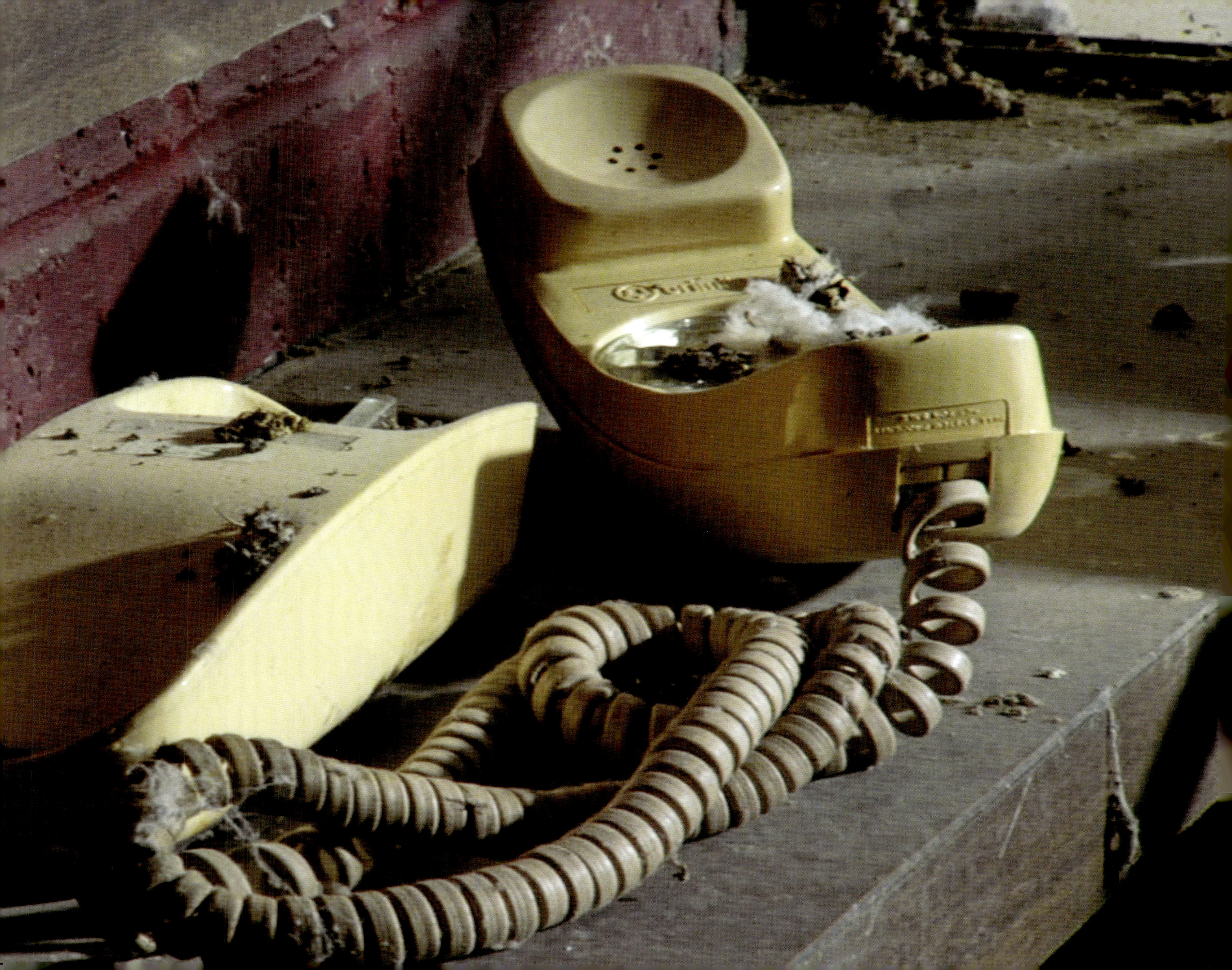

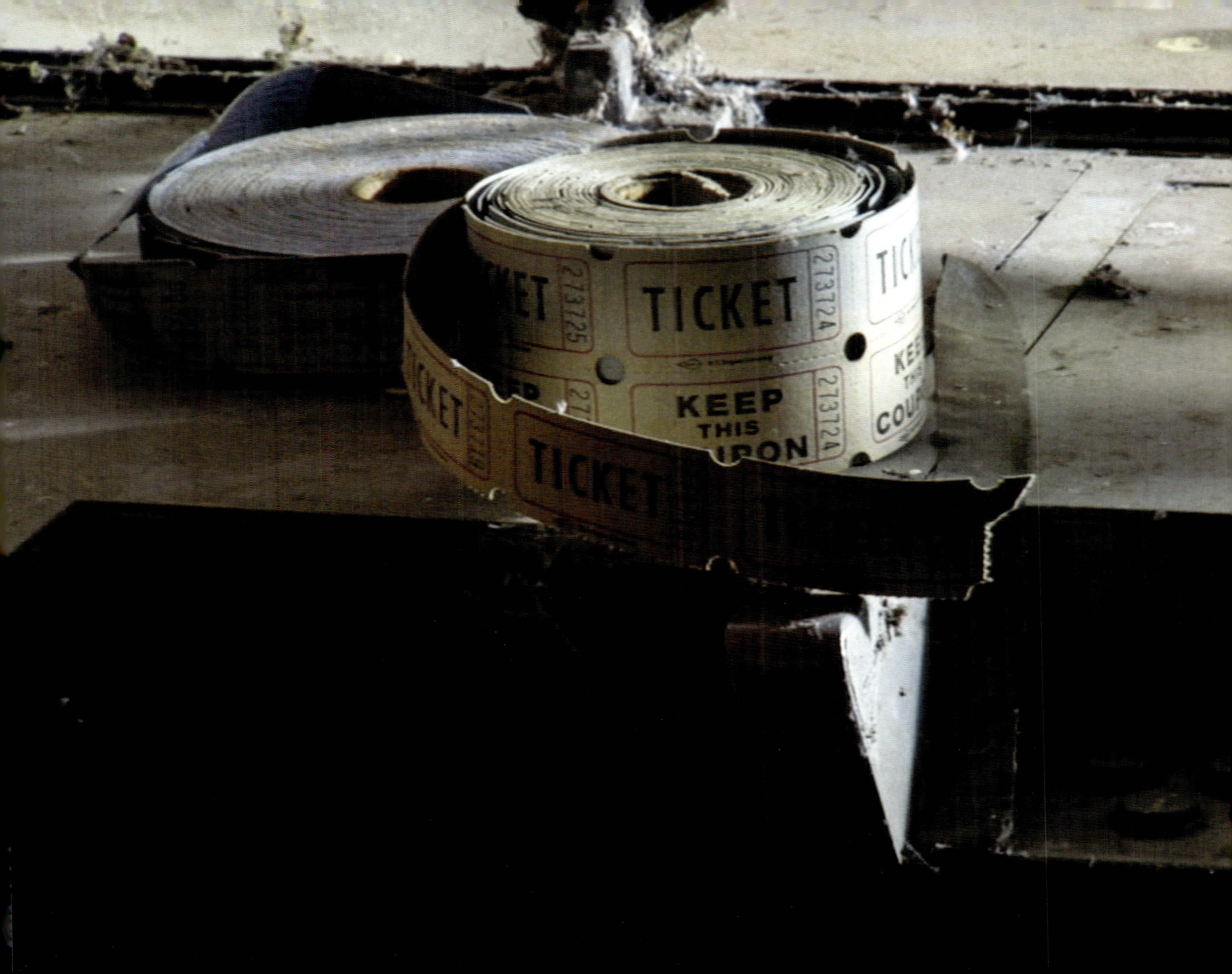
TICKET
273725
273724
TICKET
KEEP
THIS
273724
TICKET

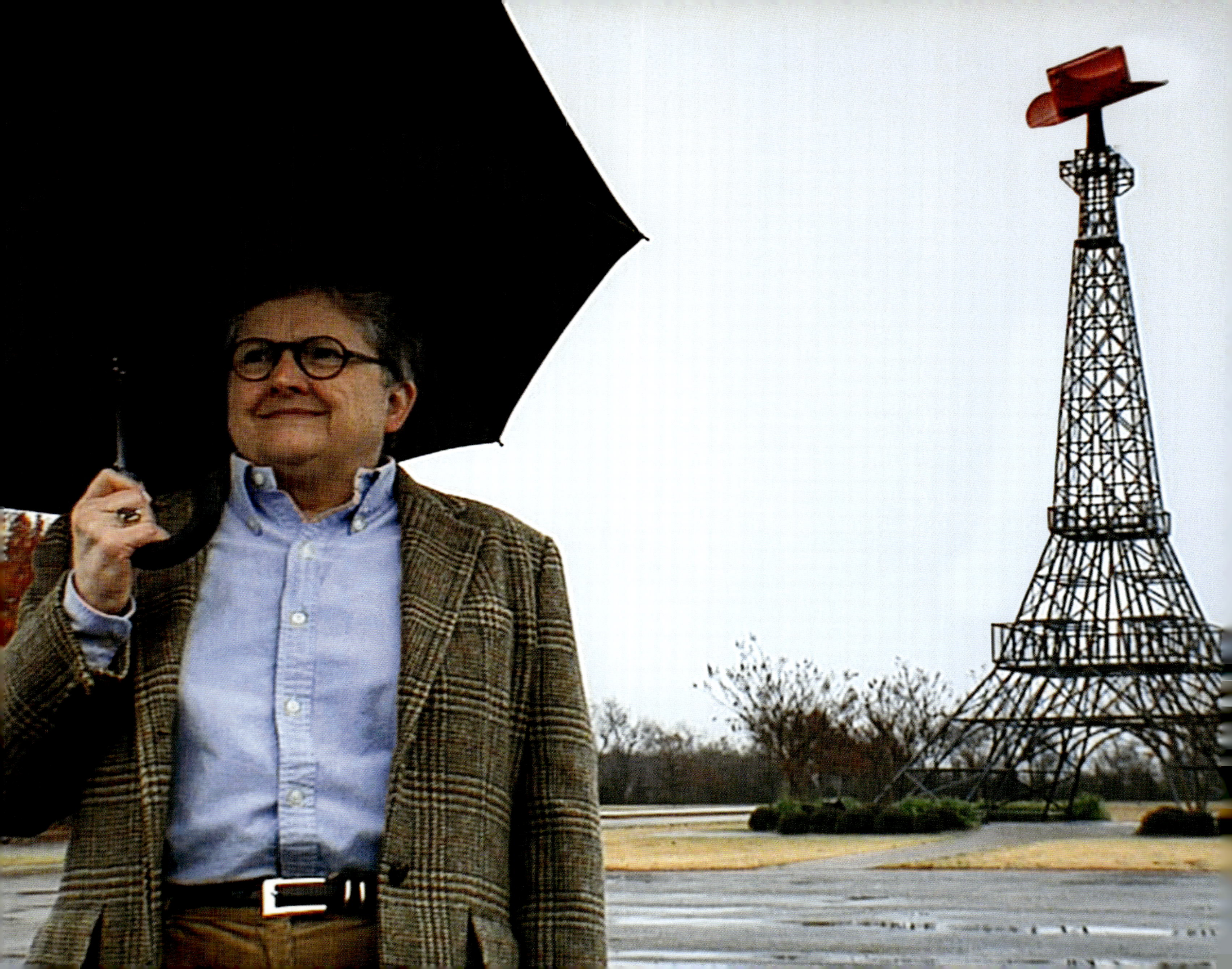

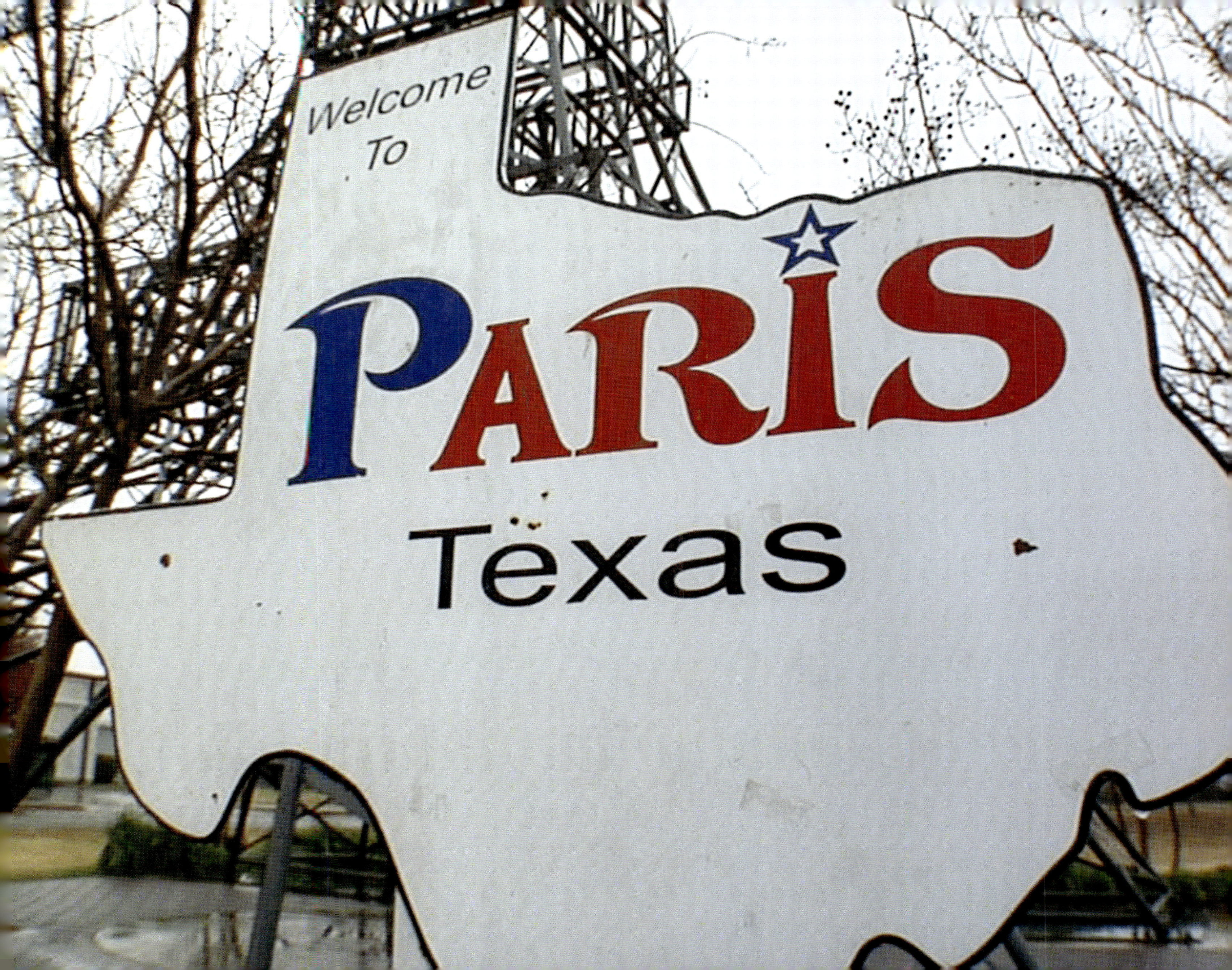
Welcome
To
PARIS
Texas

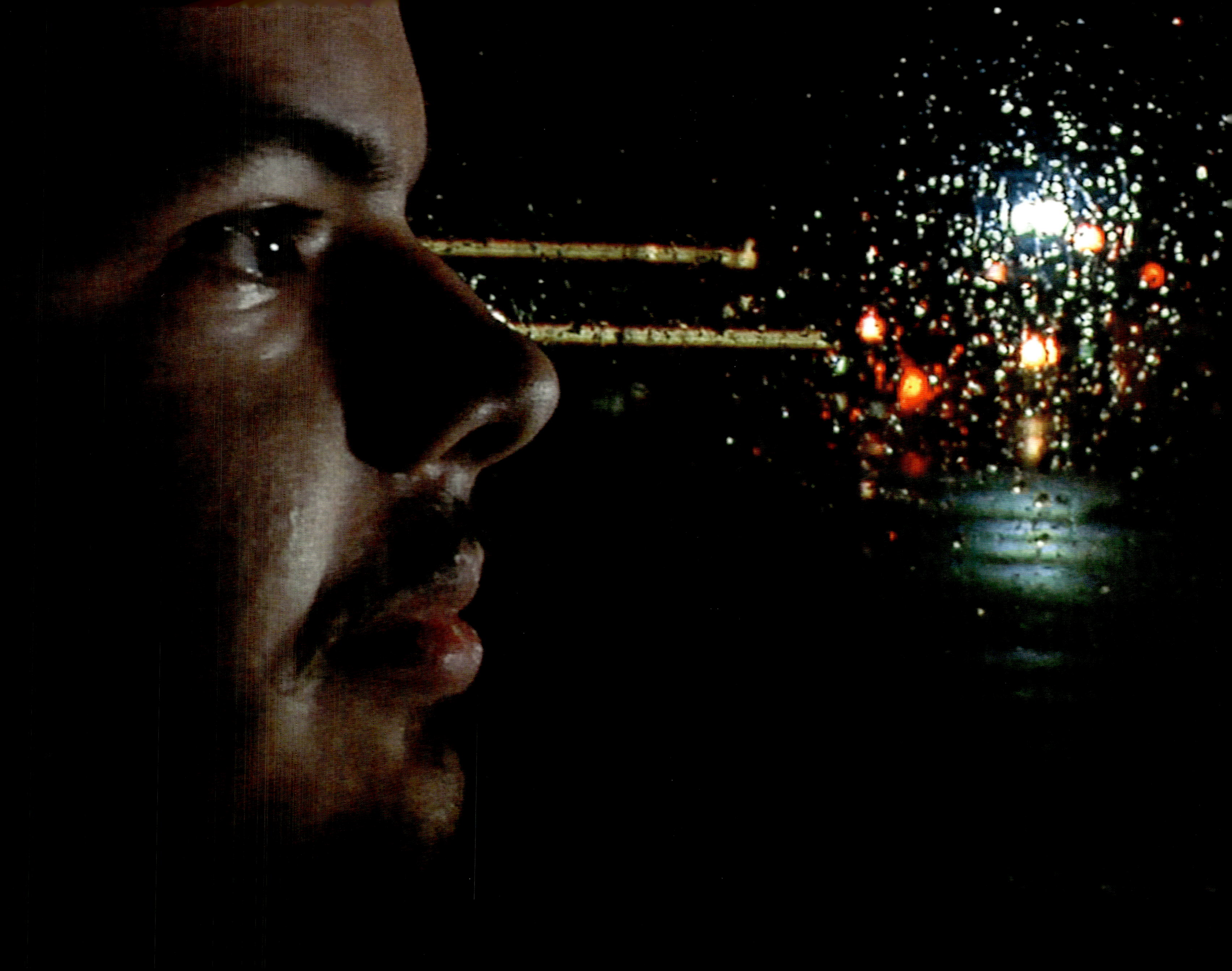

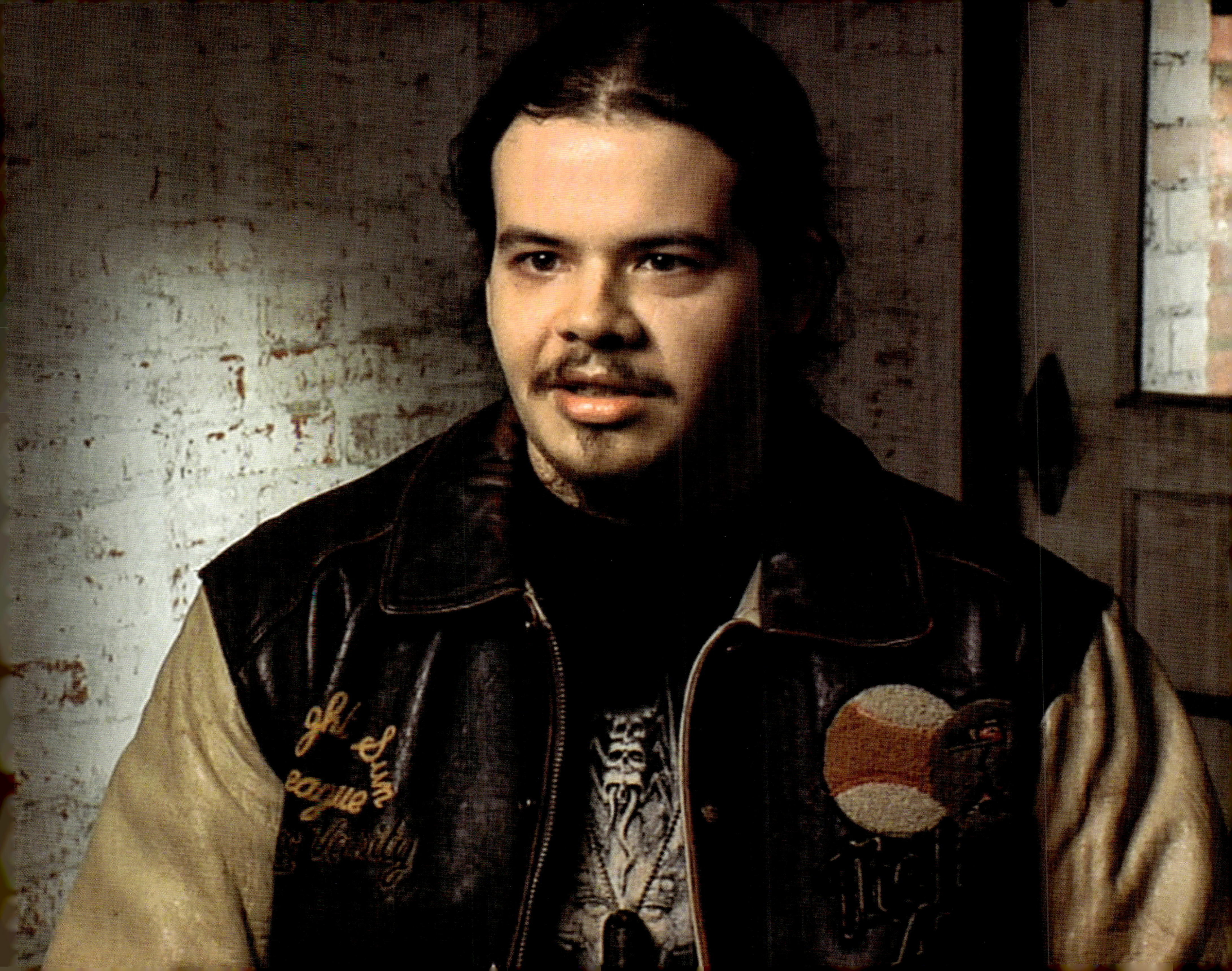

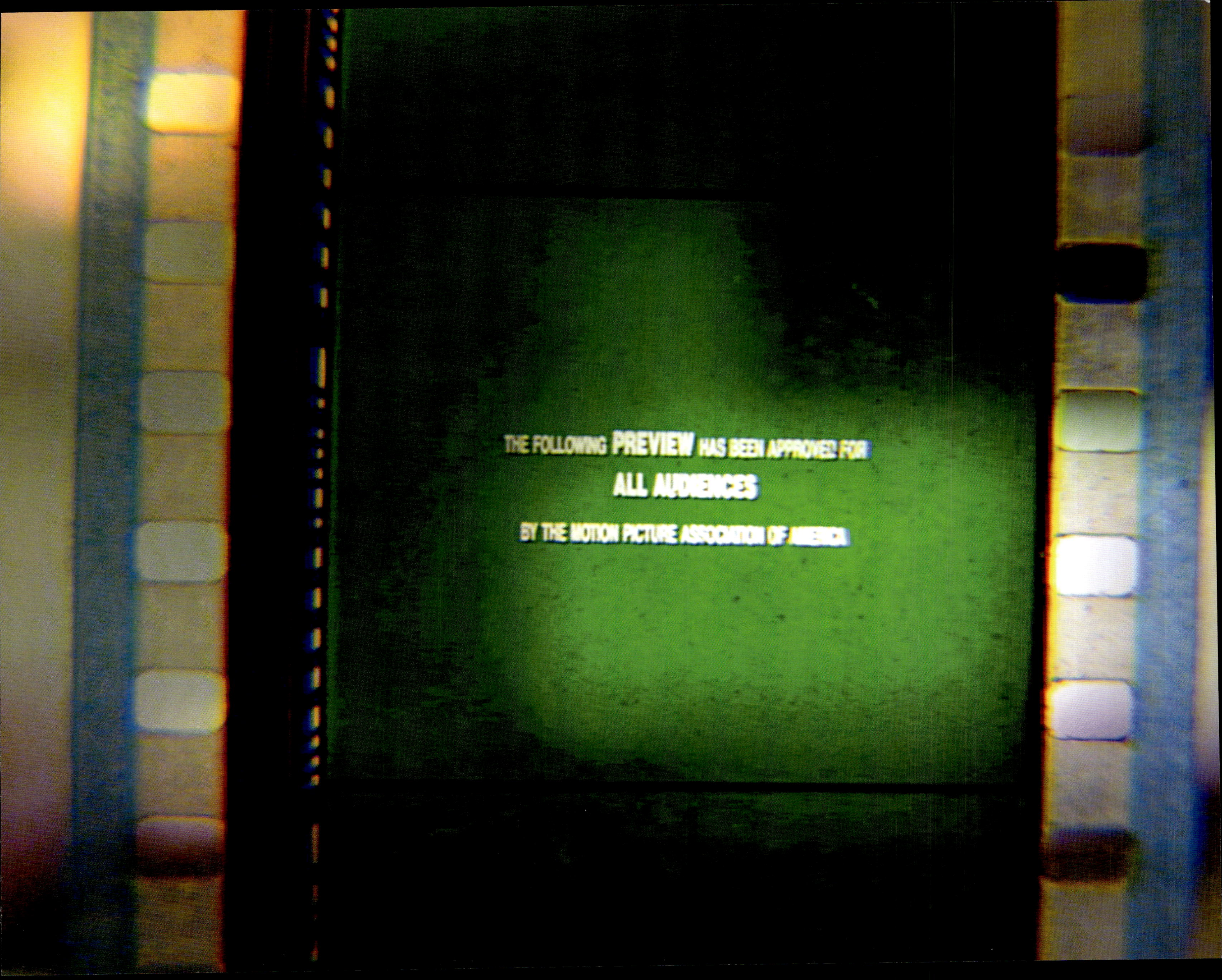
THE FOLLOWING PREVIEW HAS BEEN APPROVED FOR
ALL AUDIENCES
BY THE MOTION PICTURE ASSOCIATION OF AMERICA

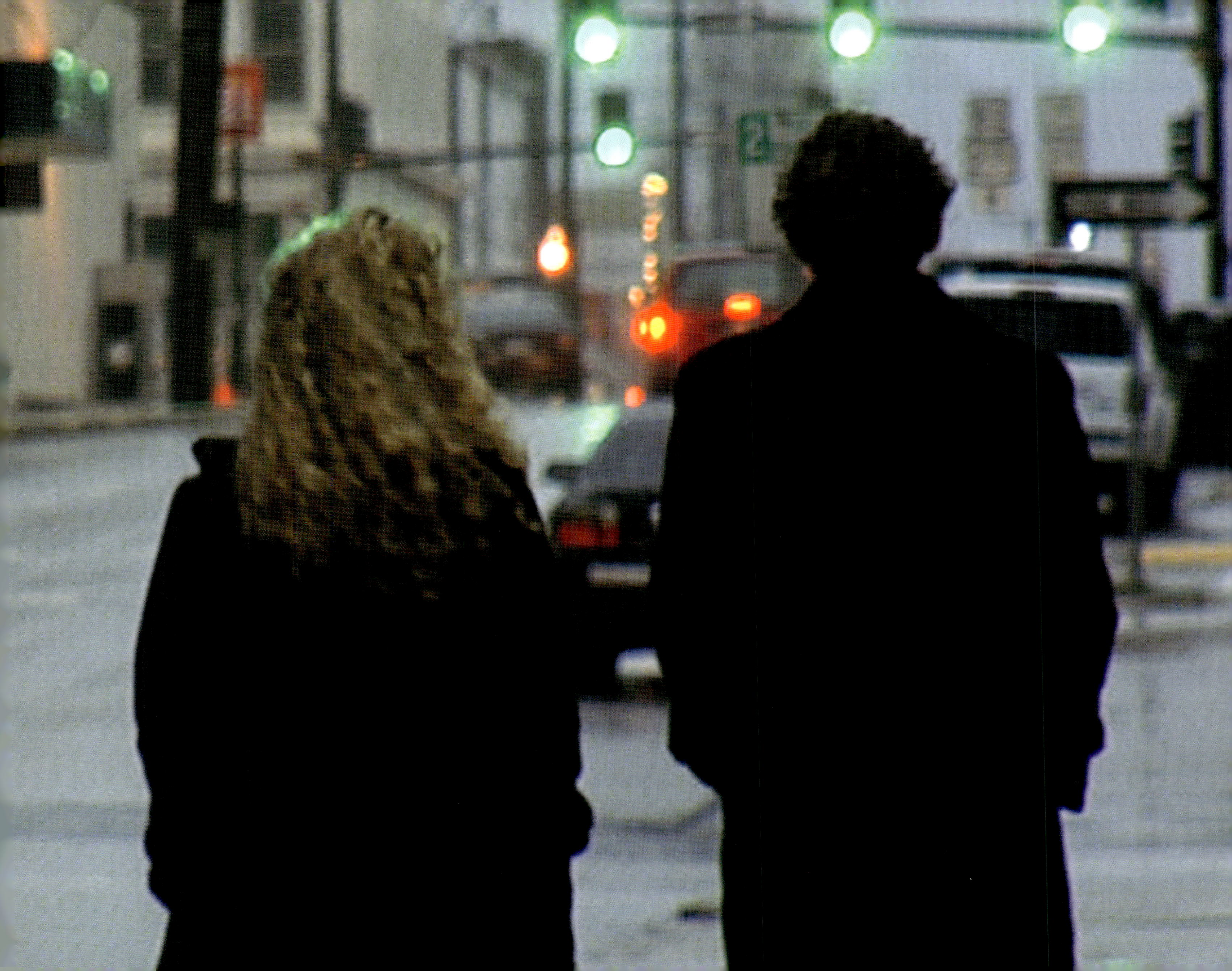

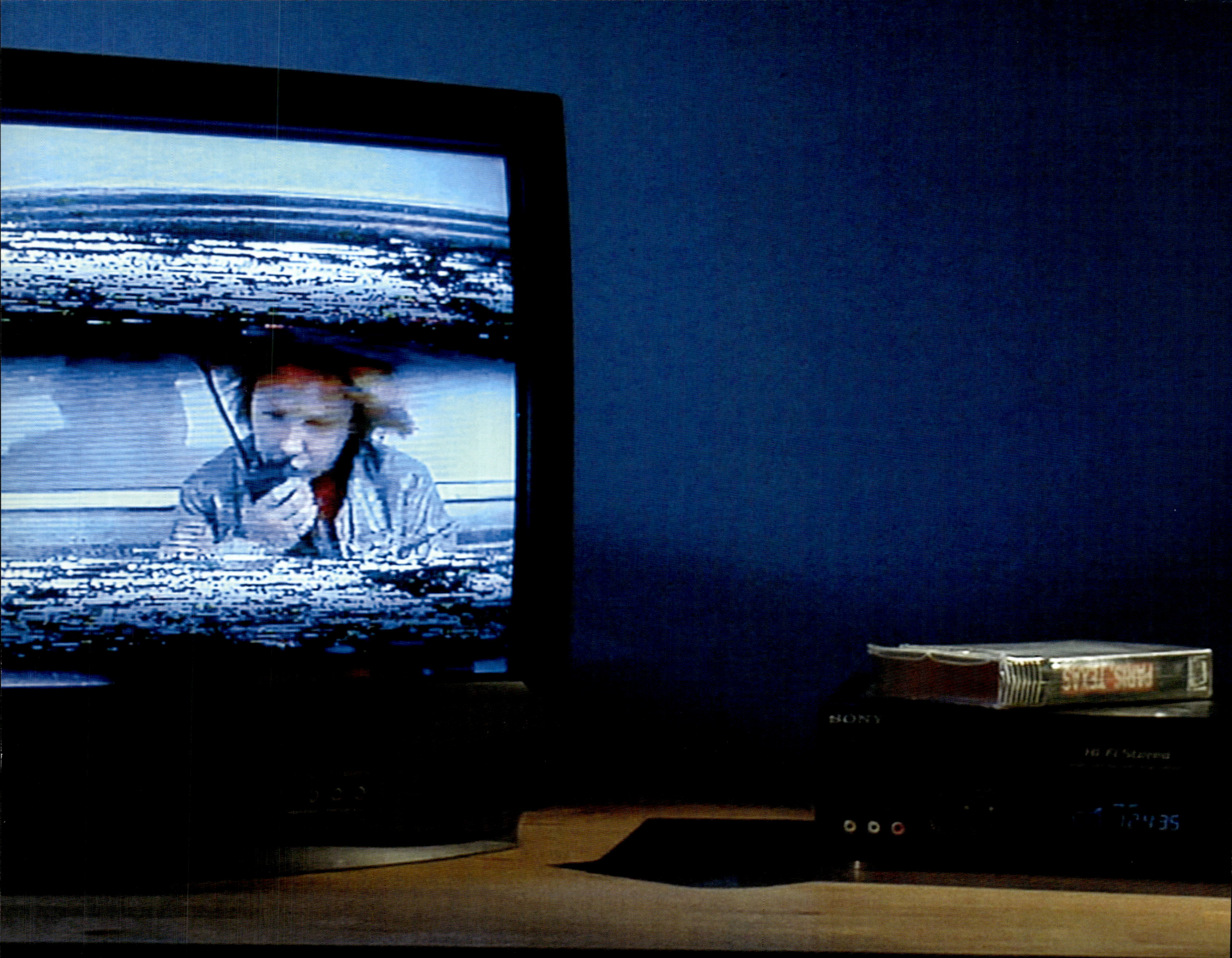
SONY

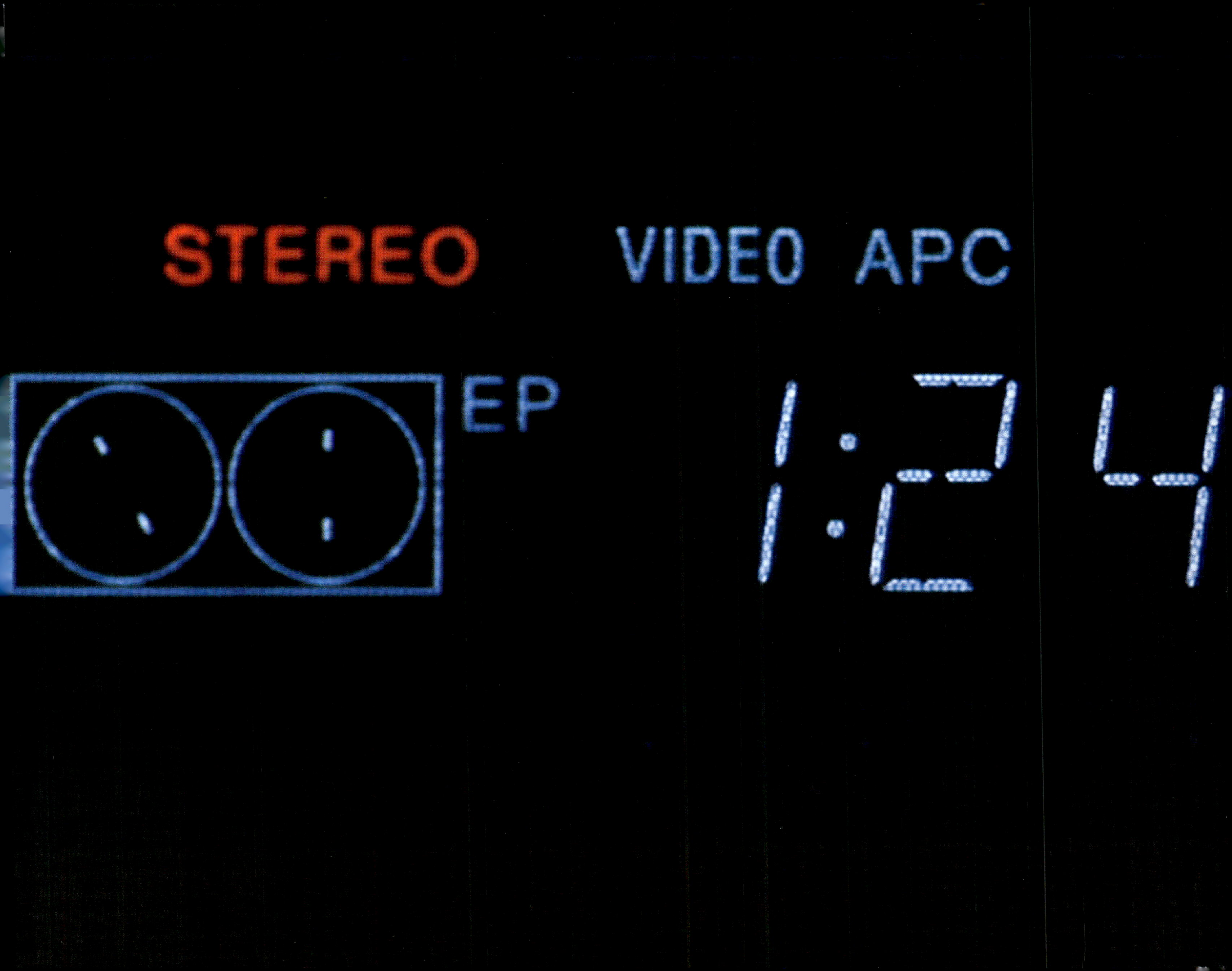
STEREO
VIDEO APC
EP
1:24

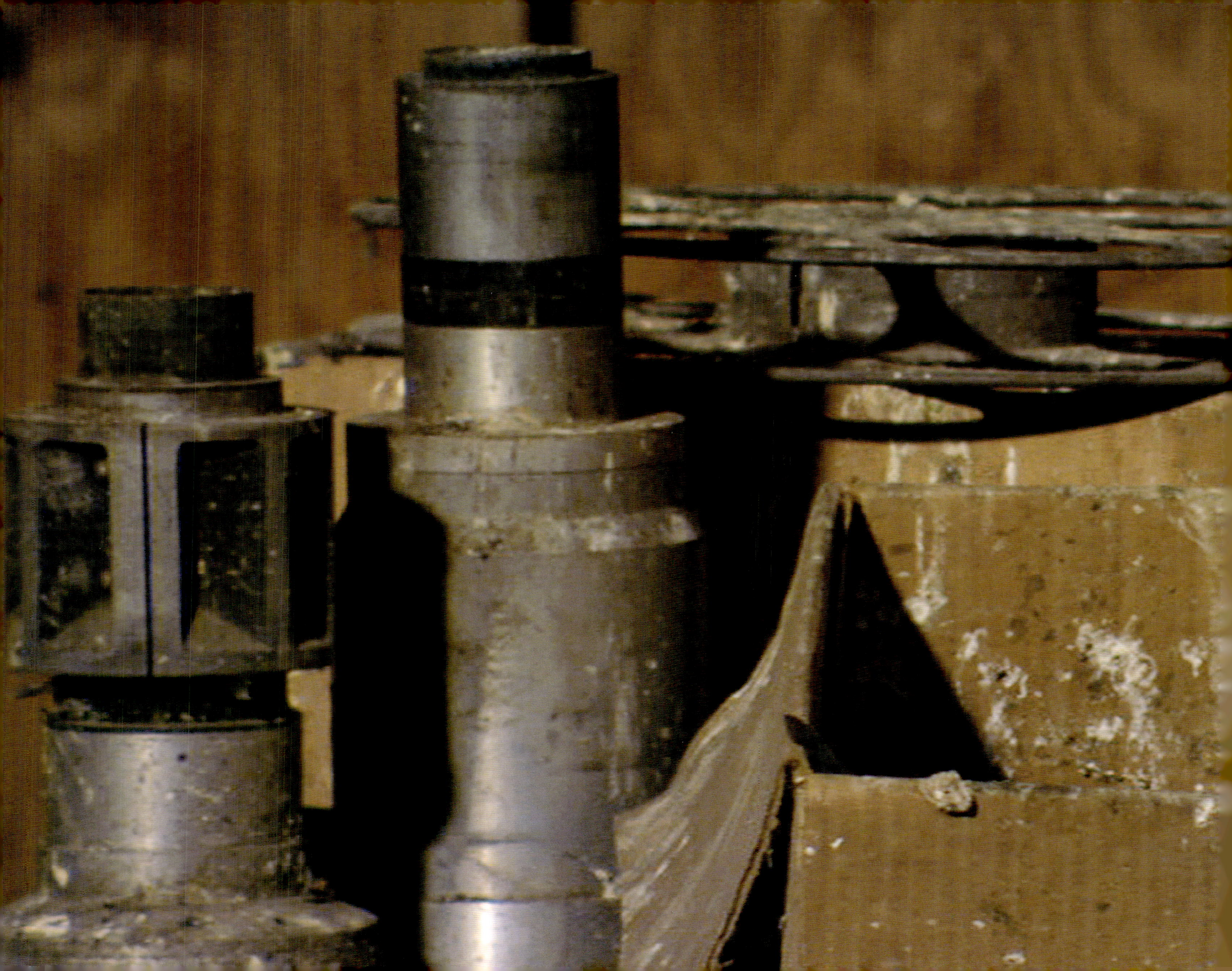

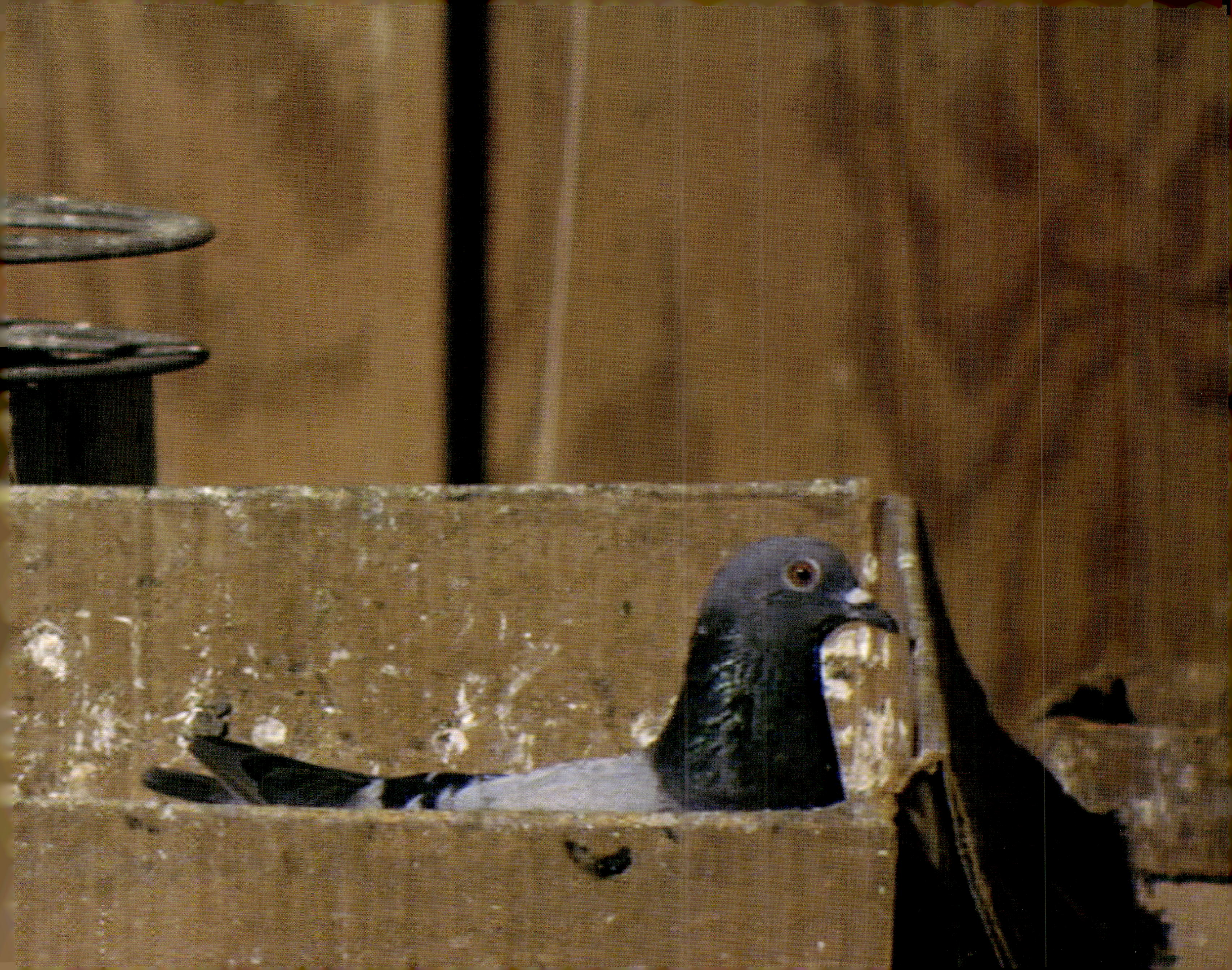

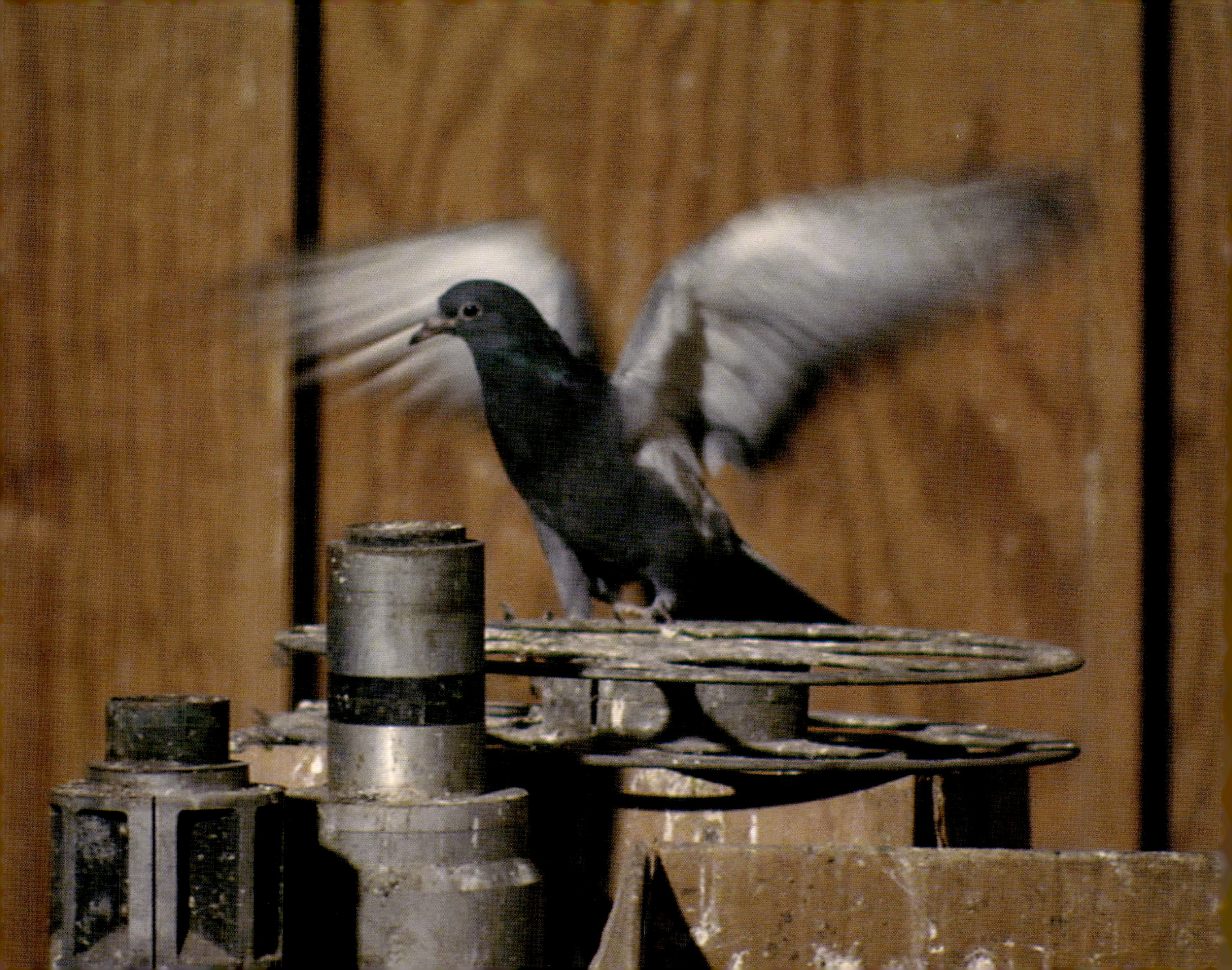

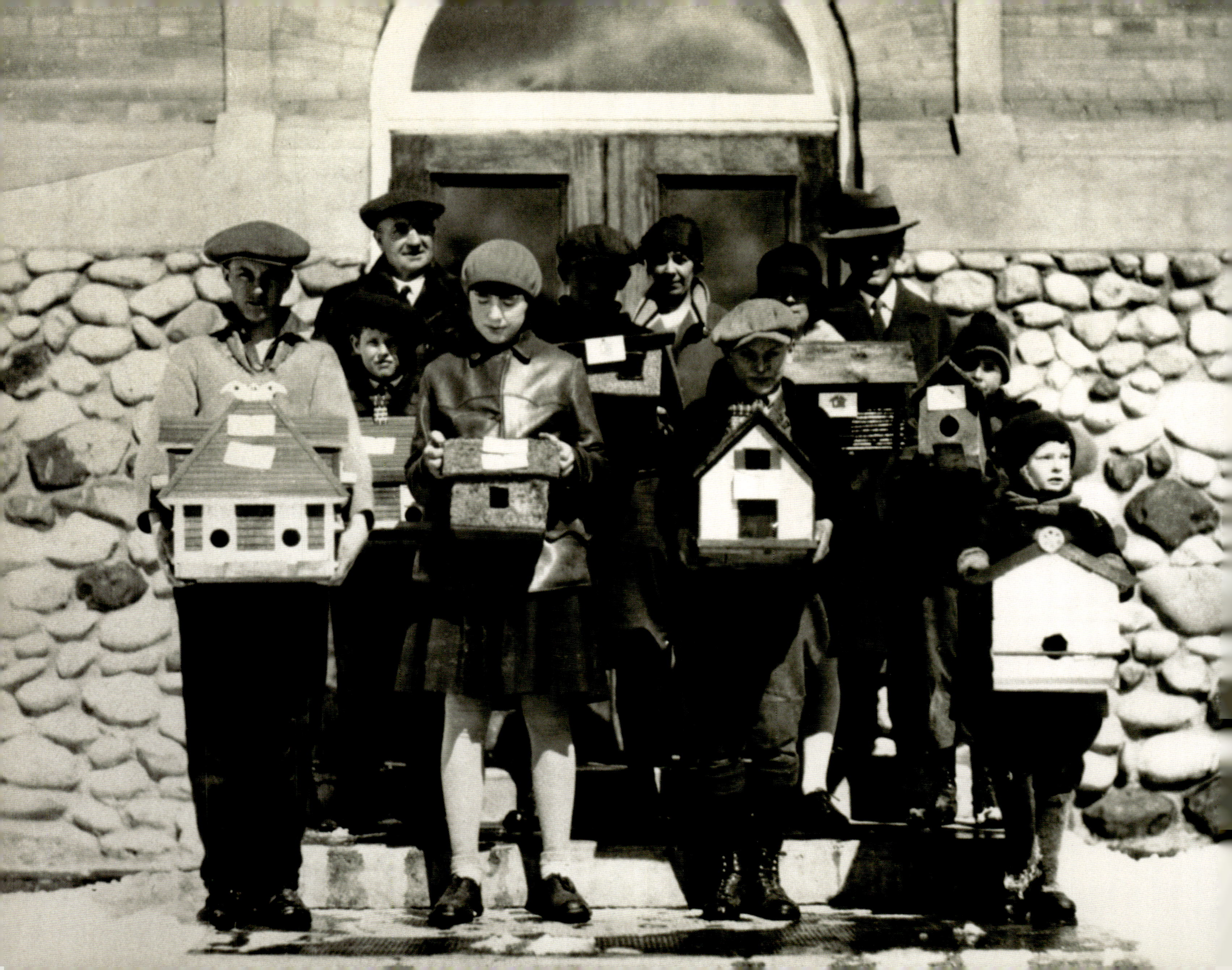

SEÁN KISSANE

This is Not a Portrait

There is a key scene in Hubbard/Birchler's video *Eight* (2001)[1] that focuses on the back of a young girl's head as she looks out a window at her own reflection. It is reminiscent of René Magritte's 1937 portrait of Edward James in which the subject's face is doubly concealed from the viewer. The title of the painting is *Not to be Reproduced* and it is a *portrait manqué*, or failed portrait—one in which the likeness of the sitter is never conveyed. Two centuries earlier Voltaire set a literary precedent with a poem called "Le Portrait Manqué" (1747) in which he expounds on his inability to portray his subject—the cryptically named "Madame La Marquise de B***"—because she is too full of mystery and contradictions.

The *portrait manqué* also provides a means to enter Hubbard/Birchler's recently completed trilogy, as this device seems to encapsulate many of the artists' current and recent concerns. With names like *Giant* (2014), *Movie Mountain (Méliès)* (2011) and *Grand Paris Texas* (2009) the videos set up the expectation that their "sitters" will be portrayed. However, like the portraits of Magritte and Voltaire, Hubbard/Birchler instead present the viewer with what is *not* known about the subjects, thus appropriating them as a sort of Surrealist Assemblage. Beginning with movies by figures as diverse as Gaston and Georges Méliès and Wim Wenders, Hubbard/Birchler take these as raw materials and create a collage or assemblage of interviews, archaeological documentation of the sets and imagined reconstructions to create new artworks that suggest another reality, another anxiety. Hubbard/Birchler's means of appropriation have already been compared to that of Cindy Sherman[2] (and thus by extension Sherrie Levine and Yasumasa Morimura), but their peculiar excavation of film history separates them from these other practitioners. Instead of re-presenting an actual historical event (like a film), their focus is on historicity—the memory or folkloric retelling of the thing rather than the fact of it as they hybridize documentary and fiction.

Magritte's *Not to be Reproduced* was created almost concurrently with Walter Benjamin's essay "The Work of Art in the Age of Mechanical Reproduction" (1936), which formed a touchstone for Hubbard/Birchler's early practice. In works like *Contestants in a Birdhouse Competition* (1991/1996), they questioned Benjamin's central assertion that part of an artwork—its aura—is lost when a reproduction (a portrait) of it is created.

In their latest work, Hubbard/Birchler create a portrait of the *production* of a portrait—a meta-portrait of sorts. But while Benjamin argued that something was lost through the mechanical reproduction of an artifact, Hubbard/Birchler continually remind the viewer that they are looking at a type of reproduction by interweaving images of the mechanisms of production into their narrative sequences. This anti-mimetic play on the naturalistic

Contestants in a Birdhouse Competition, 1991/1996
Installation detail,
Collection, Kunstmuseum Basel

RIGHT:
Not to be Reproduced, 1937, René Magritte
Oil on Canvas
81.3 x 65 cm
Collection, Museum Boijmans Van Beuningen, Rotterdam

BELOW:
The Long Road to Mazatlán, 1999
Isaac Julien
Installation view, detail

OPPOSITE:
Eight, 2001
High-Definition Video with Sound, Single Channel, 3:25 minutes, Loop
Collections, Kunsthaus Zürich, Pinakothek der Moderne, Munich, and others

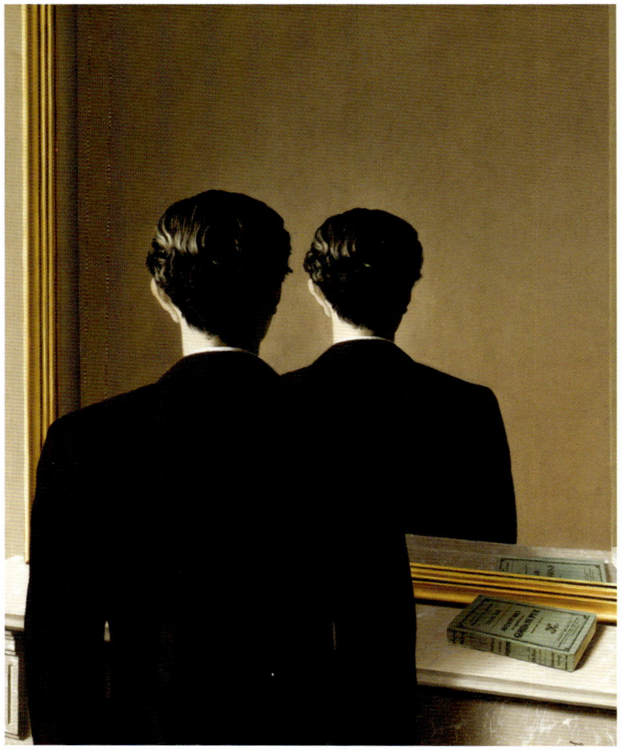

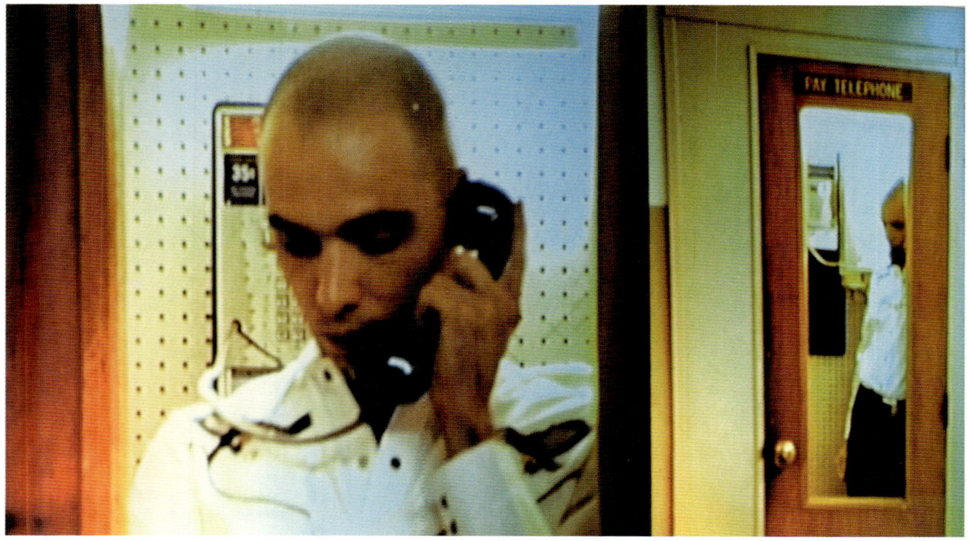

and non-naturalistic staging of pieces is something they share with the Irish artist Gerard Byrne (b. 1969), whose film projects involve reconstructing historical conversations published in popular magazines from the 1960s to 1980s. Byrne repeatedly reminds viewers that they are looking at a reconstruction; we hear the director give instruction to the actors, see repeated takes and hear the incongruity of Irish accents voicing American or French figures.

The distancing strategies employed by Byrne and Hubbard/Birchler are reminiscent of the work of Bertolt Brecht, whose practice of "Epic Theater" disallowed empathy because it "entranced" the viewer and created an uncritical and unreflective spectator who over-identified with the main characters. Brecht's renowned *Verfremdungseffekt* (distancing effect) sought to remove the naturalism of traditional theater and engender instead a recognition in the viewer that both the theater experience and the viewer's reality were constructs. Brecht hoped to create a politically activated viewer that might then go on to affect change in the real world.[3]

The location of Texas, and familiar visual tropes like cowboys, cattle and empty vistas link *Giant* and Isaac Julien's work *The Long Road to Mazatlán* (1999). "The sound design for both videos provides a note of ambivalence. The constant clatter of a train forms the backdrop of many scenes and, in Julien's video, the main figure intones the infamous line from Travis Bickle—the demented lead character in Martin Scorsese's *Taxi Driver*—"Are you looking at me?" The result is a sense of underlying apprehension. In *Giant* the viewer is brought into the realm of popular culture and the American cable television series about the New York ad industry, *Mad Men,* with its 1960s anachronisms that tweak contemporary consciousness—from smoking cigarettes and drinking whiskey in the office to strictly defined gender roles and the sexualization of women in the workplace. While the erotic

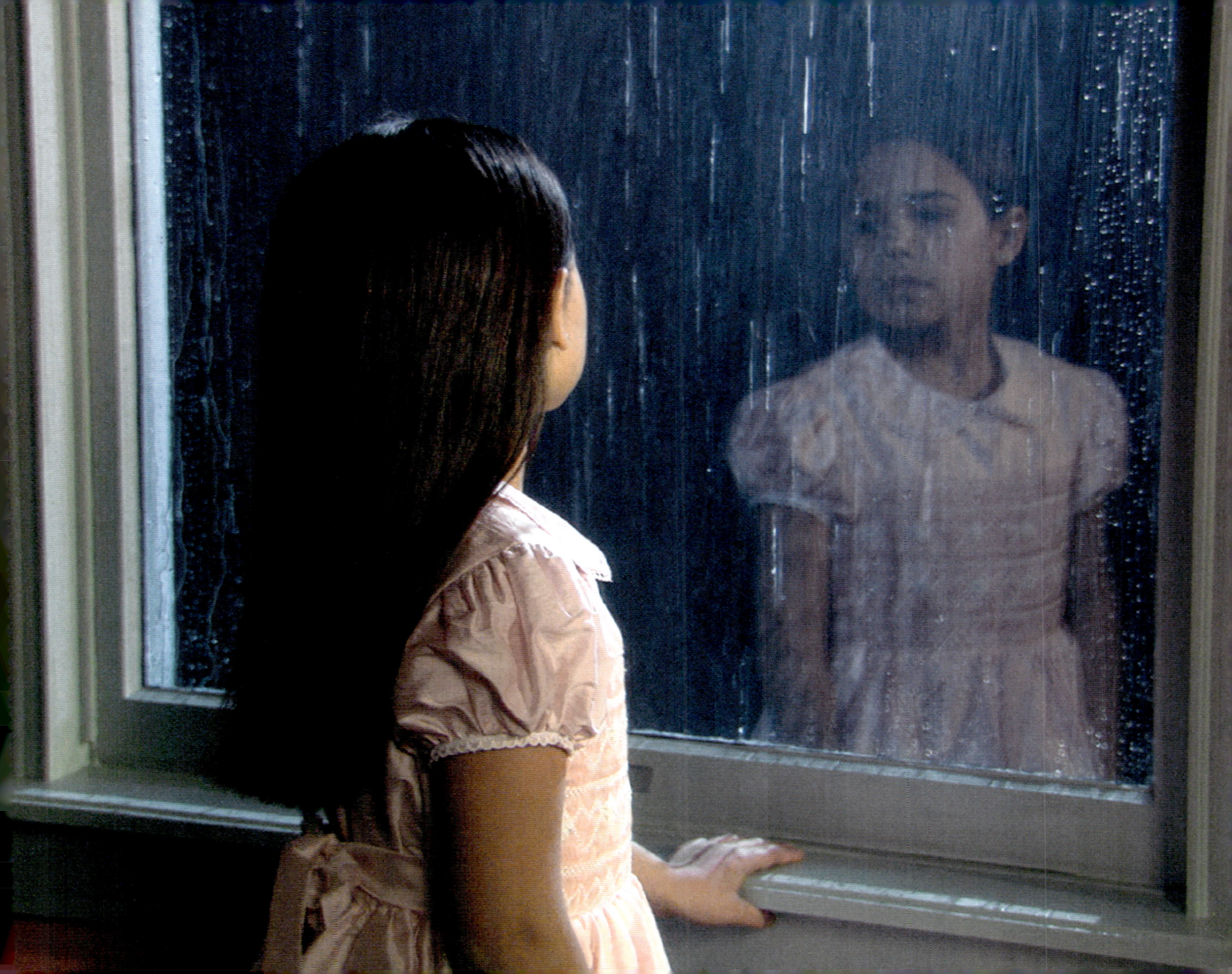

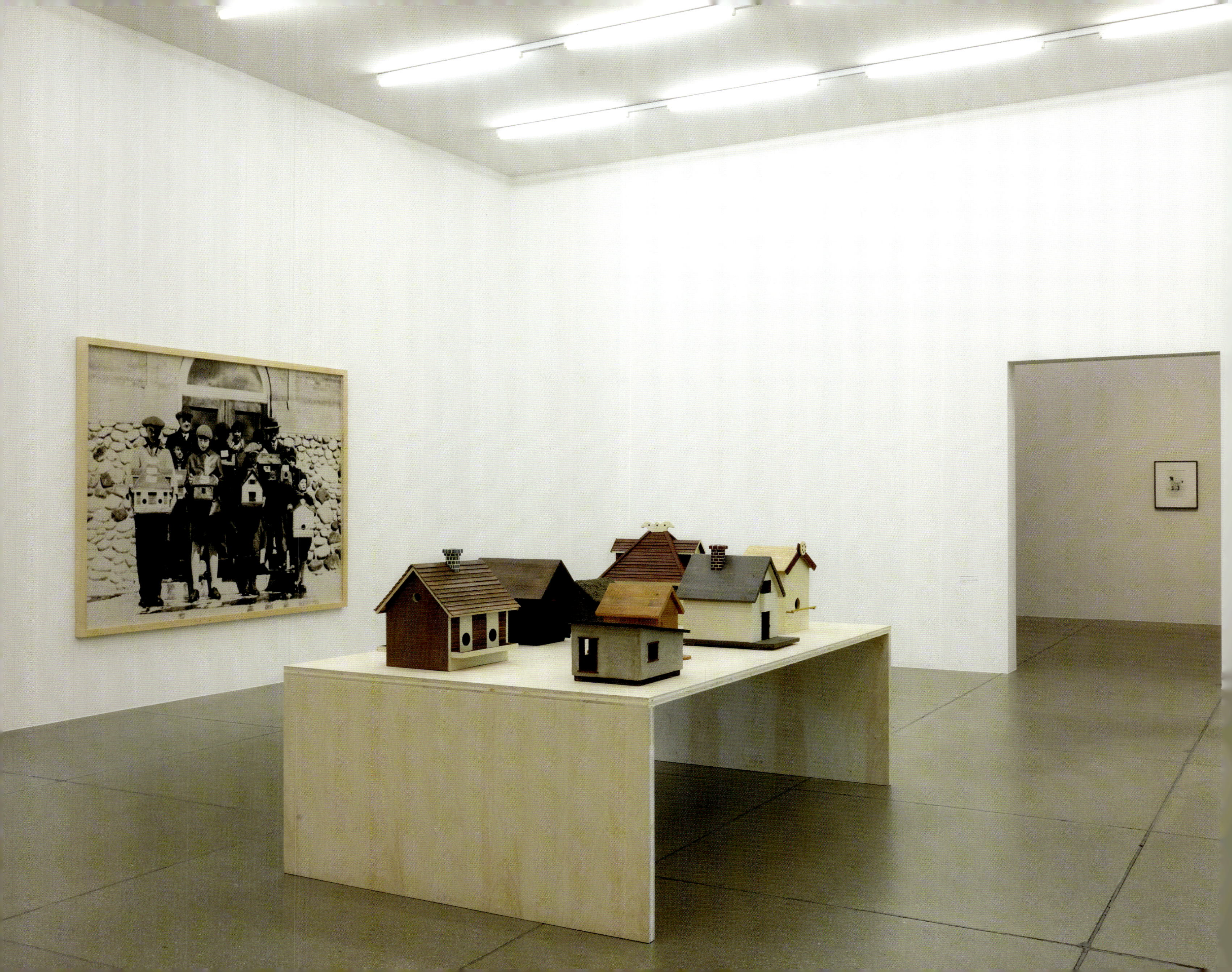

tension between the male protagonists in Julien's film remains unconsummated—theirs seems to be a love made for a different time—so too does *Giant's* female protagonist appear to look to the future, pausing from her work to gaze out the office window. The scene then cuts to the present day and a female audio engineer—a thematic nod perhaps to social and gender emancipation, but perhaps even more a Brechtian jolt that reminds us to suspend belief and distance ourselves from the emotional reaction evoked by the previous scenes. Such an interplay seems to point to a distinction that Roland Barthes made in his formative text *Camera Lucida: Reflections on Photography* (1980) between the literal meaning of an image, or the *studium*, and the entirely personal reaction of the individual viewer, the *punctum*.

As in Voltaire's *portrait manqué*, there is an air of mystery around the subjects that Hubbard/Birchler explore. The artists present us with a paradox. Although they appear to set out on a quest to disinter unknown histories, they can never quite locate the object they propose to present. Rather than constructing art through filmic *objets trouvés*, Hubbard/Birchler's trilogy is a composite of *objets manqués*. In the words of one interviewee in *Movie Mountain (Méliès)*, "I have no idea why they chose that site to take a movie."

1 *Eight* was recently presented by Hubbard/Birchler in their 2014 exhibition *Eight, Eighteen* at Tanya Bonakdar Gallery, New York.

2 Andrea Karnes, *No Room to Answer* (Modern Art Museum of Fort Worth/ Hatje Cantz, 2008), p. 23

3 Susan Best has read the work of Gerard Byrne through Brecht in her essay "Against Identification, Gerard Byrne's Brechtian Tendencies," *Australian & New Zealand Journal of Art*, Vol. 12, Issue 1 (2012): p. 224

Contestants in a Birdhouse Competition, 1991/1996
Installation view, Aargauer Kunsthaus, Aarau, Collection, Kunstmuseum Basel

MOVIE MOUNTAIN (MÉLIÈS), 2011
High-Definition Video with Sound
2 Channel, 24 minutes, Loop
Installation dimensions variable

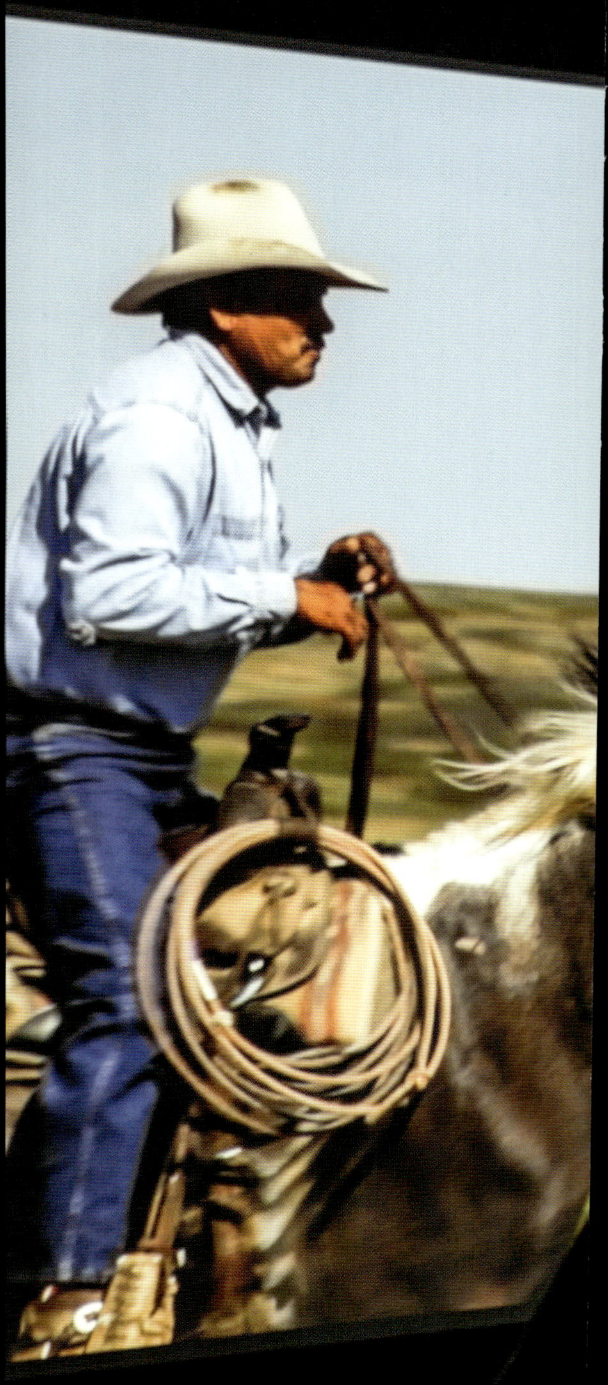

Movie Mountain (Méliès), 2011
Installation view,
Ballroom Marfa

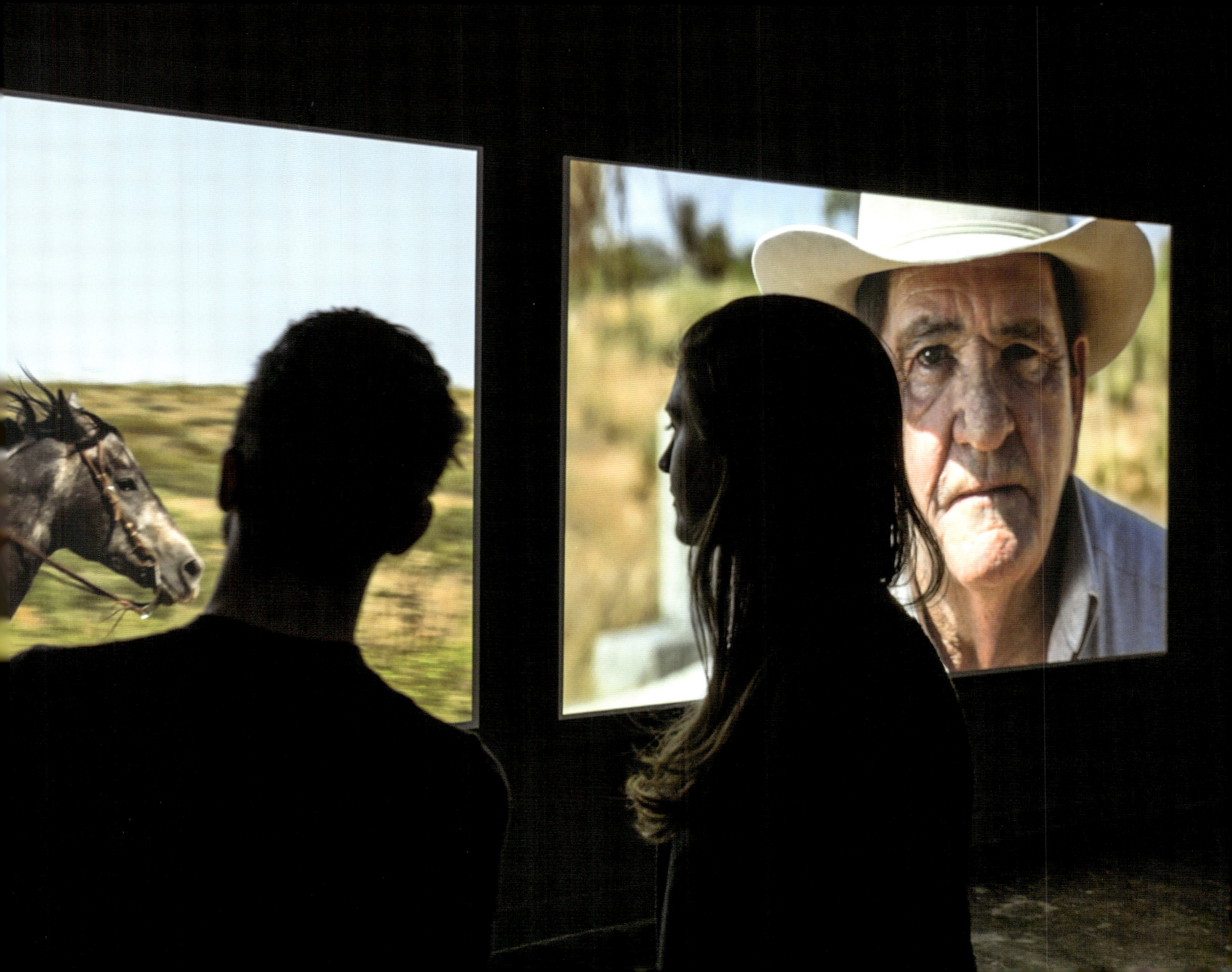

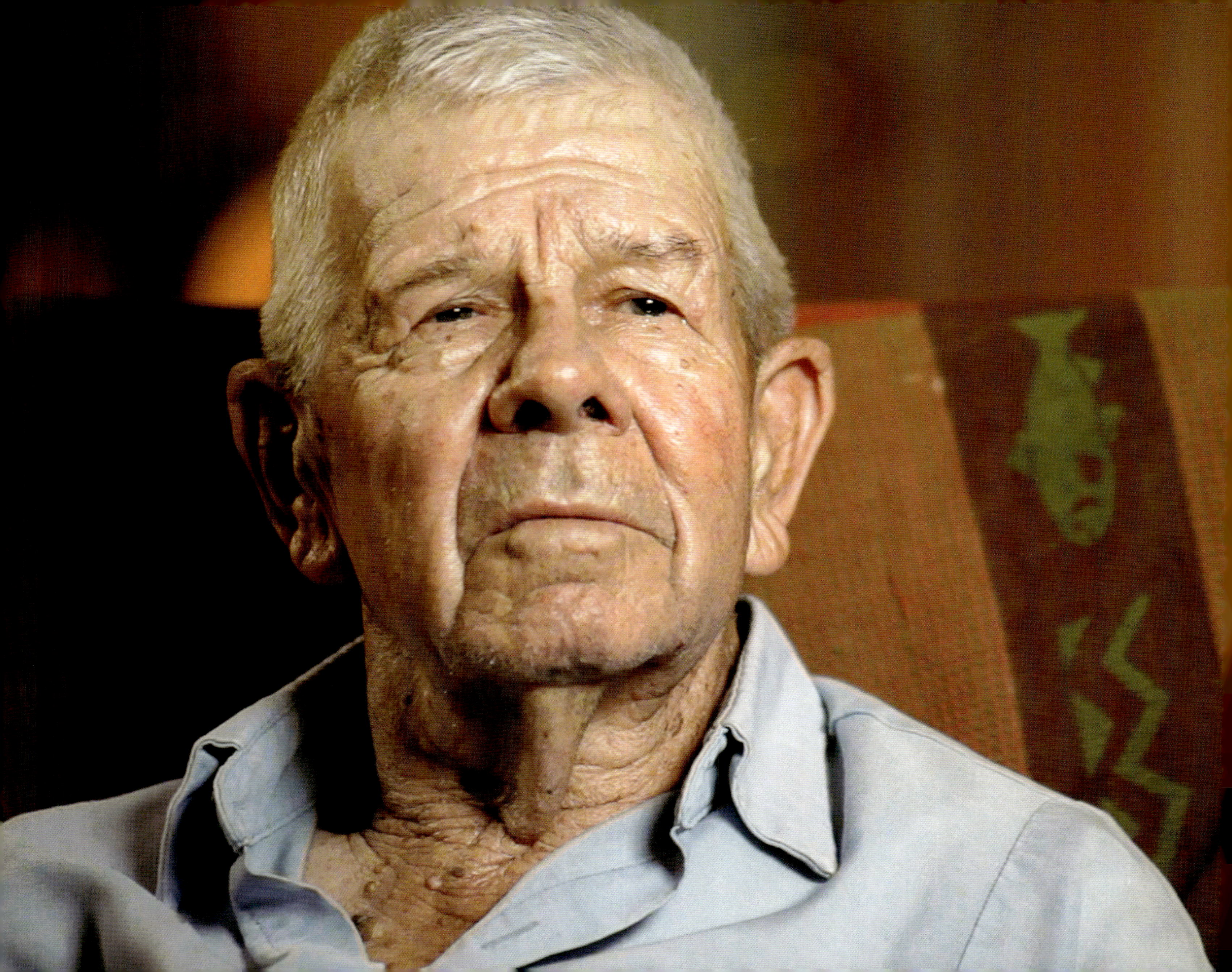

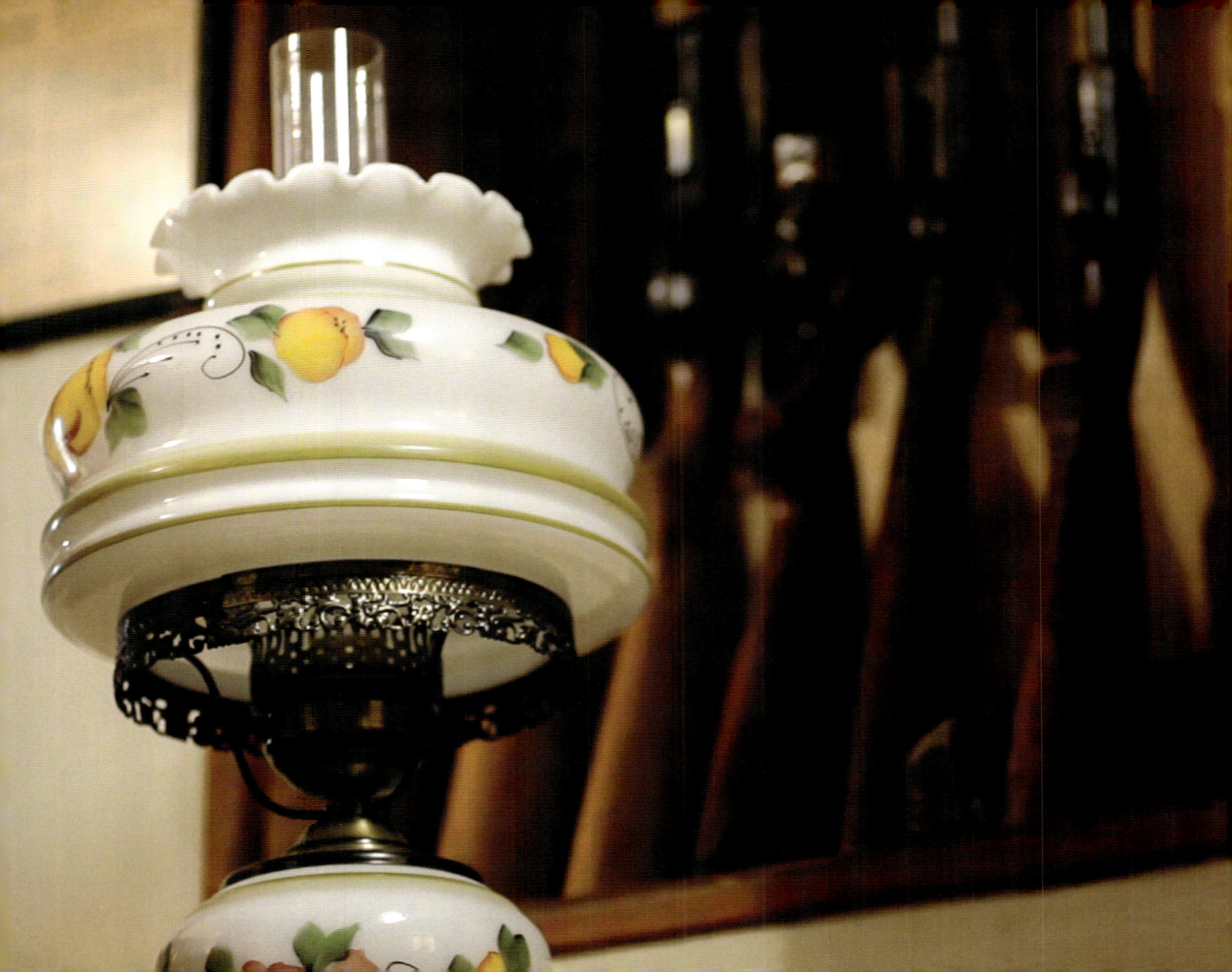

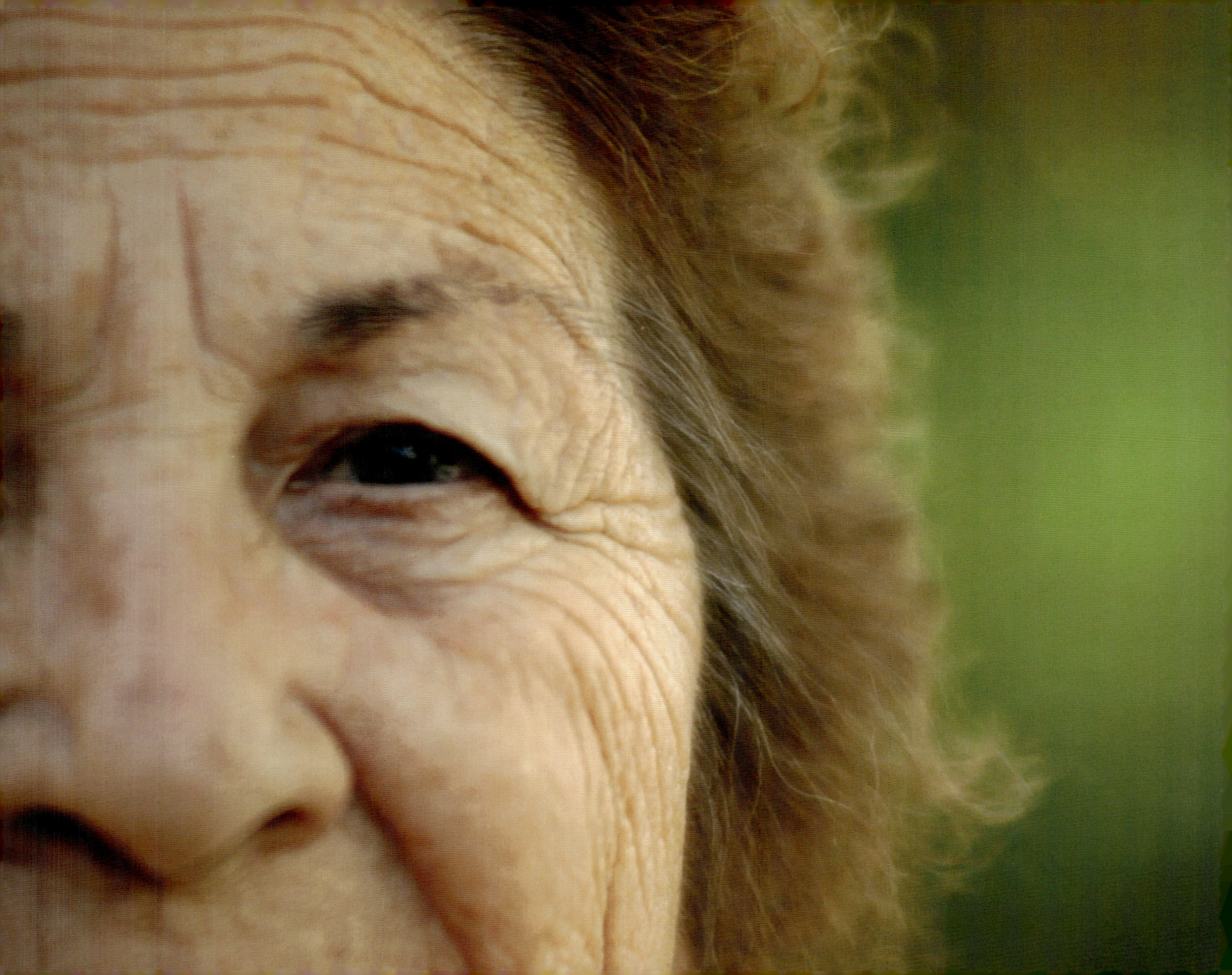

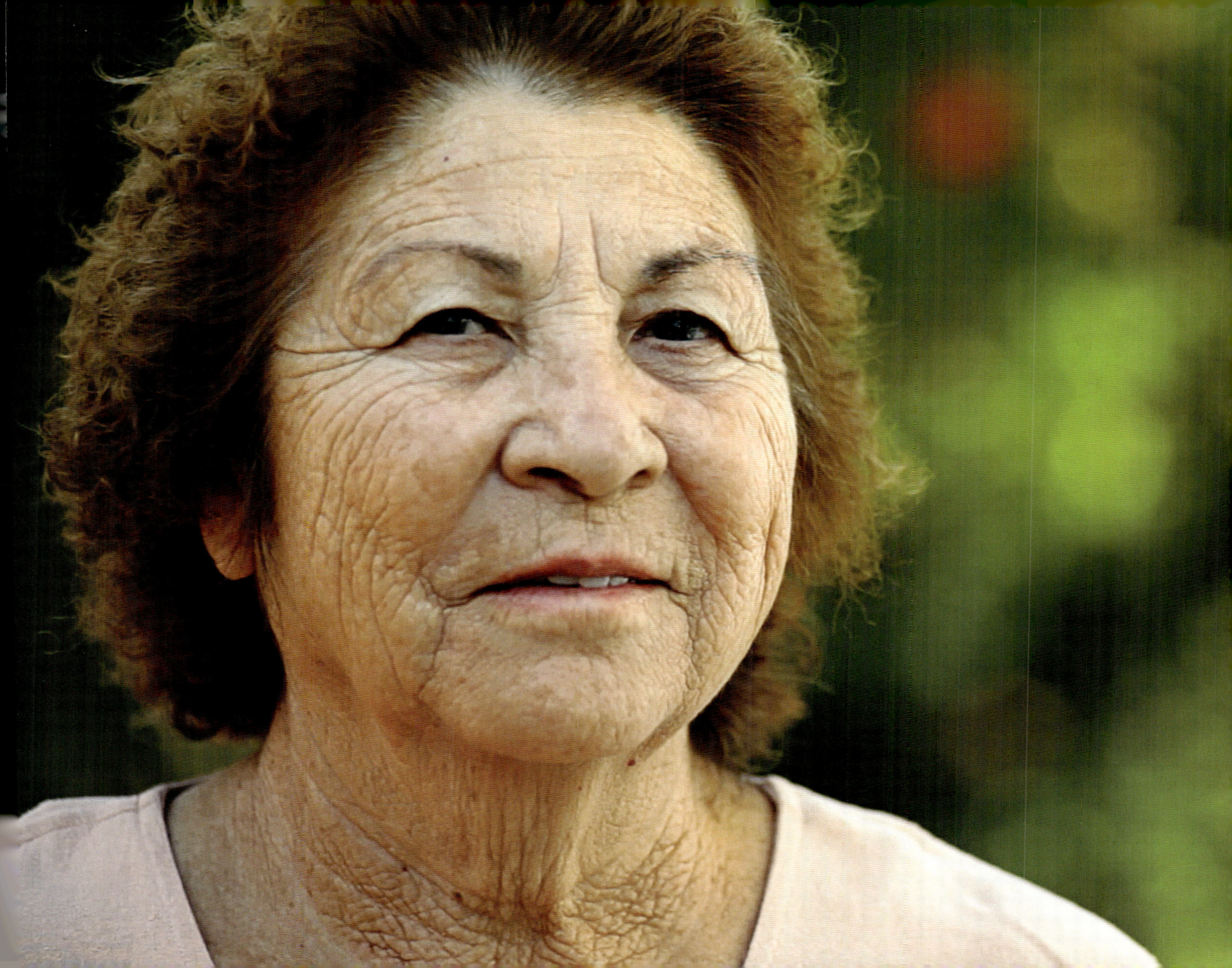

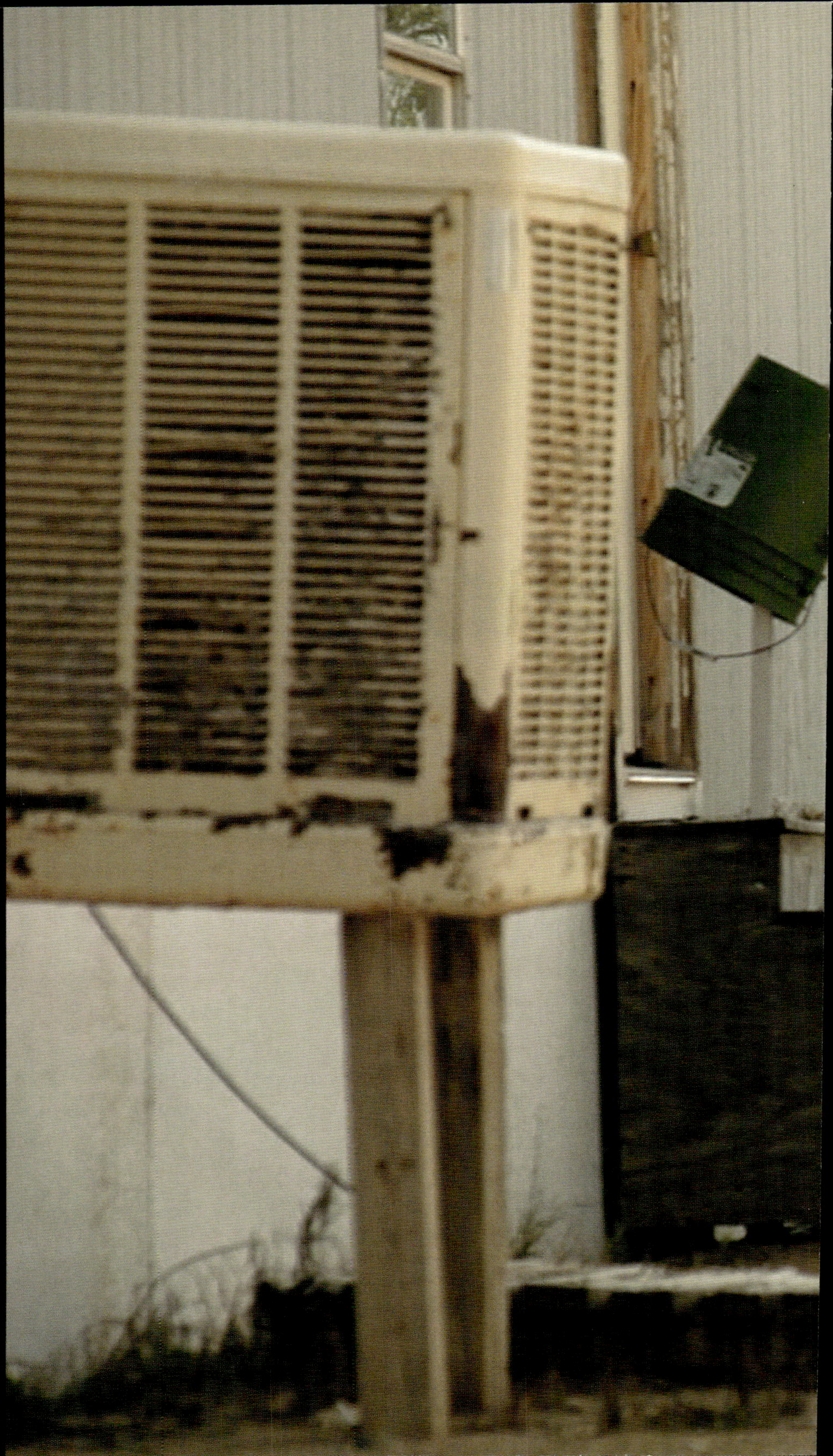

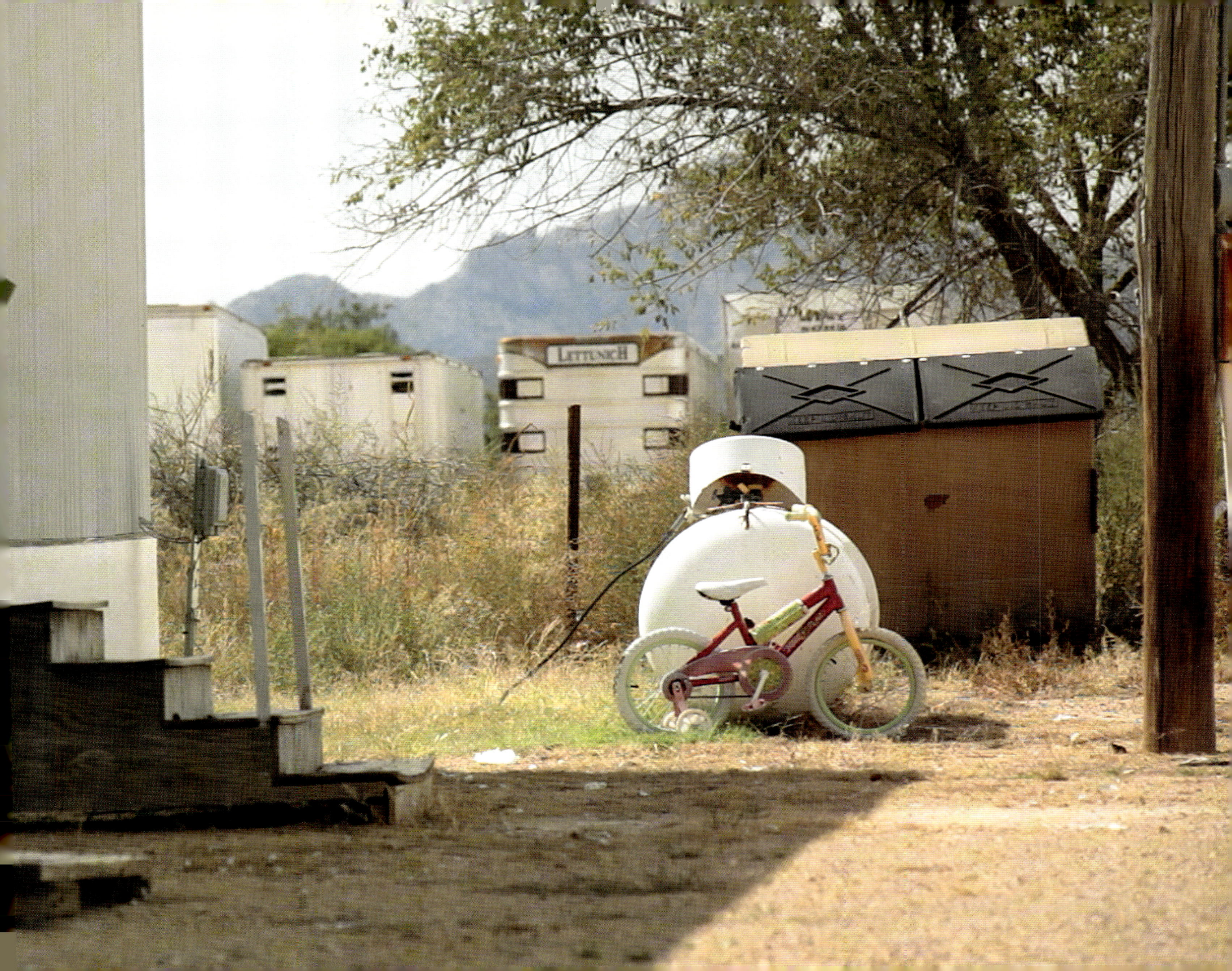
LETTUNICH

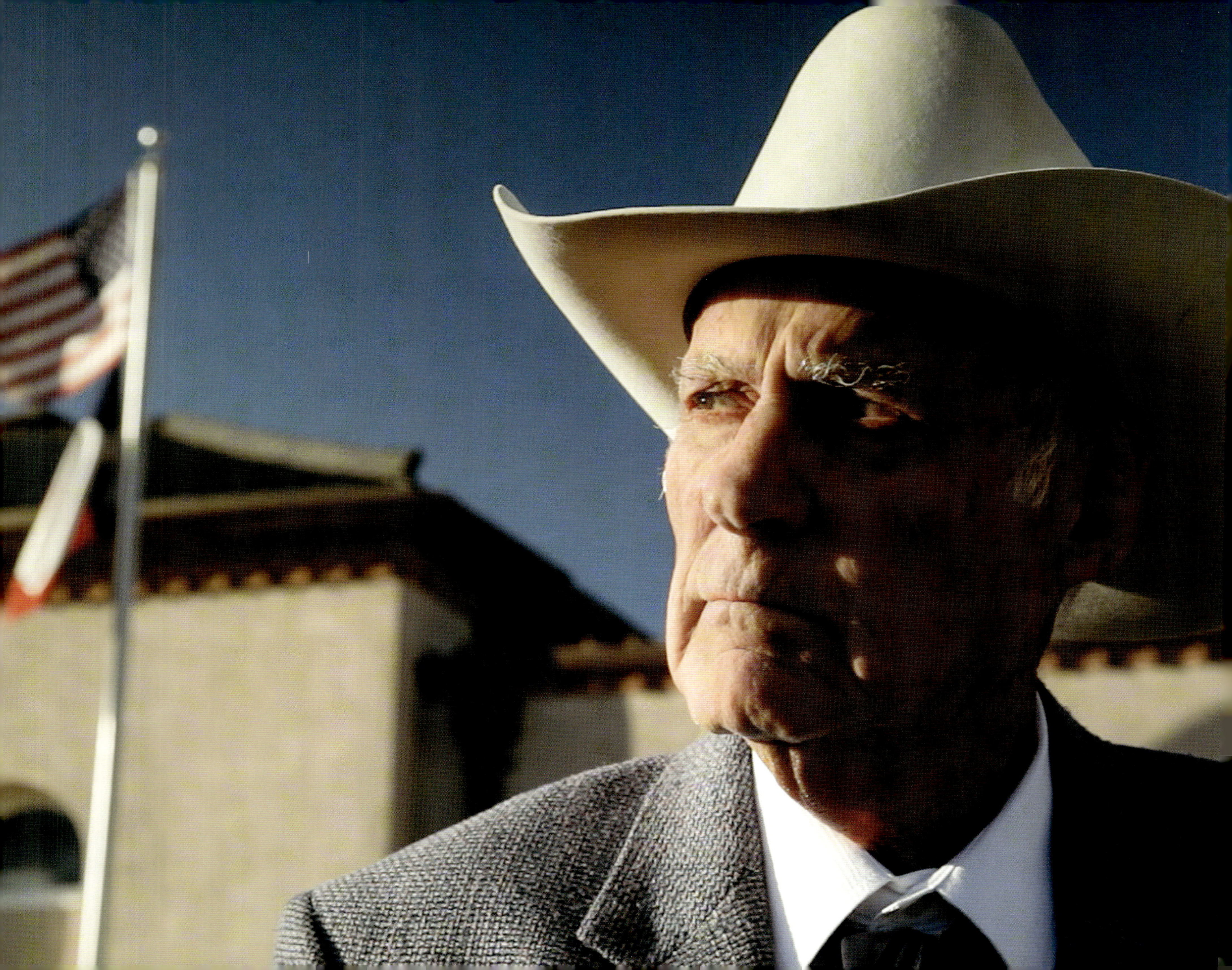

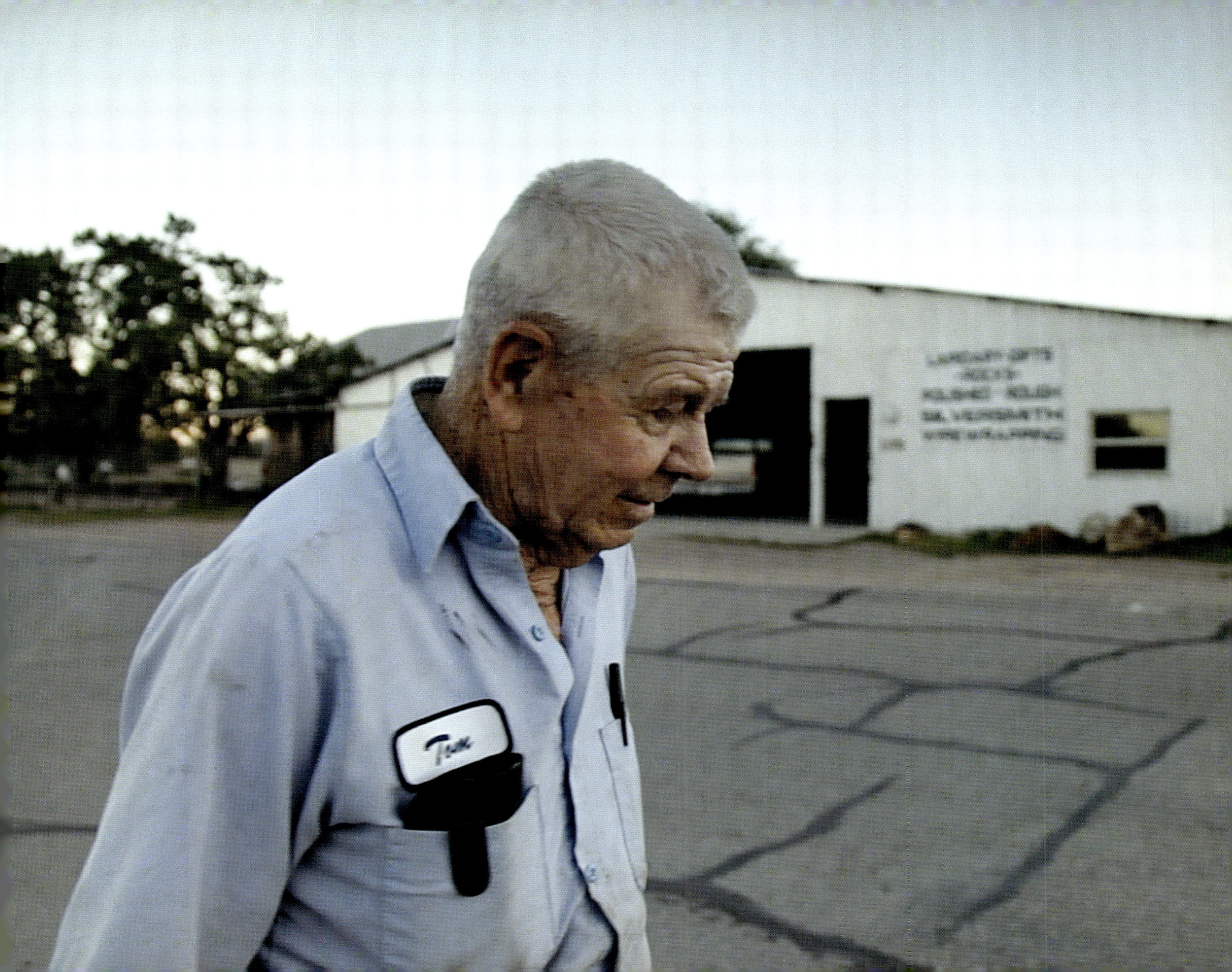

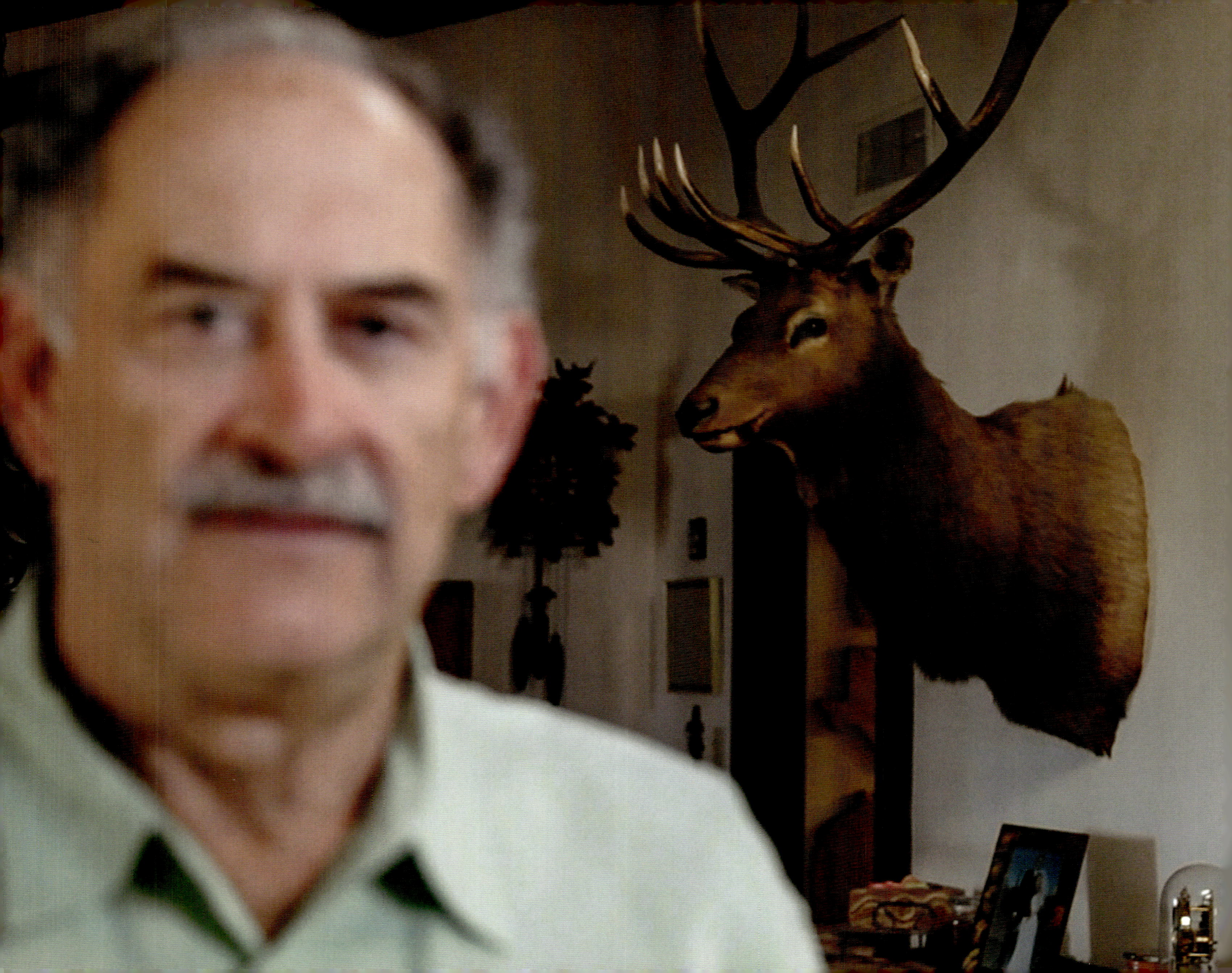

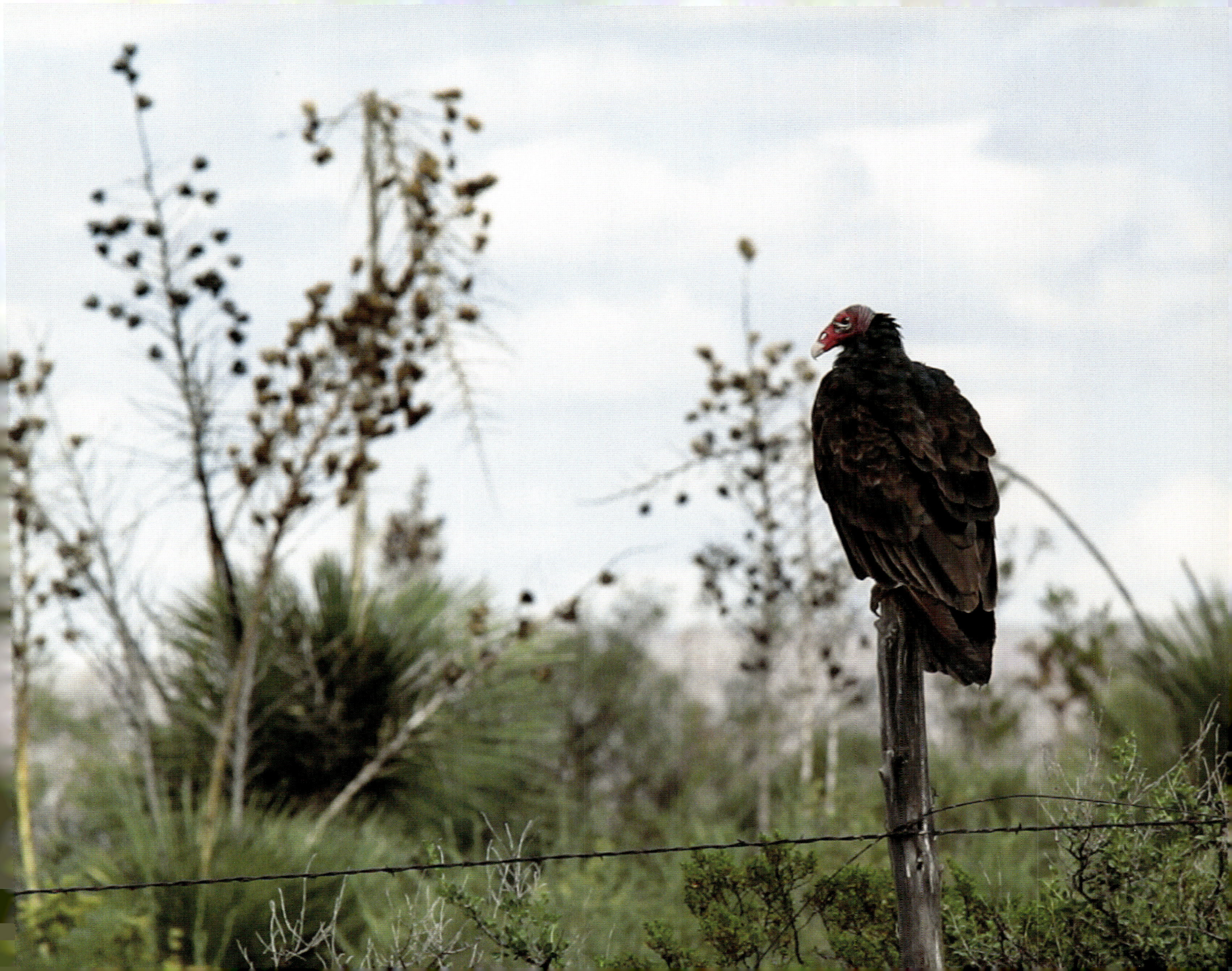

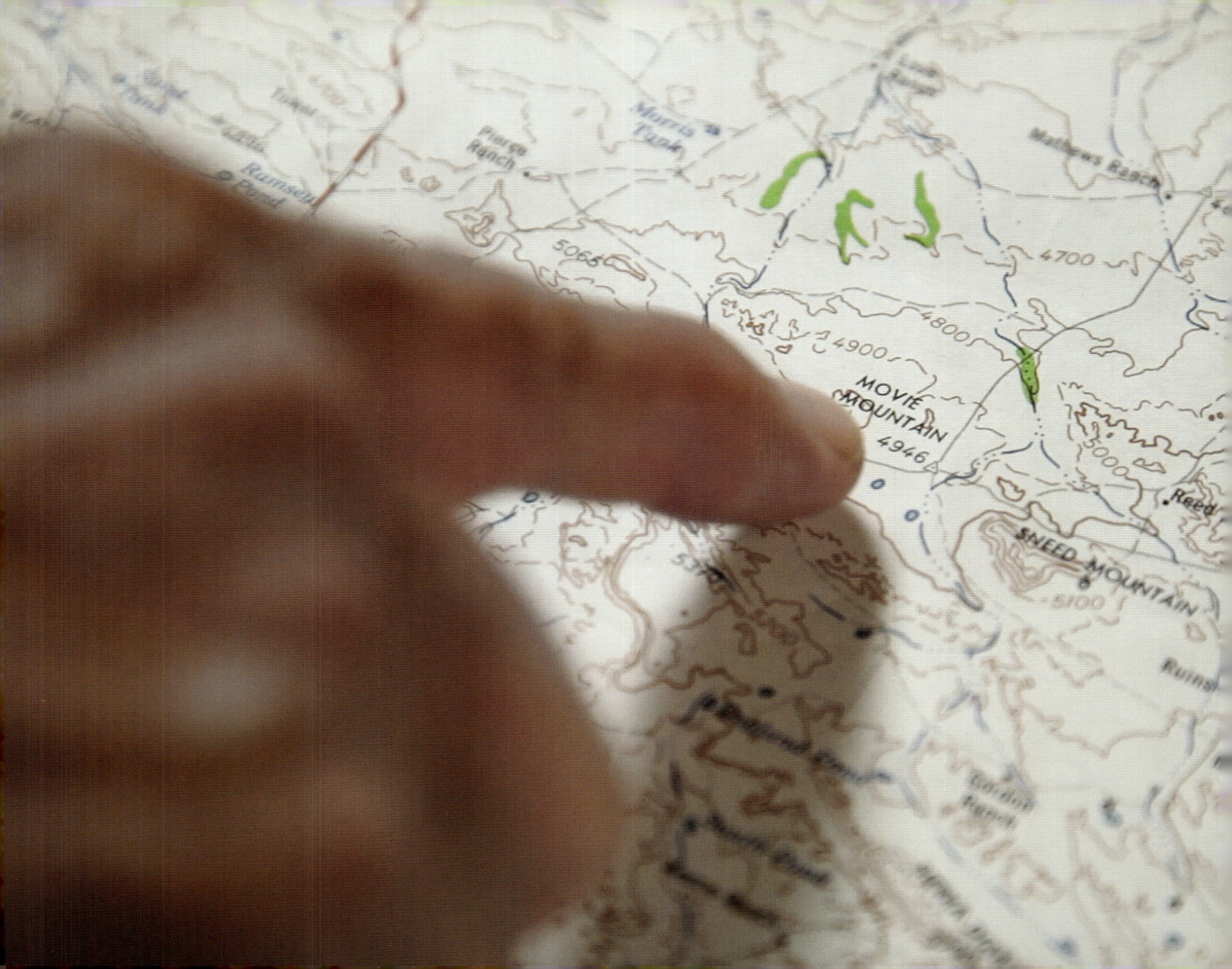
Morris Tank
Pierce Ranch
Mathews Ranch
5066
4700
4800
4900
MOVIE MOUNTAIN
4946
5000
Reed
SNEED MOUNTAIN
5100
Ruins

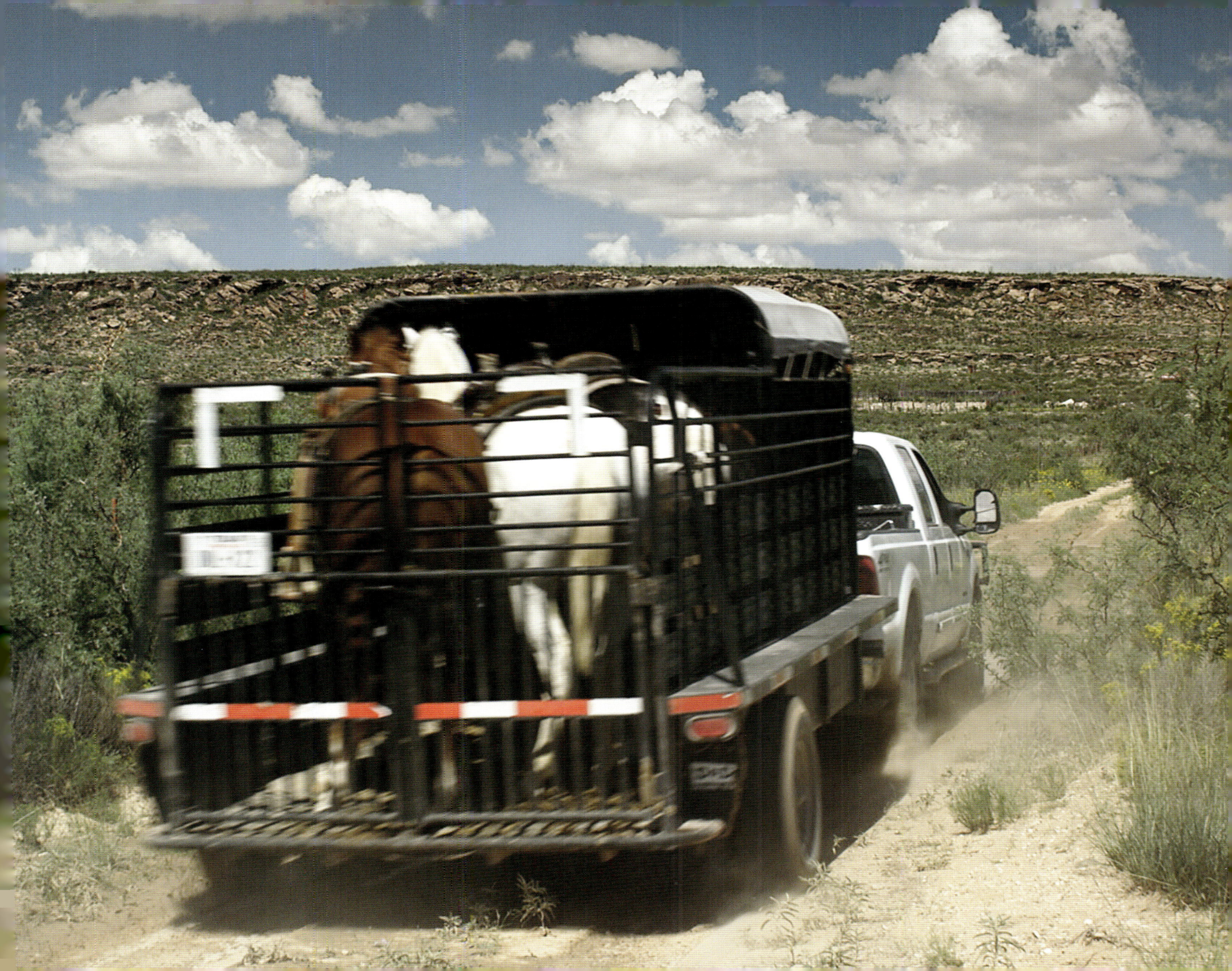

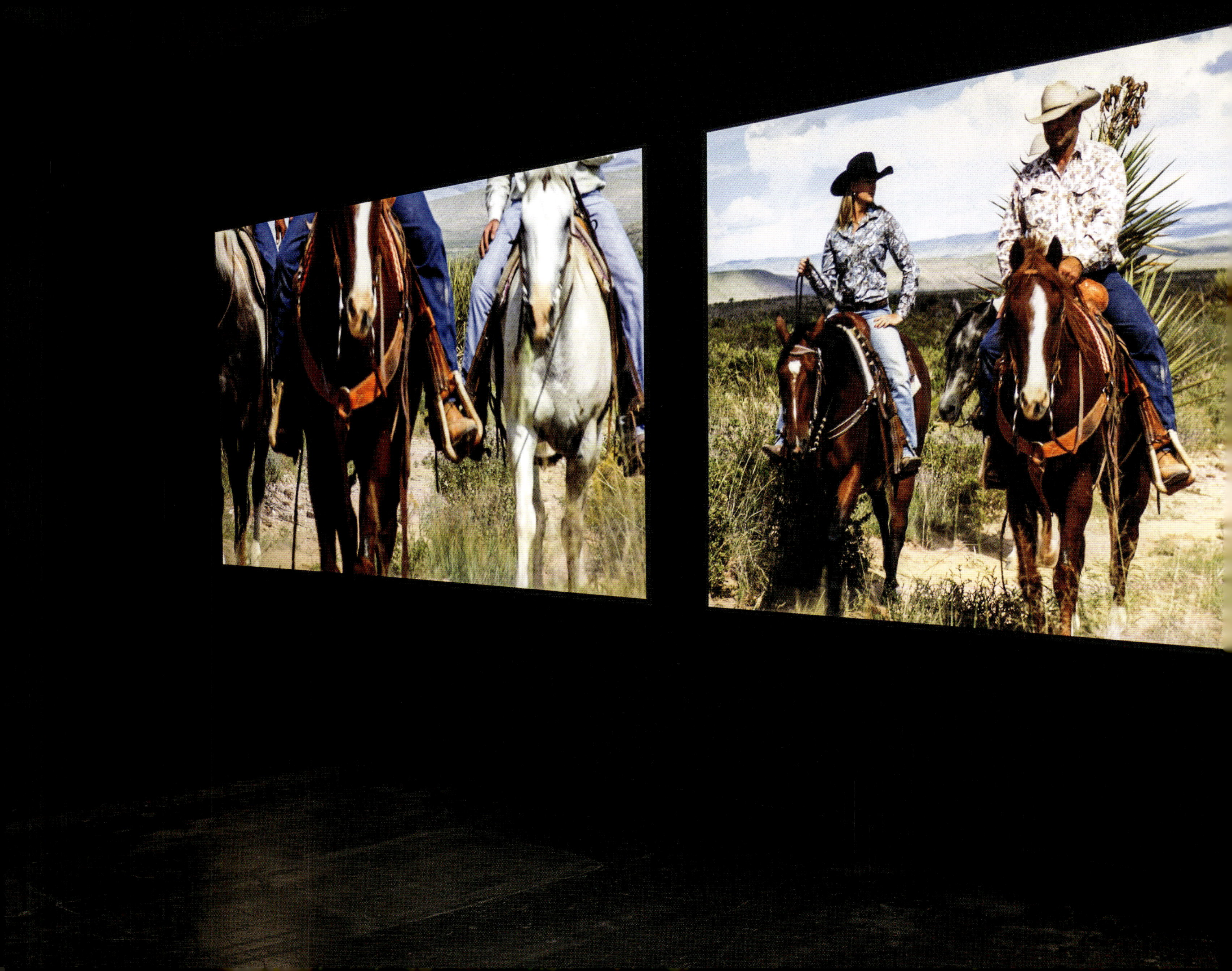

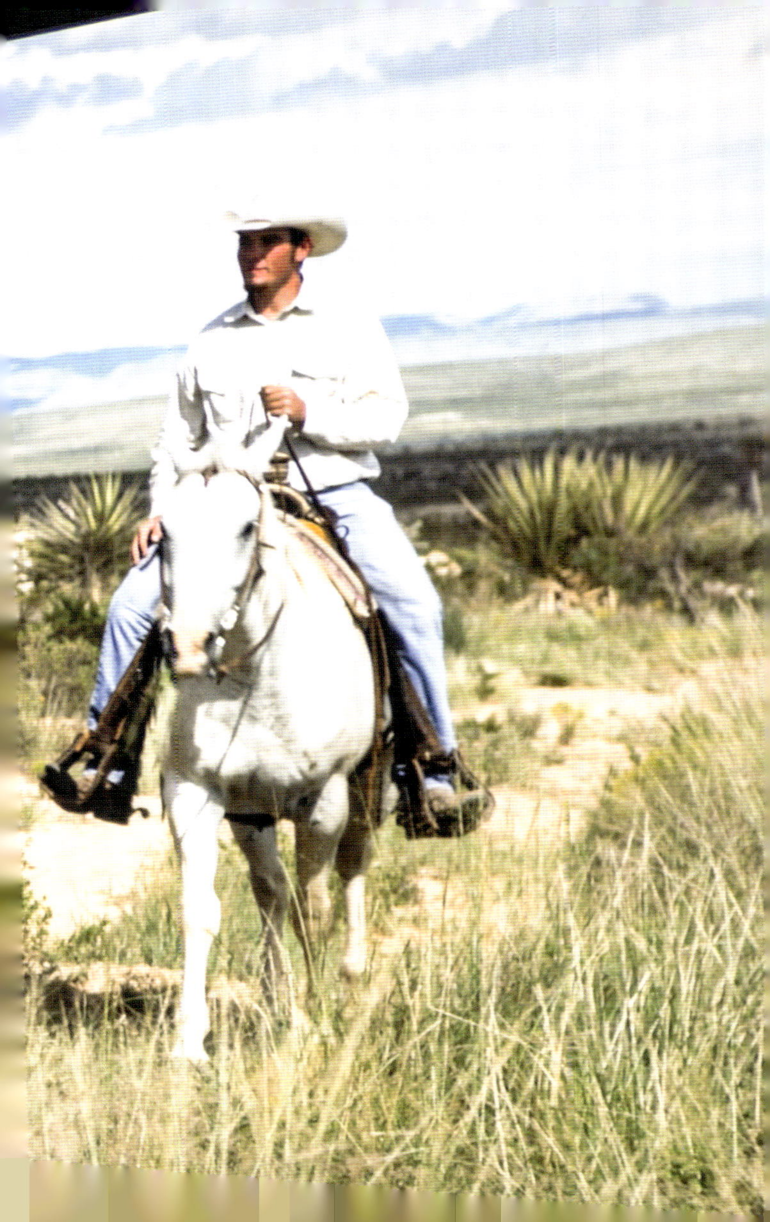

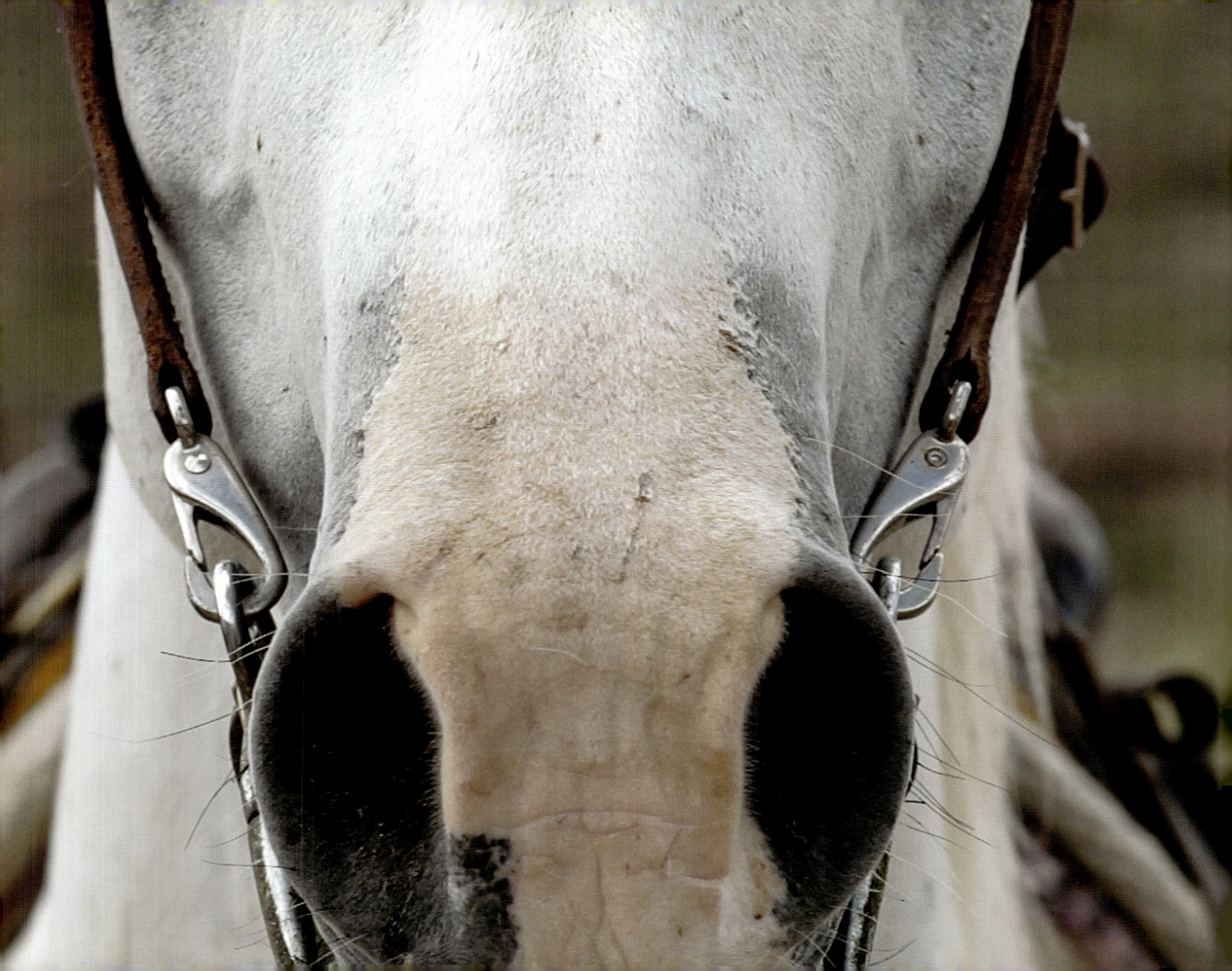

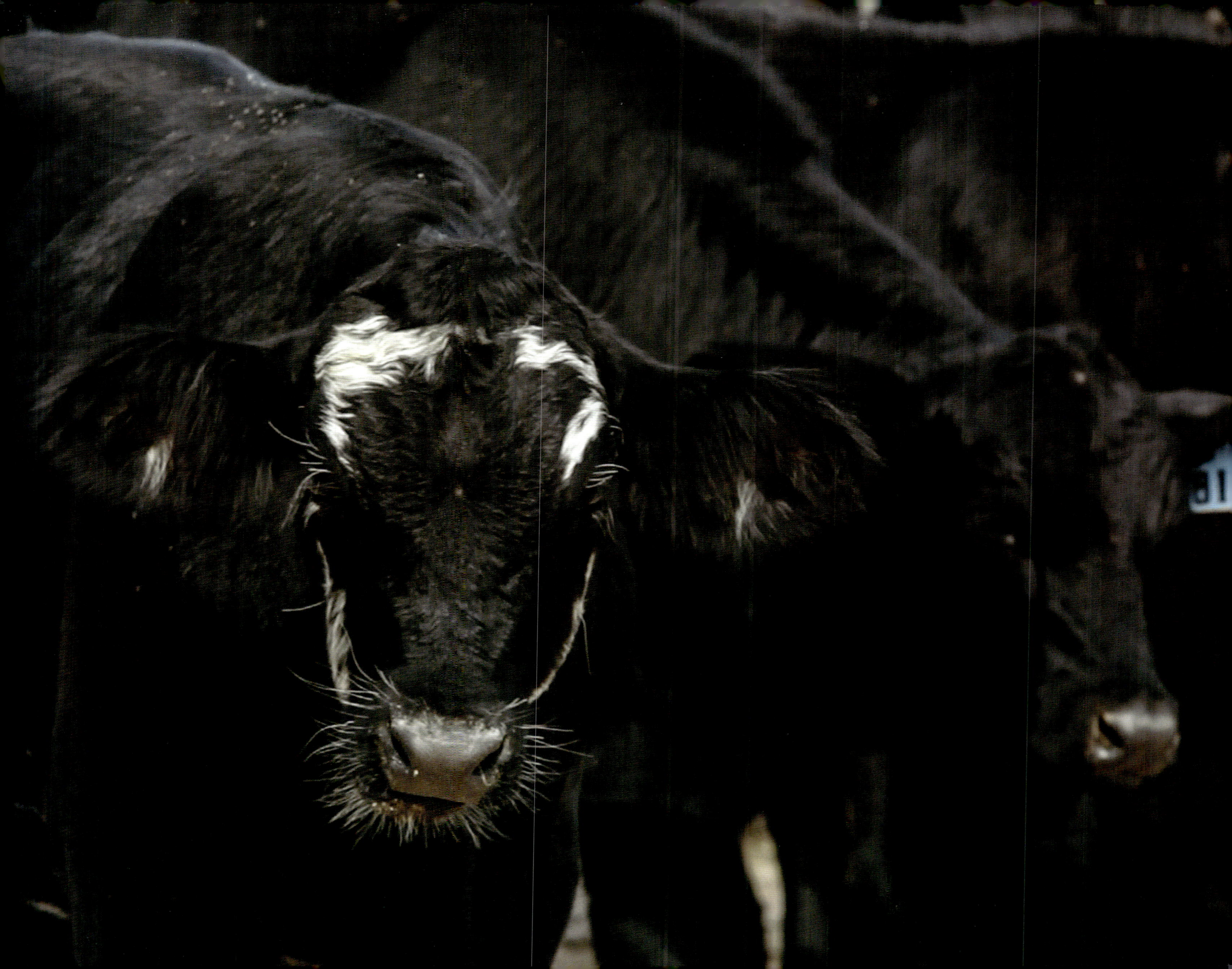

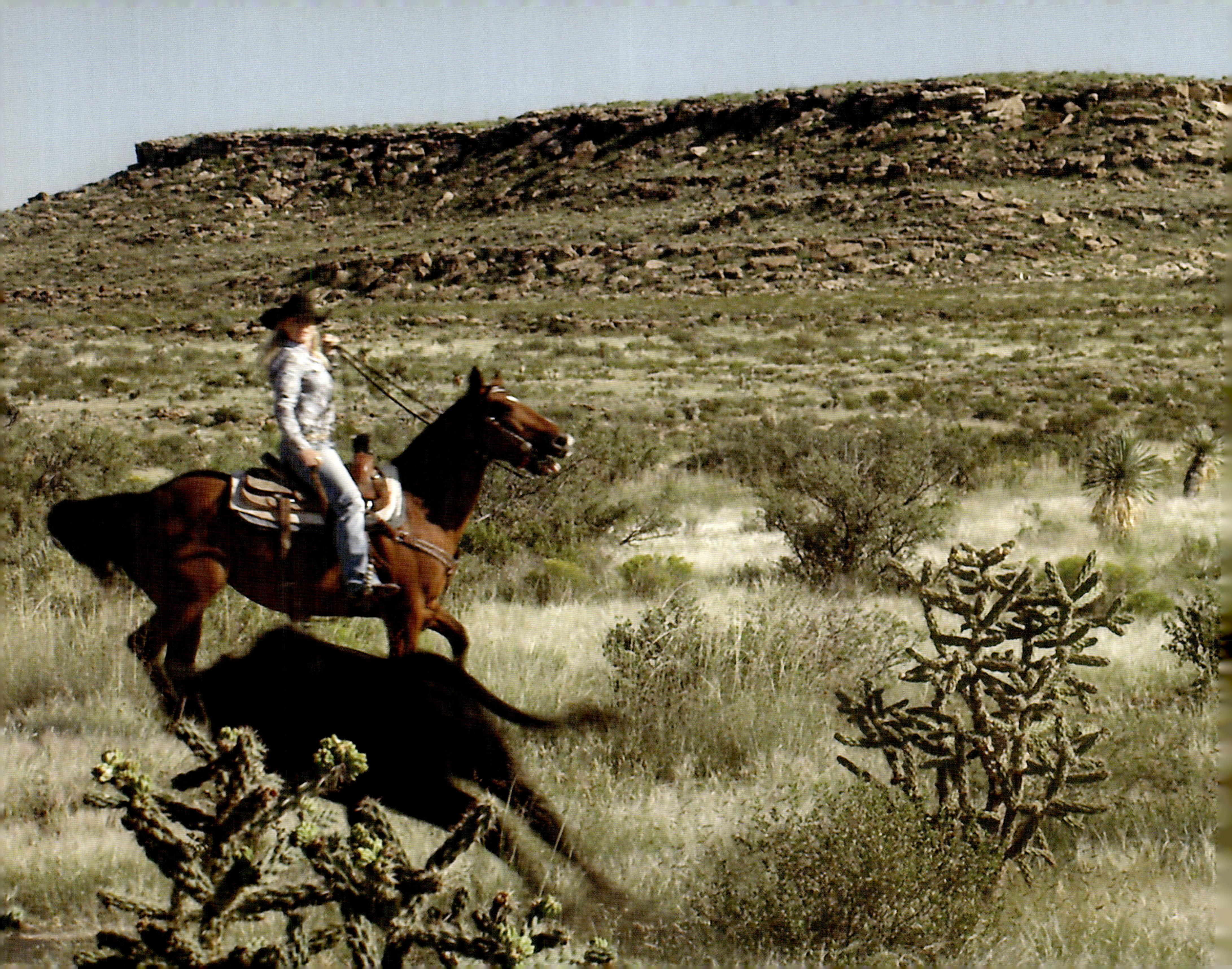

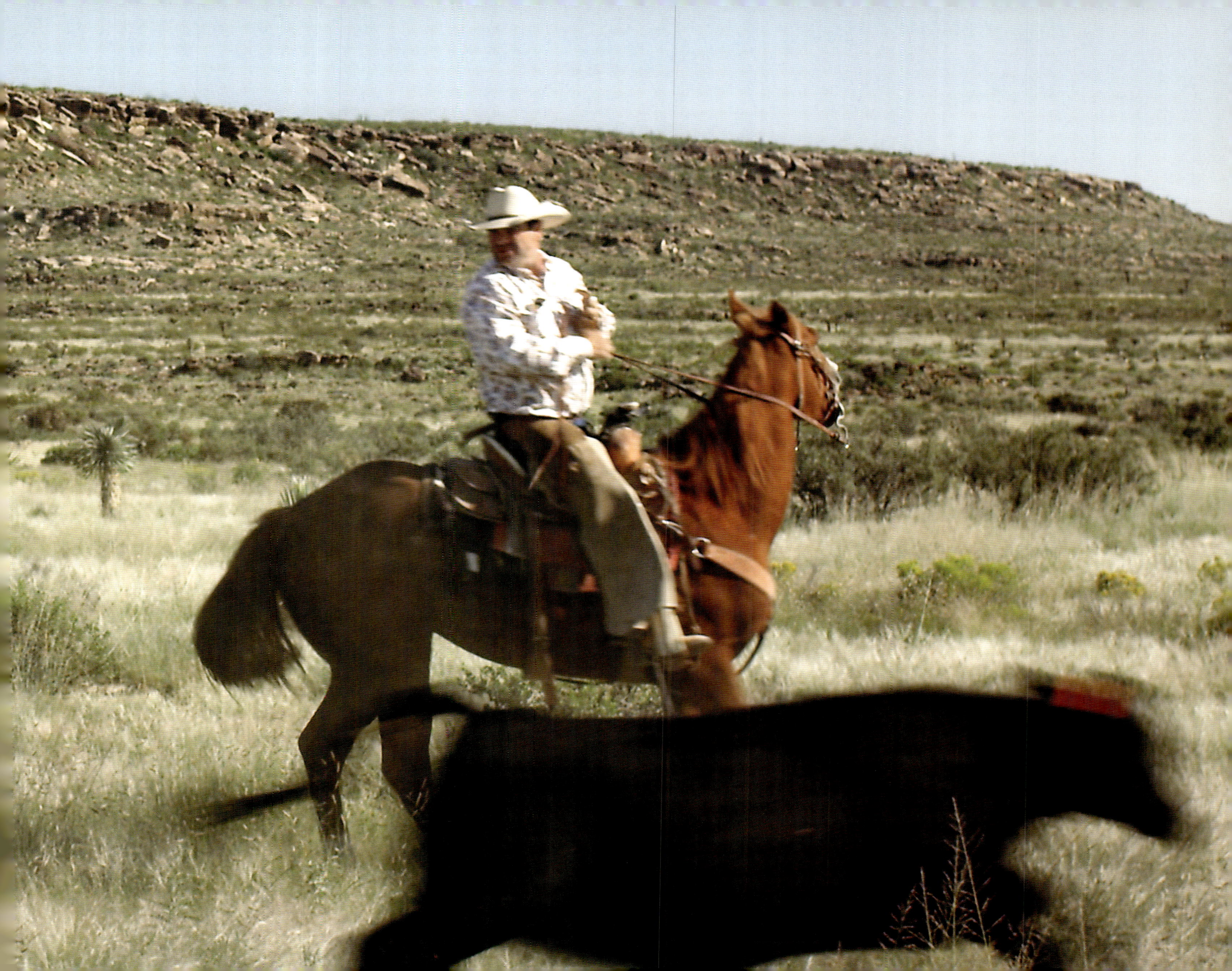

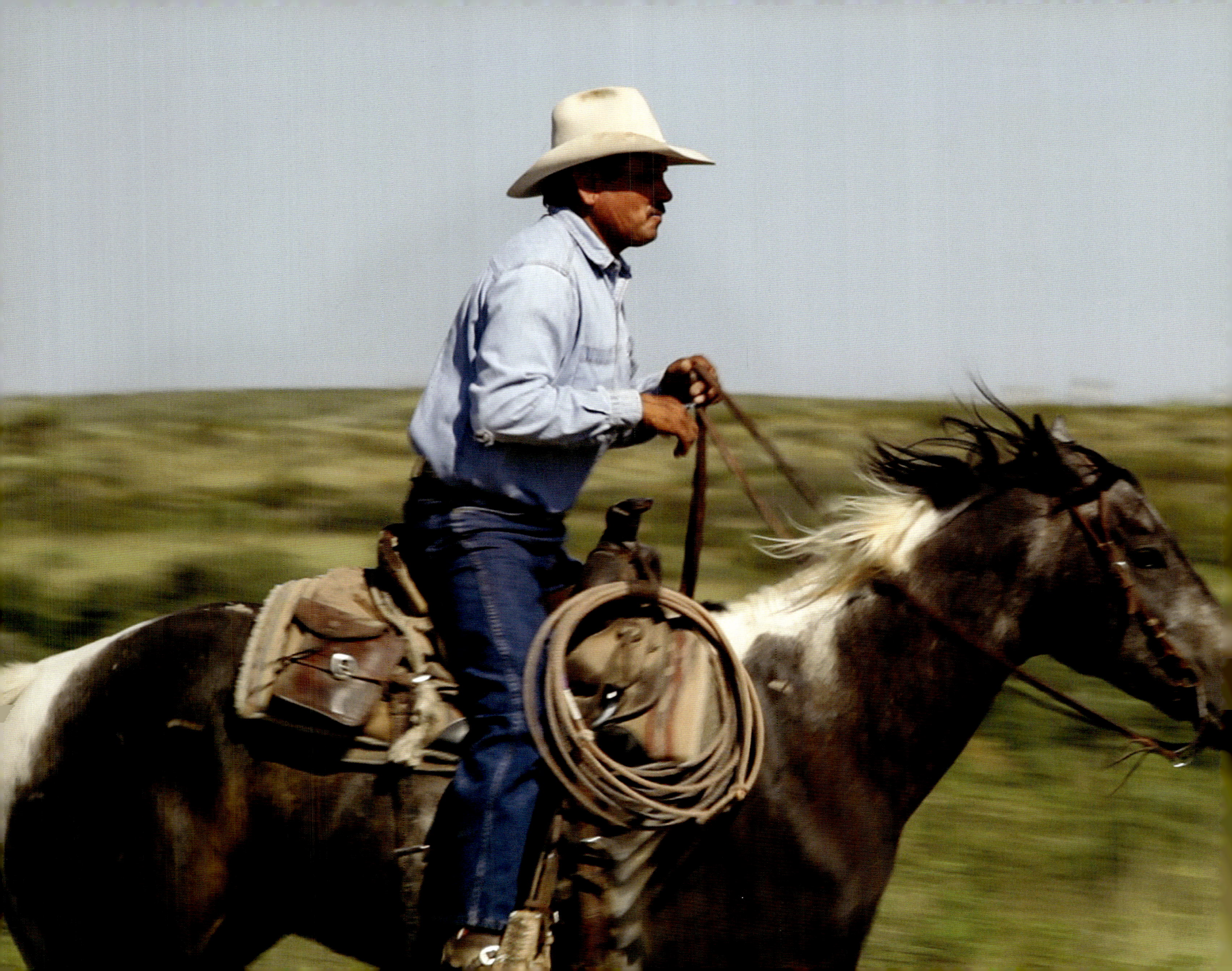

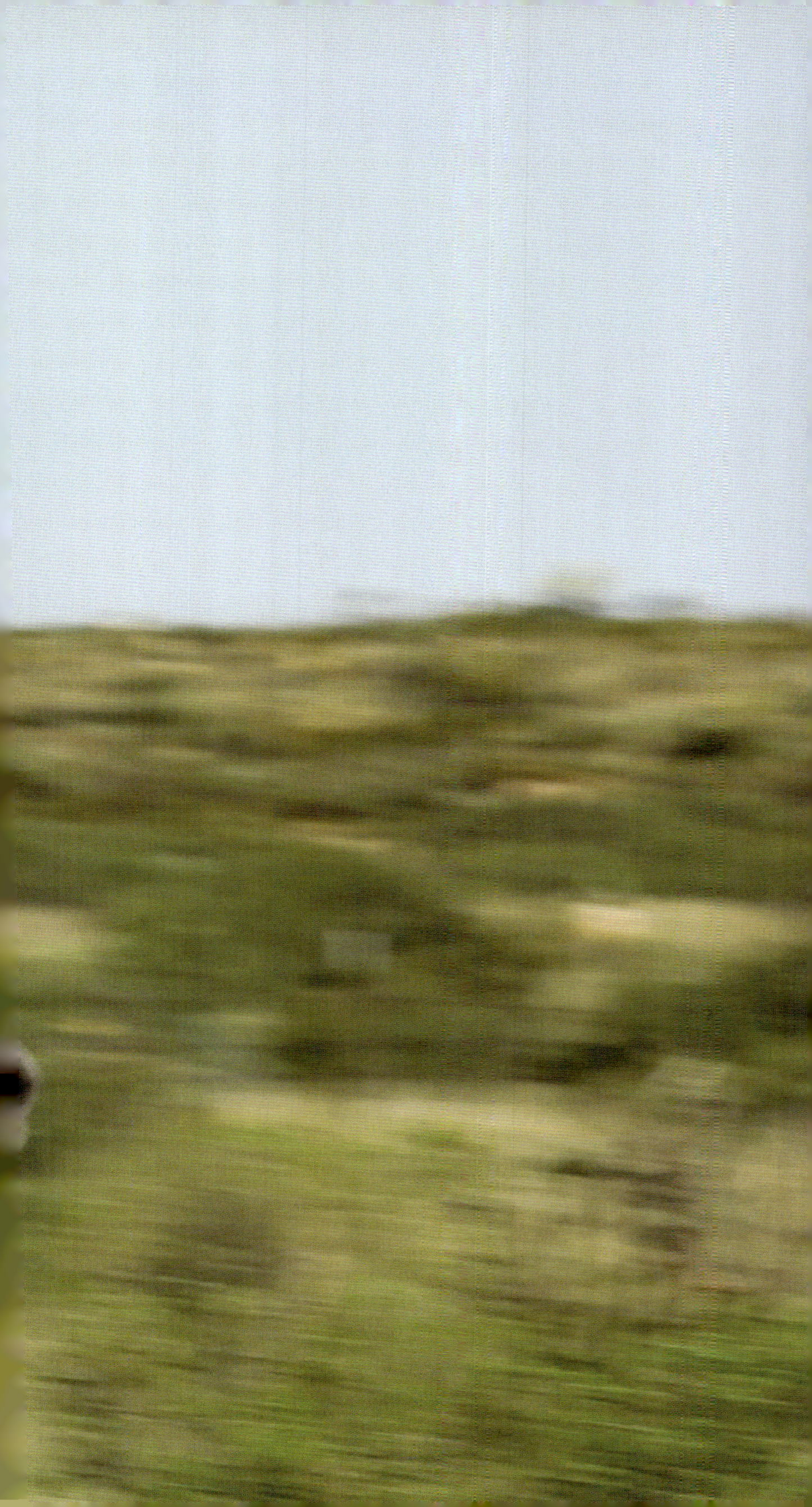

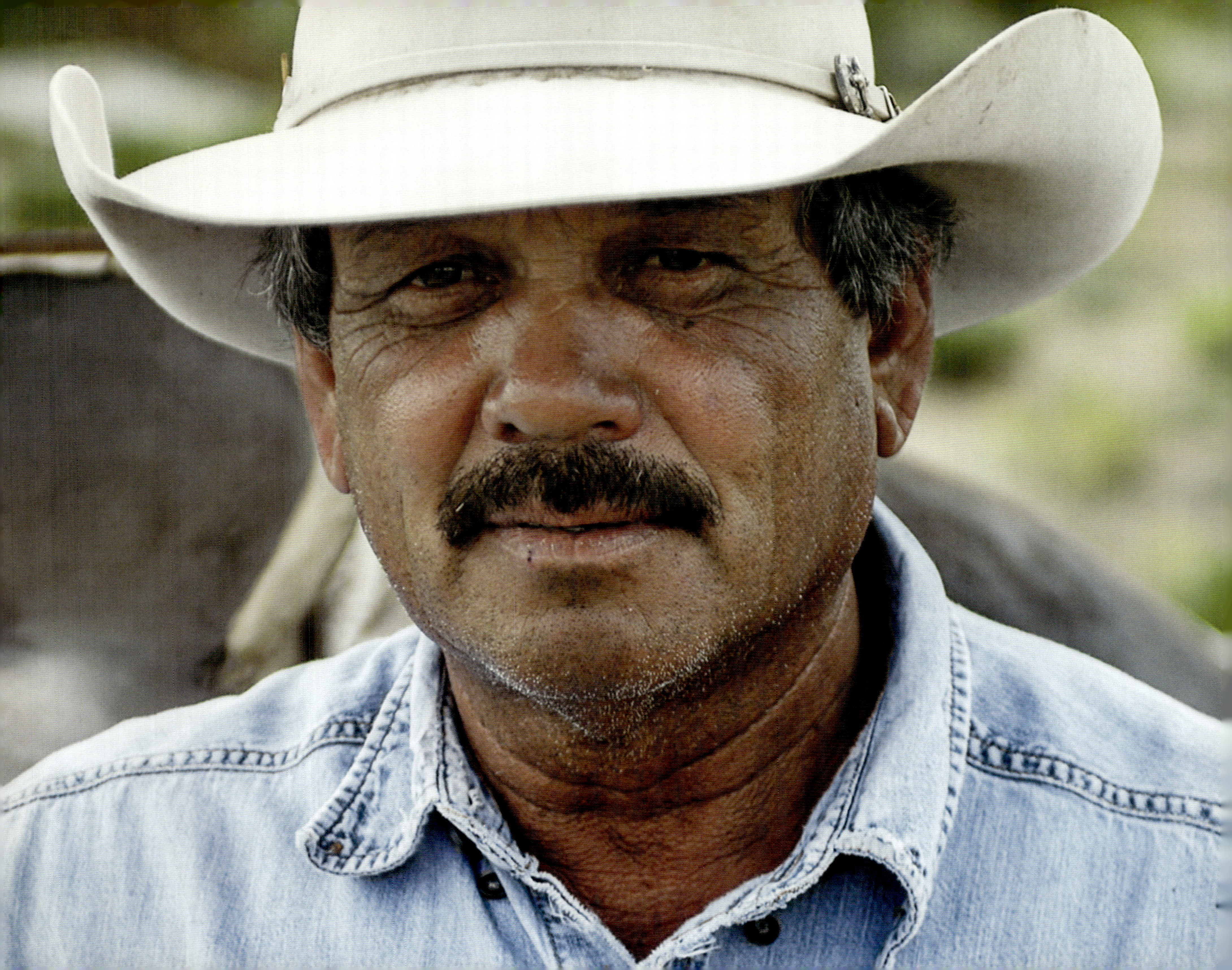

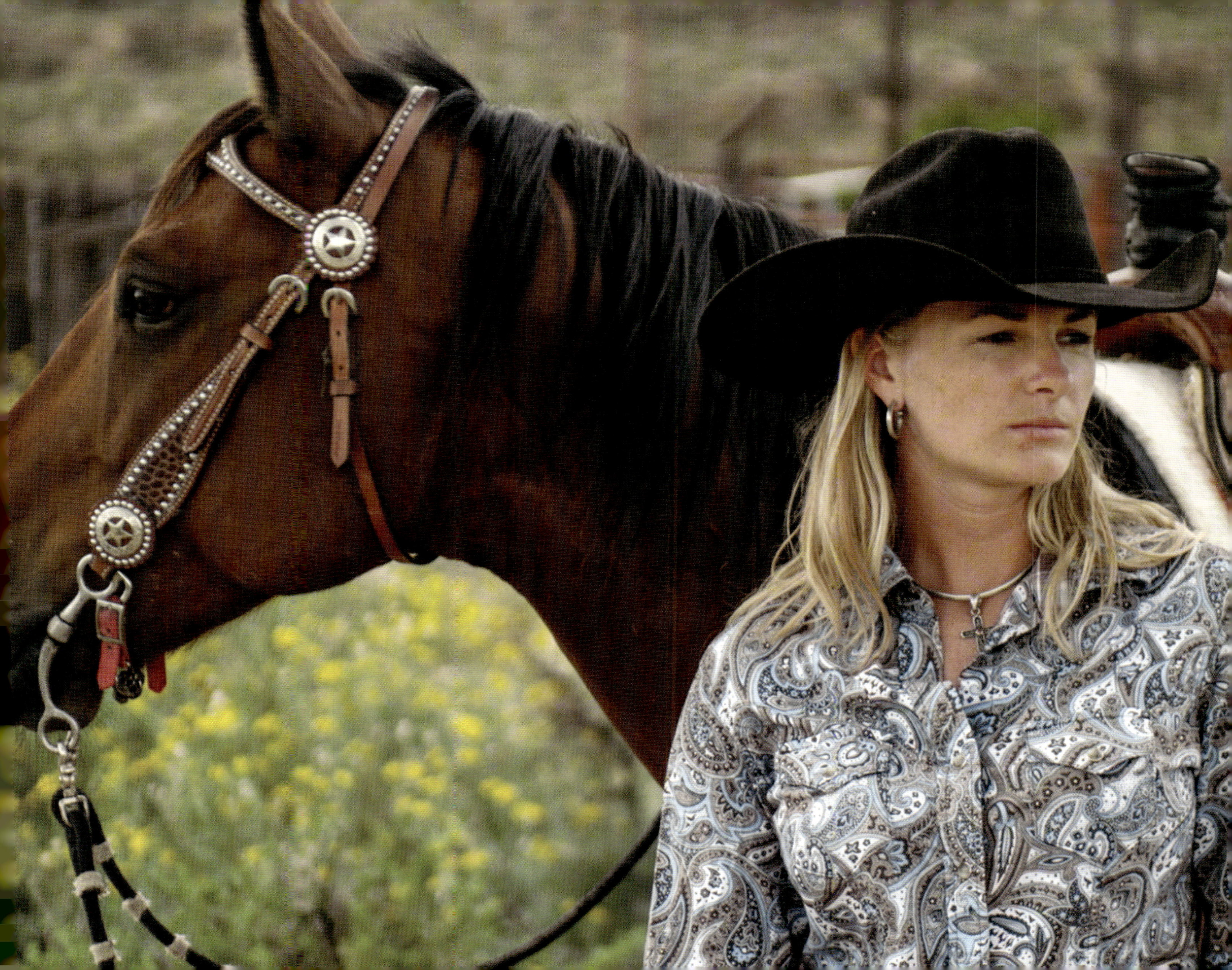

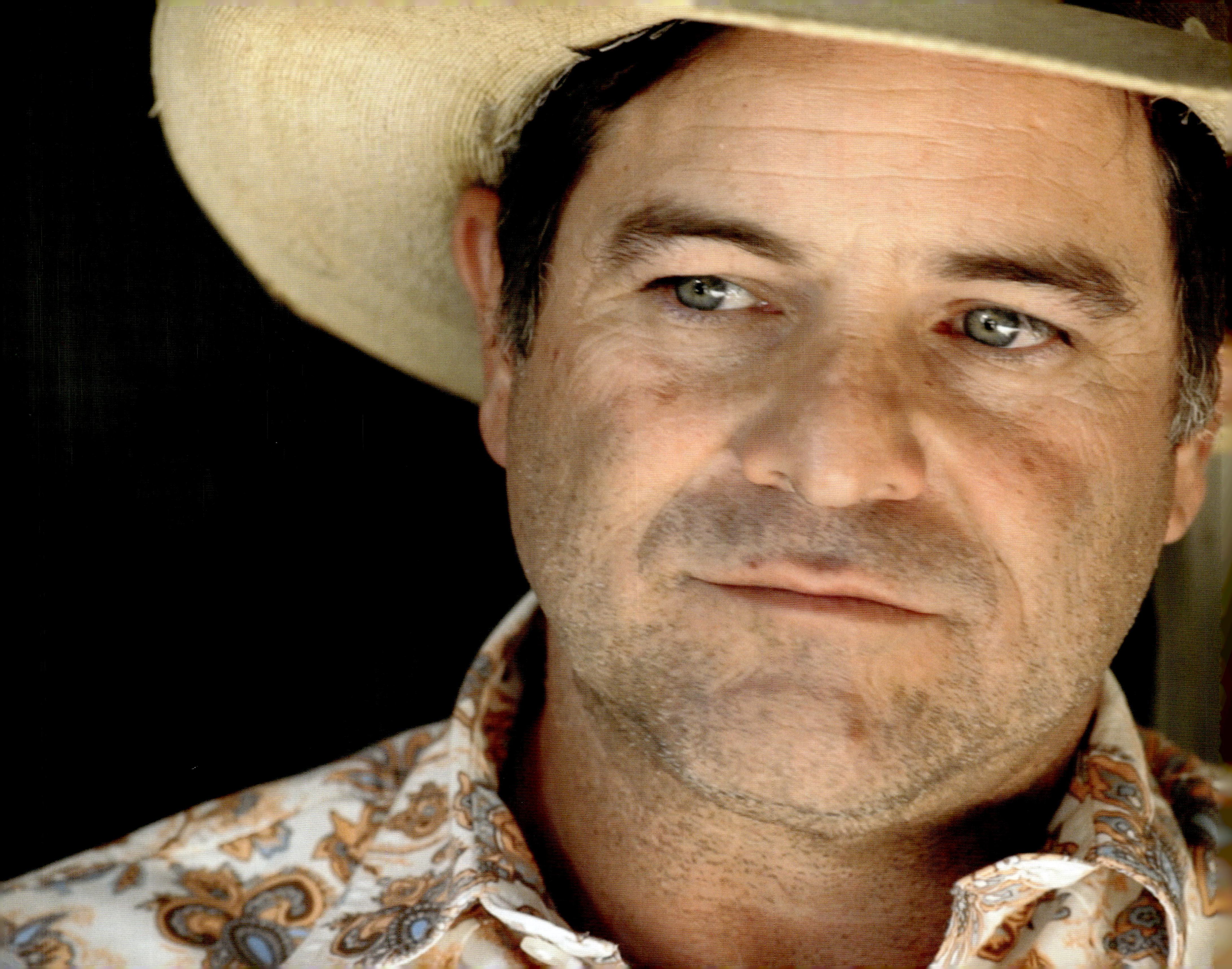

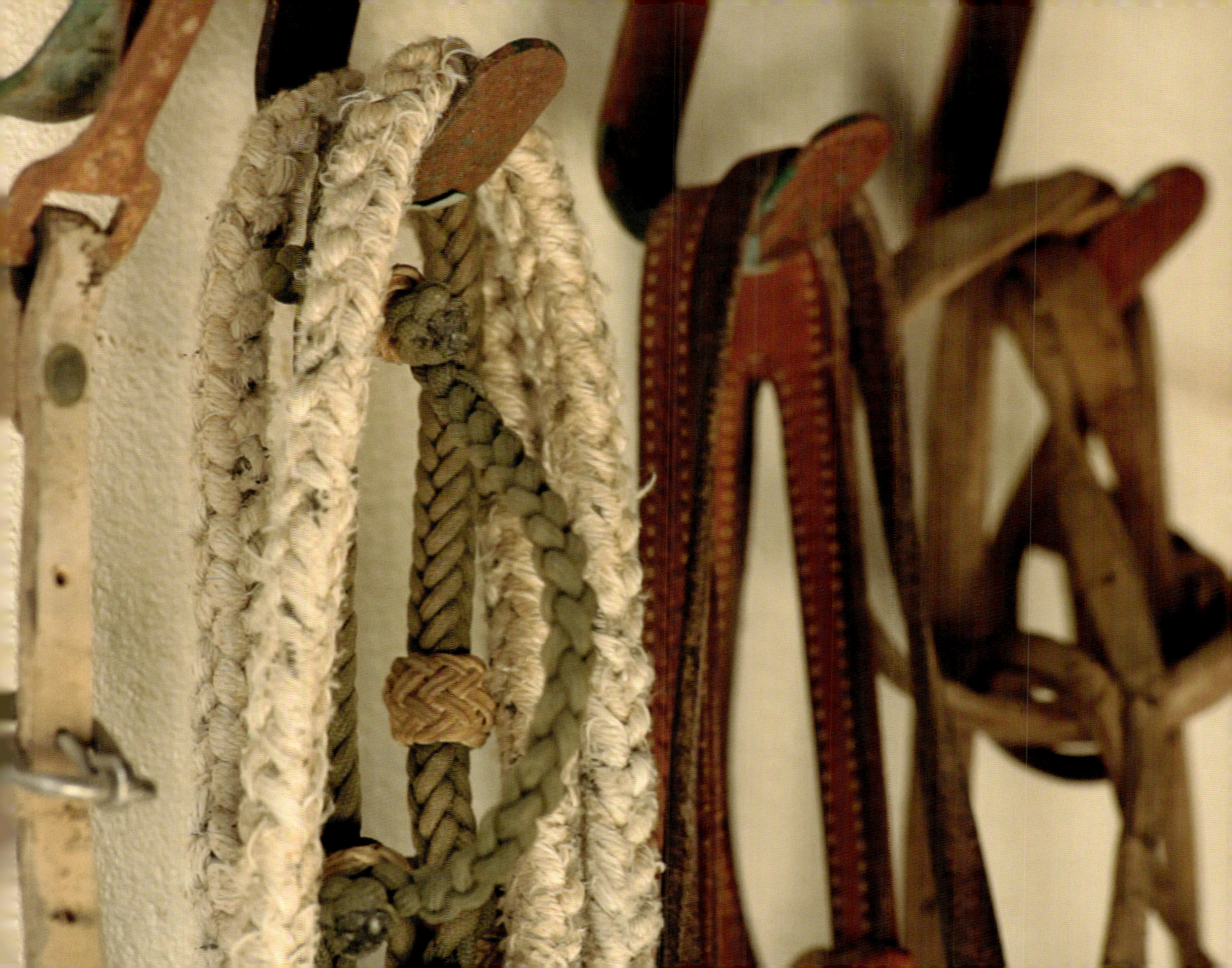

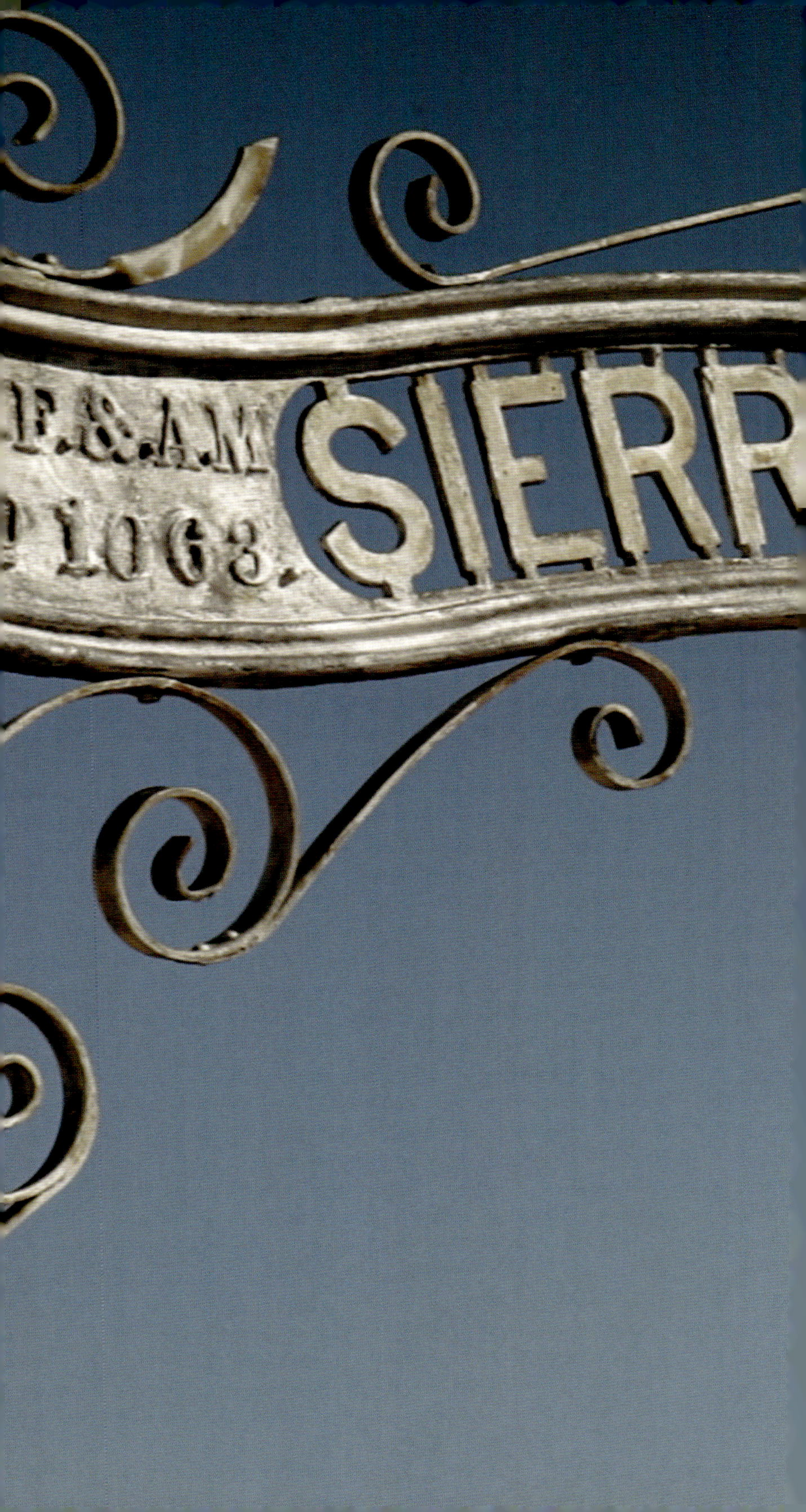
F.&.A.M
1063.
SIERR

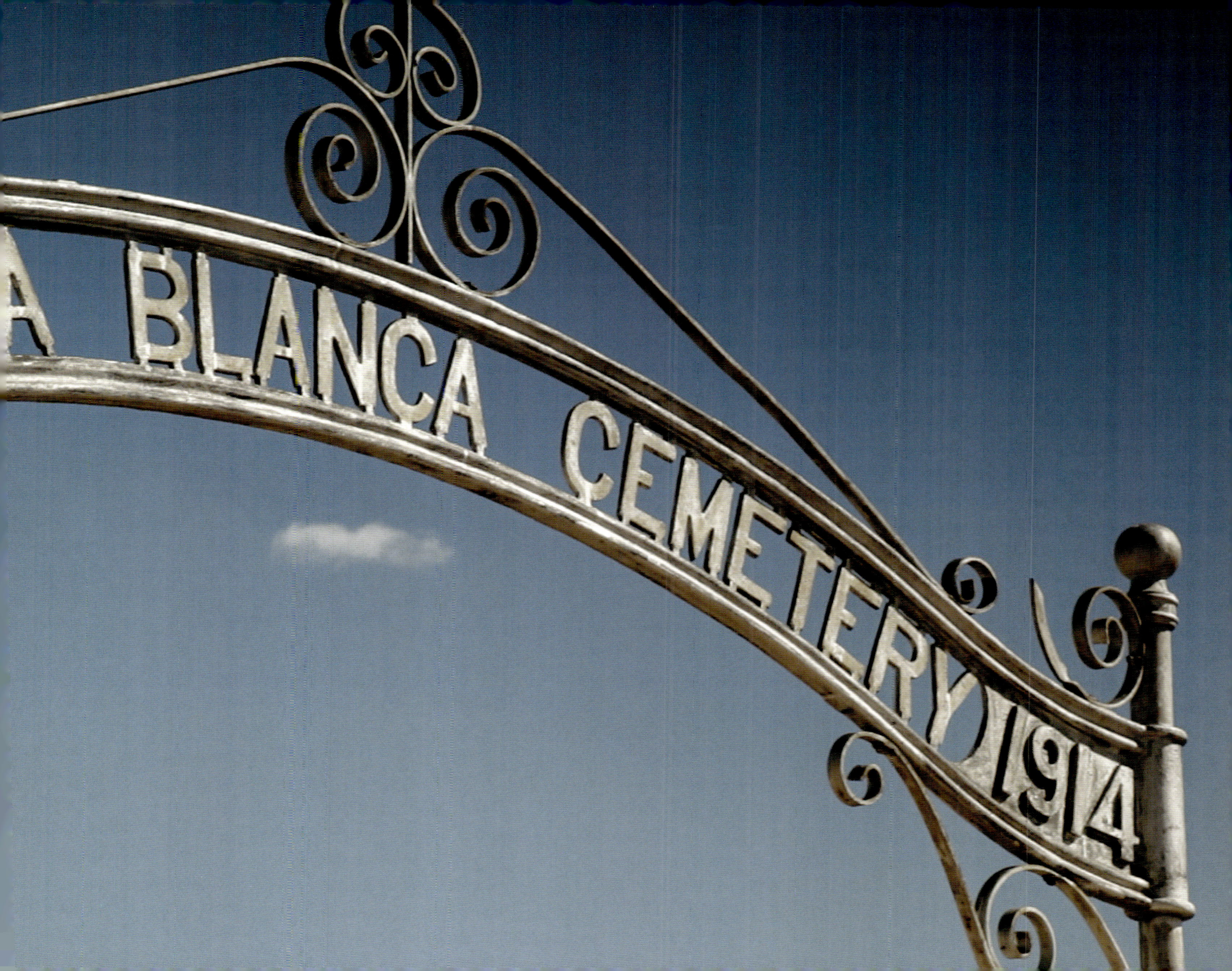
A BLANCA CEMETERY 1914

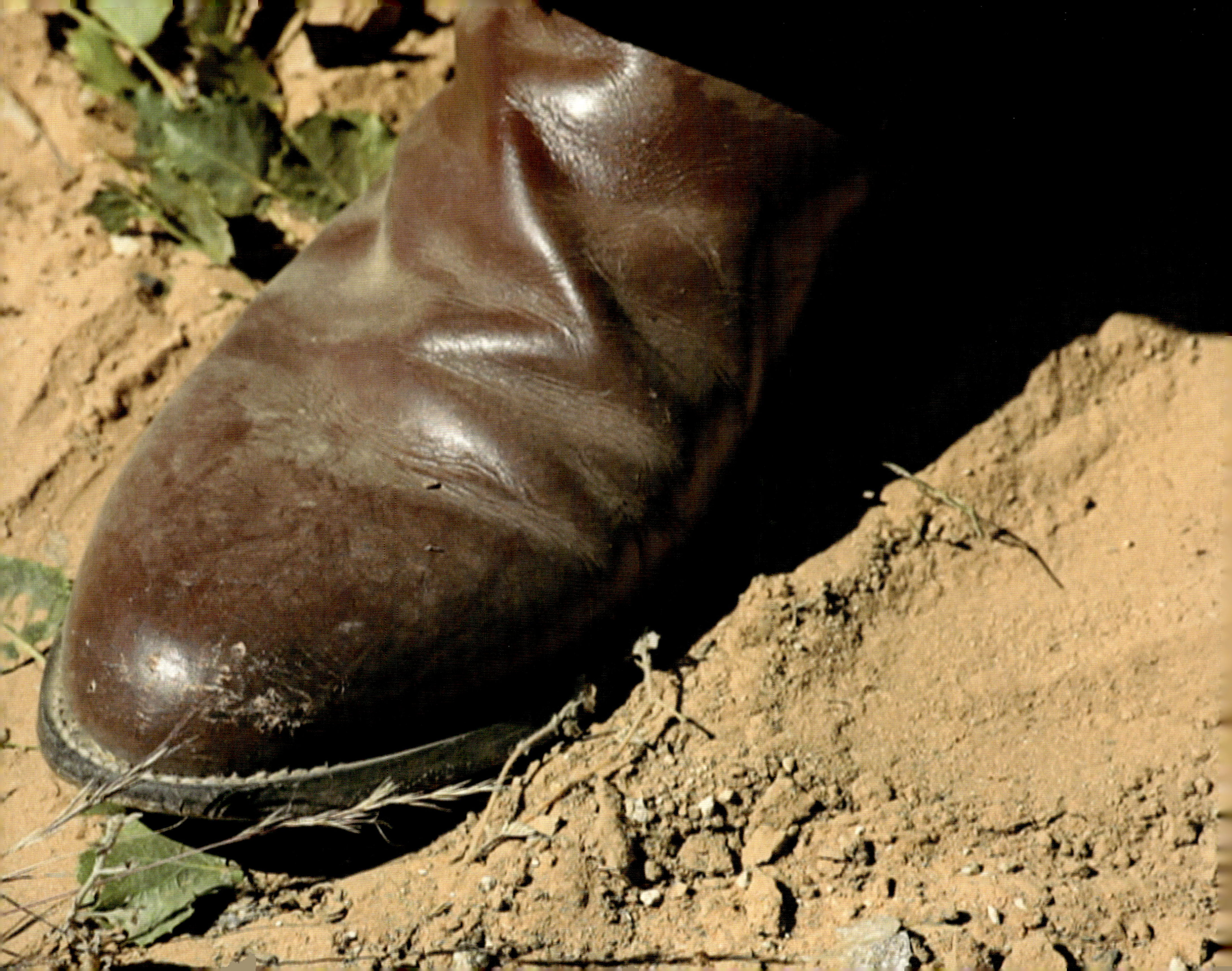

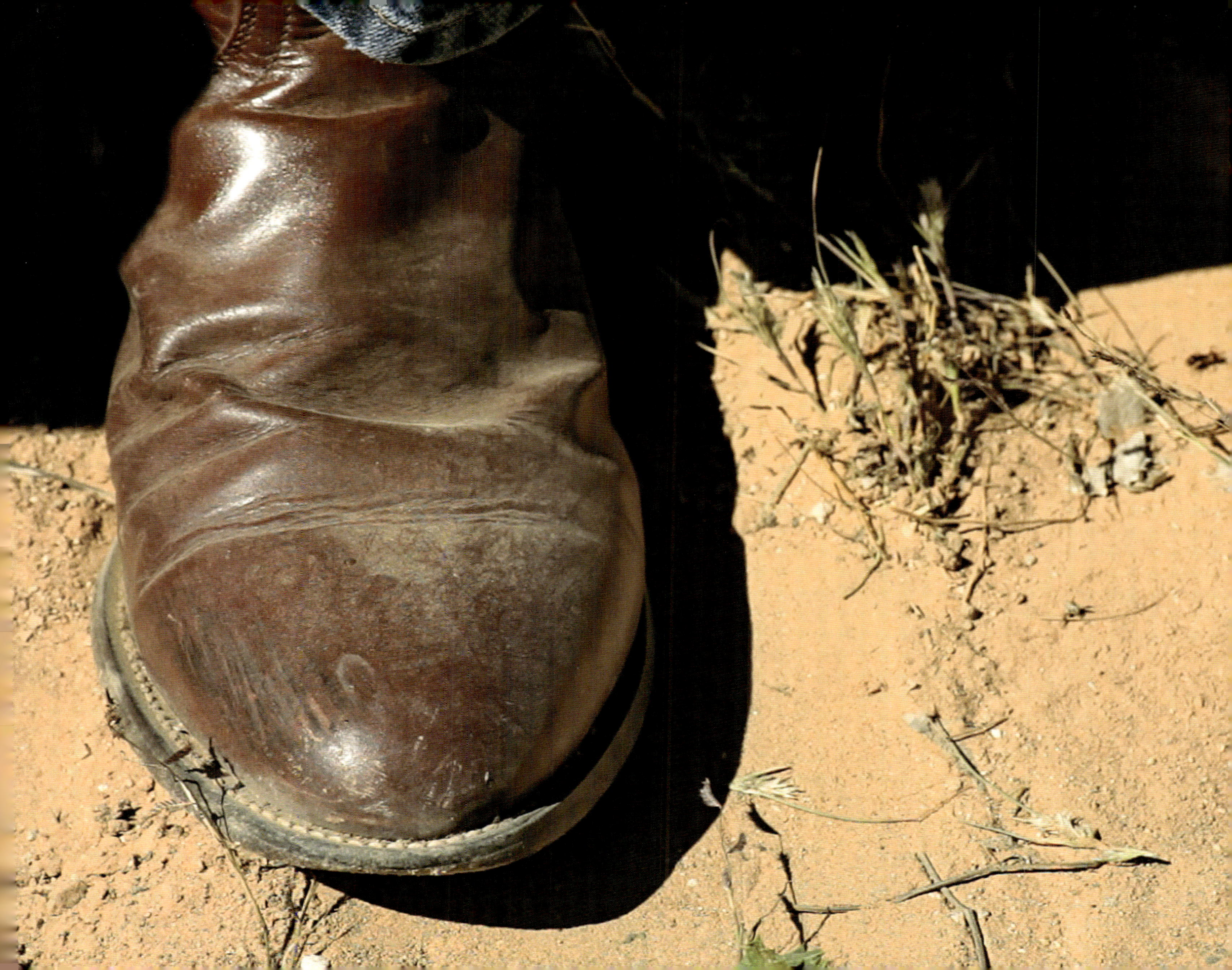

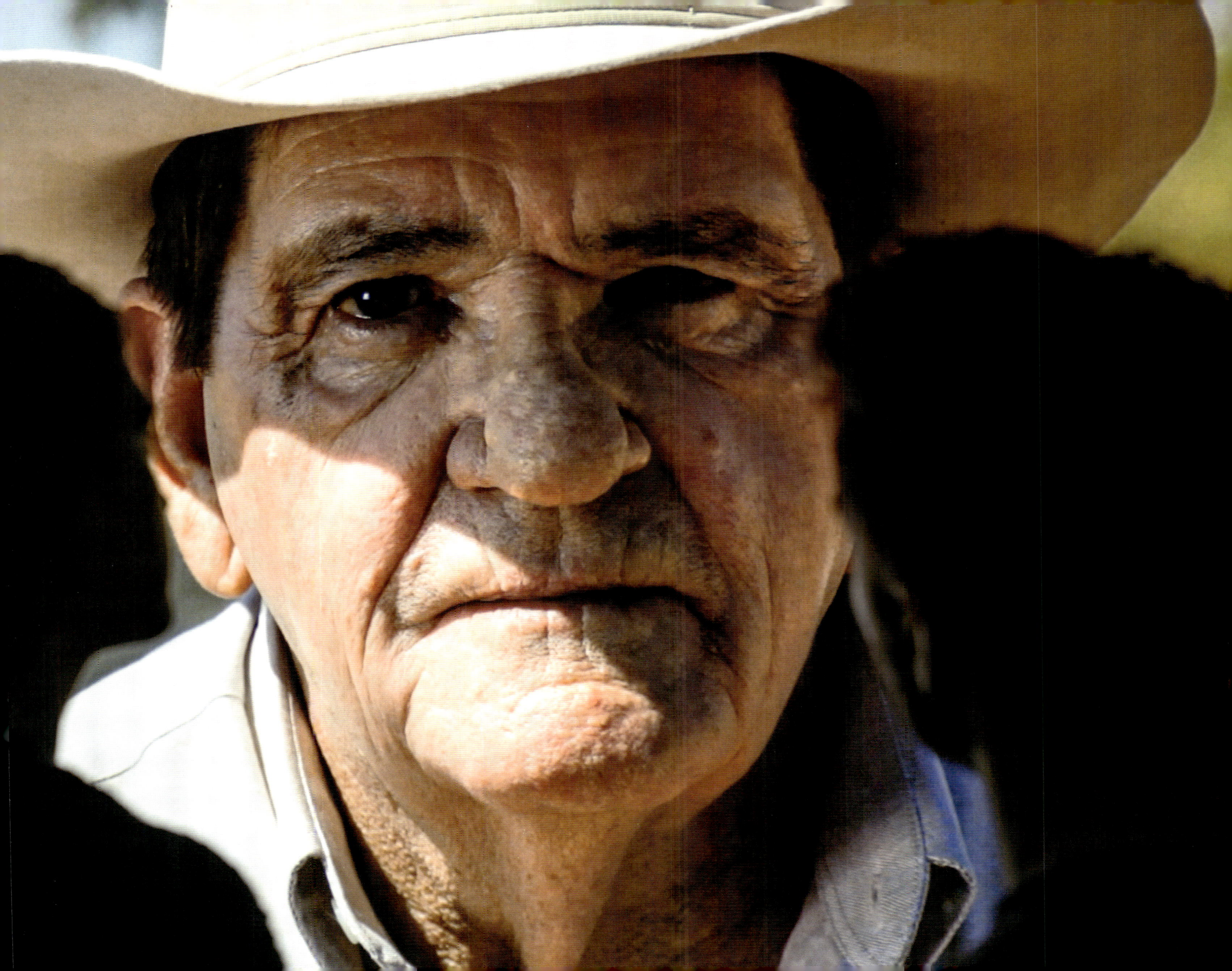

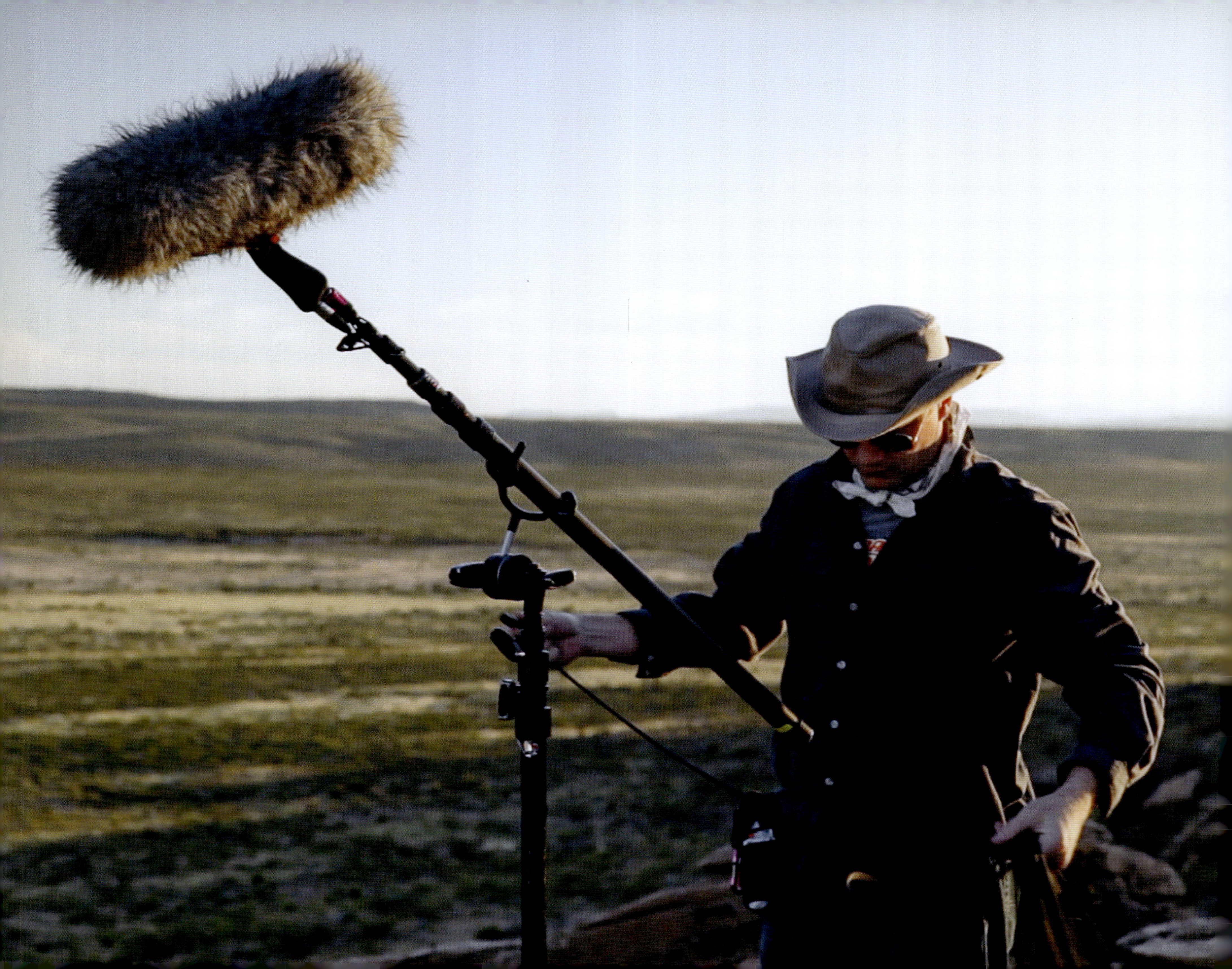

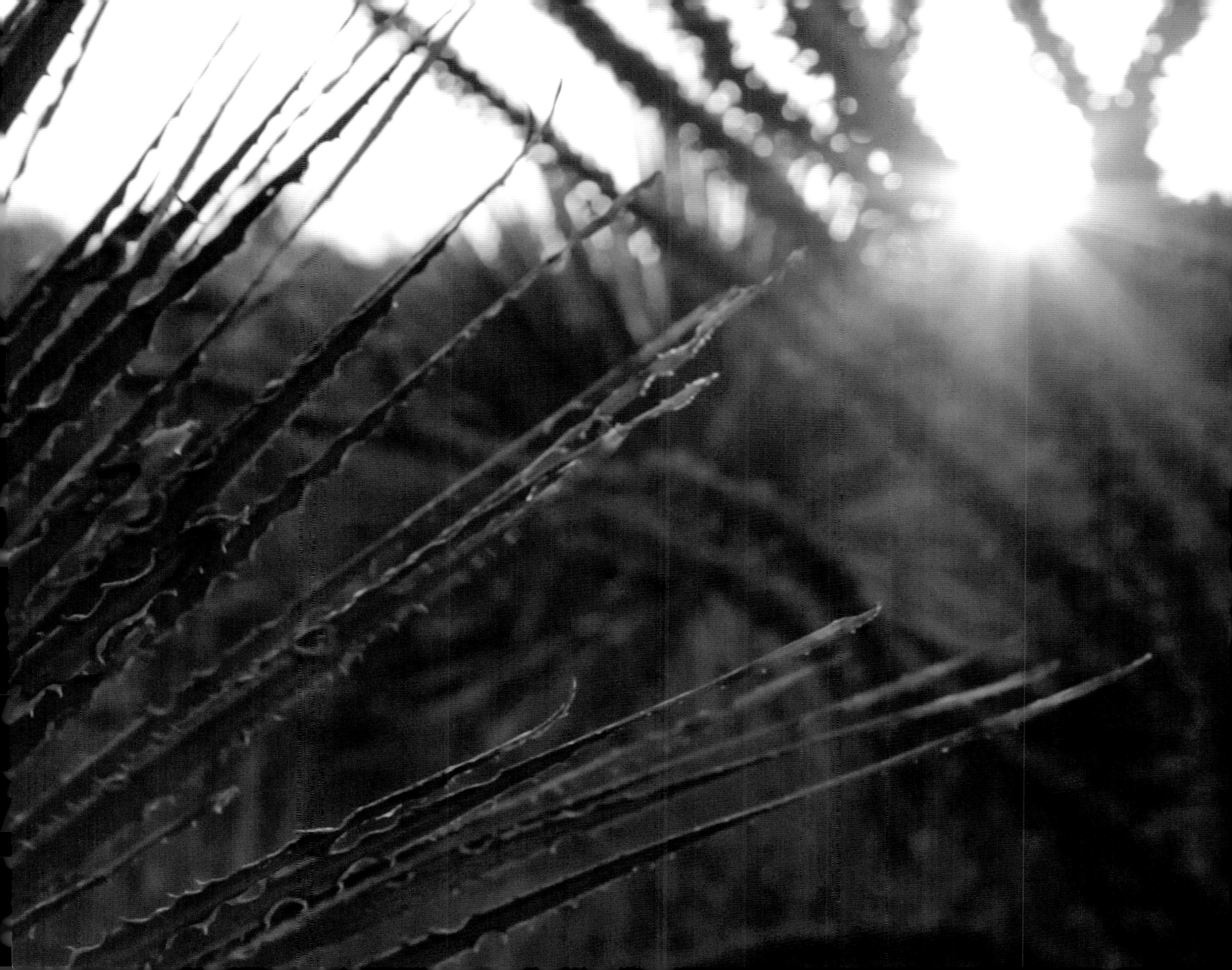

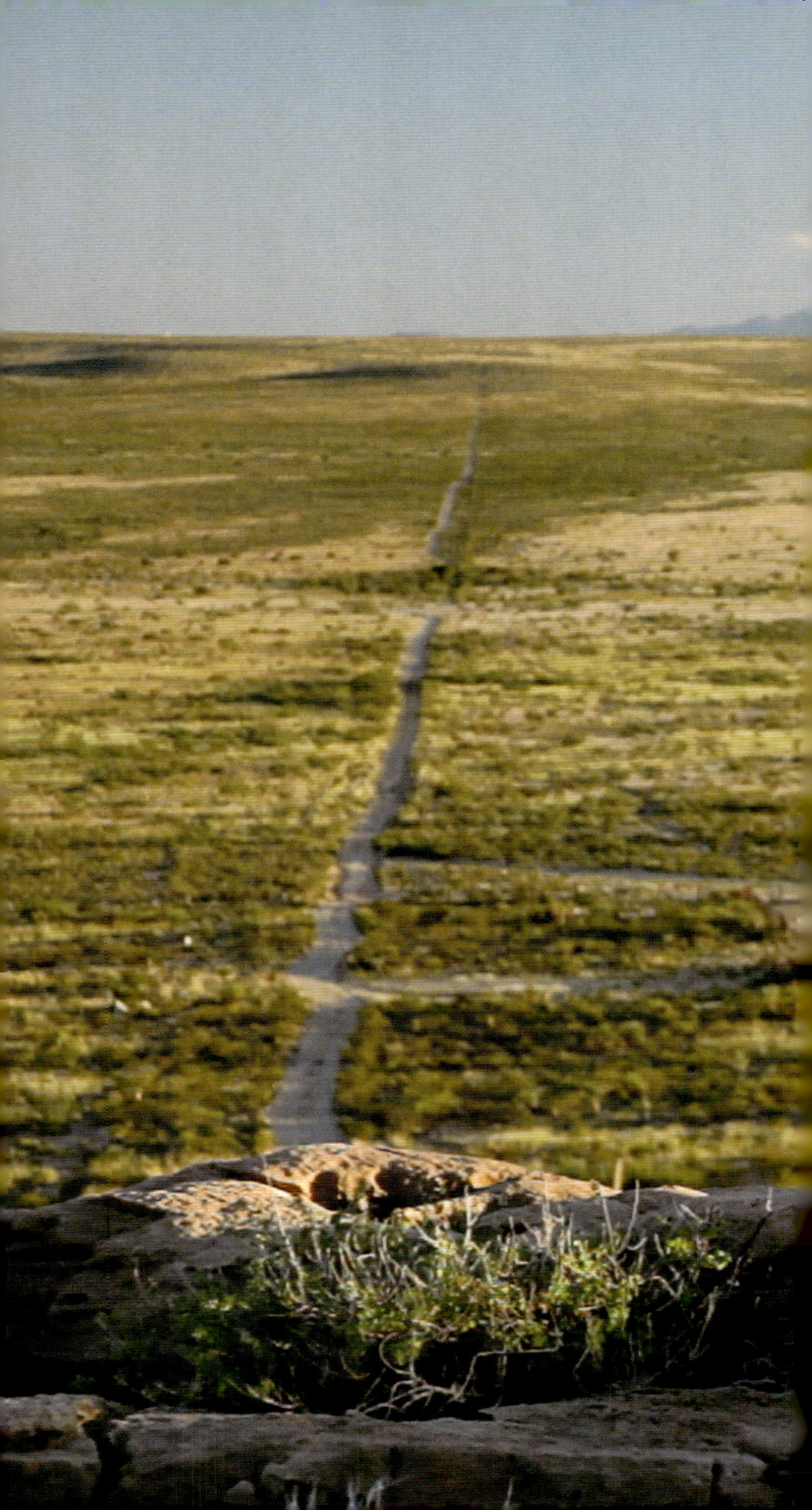

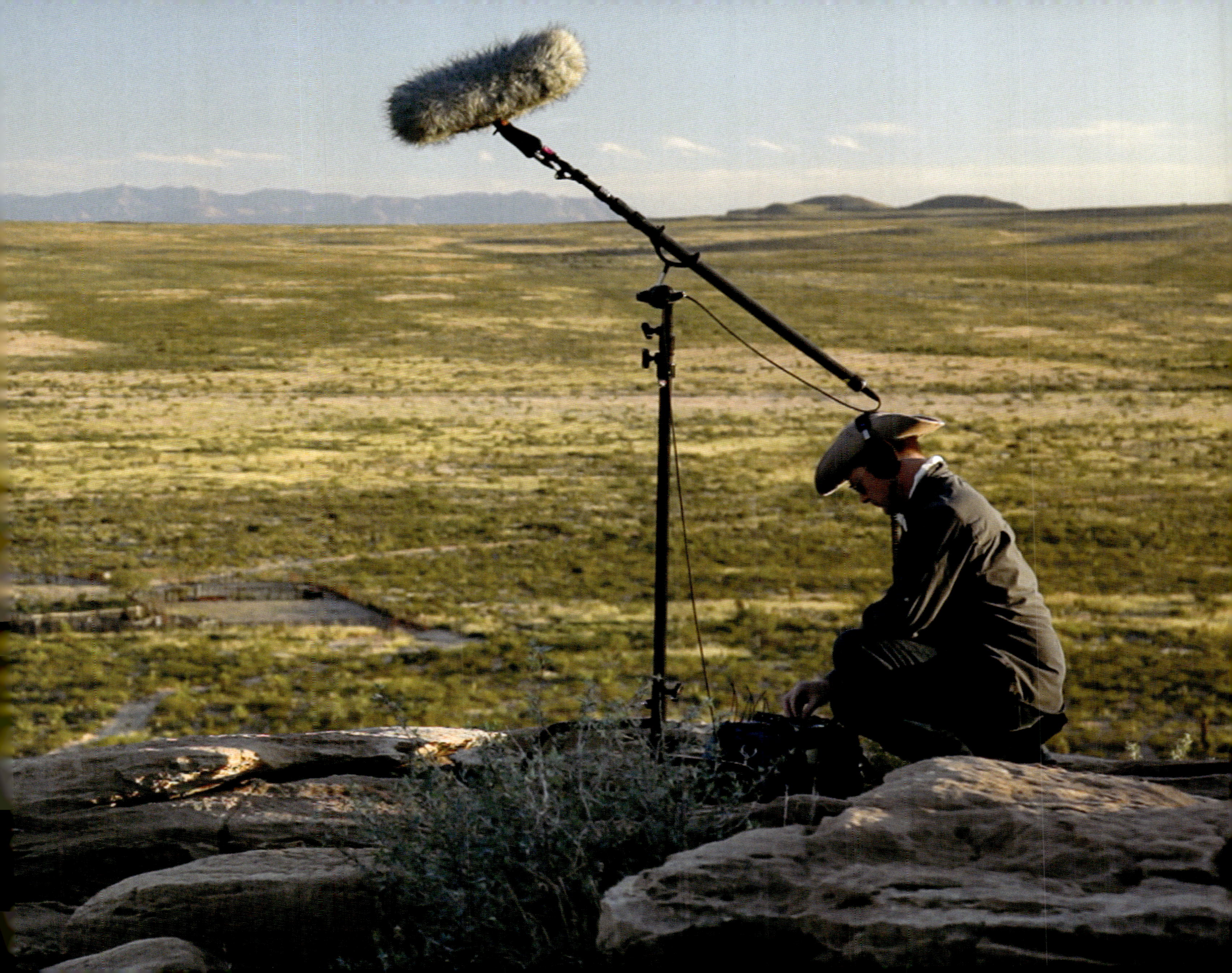

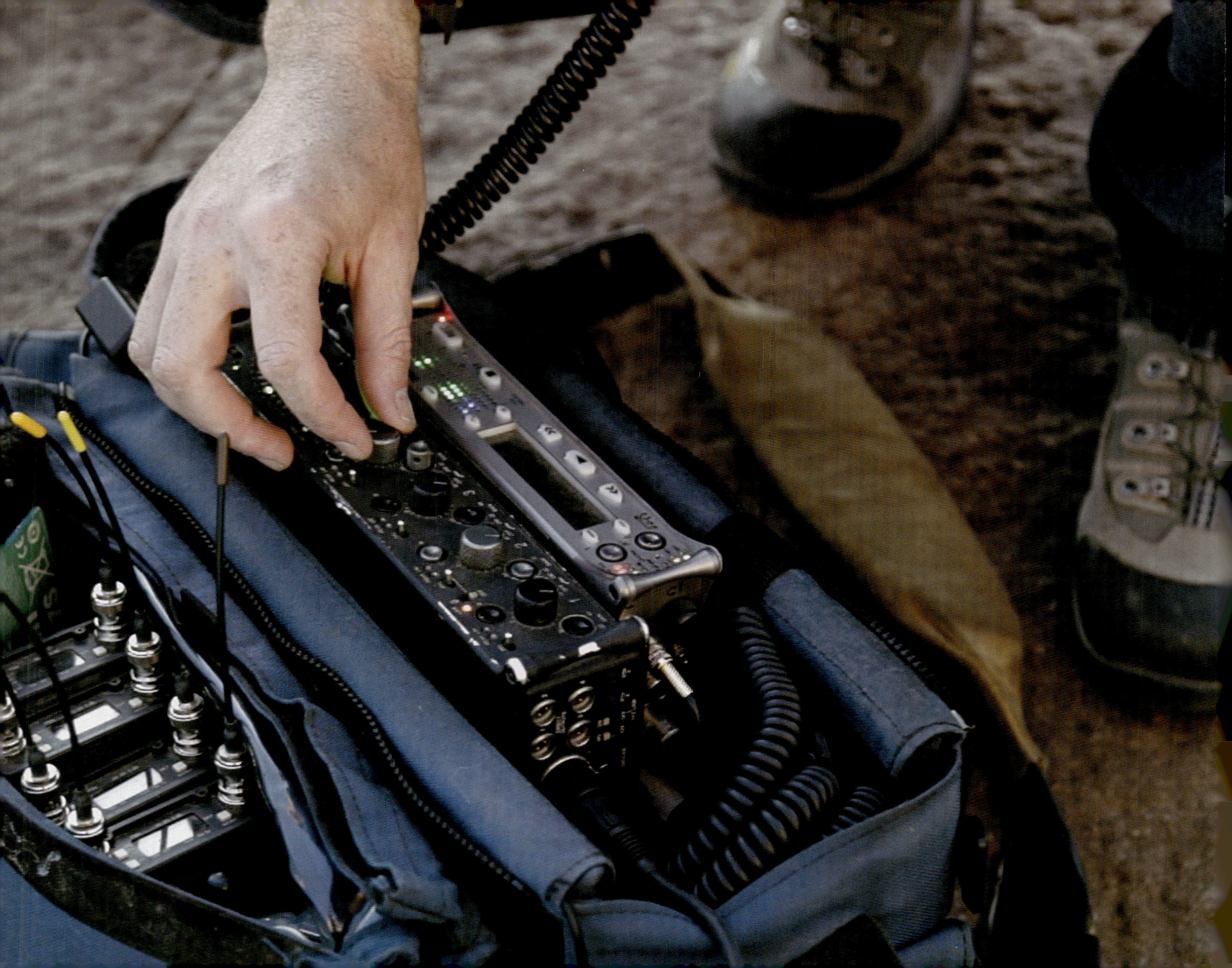

JEFFREY KASTNER

Centers of Attention: Four Essays for Teresa Hubbard and Alexander Birchler

ONE

Fortis imaginatio generat casum.
(A powerful imagination generates the event.)
—Michel de Montaigne, "On the Power of Imagination"[1]

If you've ever spent more than a half hour or so in a contemporary art gallery, it will very quickly become clear that while the rhythms of attention—the procedures of *looking*—vary widely from individual to individual, what is common to all viewers is that virtually none of them ever devotes more than five or ten minutes to a particular show. This is neither a secret nor necessarily an indictment of the quality of the work; it's just that the structure, scale and ambition of most gallery shows mean that they give themselves up to the visitor in a pretty immediate way. Of course, there are exceptions. The obligations that durational work like film and video place on the viewer in order to operate in their fullest sense are patently—perhaps even a bit defiantly—out of sync with the pace of most viewing. It's part of the reason I've always felt there was something both rather noble and a little sad about the images that loop (mostly unseen) all day inside the white cubes' black boxes. On occasion, one or two viewers are willing to settle in for something that lasts for fifteen minutes, but it must be factored into any assessment of an artwork that if it demands half an hour of your time, much less an hour, it will be experienced *in toto* by only a tiny minority of its potential audience.

House with Pool, 2004
High-Definition Video with Sound, Single Channel, 20:39 minutes, Loop
Installation view, Museum für Gegenwartskunst Basel
Collection, Hirshhorn Museum and Sculpture Garden, Washington D.C., and others

I first encountered the work of Hubbard/Birchler when they showed *House with Pool* at Tanya Bonakdar Gallery in New York in 2004. I wasn't familiar with the artists and, truth be told, I didn't make the time for the whole twenty-minute-long video, even though I remember it being gorgeous and intriguing. (In fact, I recall that I actually saw it more than once during its run, and a different part of it each time.) After that, I sort of lost track of their work and it was only in 2011 that I really was able to begin making sense of their larger practice. The occasion was again an exhibition at Bonakdar—this one comprising two videos, *Grand Paris Texas* (2009) and *Movie Mountain (Méliès)* (2011), the first and second elements of a planned trilogy, the last part of which, though I didn't know it at the time, was probably already in its preliminary stages. That was 2014's *Giant* and it, like the other two videos included in this exhibition, constitutes a meditation on the nature of place and memory—a search for a way to describe these phenomena, their effects and operations, that properly lies somewhere in the gray zone between objects

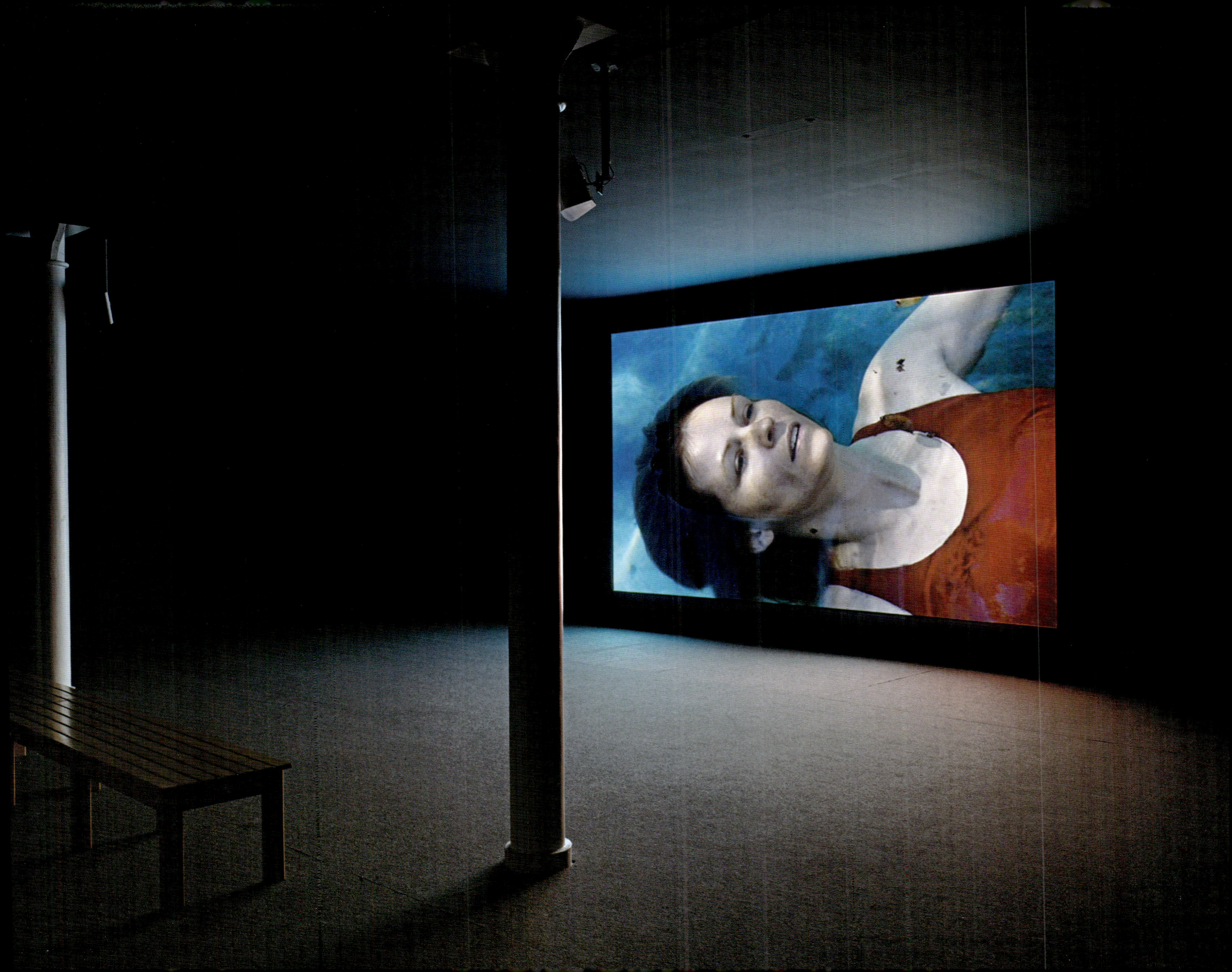

and subjects. For the artists it also completes a larger project, an elliptical consideration by the pair of their own craft attempted at a fitting midpoint some two decades into their collaboration. The works demonstrate the kinds of technical and conceptual tendencies longtime viewers have come to expect from the duo: cinematographical precision, patient observation of sites and people, a sense of the larger patterns of time and experience. Eccentric, provisional, often oblique, Hubbard/Birchler's examinations open up, rather than foreclose on, potential types of meaning, kinds of knowledge, varieties of "truth." And they put demands on the viewer, demands that rub against the grain in ways that reveal important things about the nature of spectatorship and the mechanisms of attention. The work quite literally expects, as Alexander Birchler once put it, "that a viewer participate in the authorship of the story."[2] After spending an hour and a half watching the two videos in succession that day in the gallery (one of the longest amounts of time I've ever spent in a single gallery show), it was clear that in some way I surely had. It was an experience of work that seriously challenged my expectations as a viewer and it's stayed with me, as have the stories the videos tell and the often unexpectedly moving ways they tell them.

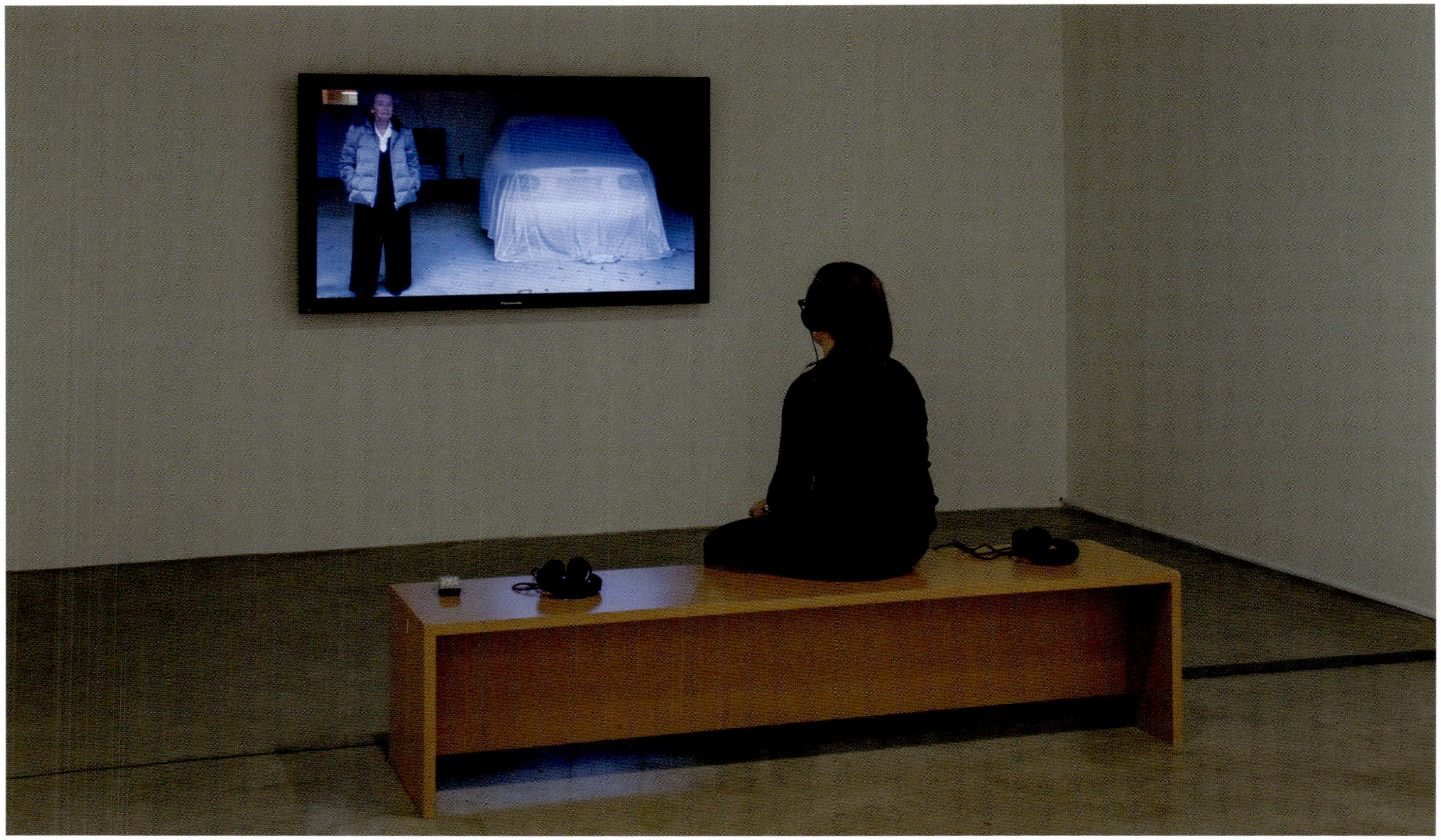

Grand Paris Texas, 2009
Installation view,
Tanya Bonakdar Gallery,
New York

OPPOSITE:
Dead Cat on Movie Mountain, Sunrise, 2011
Dead Cat on Movie Mountain, Sunset, 2011
Installation view,
Tanya Bonakdar Gallery,
New York

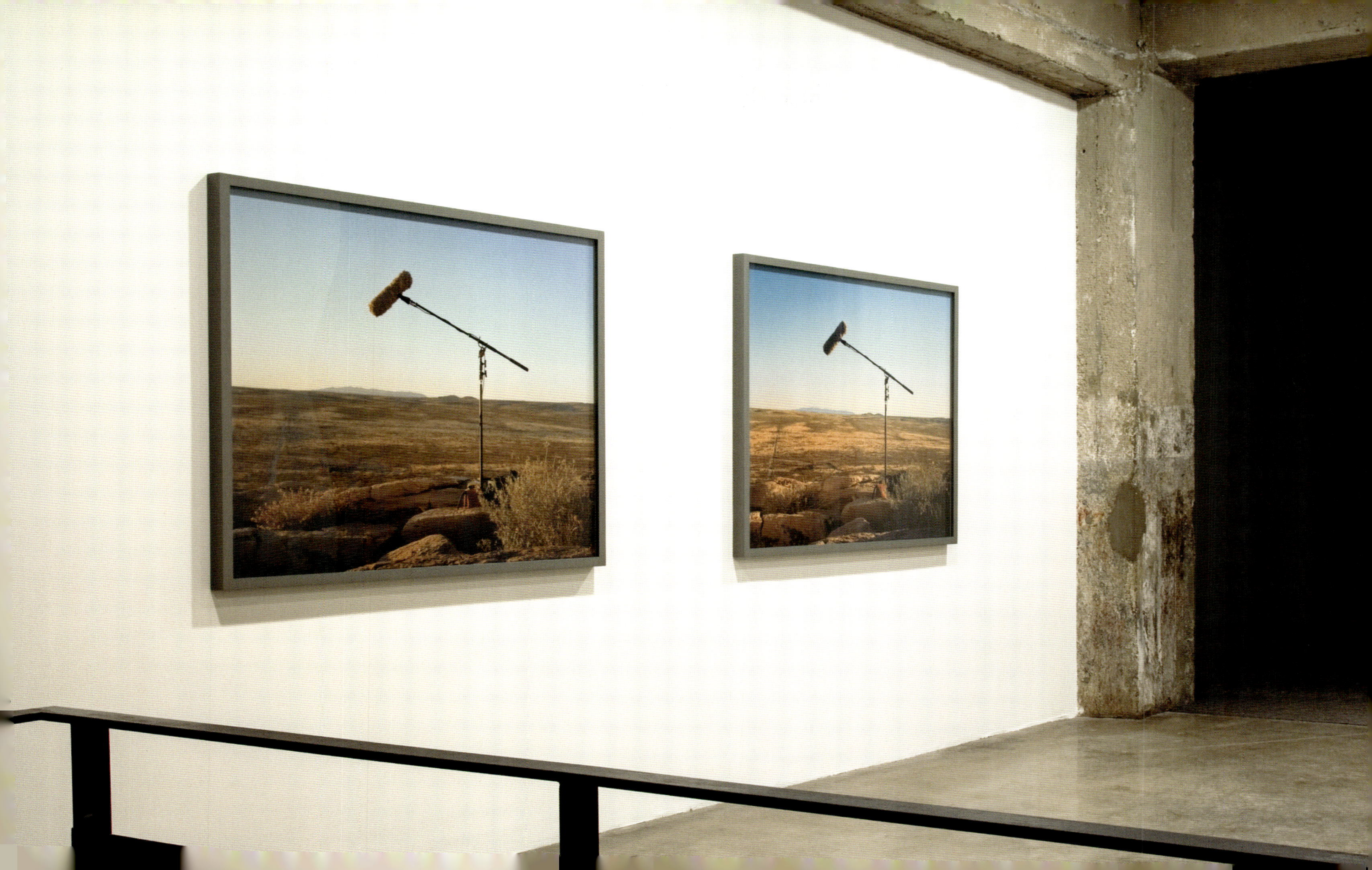

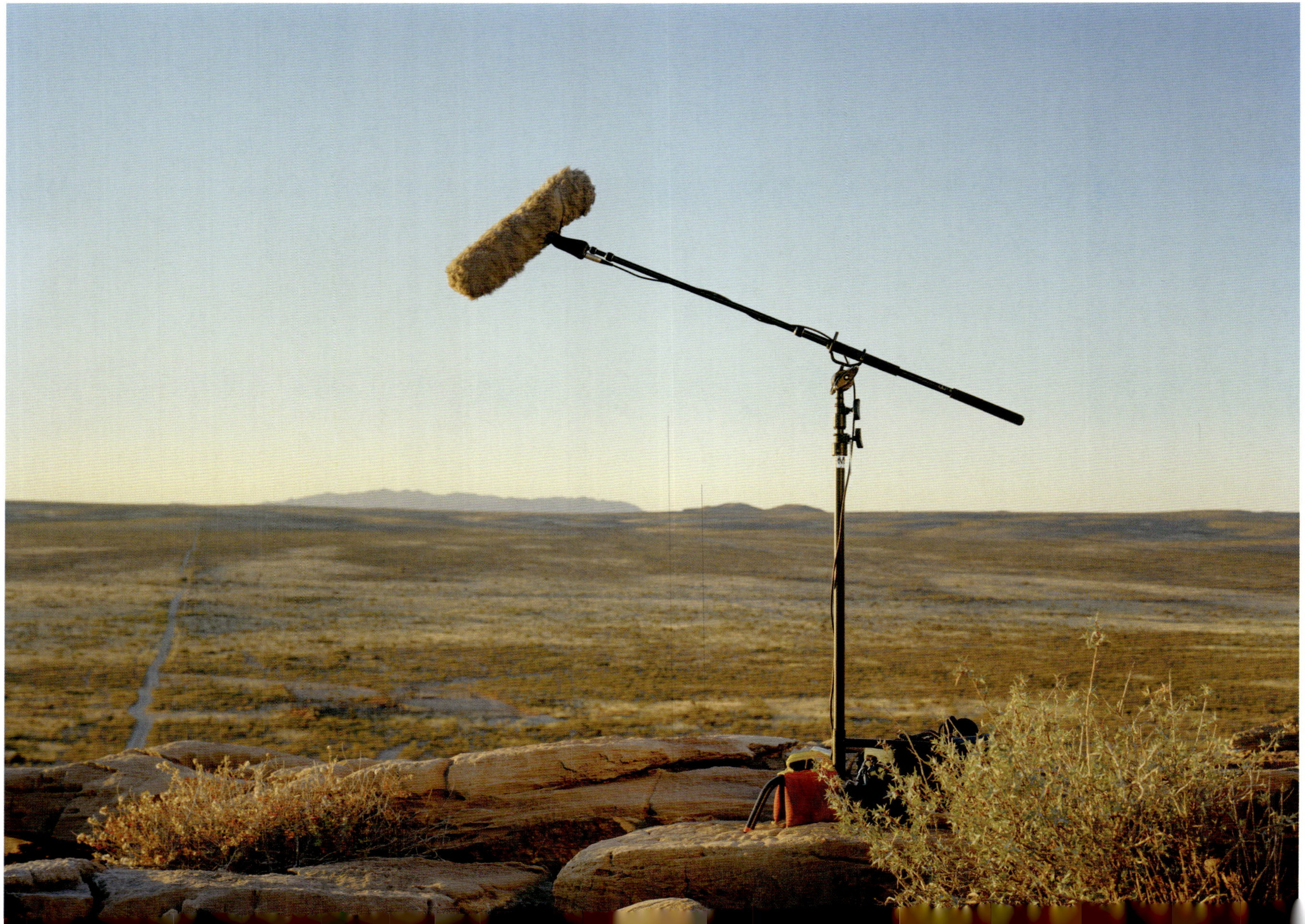

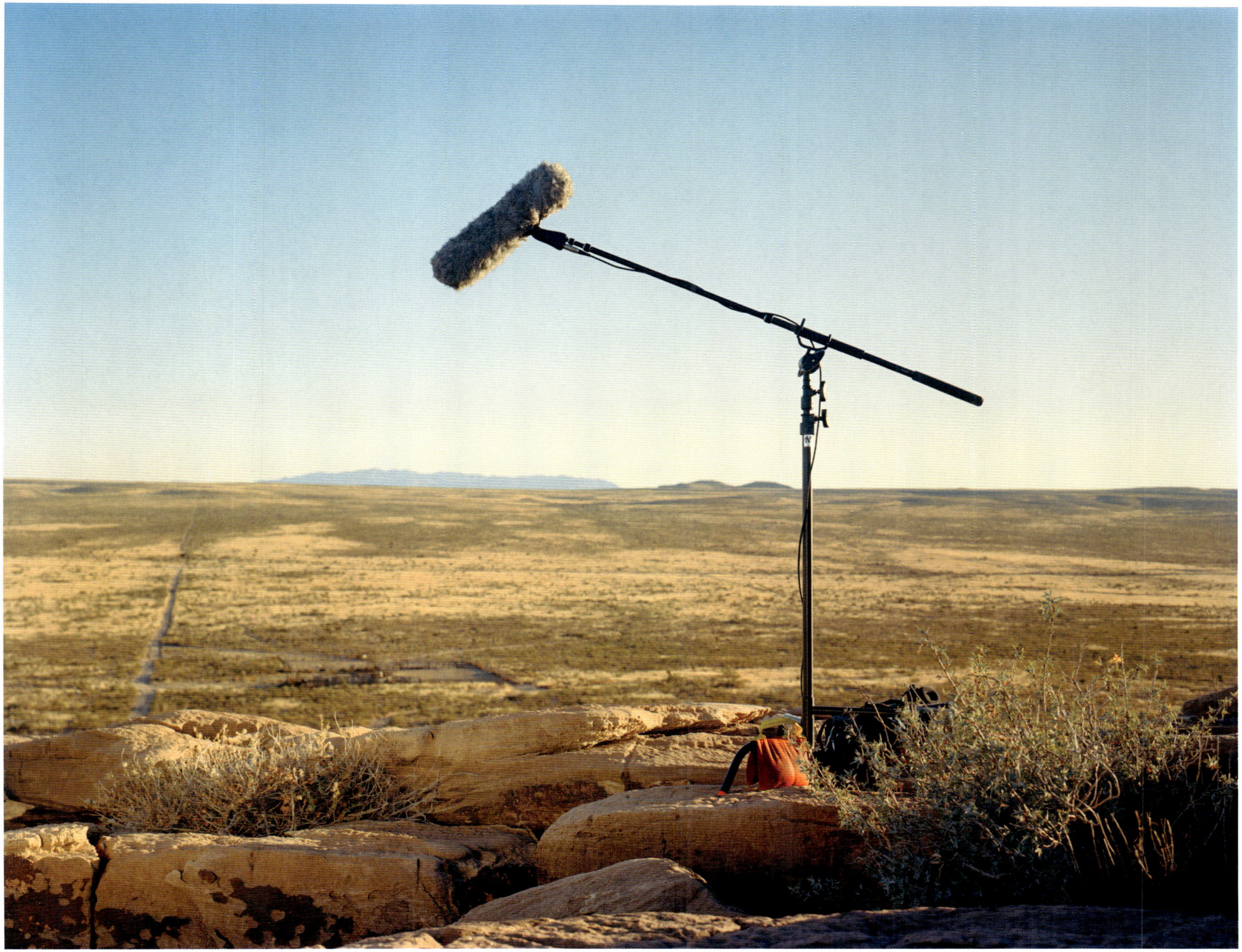

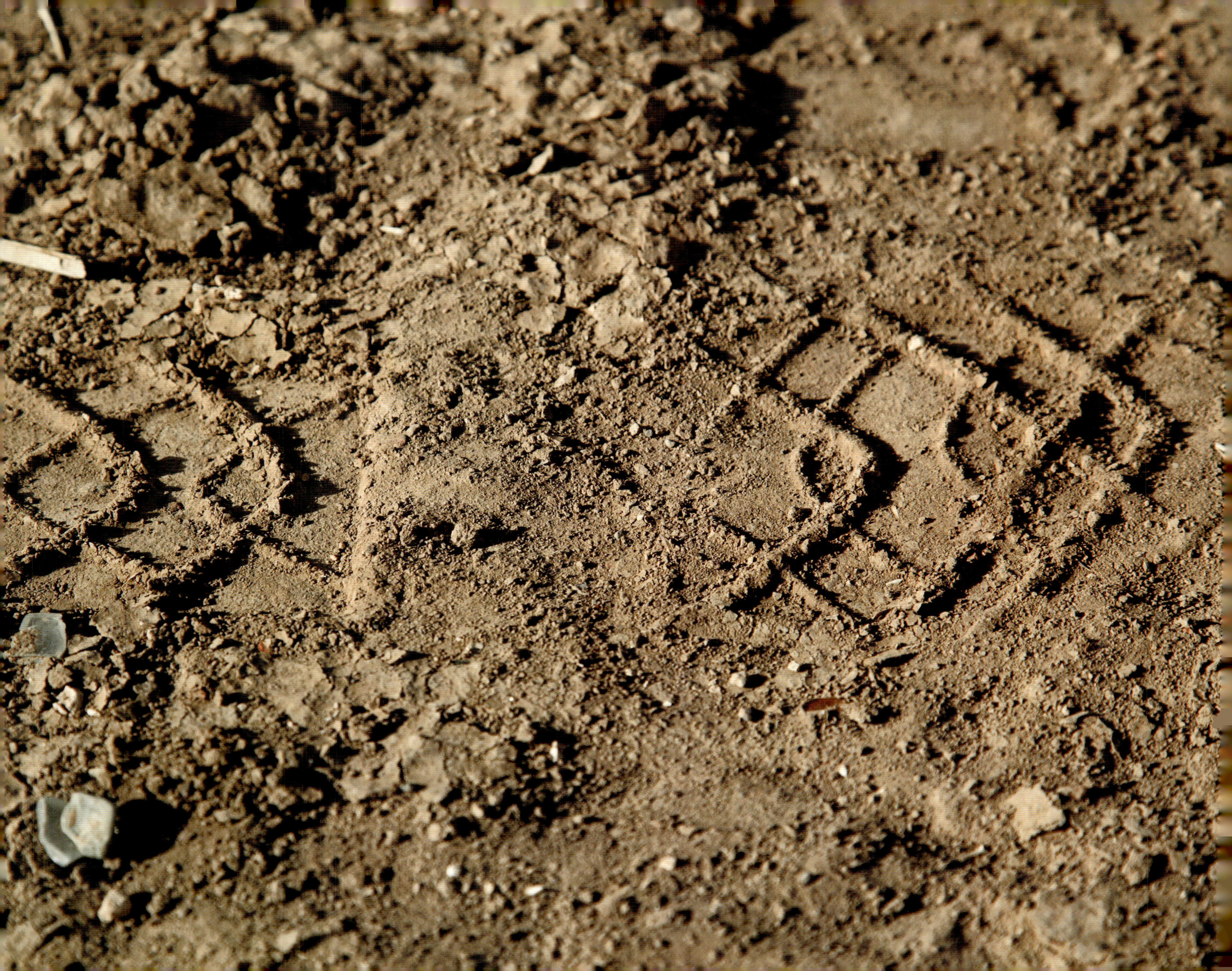

TWO

The hero of the essay is its author in the act of thinking things out, feeling and finding a way; it is the mind in the marvels and miseries of its makings, in the work of the imagination, the search for form.
—William Gass, "Emerson and the Essay"[3]

Hubbard/Birchler's work might properly be thought of within the tradition of the so-called "essay film," a loosely defined, if increasingly theorized form that might be understood as a kind of personal or quasi-performative documentary; focused on the accumulation of information but also diaristic; a hybrid species of non-fiction storytelling of which strategic digression is not just a feature but a structuring element. All Hubbard/Birchler's filmic essays are also in their way detective stories, with all the poetic and philosophical resonance that the form at its best can offer. Not run-of-the-mill whodunnits, but examinations of the ways in which knowing and not-knowing are related and how tangential information—unrelated or even opposing viewpoints, individualized experiences of larger phenomena—can be woven together to tell stories that bear as much on ontological conditions as they do on epistemological ones.

The essayistic form has become such a commonplace mode of address in both print and digital media (what after all are our ubiquitous blogs but ever-proliferating collections of essays?) that it's easy to forget the outlier status it long held in the literary canon—just as the cinematic equivalent (work by artists as diverse as Chris Marker, Jean-Luc Godard, Jonas Mekas, D. A. Pennebaker, Agnes Varda, Werner Herzog and Errol Morris, to name just a few) continues to elude fully stable definition within the history of filmmaking.[4] A discursive mode that sifts together

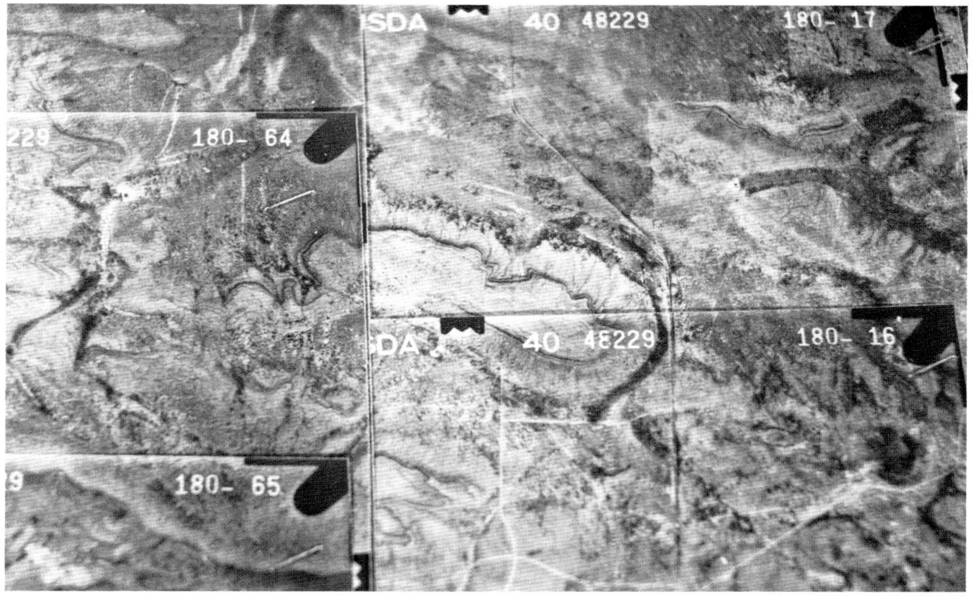

objective facts and subjective assessment, the observational and the speculative, the essay—whether literary or cinematic—is always a study in both its ostensible topic and in the inclinations and preoccupations of its author. "I myself am the subject of my book," wrote Montaigne, the father of the modern, self-reflexive essay form, at the end of the 1500s.[5] This peculiar state of affairs—a figuring of the world at once faithful to its conditions but also rich with the potential for the revelation of a unique authorial sensibility—has meant that the device has continued to be the subject of discussion, often in the guise of a mode of introspection that turns the inquisitional techniques native to the form back onto the form itself. In some sense, then, every essay is not just about its topic, or indeed, even (as Montaigne had it) about its *auteur*, but also about the condition of the essay itself. When Aldous Huxley famously touted the essay as "a literary device for saying almost everything about almost anything,"[6] he did so by way of presenting his own. One can't help but wonder if rather

PREVIOUS TWO PAGES:
Dead Cat on Movie Mountain, Sunrise, 2011
Archival Pigment Inkjet Print
Dead Cat on Movie Mountain, Sunset, 2011
Archival Pigment Inkjet Print

ABOVE:
Aerial Photographs, U.S. Department of Agriculture, Hudspeth County, Texas, 1981

OPPOSITE:
Giant, 2014
Production still

than simply the conviction of the author, it is something in the very nature of the essay that demands such a strongly reflexive move—a clear staking-out of a terrain for its operations—and also a kind of constant reassessment of its aims and potential. It's no stretch, I think, to detect in the recursive consideration of the medium of cinema in the three films that comprise *Sound Speed Marker*—the show's title itself comes from the verbal cues given on a movie set, recalling the nuts and bolts praxis of filmmaking—some of this broadly essayistic tendency toward reflexivity. It's very much of a piece with the self-aware oscillations regularly seen in Hubbard/Birchler's films: their deft management of the viewer's immersion in (and distance from) both the story of the video and its form. Like the literary essay, their work at its best holds belief and the suspension of belief in productive tension, allowing for what the artists have described as a process of moving between states of absorption and of de-absorption, of full engrossment in an artwork and of self-consciousness regarding the way that artwork acts to foster it.

Grand Paris Texas, 2009
Production still

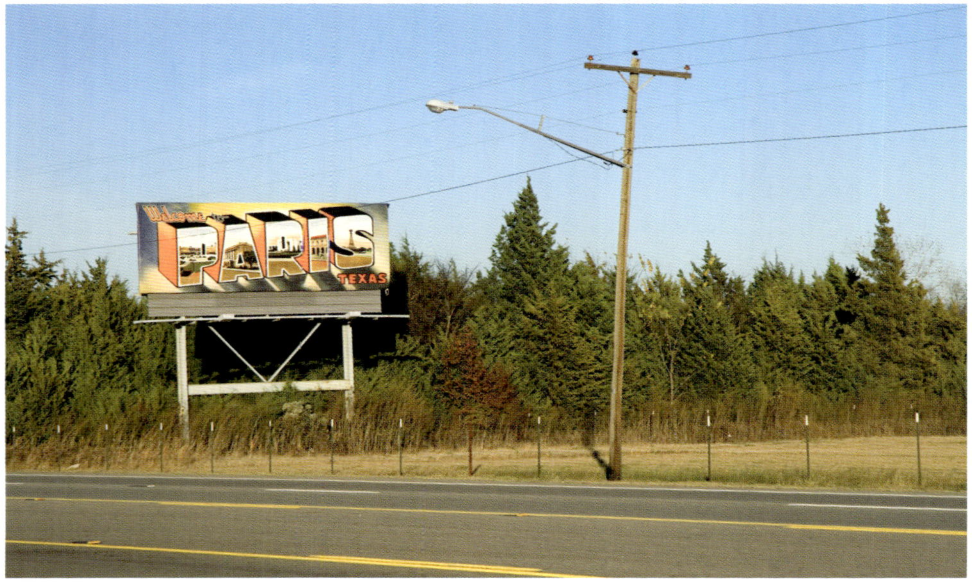

THREE

In the essay, concepts do not build a continuum of operations, thought does not advance in a single direction, rather the aspects of the argument interweave as in a carpet. The fruitfulness of the thoughts depends on the density of this texture.
—Theodor Adorno, "The Essay as Form"[7]

The word *essay* originally carried with it the sense of an *attempt*, of a *weighing* of evidence, a test of sorts—the modern French word *essayer*, "to try," reflects these etymological origins. In his final summary essay, "On Experience," Montaigne writes that "No desire is more natural than the desire for knowledge. We assay all the means that can lead us to it. ... Truth is so great a matter that we must not disdain any method which leads us to it."[8] Montaigne's *assay* (the word that in our time has retained these early meanings) of the potential means to knowledge echoes in part all of these aspects: a trying of the world around us, a shot at finding, and making, meaning in the spaces where the past and the present, people and places, things and ideas bump up against each other. Hubbard/Birchler's films each attempt to subtly gather up information about a site and to understand the individual and the collective figuring of that site through (always partial; always faulty; always, finally, personal) memory. Their routing of a kind of documentary methodology—with their minute attendance to factual details—through a highly individual conceptual lens produces what Robert Musil in his *Man Without Qualities* called *Essayismus*, or essayism: a third way that finds new meaning in the spaces between the objective and the subjective.

This dialectic of facts and interpretations is echoed in Hubbard/Birchler's work by its many oscillations between site/non-site.

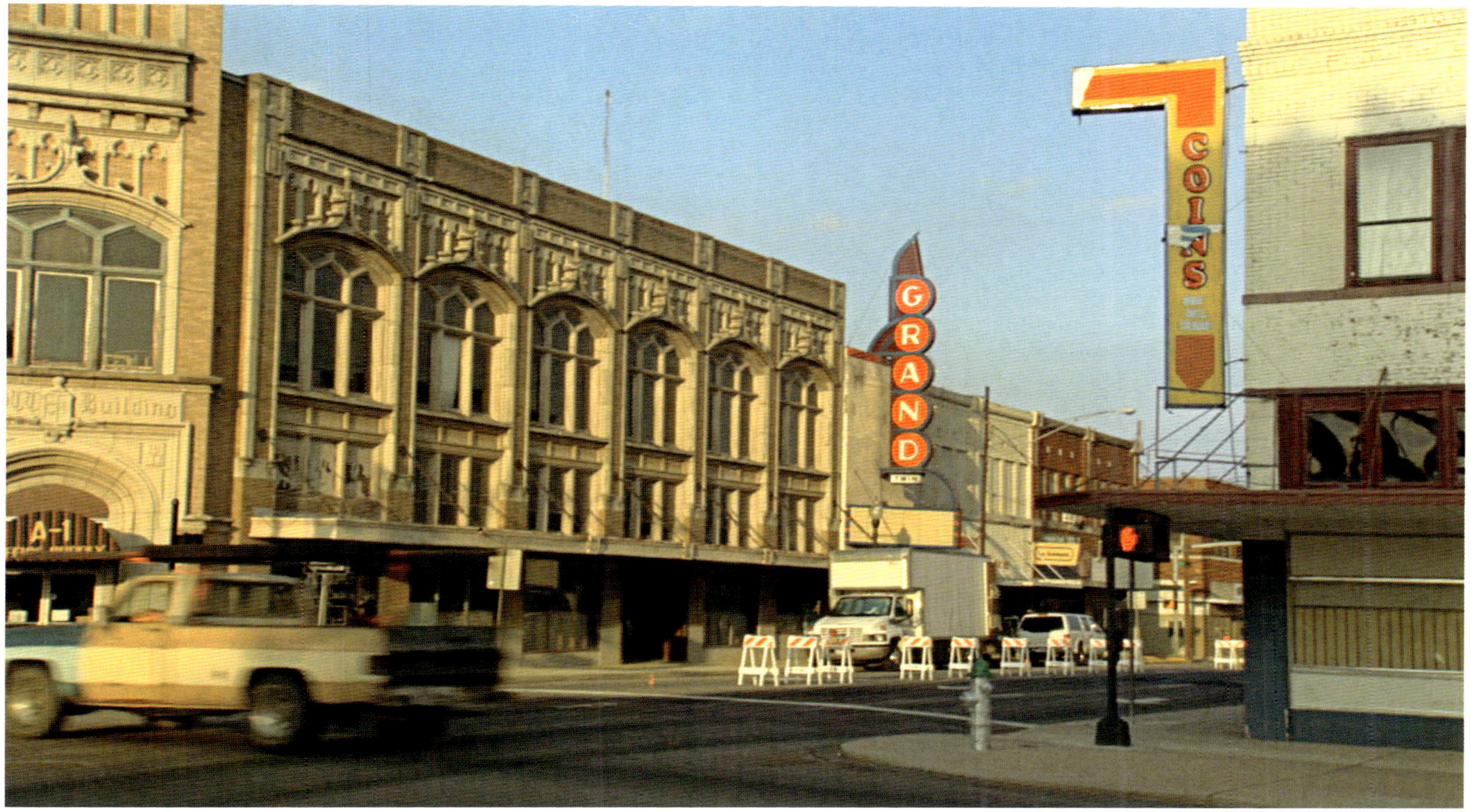

Grand Paris Texas, 2009
Video still

Famously articulated by Robert Smithson, the influence of the concept—in his case, the relocation of materials from an actual location into the space of the gallery to produce what he described as "a three-dimensional logical picture that is *abstract*, yet ... *represents* an actual site"[9]—can be seen in each of the three films in *Sound Speed Marker*. All are focused on sites that are at once present and absent, that sit at the intersection of physical actuality and metaphorical consequence: a bit of unremarkable landscape where some activity may have taken place in *Movie Mountain (Méliès)*; the ruins of a fictional, constructed place in *Giant*; and perhaps most complexly in *Grand Paris Texas*, which considers places and artifacts that exist precisely on the threshold between there and not-there (the somewhat dusty town about two hours northeast of Dallas; the abandoned Grand cinema, once a major social and cultural hub there; a film whose title would seem to refer to a place but is instead an ever-receding *placeholder*, a destination constructed by loss toward which no actual journey is directed).

Of course photographic and filmic representation by its nature has some of Smithson's notion of the non-site in it. "By drawing a diagram, a ground plan of a house, a street plan to the location of a site, or a topographic map, one draws a logical two-dimen-

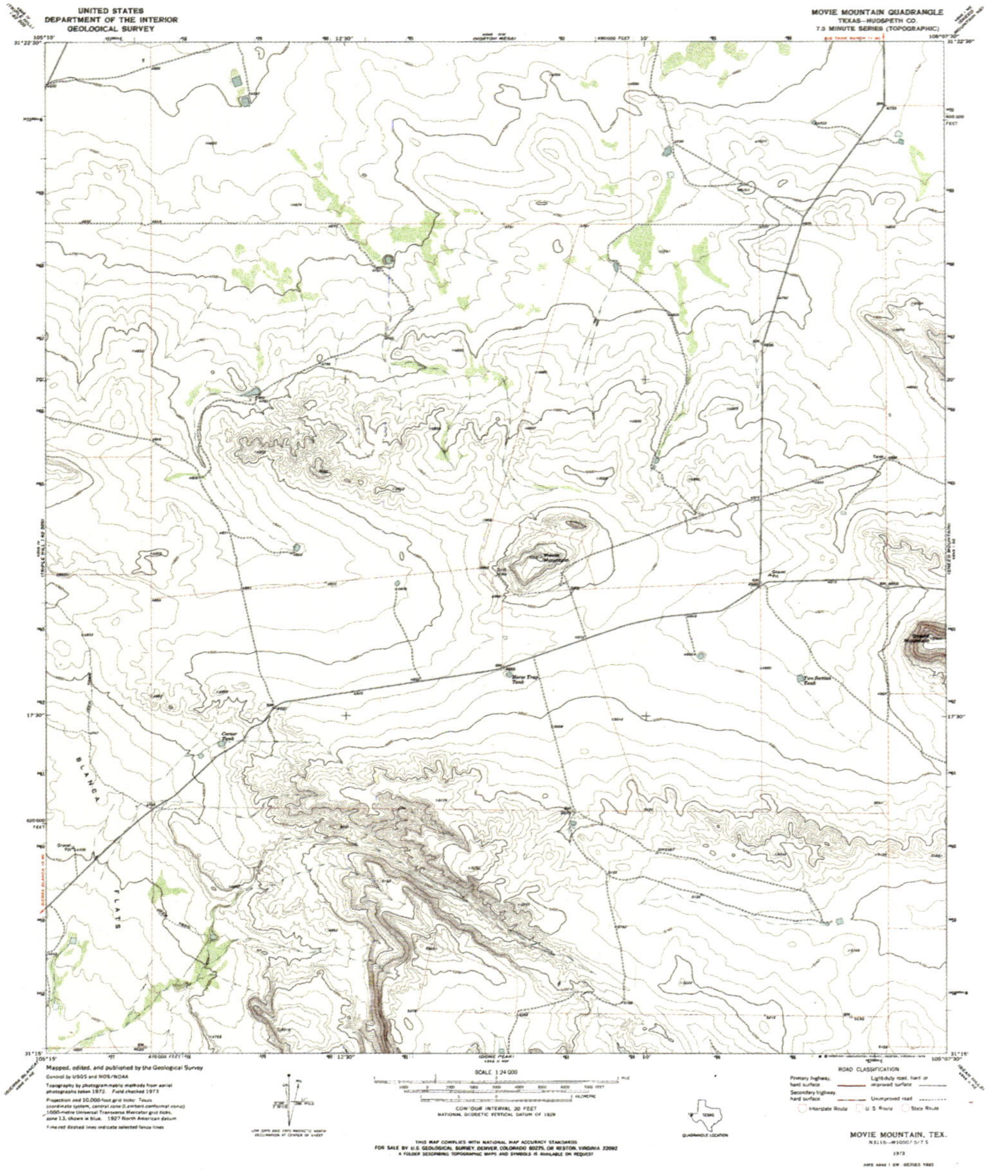

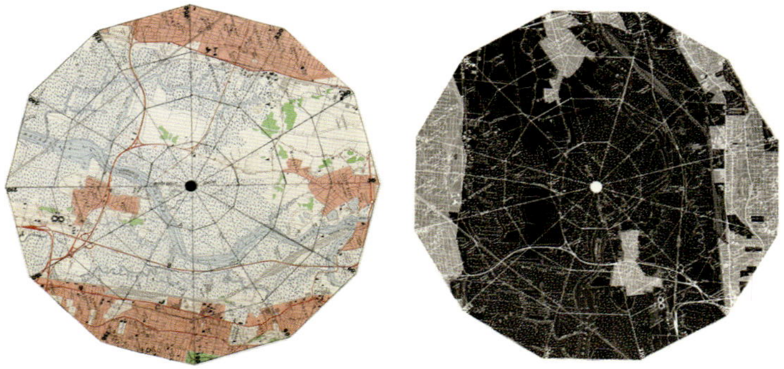

ABOVE LEFT AND OPPOSITE:
United States Department of the Interior Geological Survey, Movie Mountain Quadrangle, Texas–Hudspeth CO., 1973

ABOVE RIGHT:
Robert Smithson,
Entropic Pole, 1967
Art © Estate of Robert Smithson/Licensed by VAGA, New York, NY

sional picture,'" he wrote. "A 'logical picture' differs from a natural or realistic picture in that it rarely looks like the thing it stands for. It is a two-*dimensional analogy or metaphor*—A is Z."[10] The three films included in this exhibition all, in some sense, act as analogies for the places they investigate; they are diagrams that describe the "metaphorical significance" that Smithson saw operating between the site and its stand-in. Unlike Smithson's gallery non-sites, Hubbard/Birchler's filmic non-sites do, strictly speaking, "look like" the things they stand for. But they also are constantly aiming to trouble the relationship between resemblance and actuality. They do so by orchestrating highly complex narrative and pictorial tangents that extend the stories they tell into zones of interwoven personal experience and memory that somehow *exceed* the reality on the ground. These surplus textures produce both a startlingly clear sense of the work's subjects—whether charming cowboys or philosophical funeral directors, abandoned offices or ruined movie sets—and engineer a kind of dis-placement, an estrangement (literally a making-strange) of the superficially unremarkable.

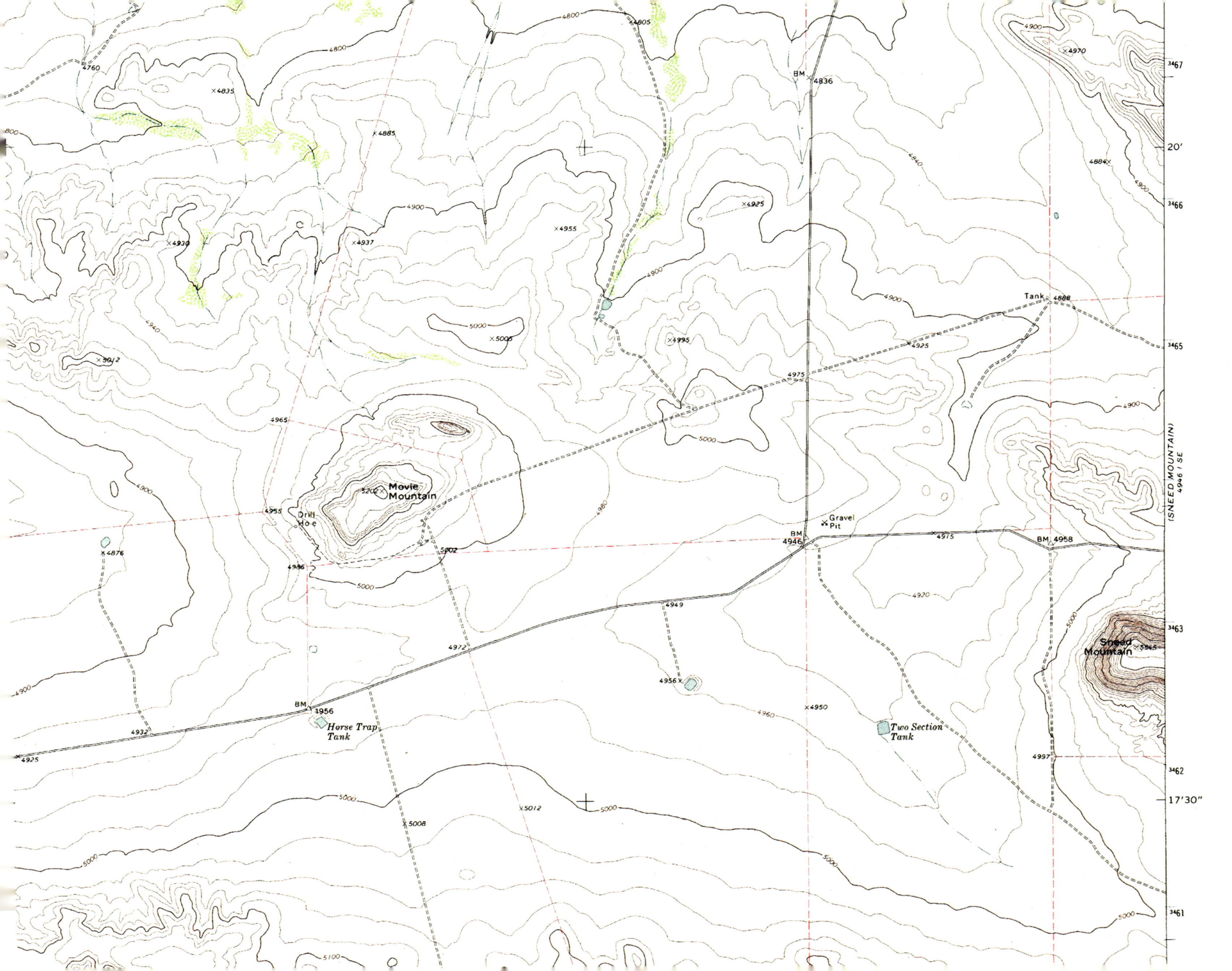
Movie Mountain
Sneed Mountain
Horse Trap Tank
Two Section Tank
Drill Hole
Gravel Pit
Tank
BM 4836
BM 4946
BM 4958
BM 1956
(SNEED MOUNTAIN)
4946 I SE
20'
17'30"
3467
3466
3465
3463
3462
3461

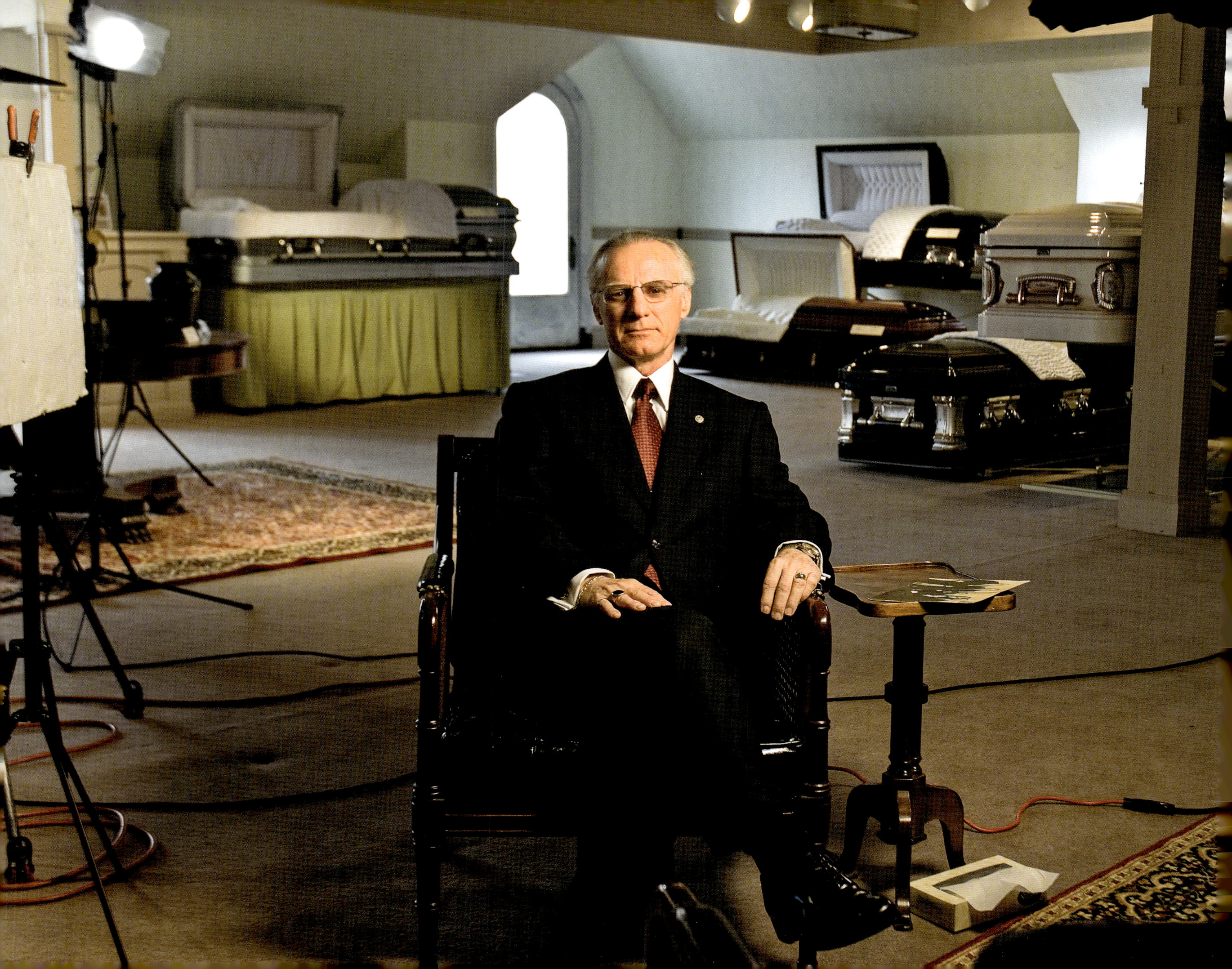

FOUR

When I talk about pictures in my mind I am talking, quite specifically, about images that shimmer around the edges. Look hard enough, and you can't miss the shimmer. It's there. You can't think too much about these pictures that shimmer. You just lie low and let them develop. You stay quiet.

—Joan Didion, "Why I Write" [11]

Perhaps it's because their practice has always included photography as well as videos, but I often find myself thinking about particular images—or, more generally, isolated moments—from Hubbard/Birchler's work. They do "shimmer," to use Didion's phrase, and they do so within the artists' cinematic essays precisely because of their conceptual quietness, the way they are given the space they need to develop. About halfway through *Grand Paris Texas*, for example, the artists turn their camera on a funeral director in the town, Marcus Roden. All of the interview subjects in the film are speaking about the physical and emotional space of cinema—the critic, the former theater operator, the now-elderly former candy counter girl, the various young people whose lives have intersected in some way or another with the world of the movies—but it's Roden who engages most directly with the activities of the artists. Directing a funeral has a lot in common with directing a film, he offers, as he sits in the soberly elegant rooms of his family's funeral home. "If it is done properly it requires a director," Roden says, "a person who is at the helm and in charge—and that person has to have the overall picture of what they're wanting to accomplish. You cannot conduct a good funeral in my judgment if you are an observer. You cannot be watching the funeral going on; you have to be the one causing the funeral to go on." It's at once a rather zen proposition and a fully pragmatic observation, and it's in this space between laying low and making something happen that Hubbard/Birchler operate.

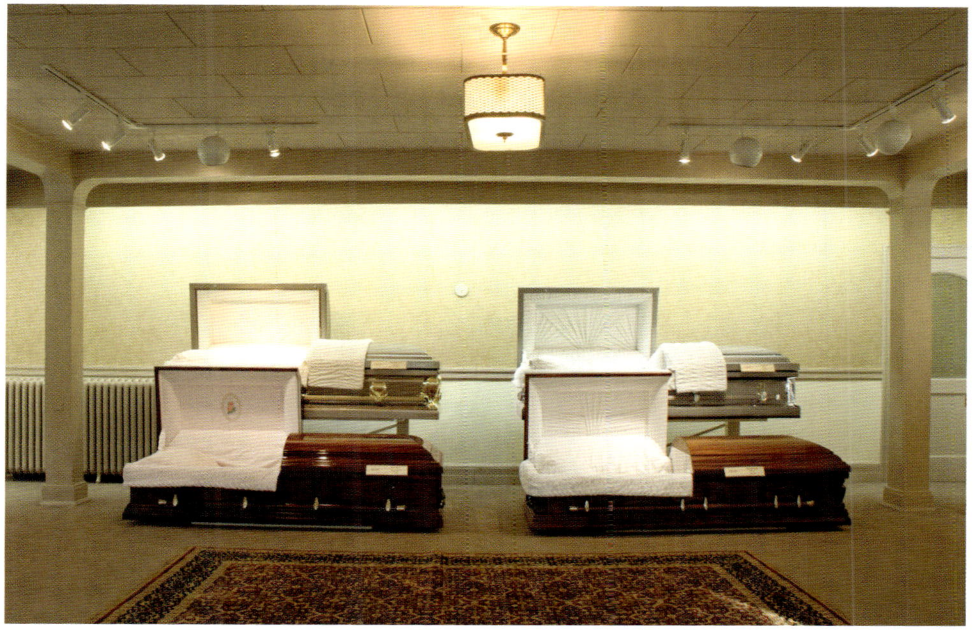

The artists are absent from the interview, as they are in all the interviews in these films; they are invisible "observers" that nonetheless initiate the event. Yet they crucially do appear elsewhere in *Grand Paris Texas*, seen in the dis-placing moments that take the viewer "behind the scenes," to the set up and filming of the old cinema. This turning of the work's attention back not only on themselves but more pointedly on the mechanics of film production occurs at several moments in both *Movie Mountain (Méliès)* and *Giant*, as well—it's a device that not only represents a vital up-rushing of the real into the fictive space of the film but also in its content (the careful preparations taken to best *record* the evidence they seek) expresses what might be thought of as the ethical stance of their work, one that

ABOVE:
Grand Paris Texas, 2009
Production still, Starrett funeral home

OPPOSITE:
Grand Paris Texas, 2009
Production still

makes a point and a practice of sustained attention and patient observation. Perhaps no moments in these films encapsulate this more clearly than the scenes that bracket the narrative "action" of *Movie Mountain (Méliès)*. The film begins and ends with sequences focusing on a solitary sound recordist carrying a large boom microphone: in the opening moment of the work, he stands in the middle of a dirt road, the sky behind him blue-black and lowering as a storm front approaches, and adjusts the controls on a sophisticated recording device he carries in a bag over his shoulder as he looks into the distance. As it ends, he's seen again with his gear, this time on a bluff high above a wide expanse of open pasture land. It's the artists' way of saying that they too are waiting—and listening.

Department of the Interior, U.S. Geological Survey, Texas (El Paso County) Sierra Blanca Sheet, 1895. Movie Mountain, not yet named, is visible between Round Mountain and Tabernacle Mountain.

1 Montaigne is paraphrasing a well-known medieval axiom. See Michel de Montaigne, "On the Power of the Imagination" (1580) in *Michel de Montaigne: The Complete Essays*, trans. M. A. Screech (London: Penguin Books, 2003), p. 109.

2 See "Hubbard/Birchler: Storytelling," available at www.pbs.org/art21/texts/hubbard-birchler/interview-hubbard-birchler-storytelling.

3 William Gass, "Emerson and the Essay," in *Habitations of the Word* (Ithaca, NY: Cornell University Press, 1997), pp. 19–20.

4 For a useful recent examination of the genre, see Timothy Corrigan, *The Essay Film: From Montaigne, After Marker* (Oxford: Oxford University Press, 2011).

5 Michel de Montaigne, "To the Reader" (1580) in Montaigne, op. cit., p lxiii.

6 Aldous Huxley, "Preface" in *Collected Essays* (New York: Harper, 1959), p. 1.

7 Theodor Adorno, "The Essay as Form" (1958), trans. Robert Hullot-Kentor and Frederic Will, *New German Critique* no. 32 (Spring–Summer 1984): p. 160.

8 Michel de Montaigne, "On Experience" (ca. 1588) in Montaigne, op. cit., pp. 1207.

9 Robert Smithson, "A Provisional Theory of Non-Sites," in Jack Flam, ed., *The Collected Writings of Robert Smithson* (Berkeley: The University of California Press, 1996), p. 364.

10 Ibid.

11 Joan Didion, "Why I Write," in *The Writer on Her Work*, ed. Janet Sternburg (New York: W.W. Norton & Company, 2000), p. 20.

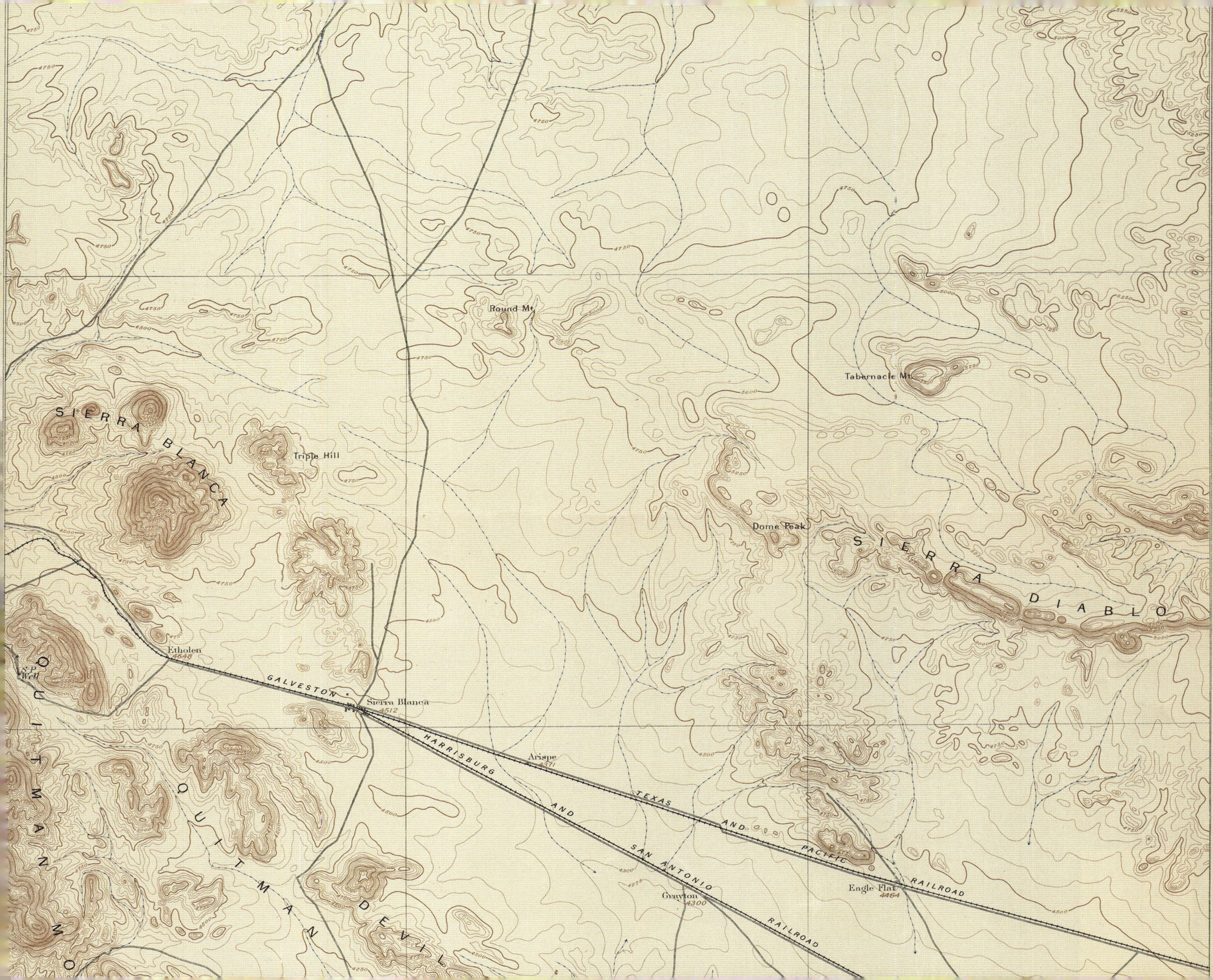

TEXAS - SIERRA BLANCA SHEET - EL PASO COUNTY

GIANT, 2014
High-Definition Video with Sound
3 Channel, 30 minutes, Loop
Installation dimensions variable

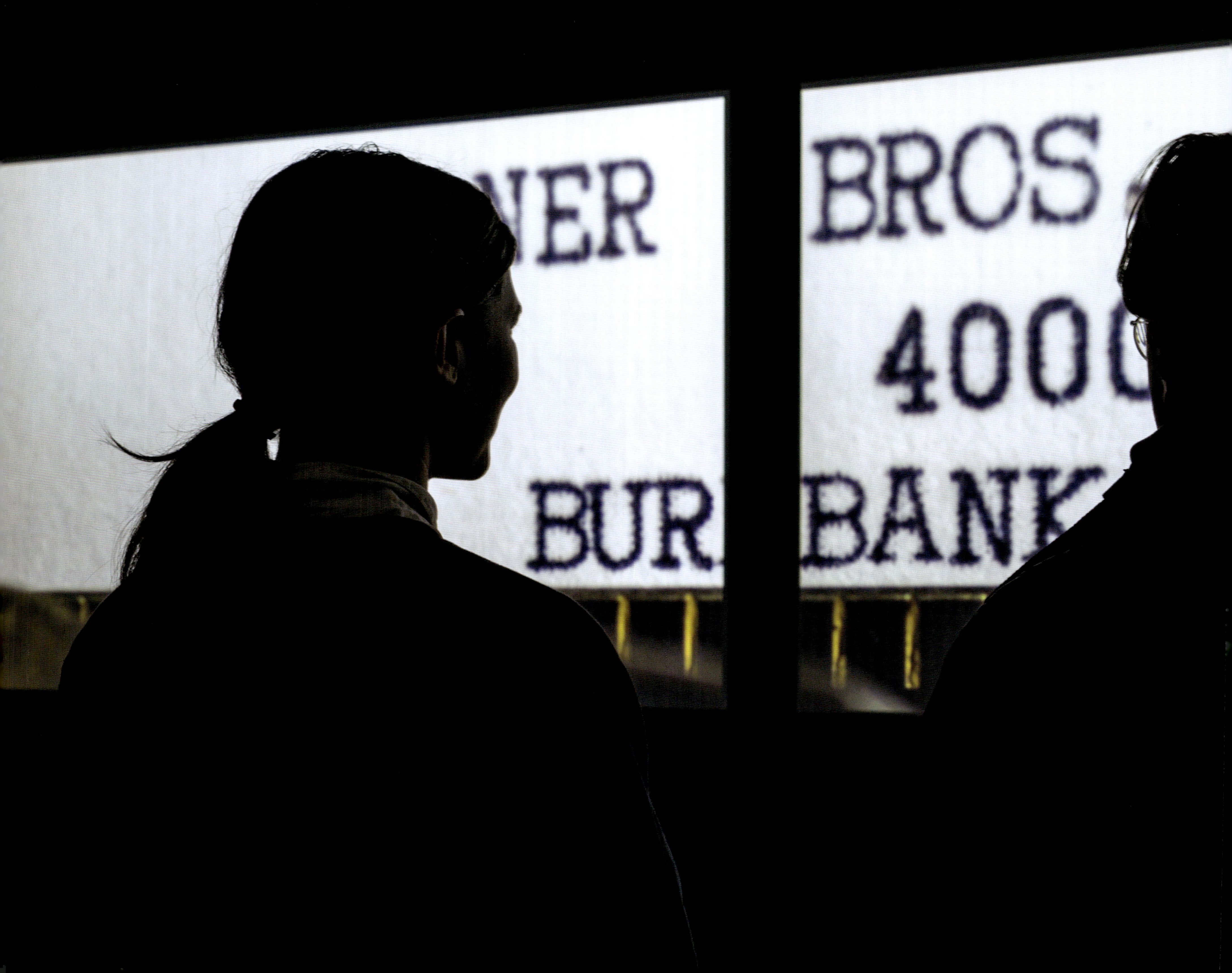
NER BROS
4000
BUR BANK

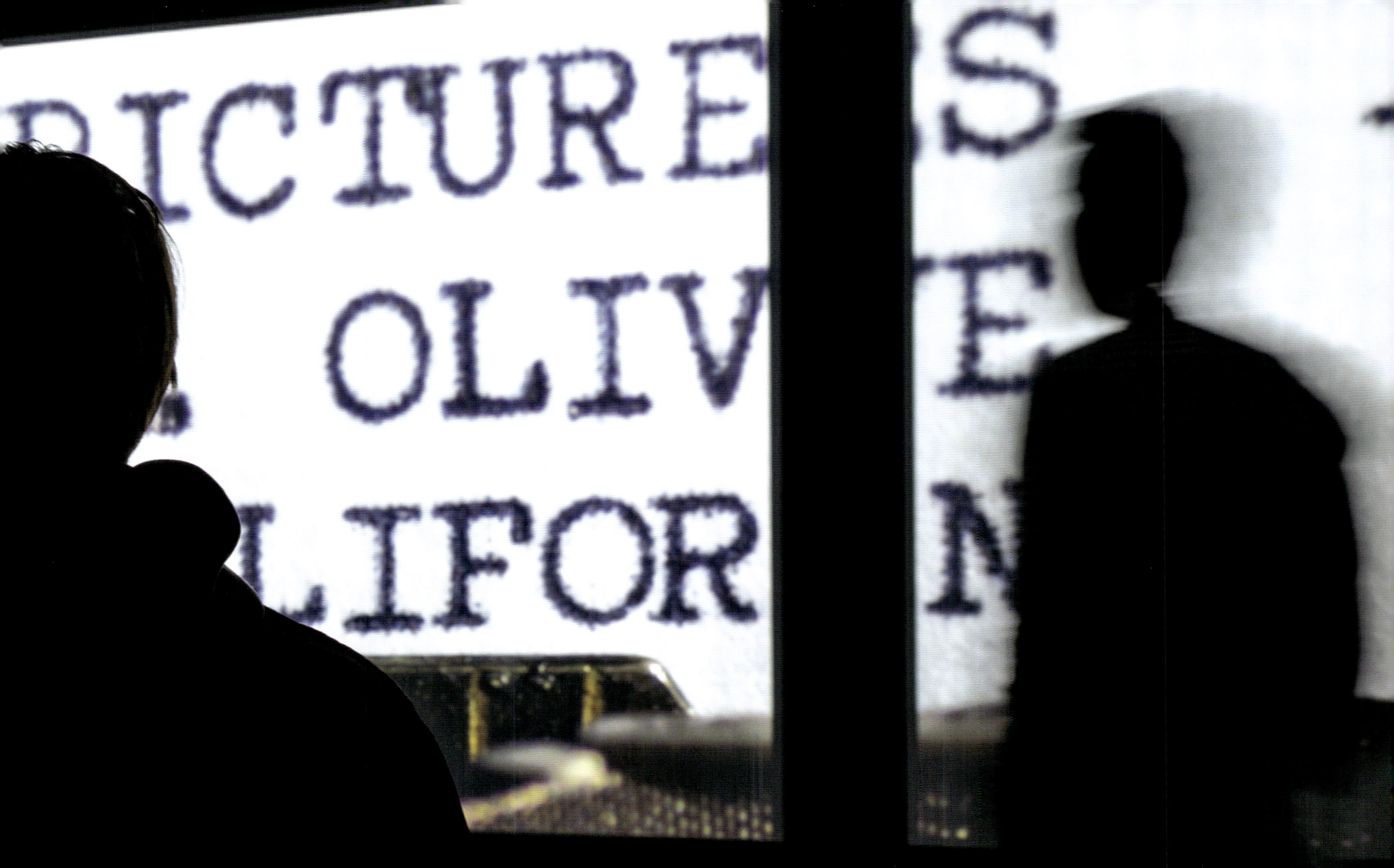

Giant, 2014
Installation view,
Ballroom Marfa

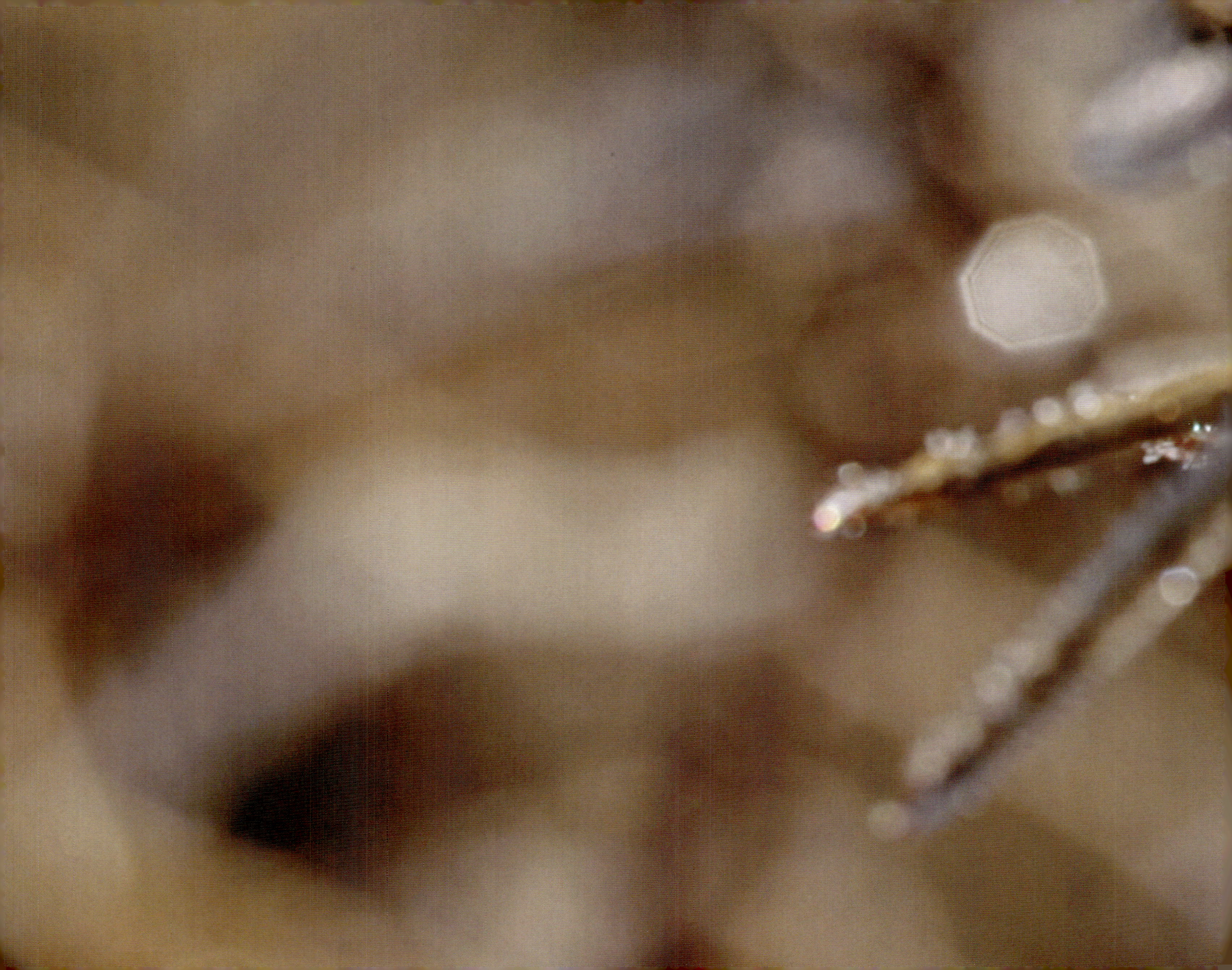

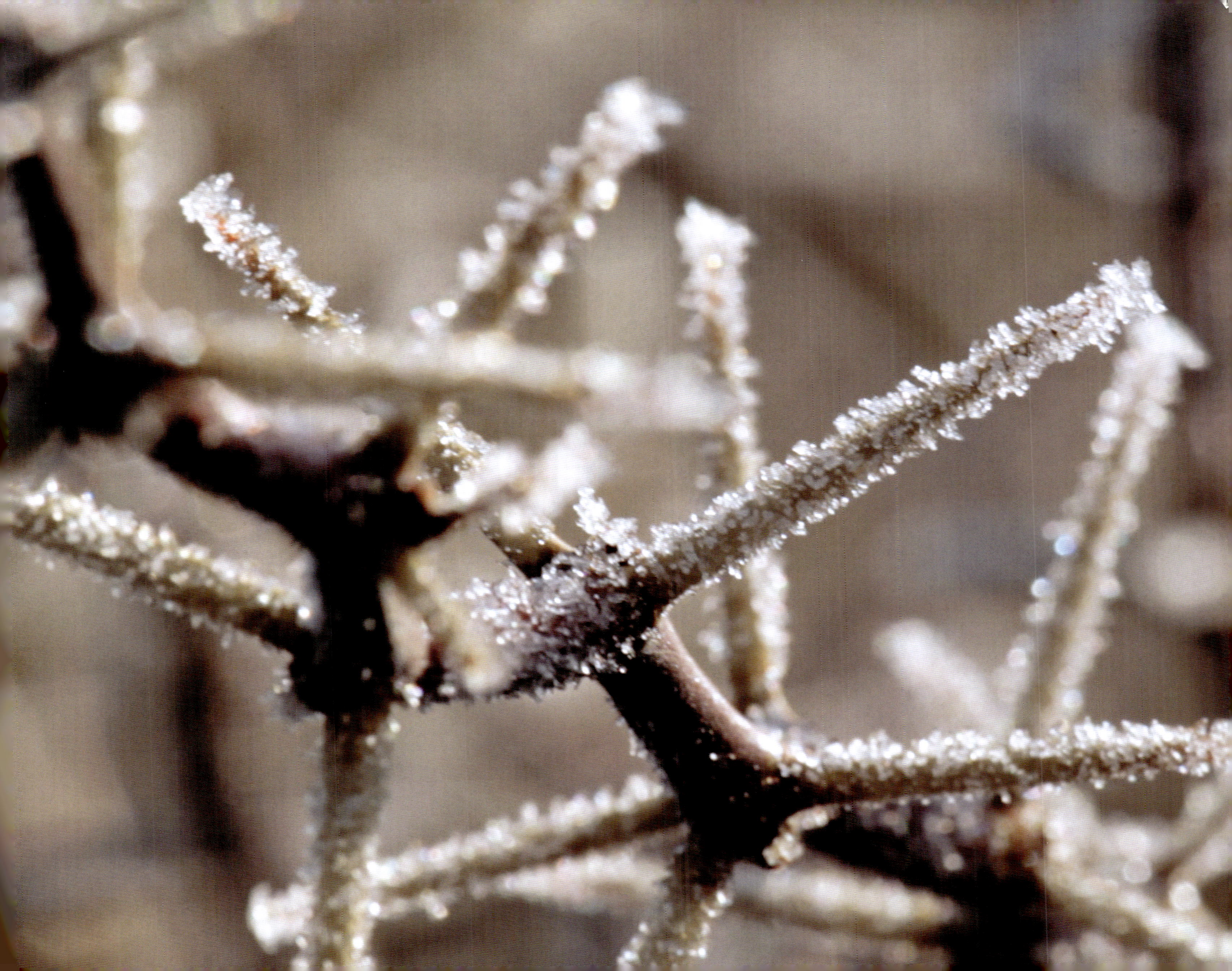

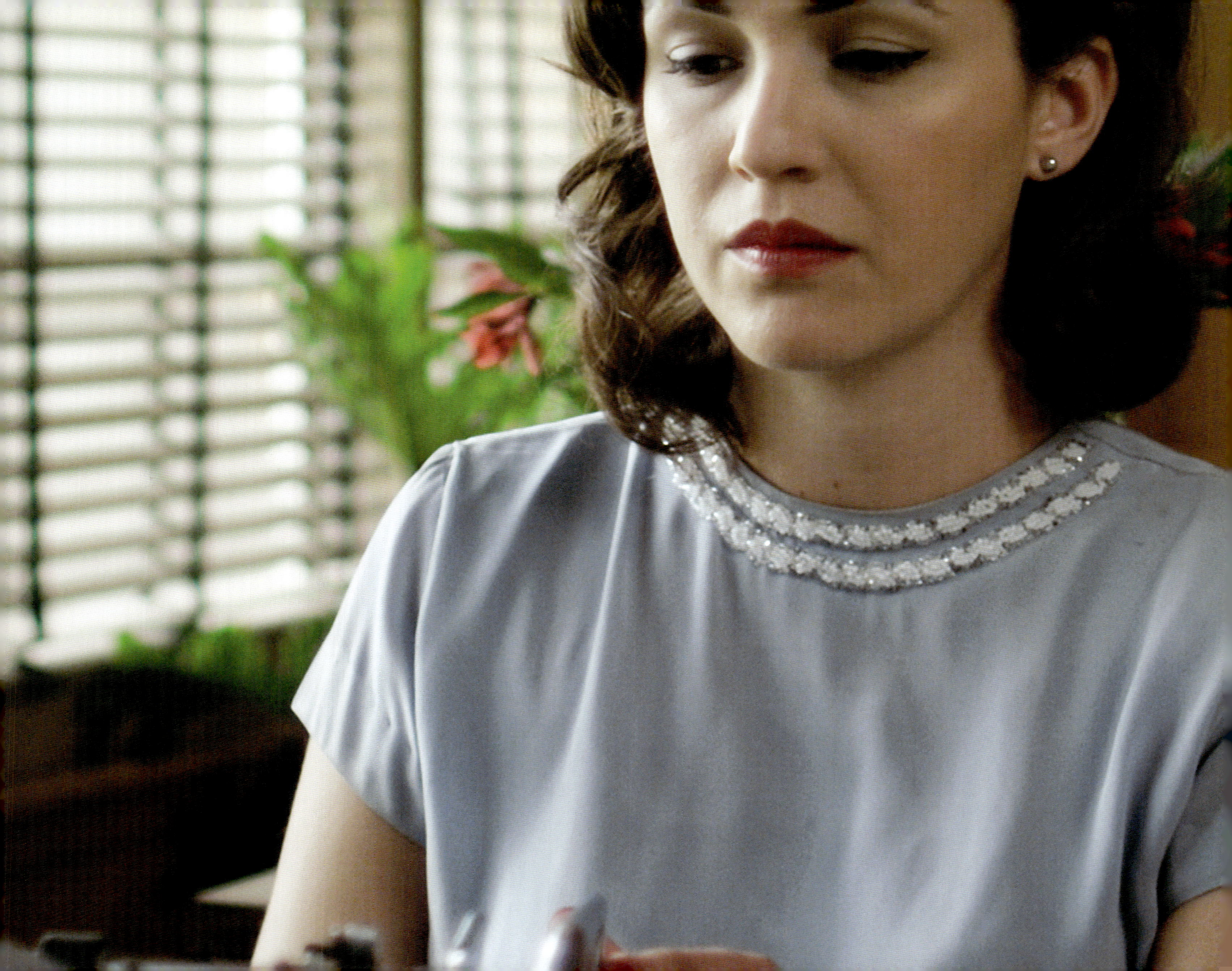

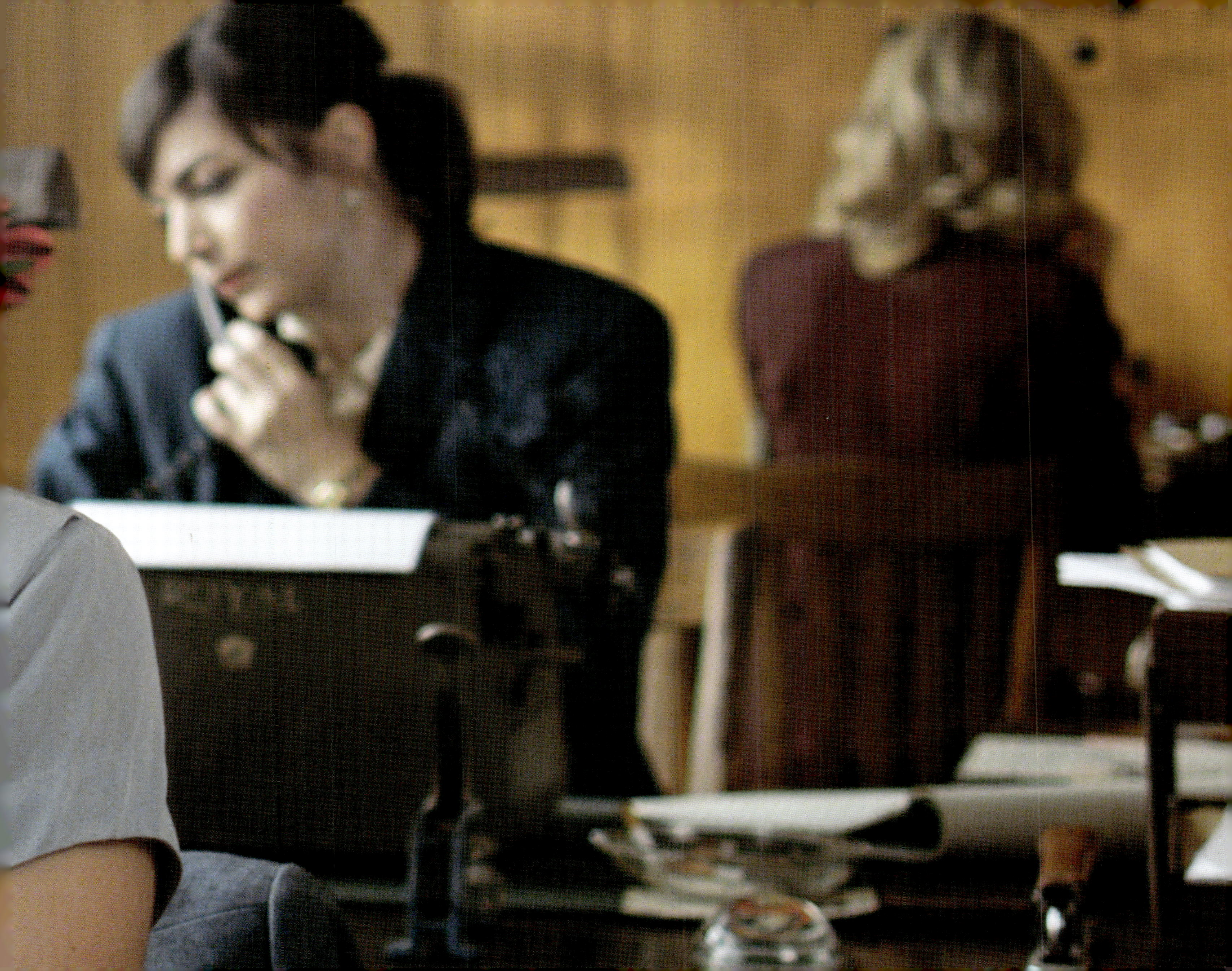

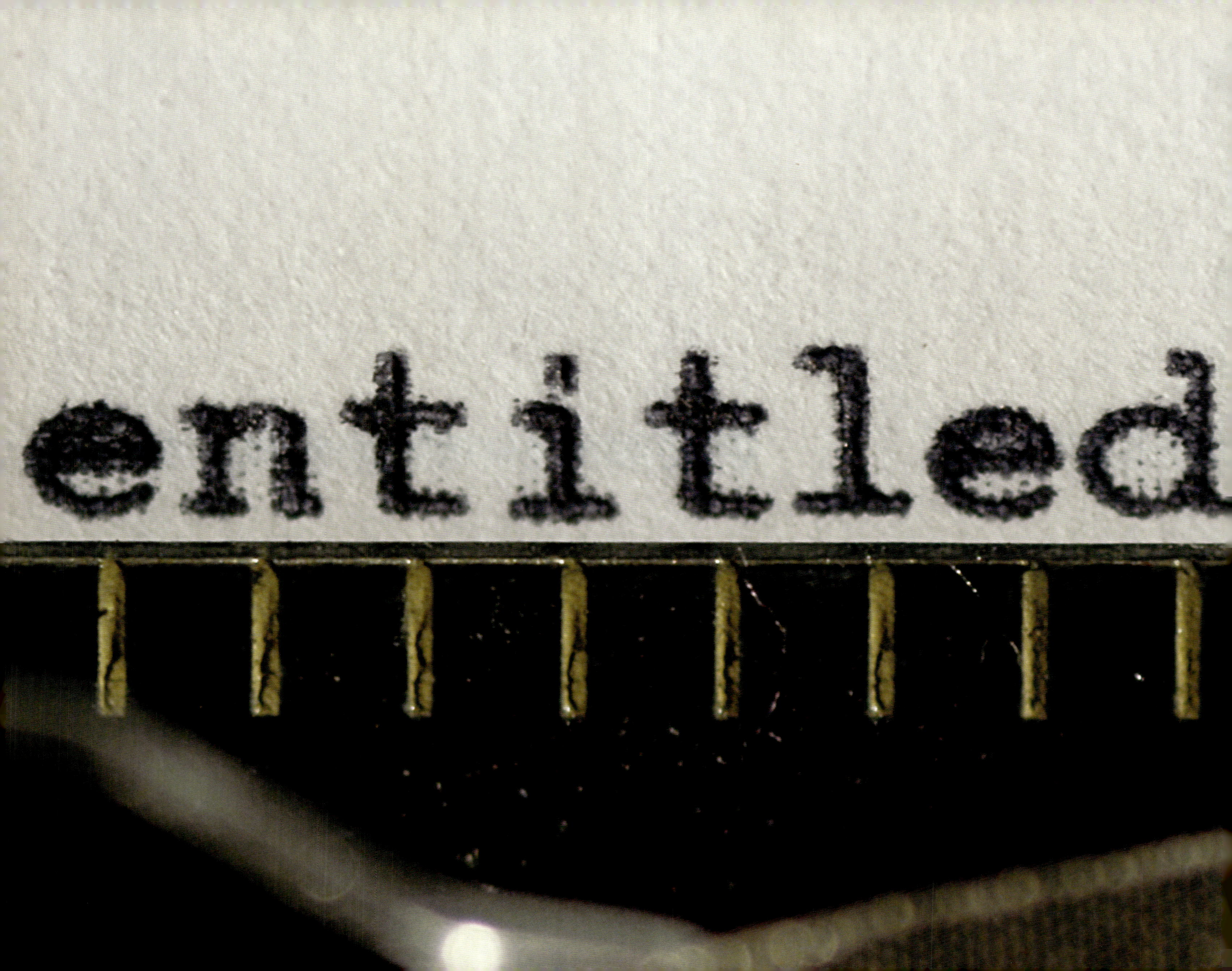
entitled

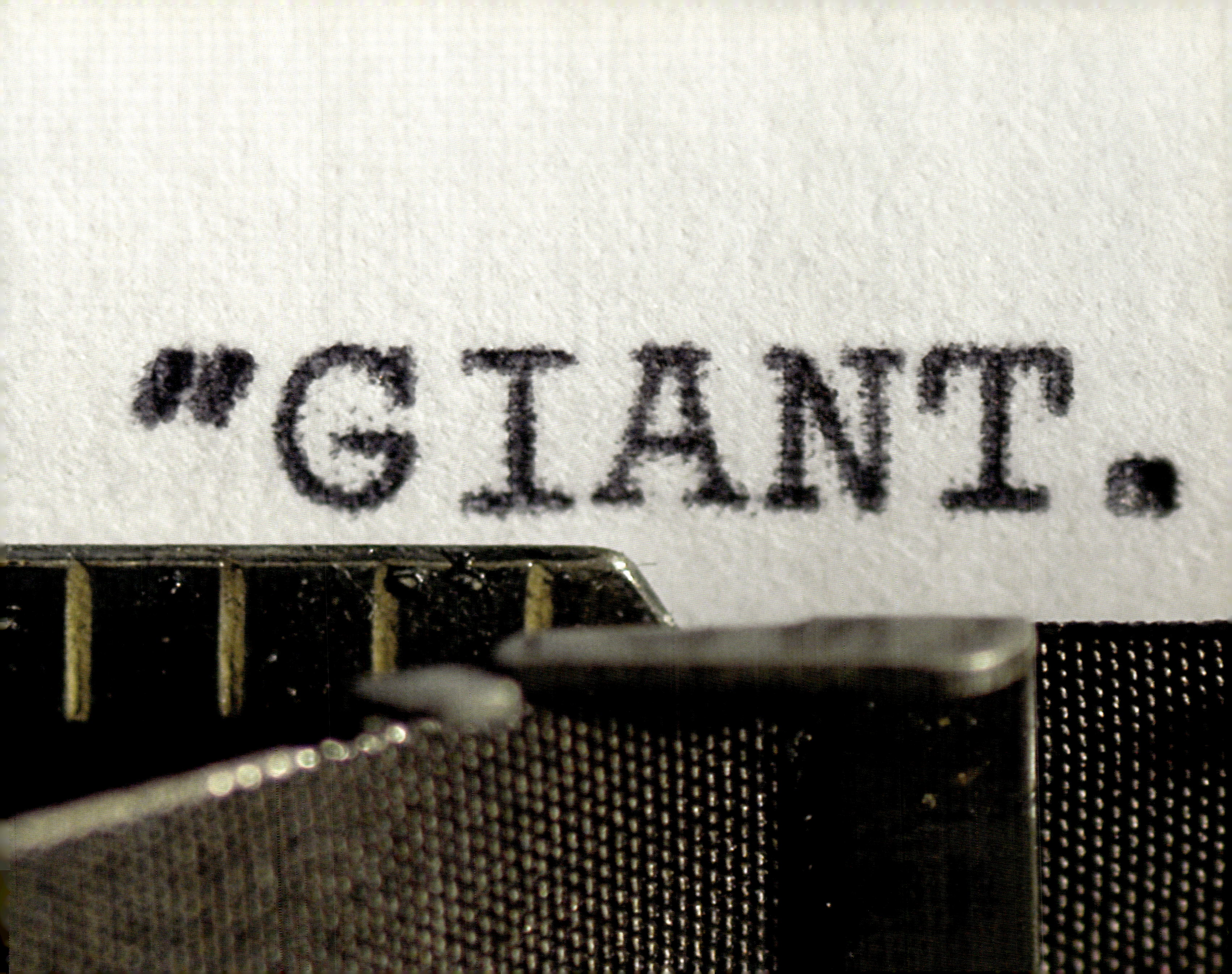
"GIANT.

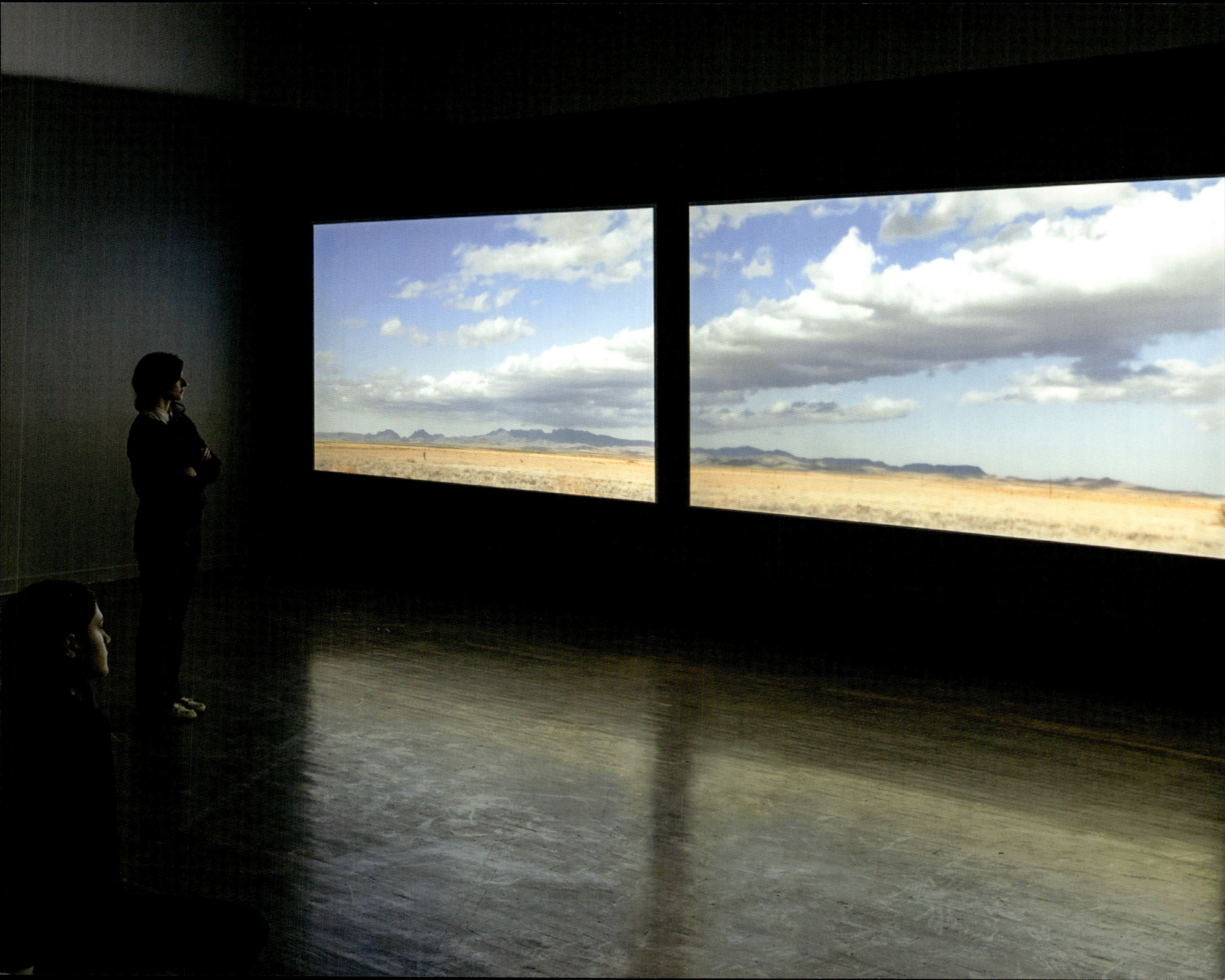

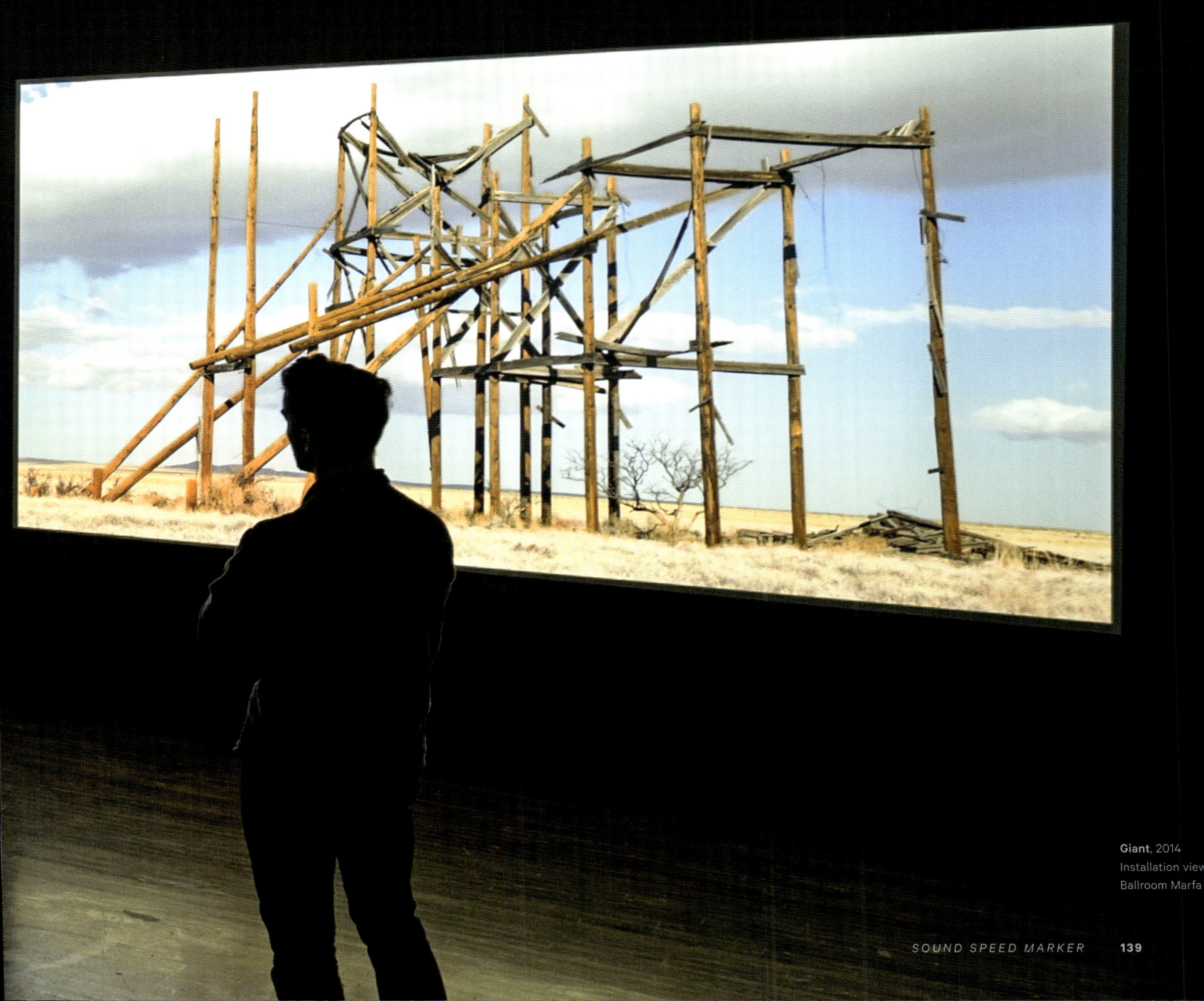

Giant, 2014
Installation view
Ballroom Marfa

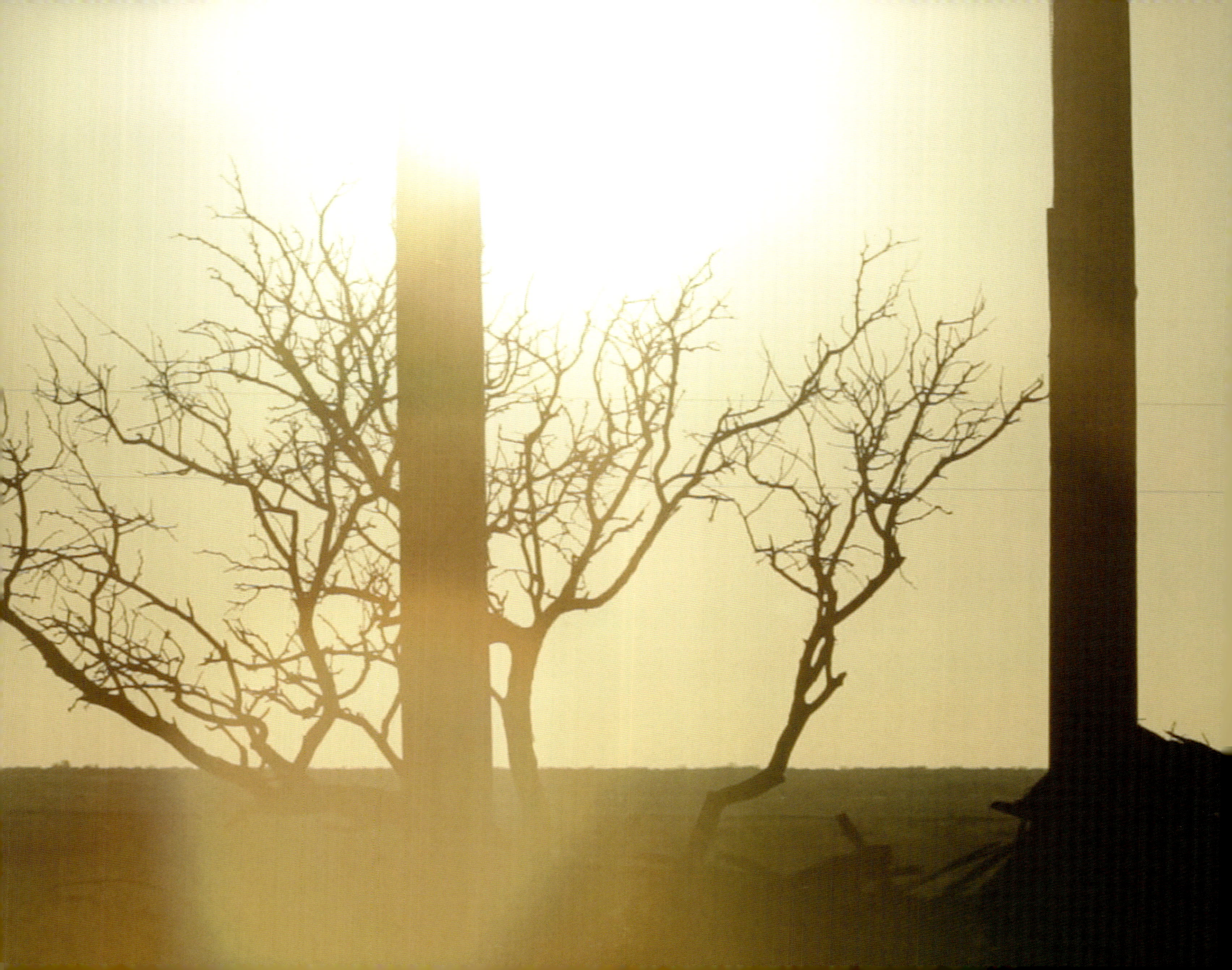

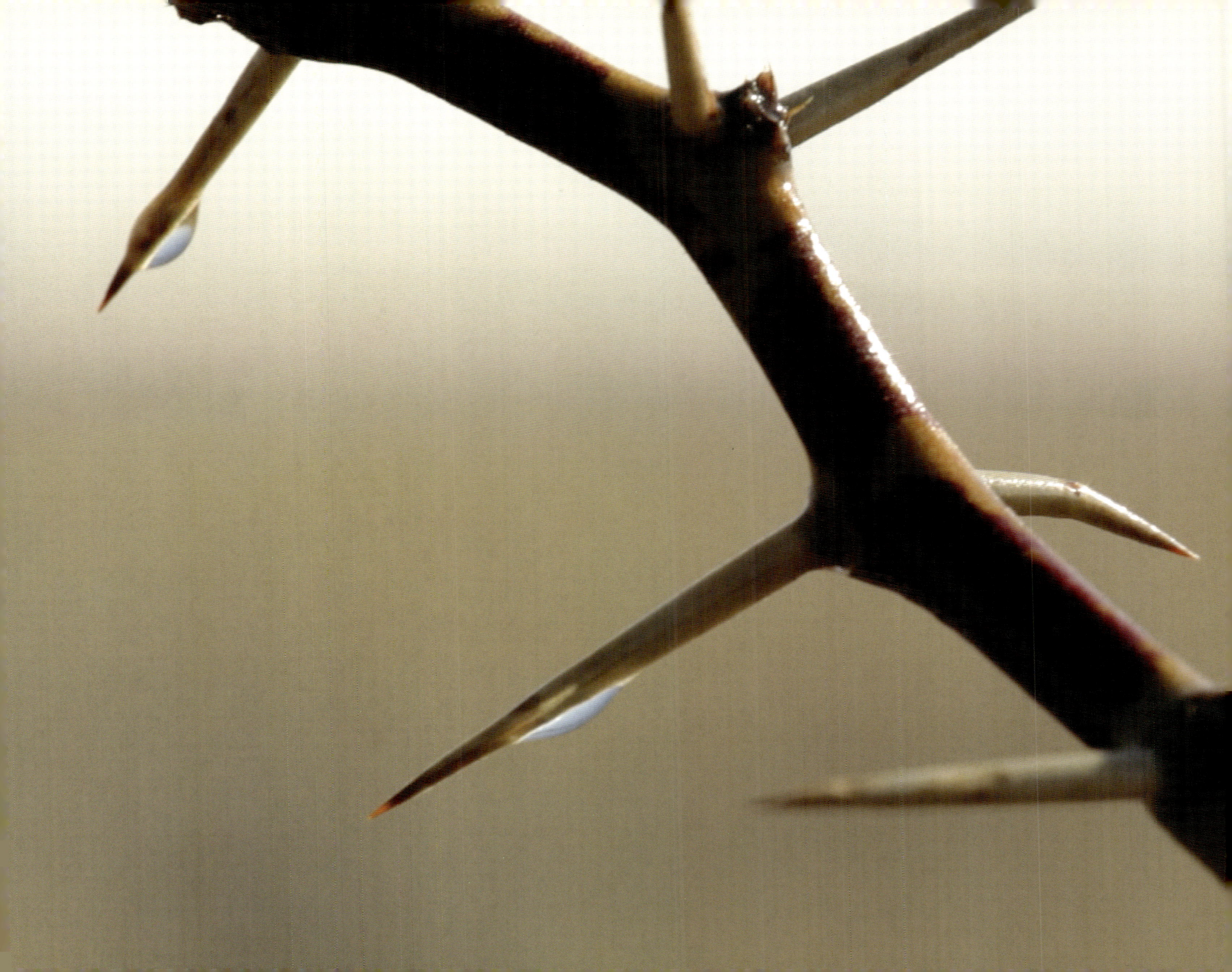

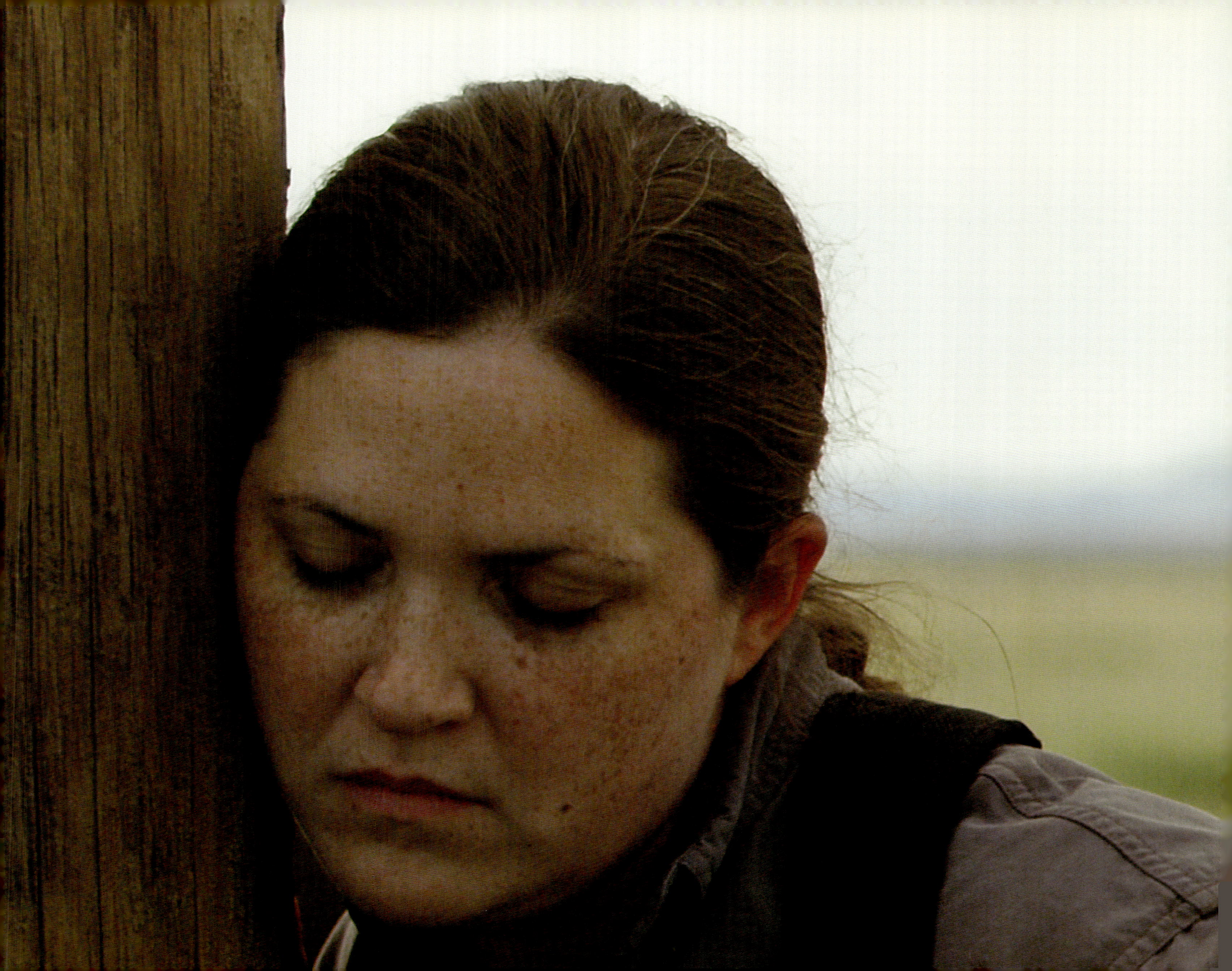

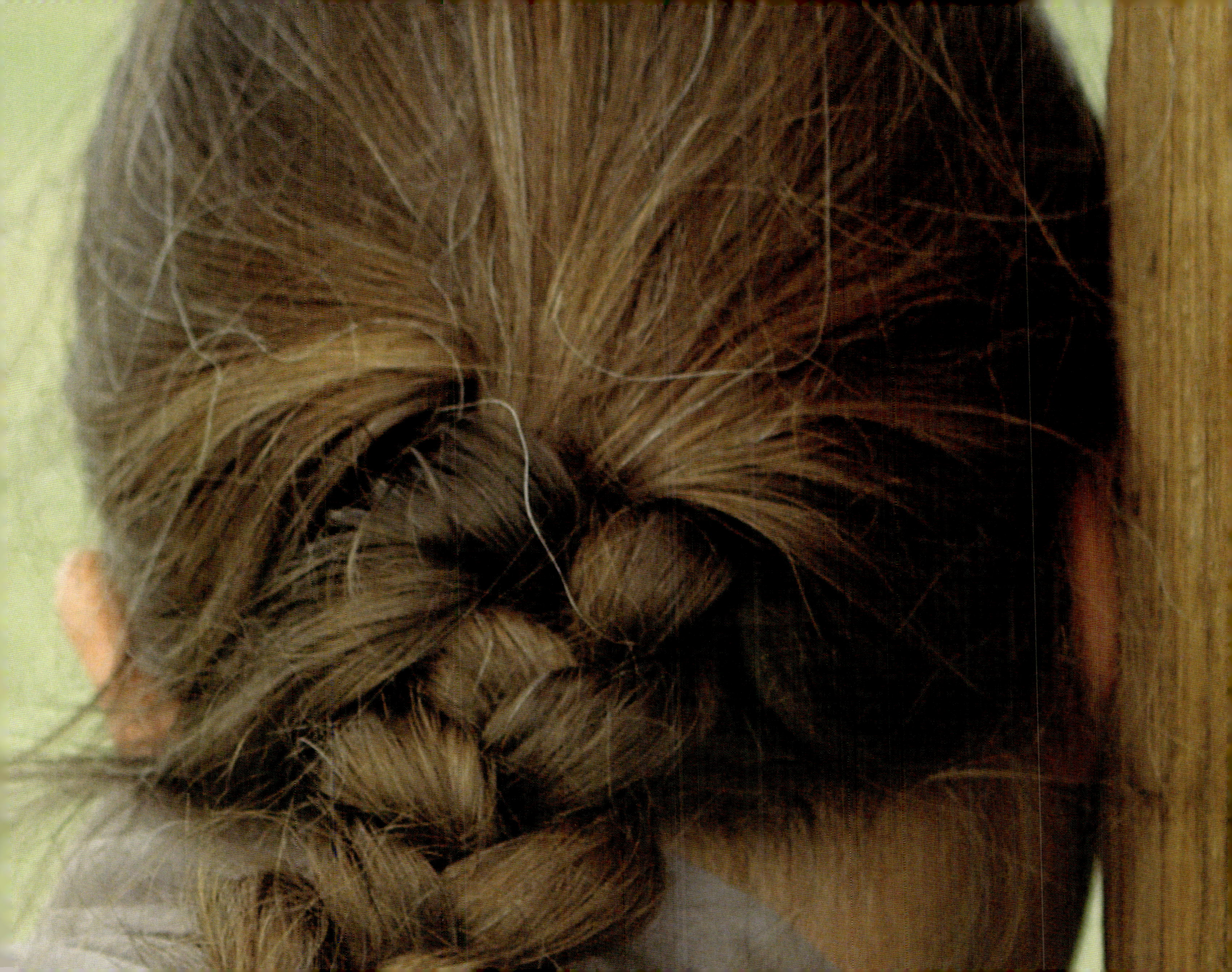

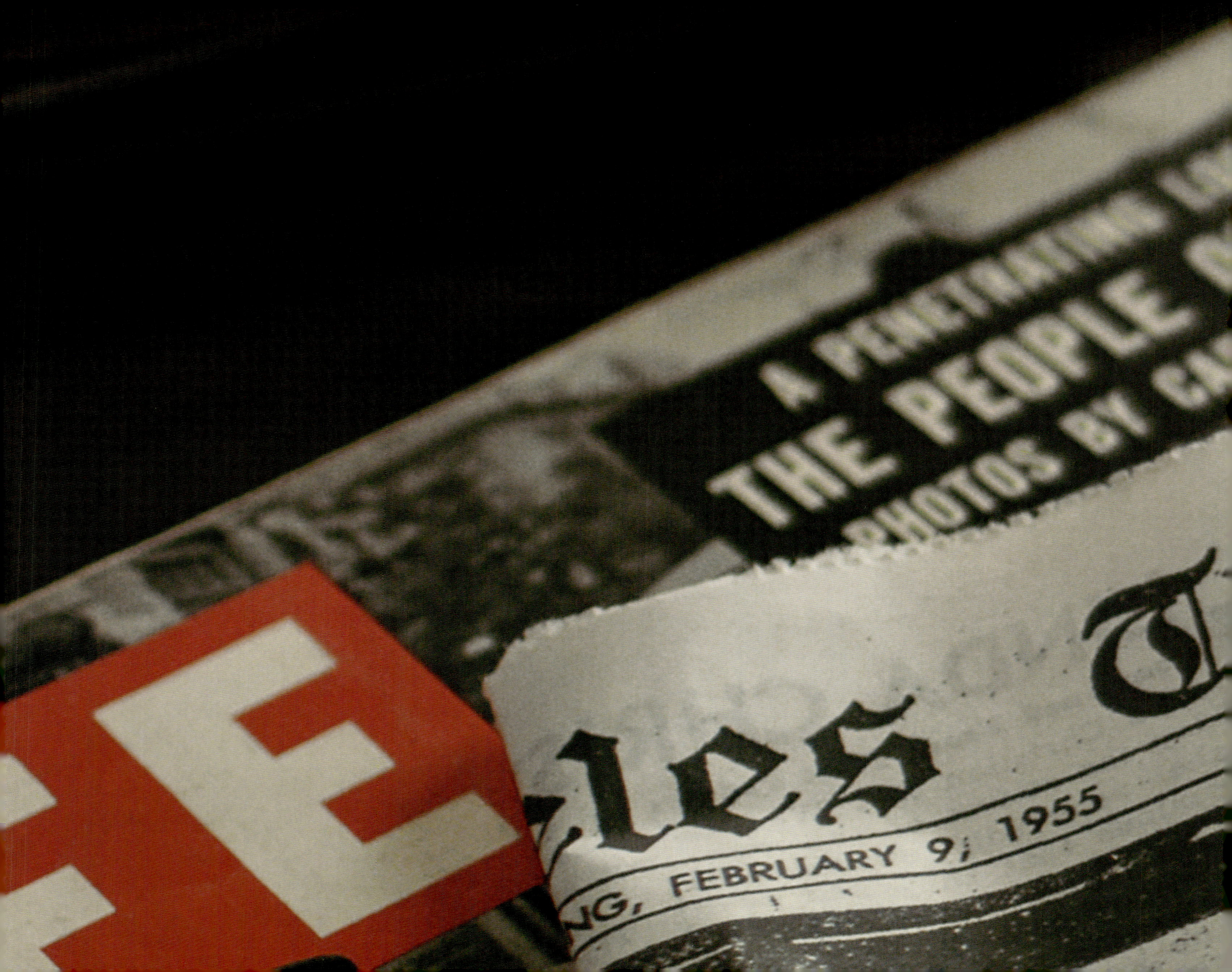
A PENETRATING
THE PEOPLE
PHOTOS BY
FEBRUARY 9, 1955

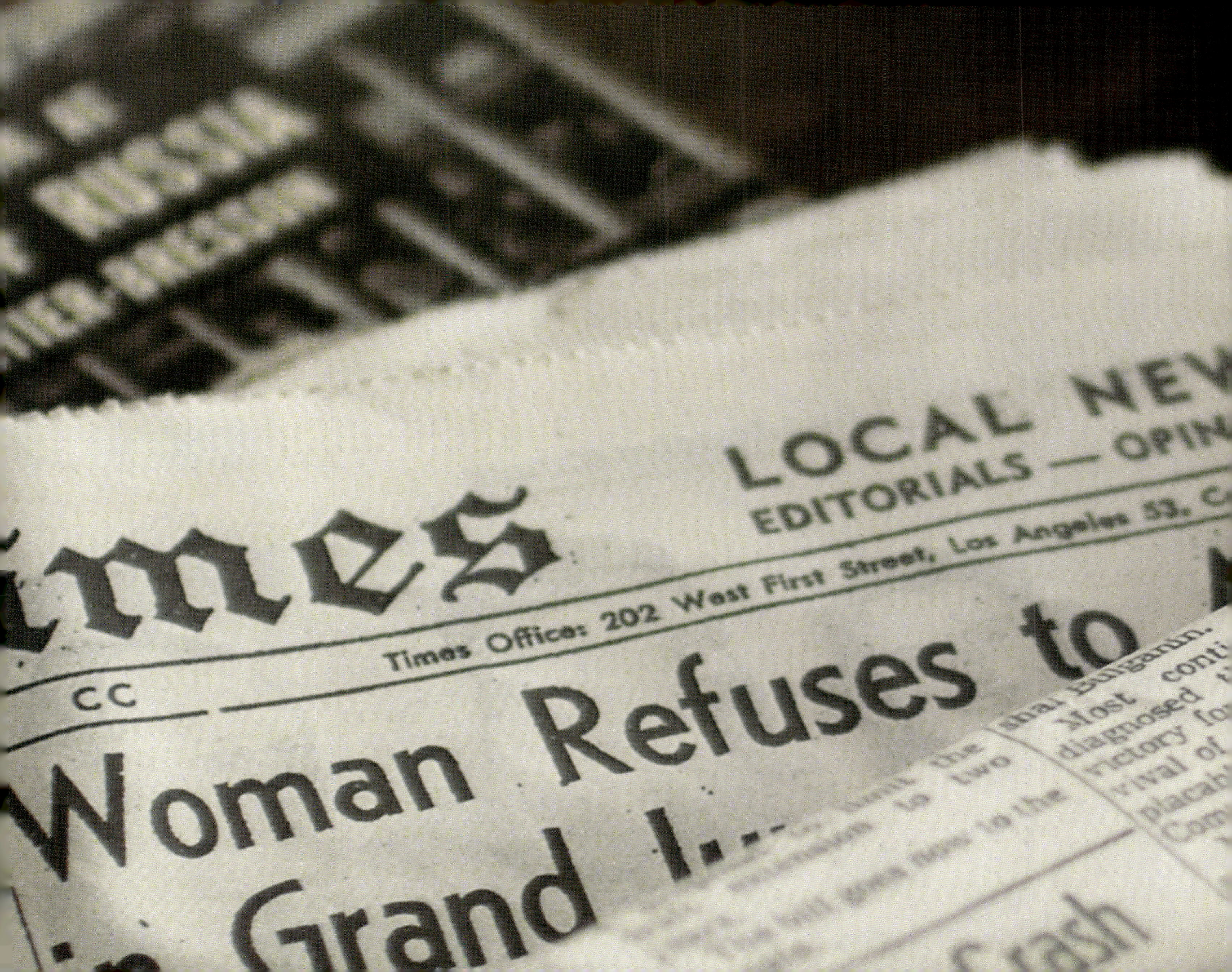
imes
LOCAL NEW
EDITORIALS — OPIN
Times Office: 202 West First Street, Los Angeles 53,
CC
Woman Refuses to
Grand

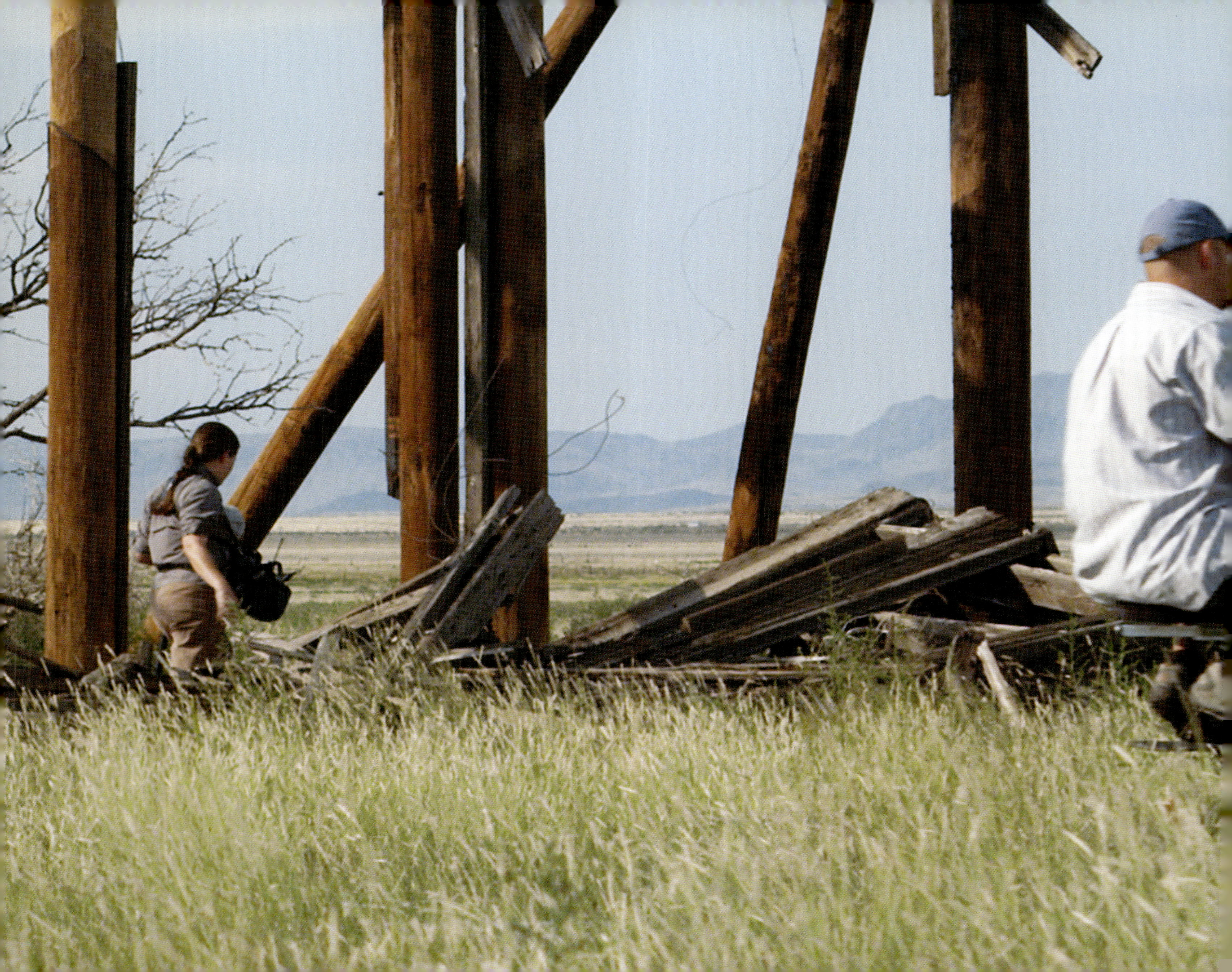

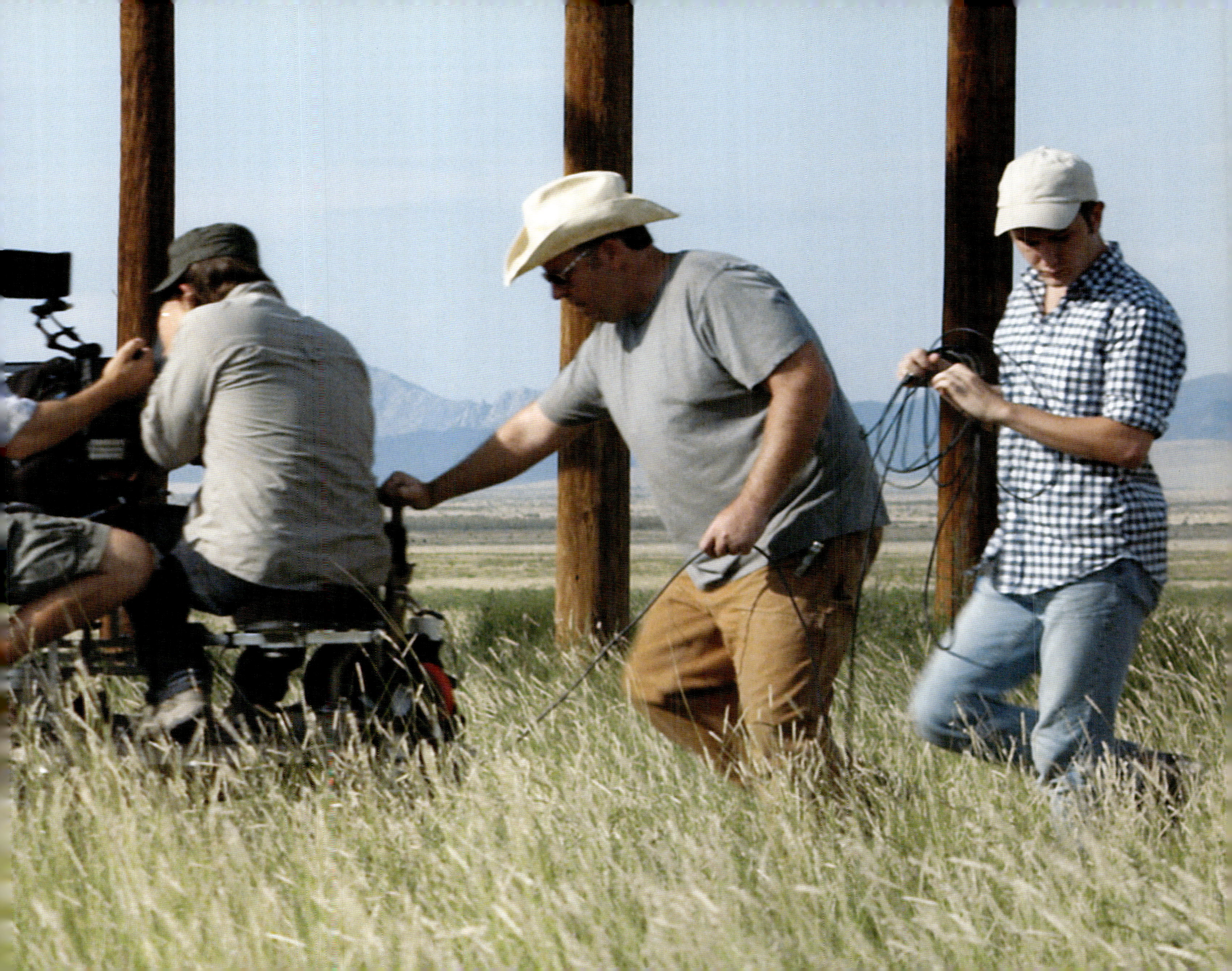

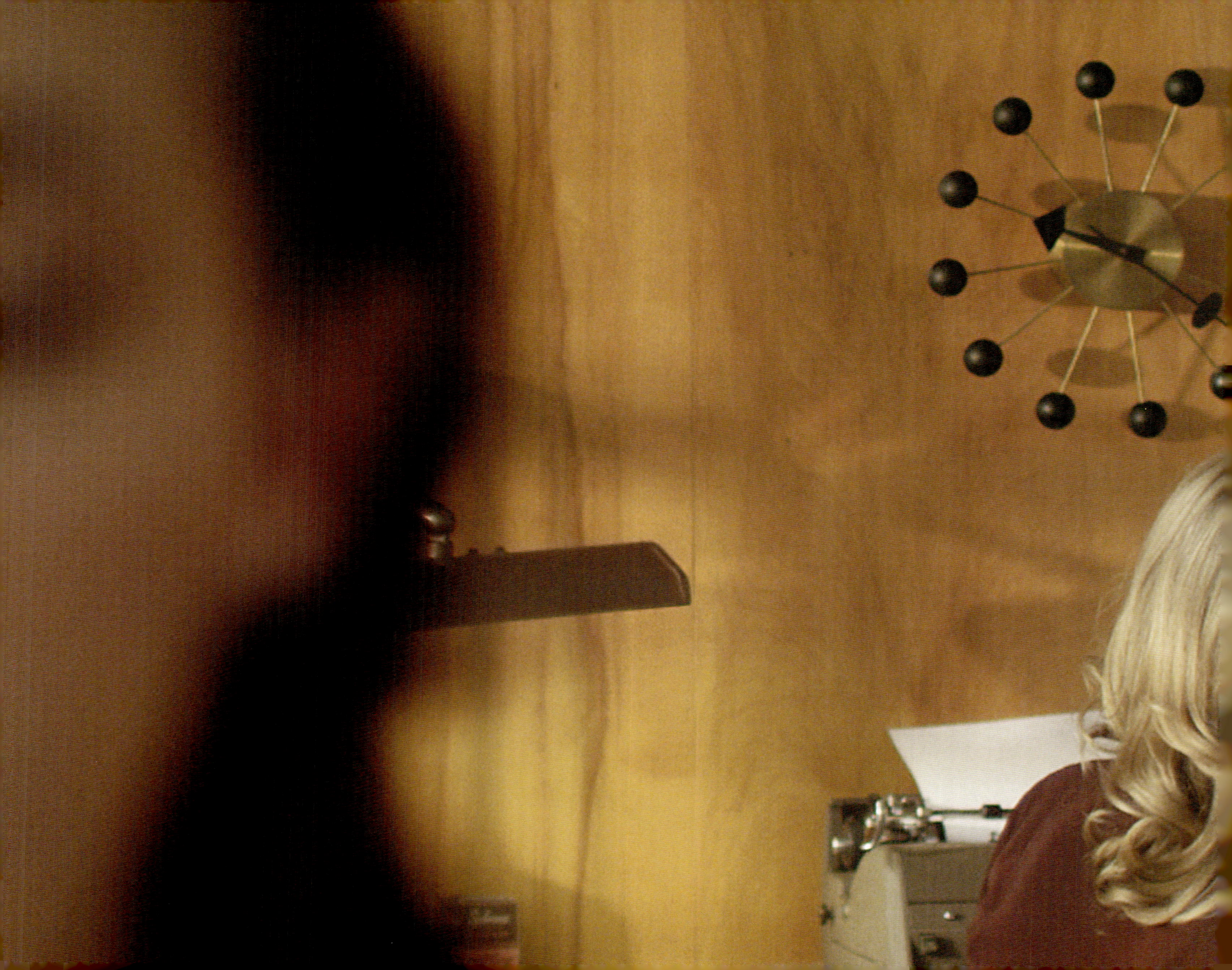

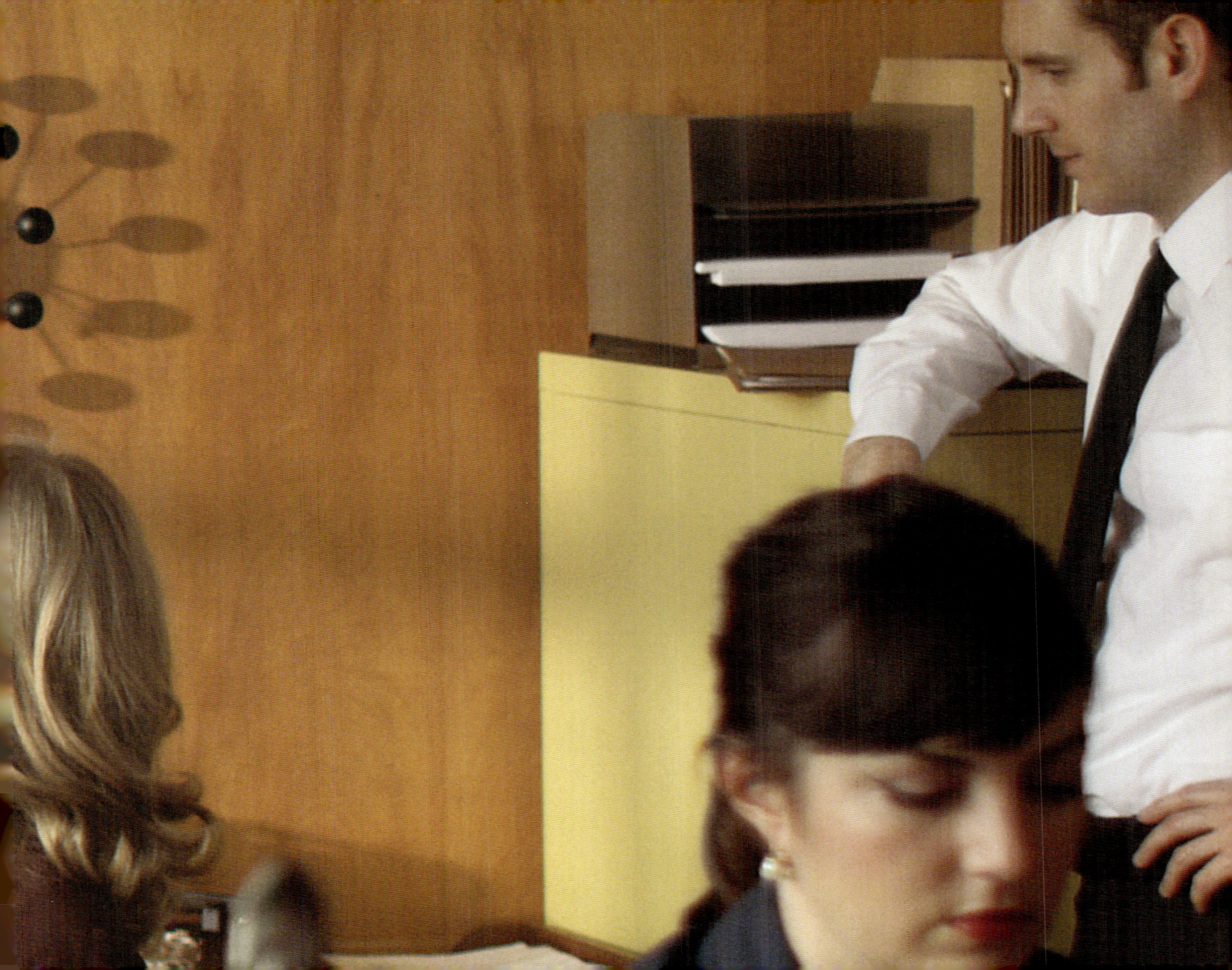

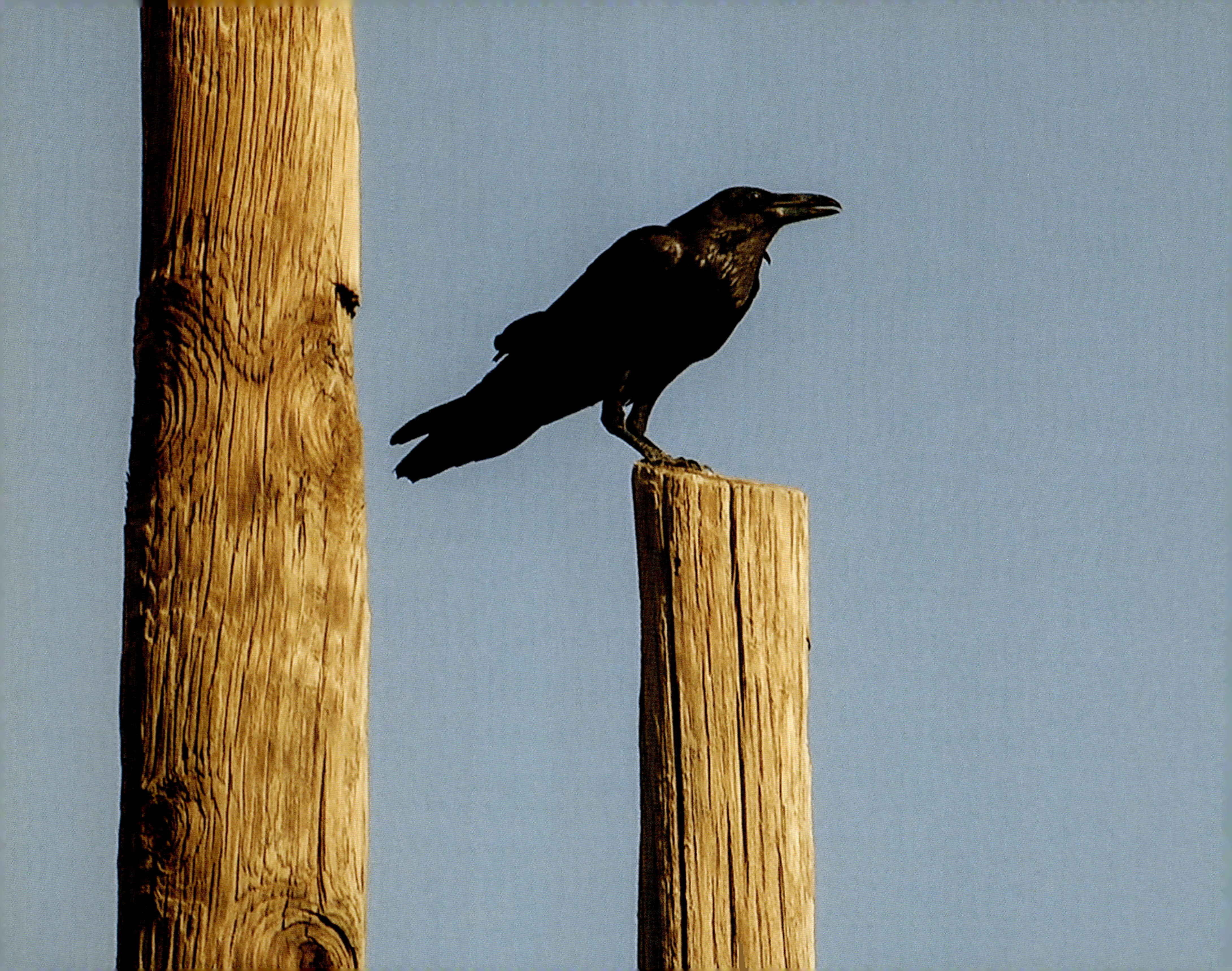

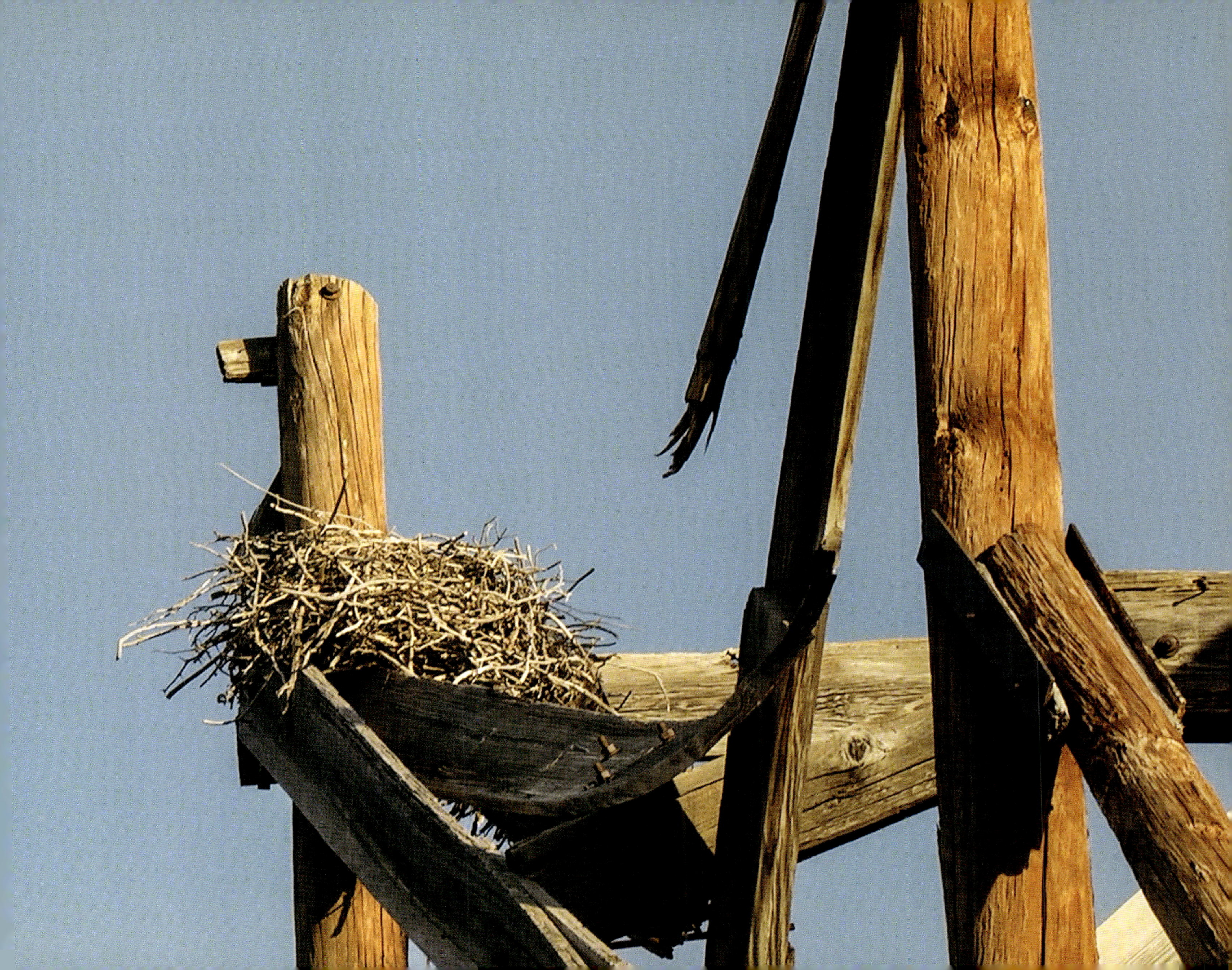

have the
r buildi

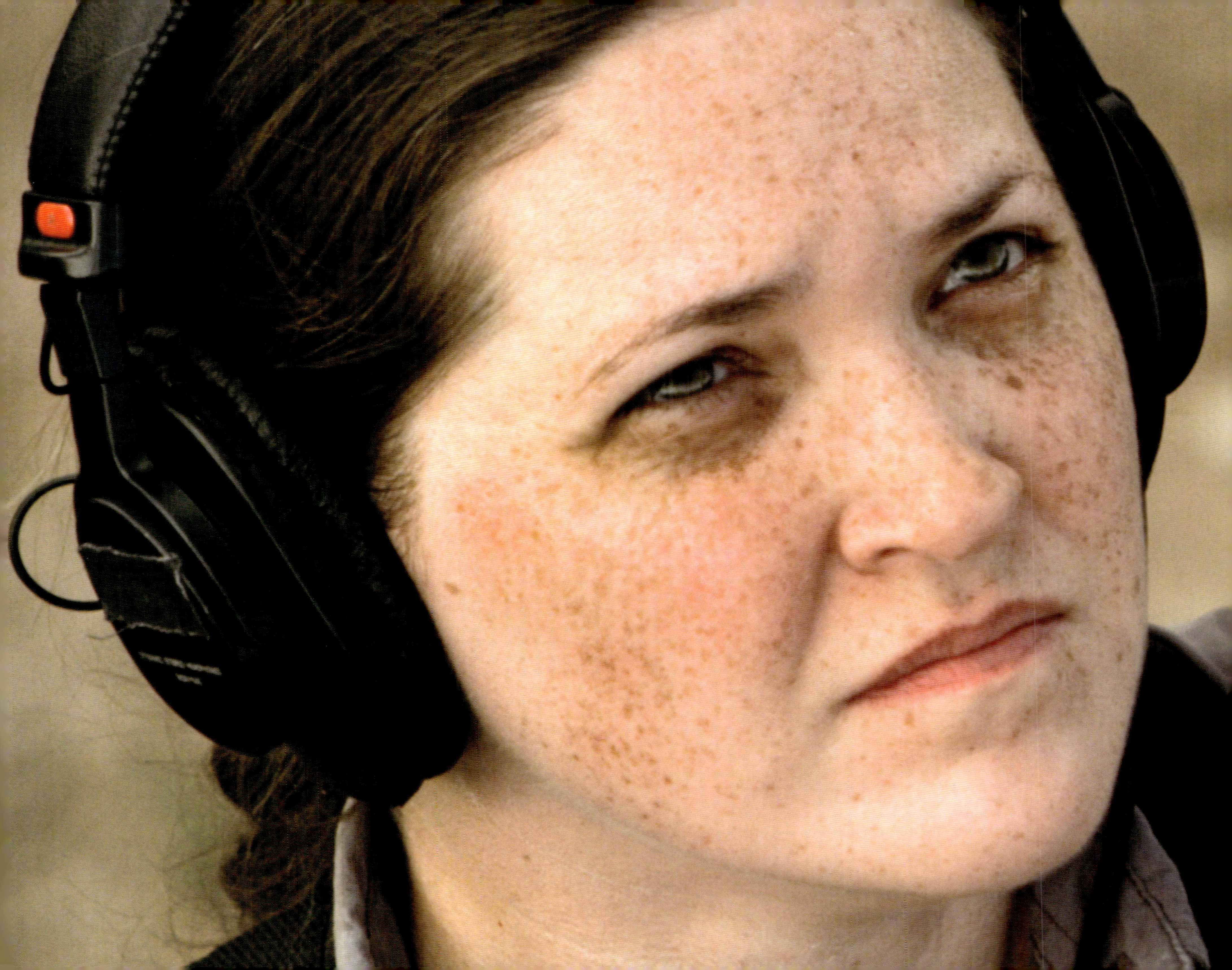

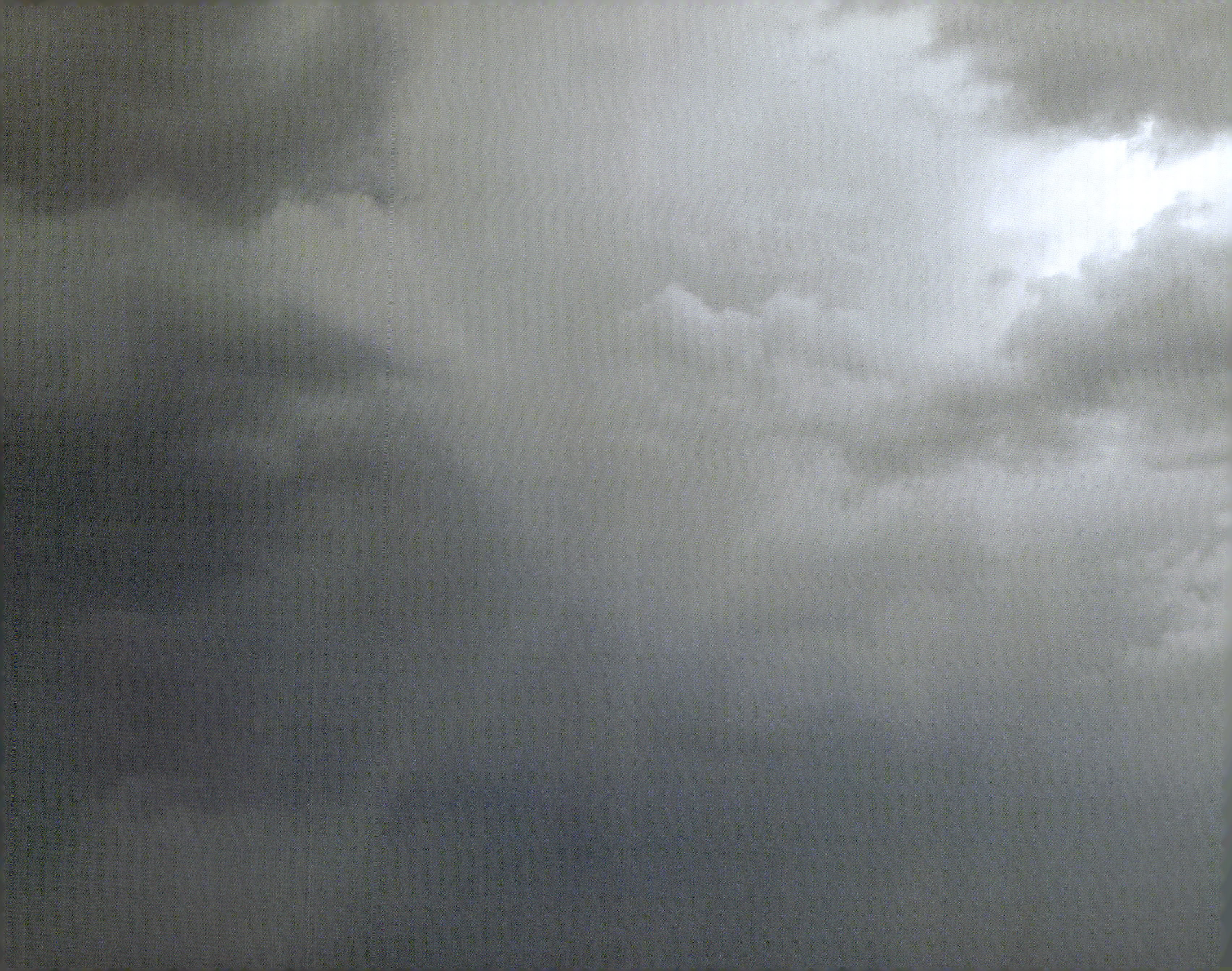

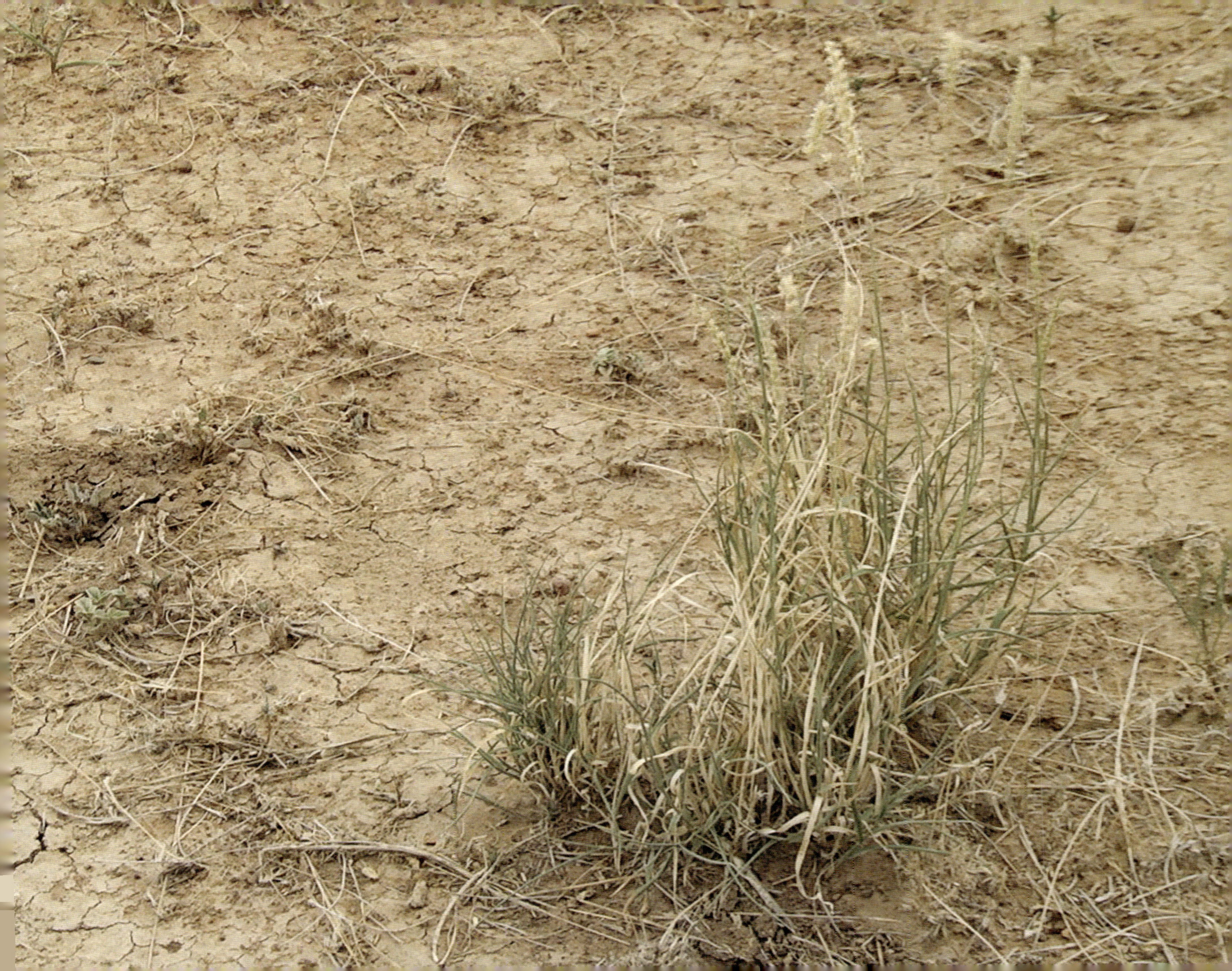

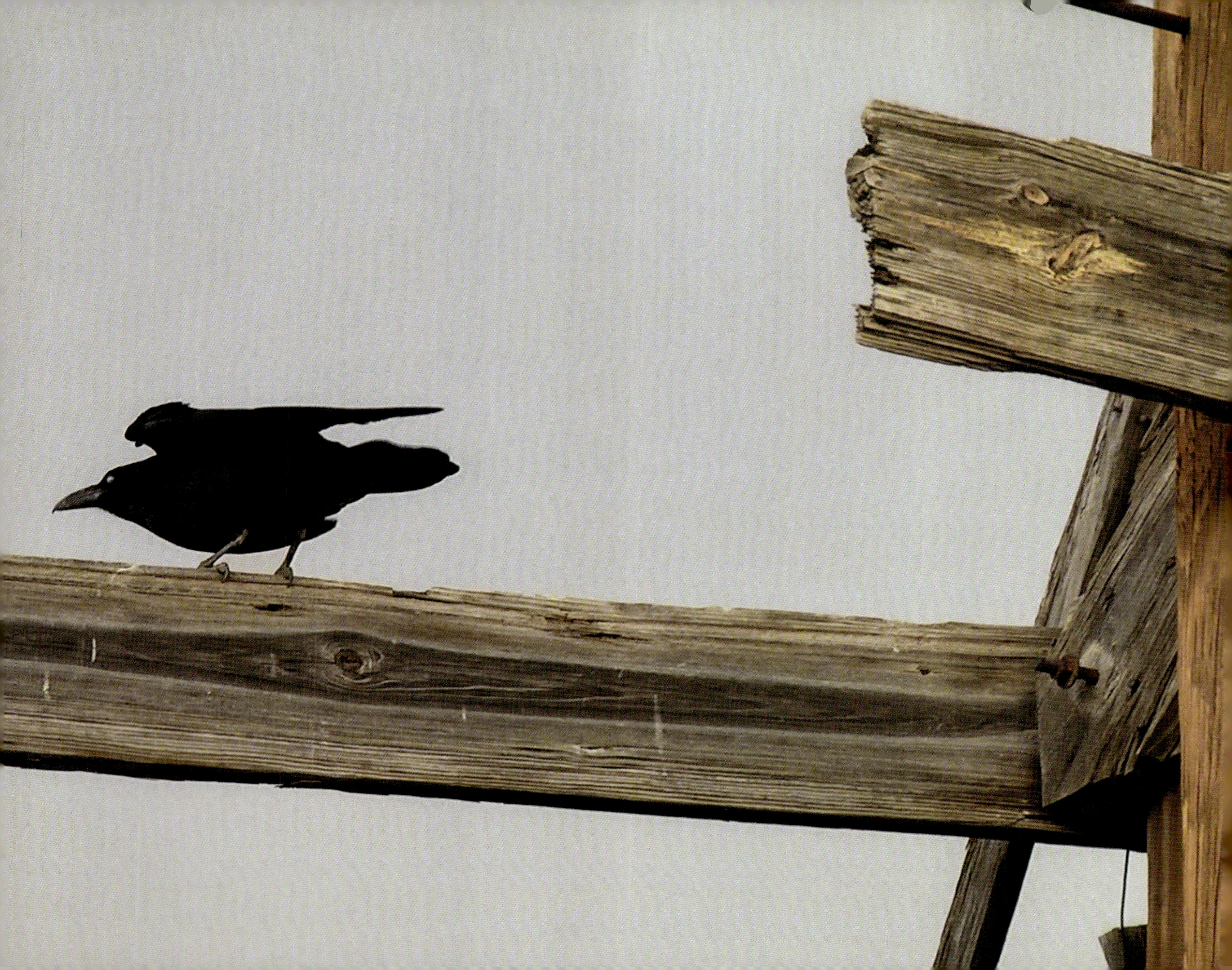

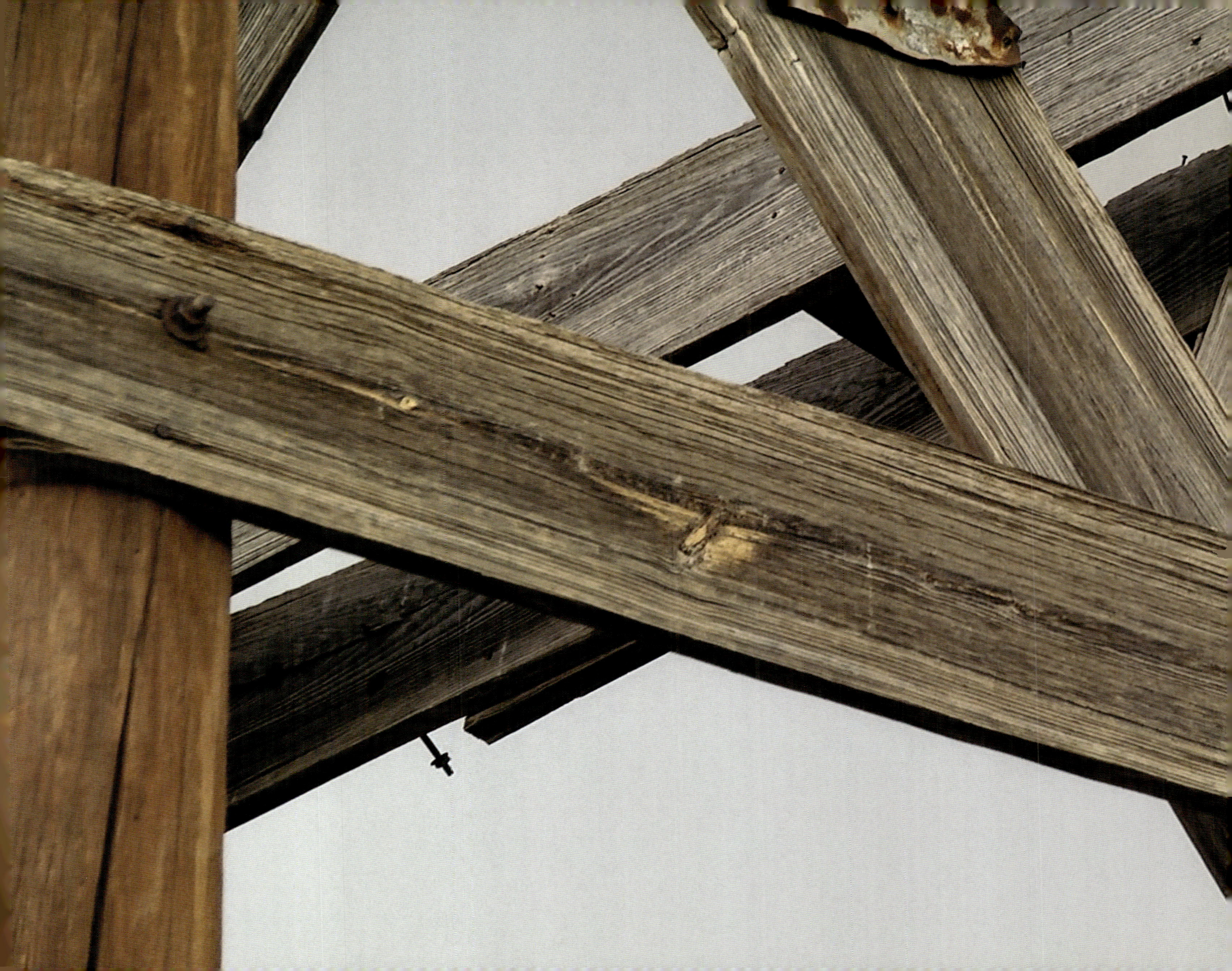

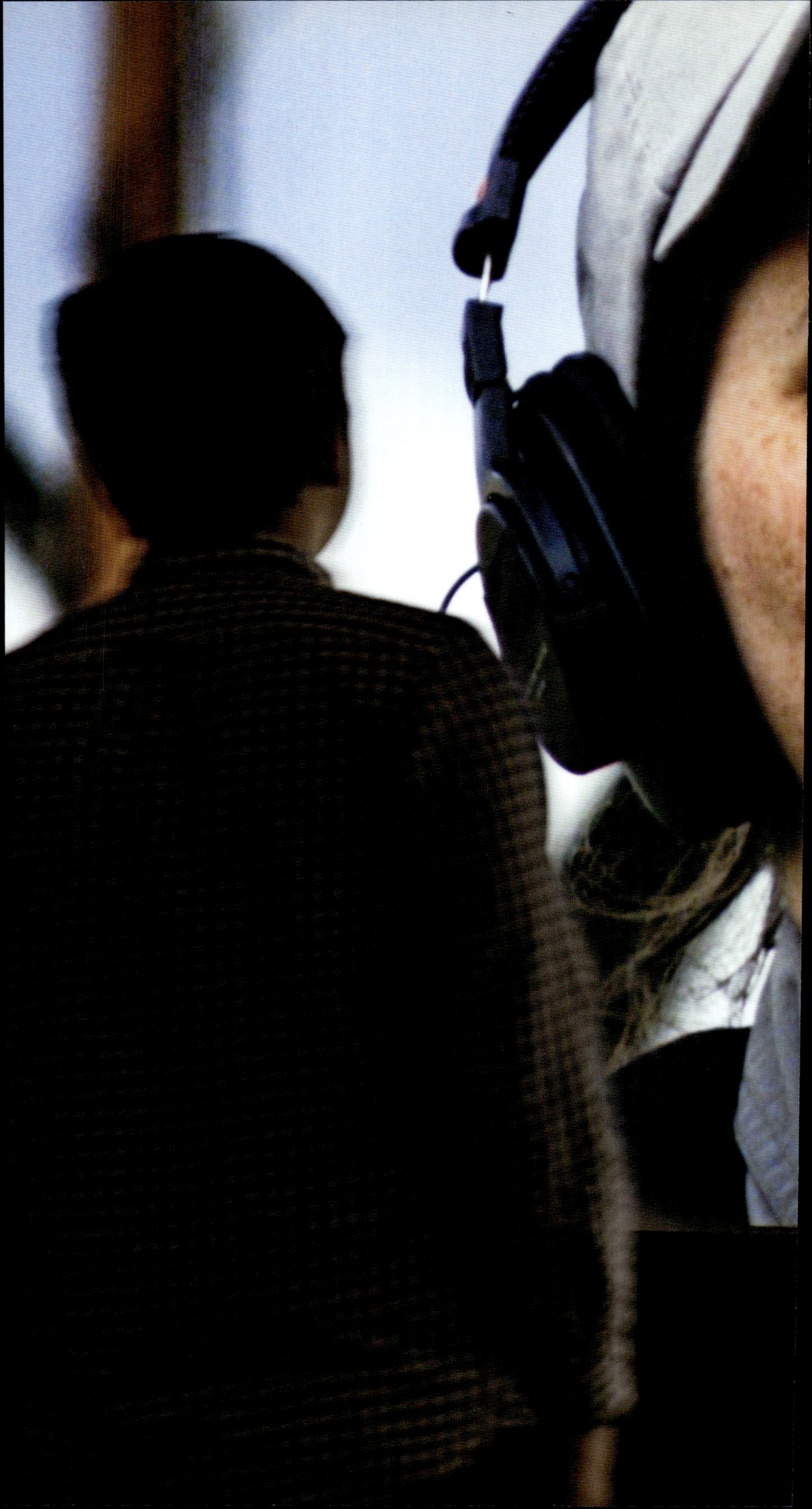

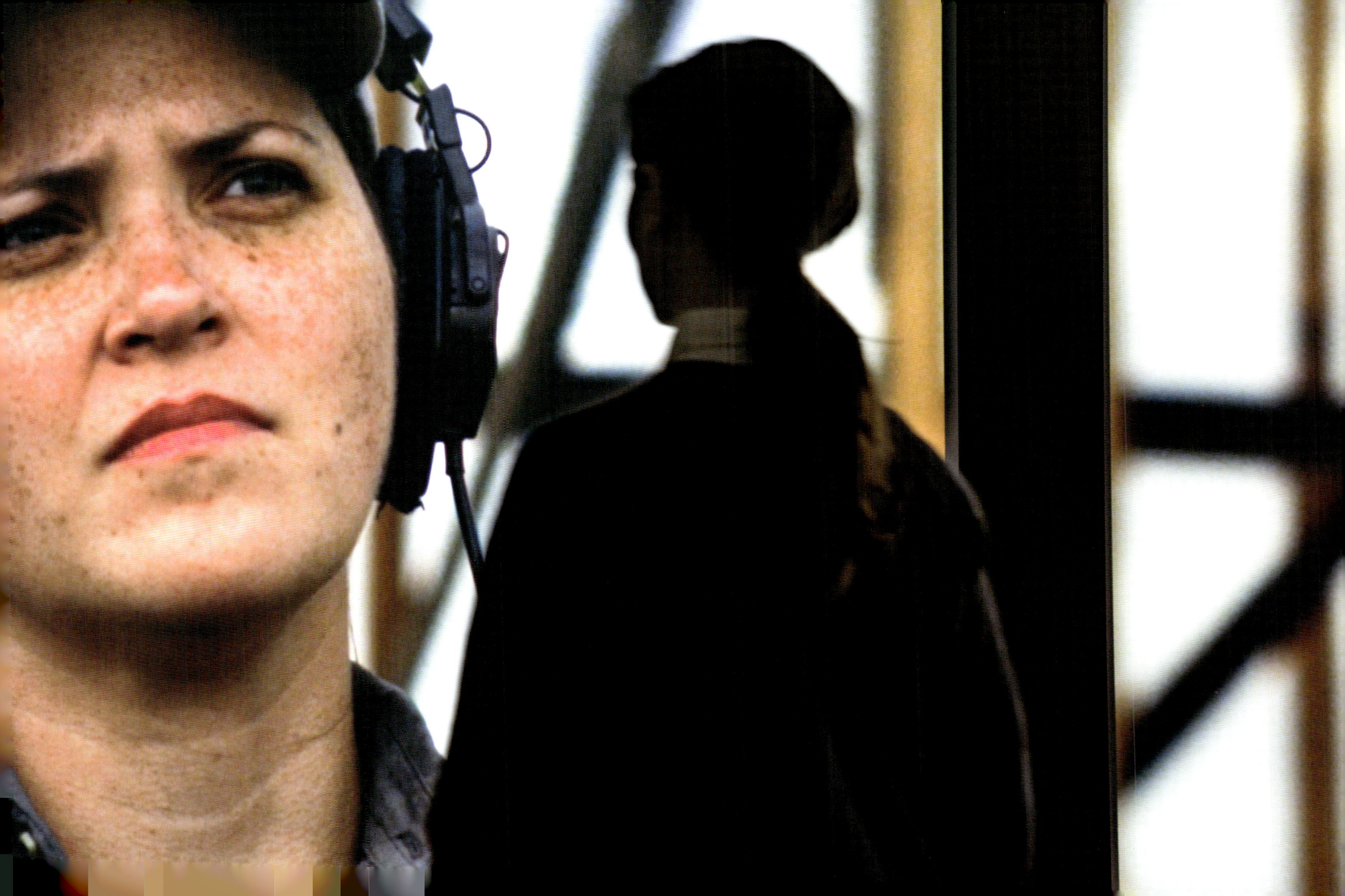

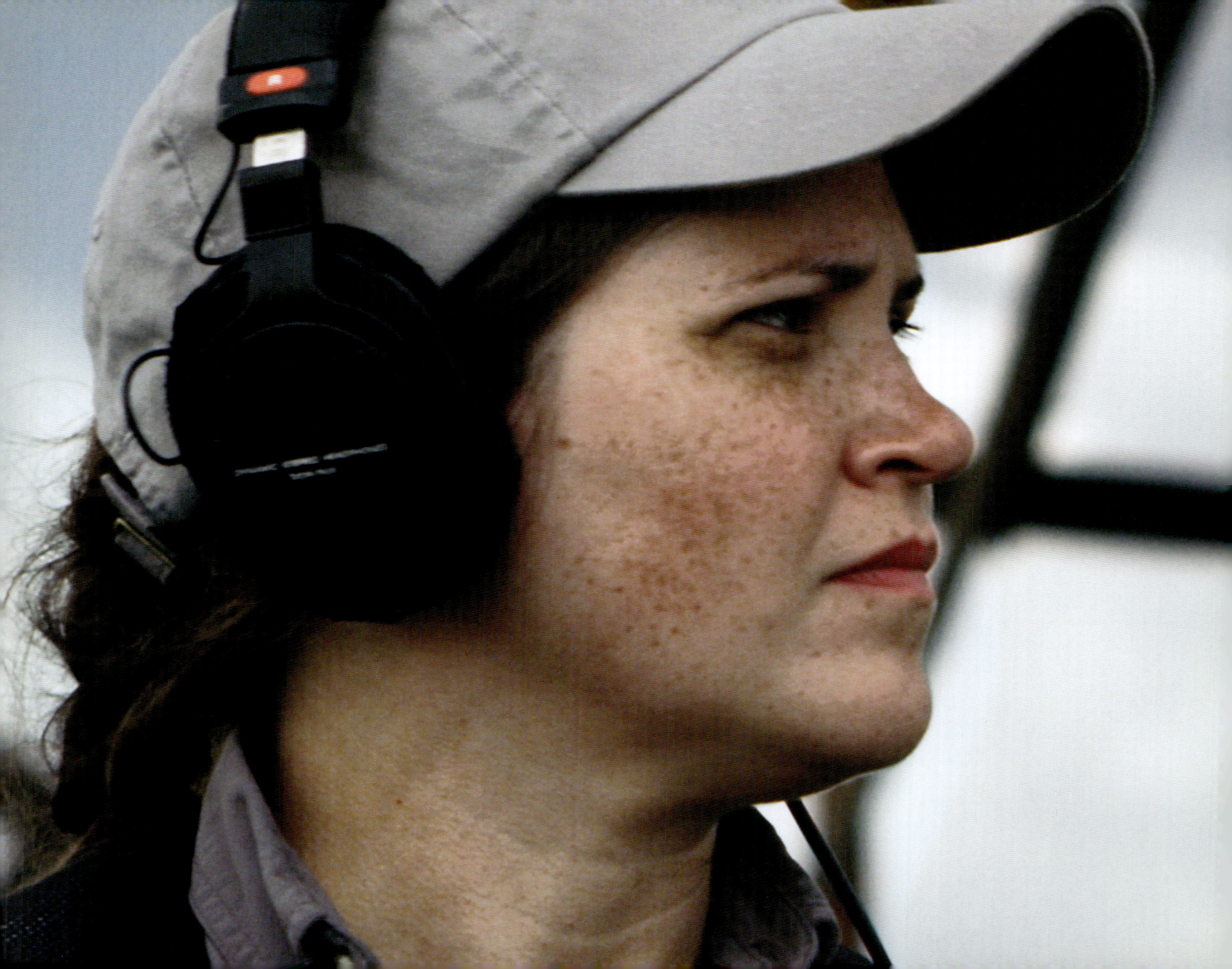

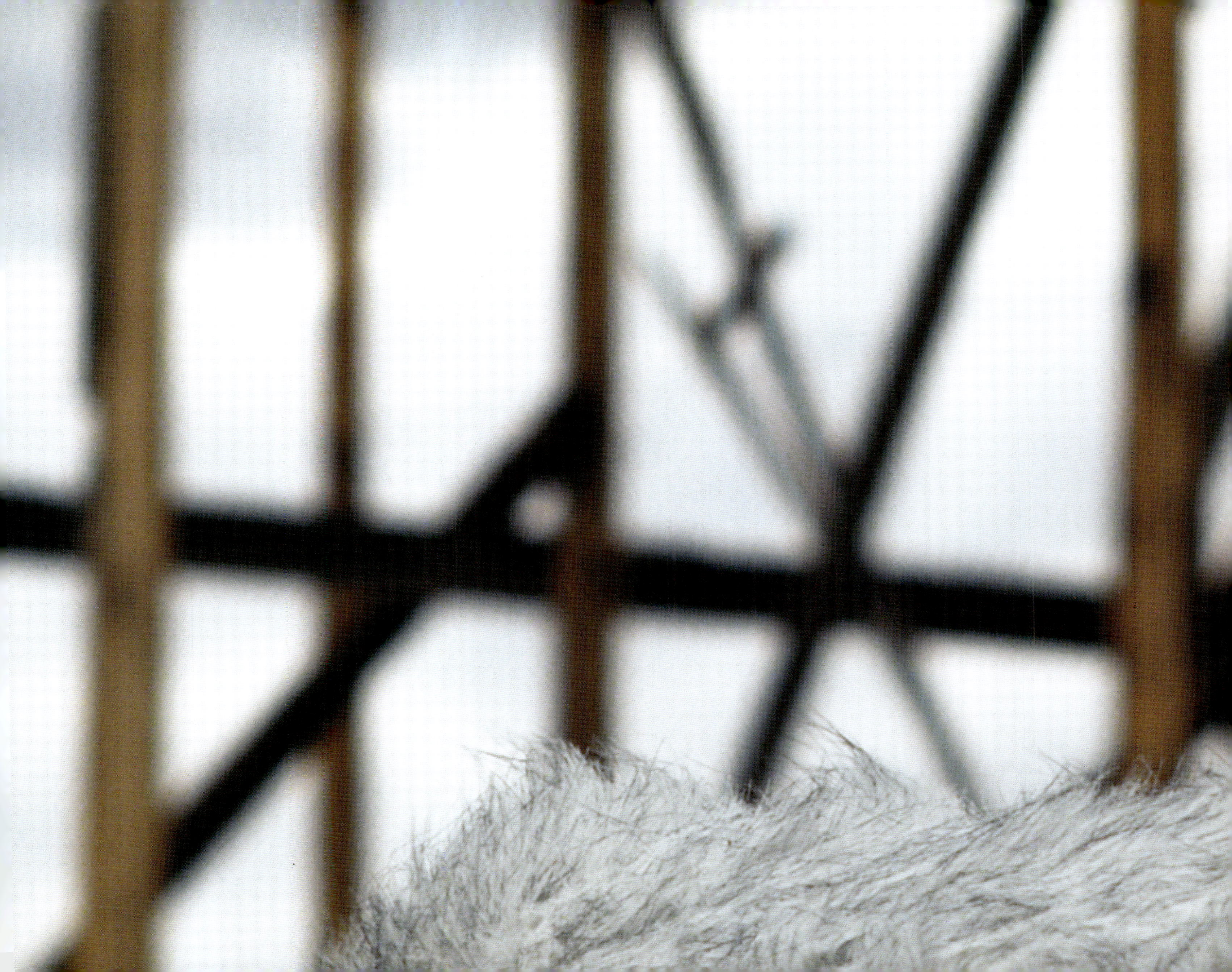

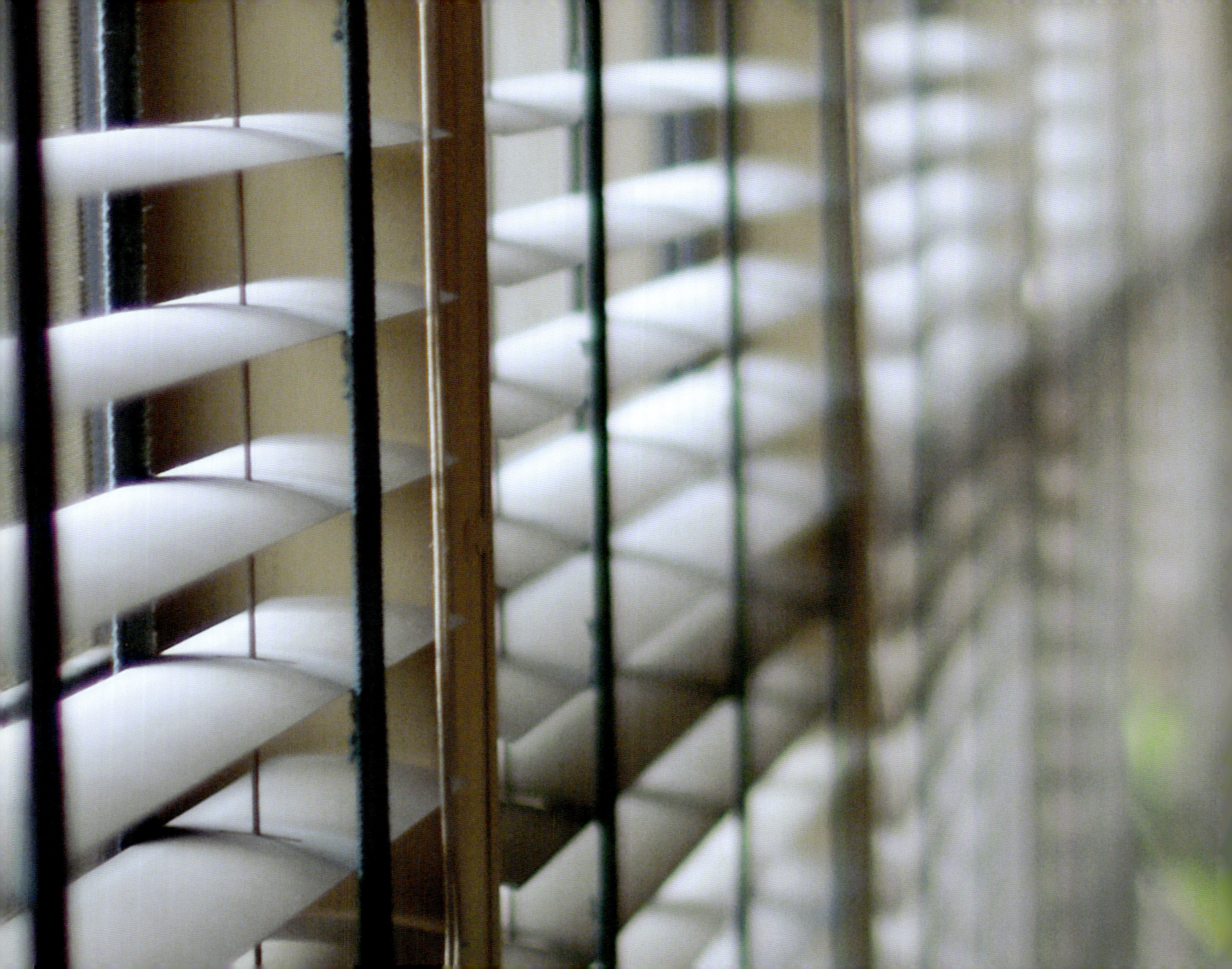

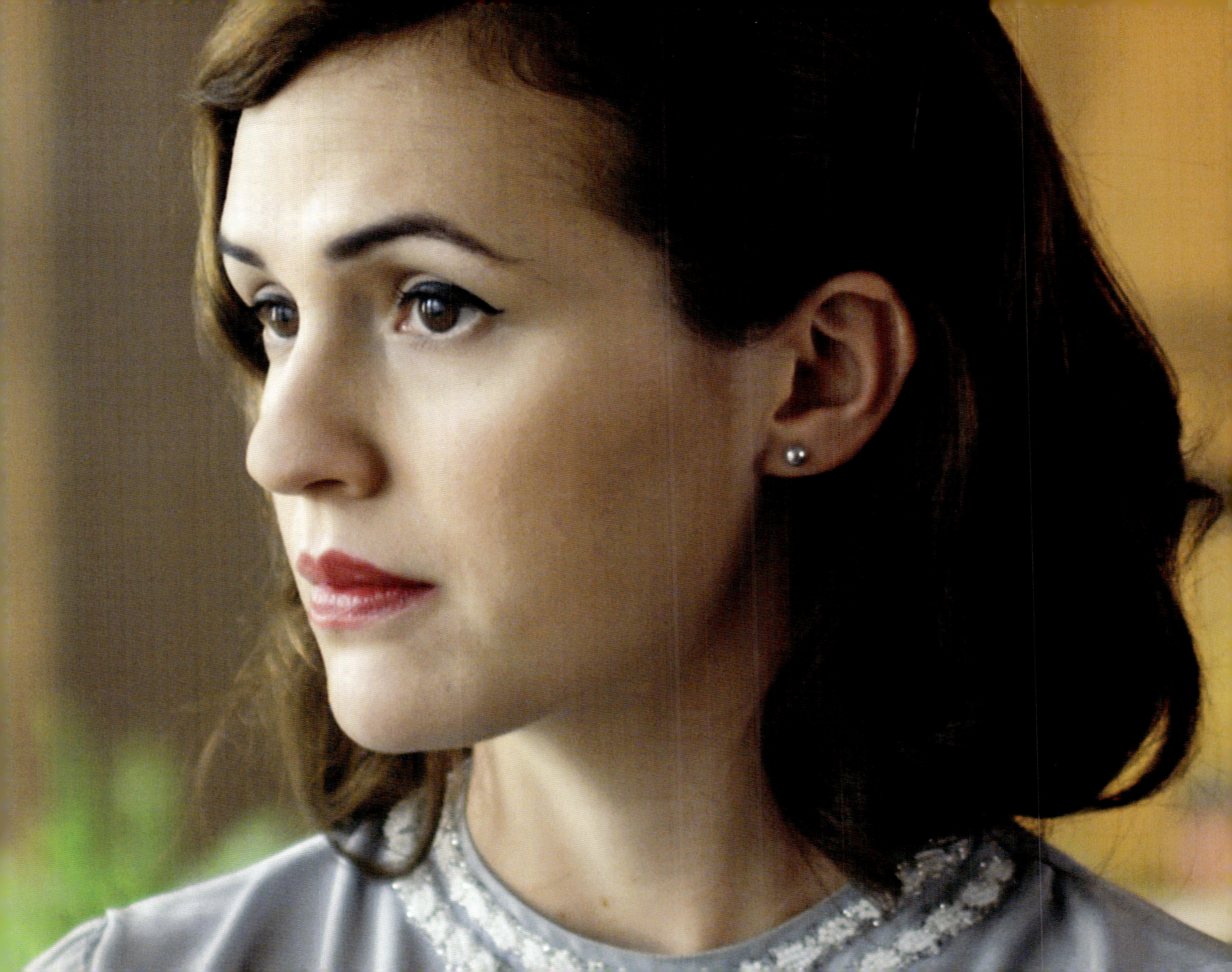

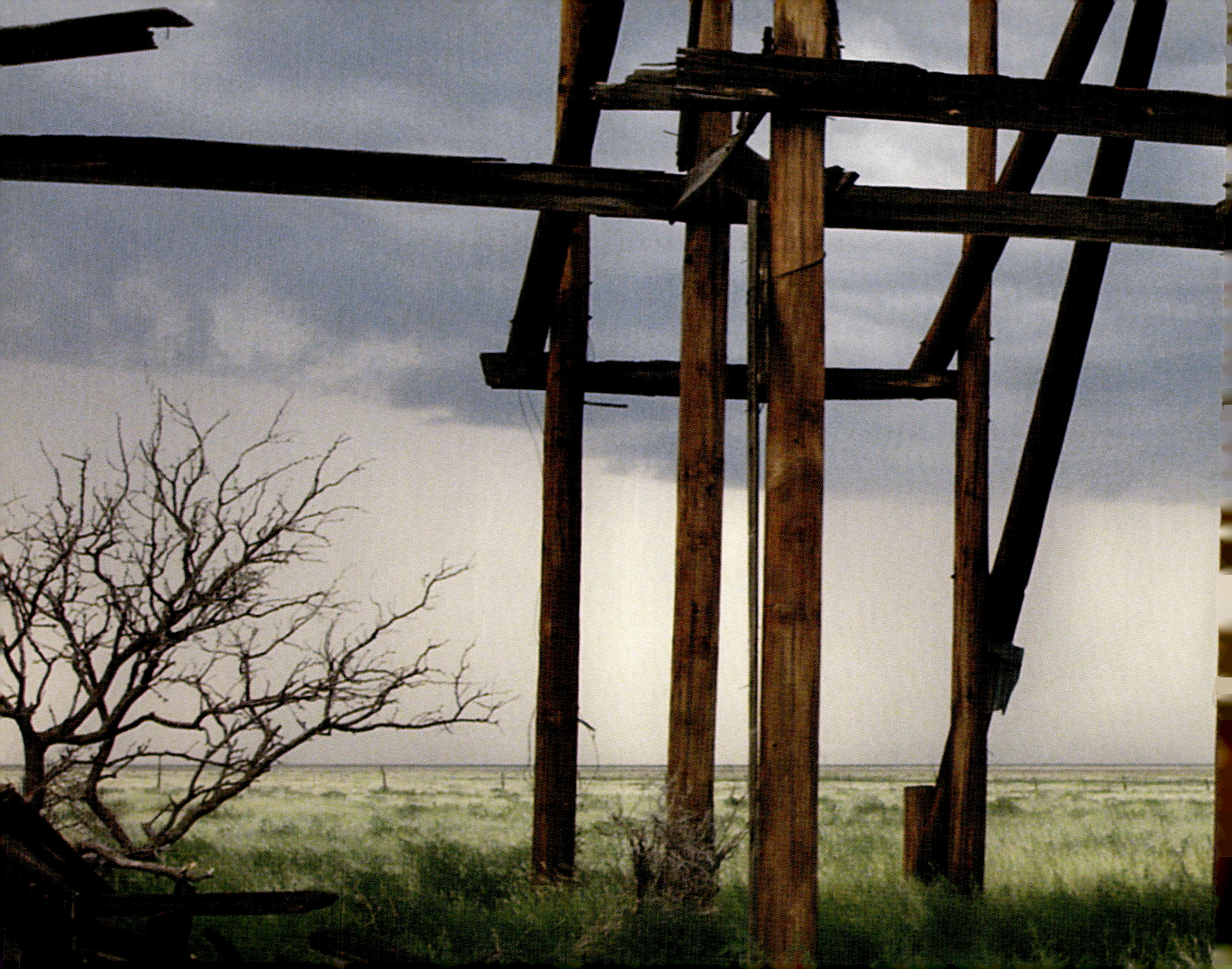

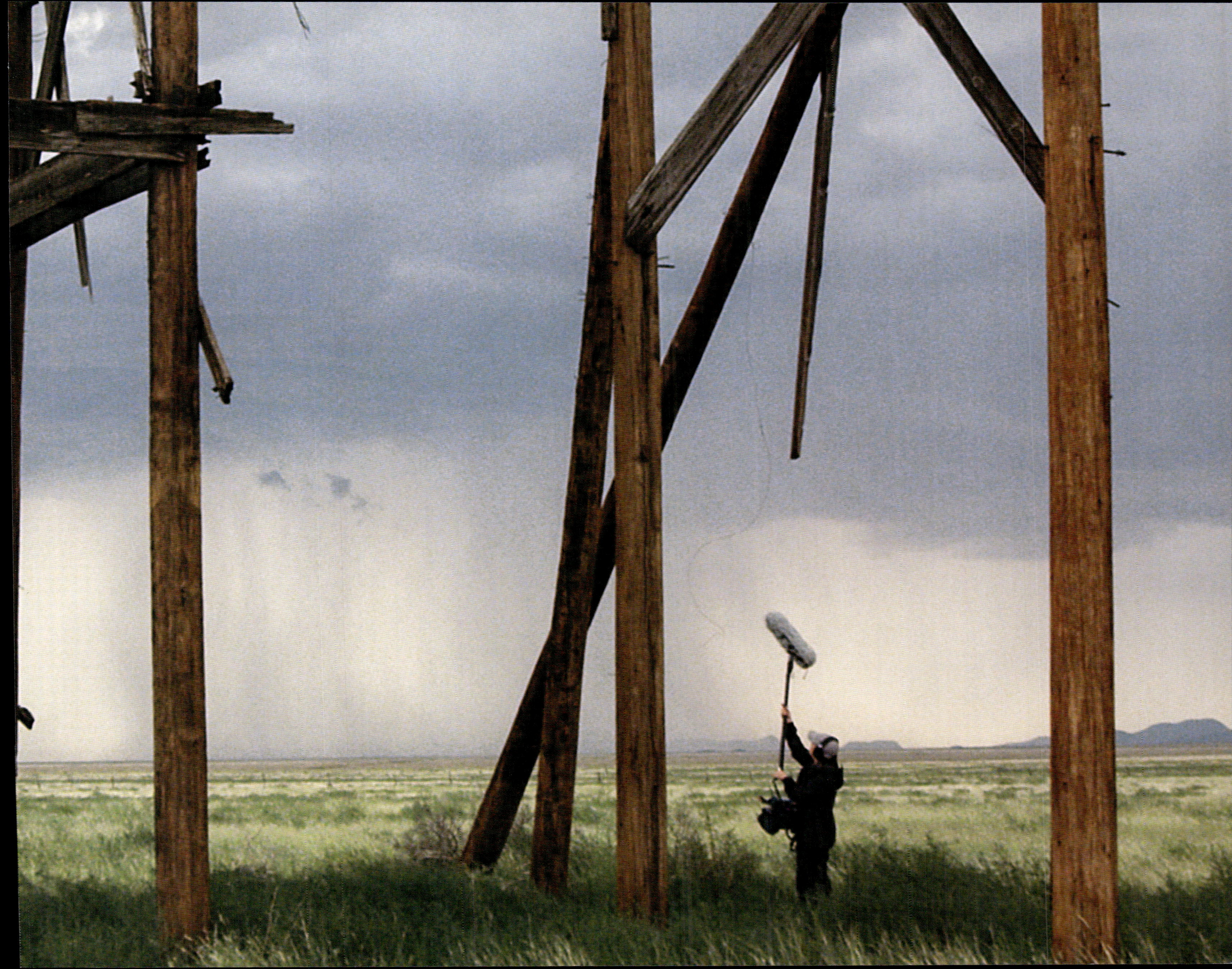

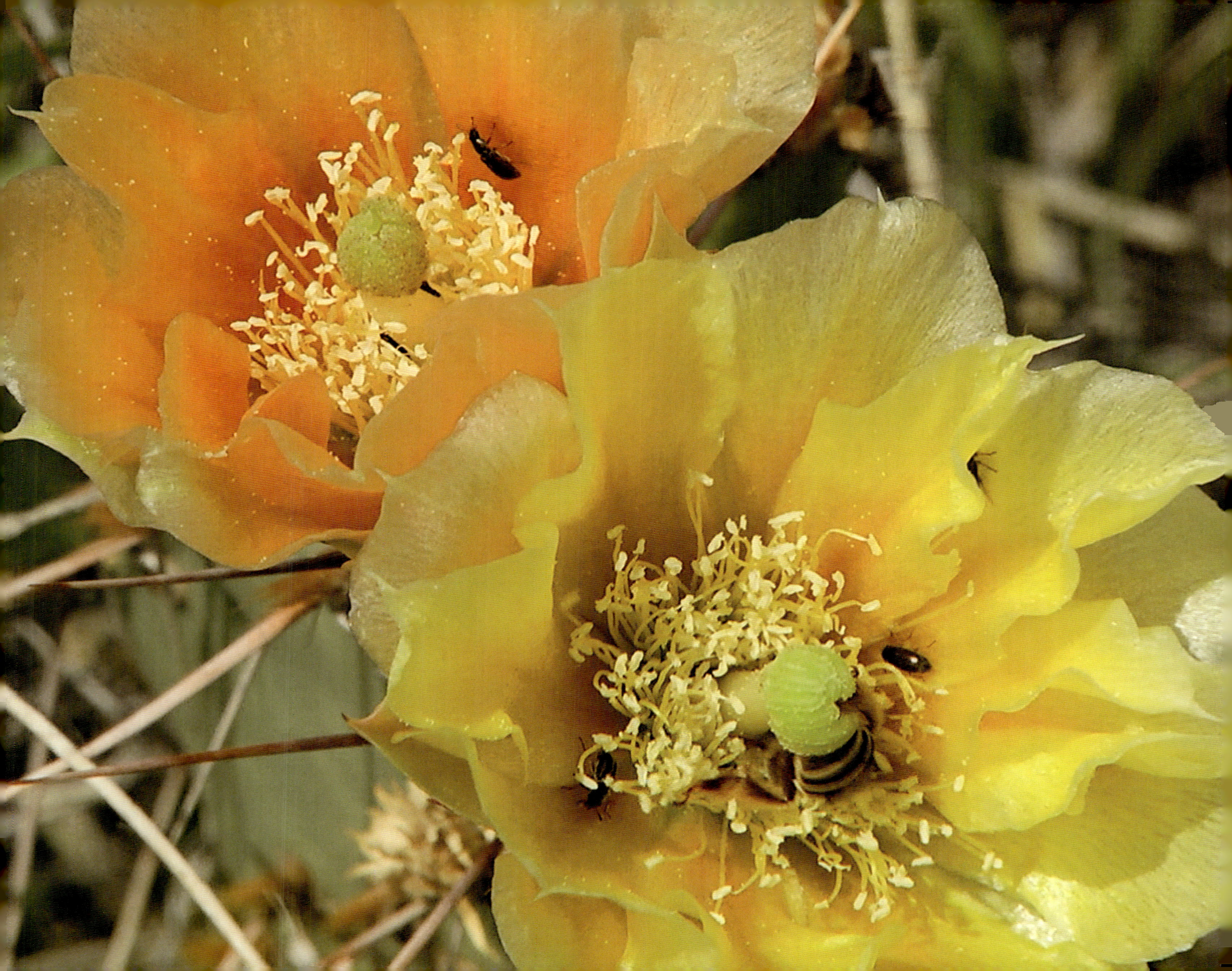

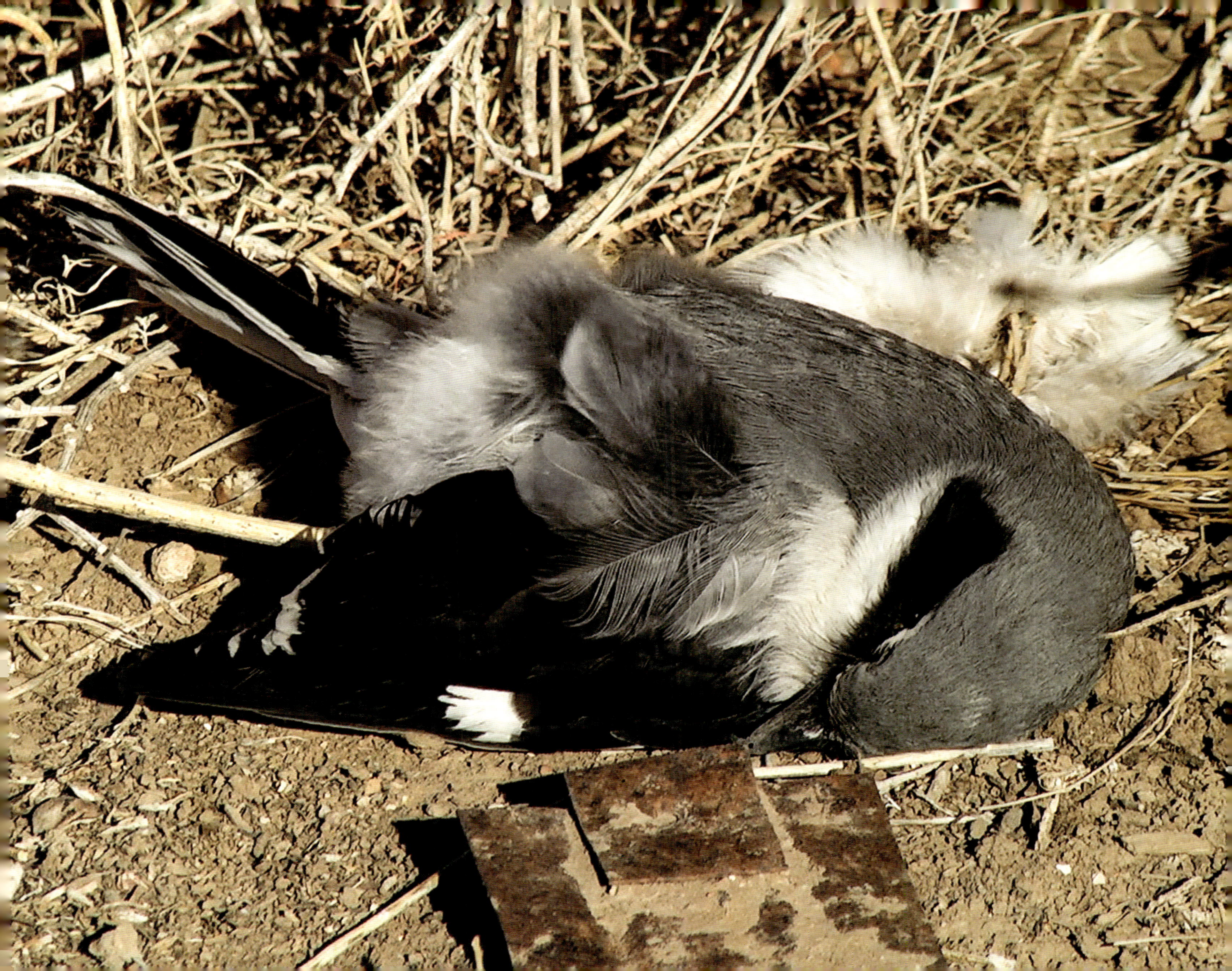

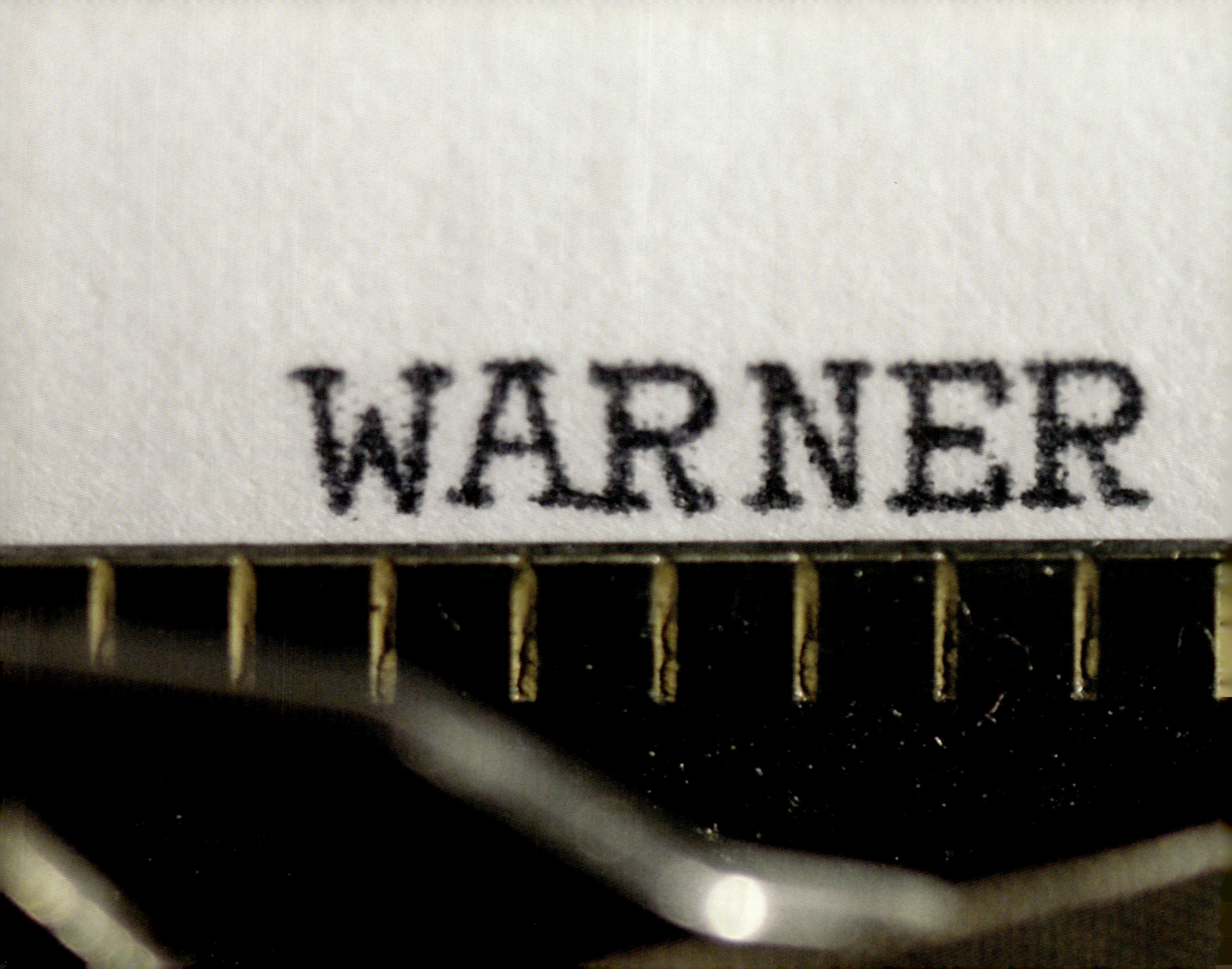
WARNER

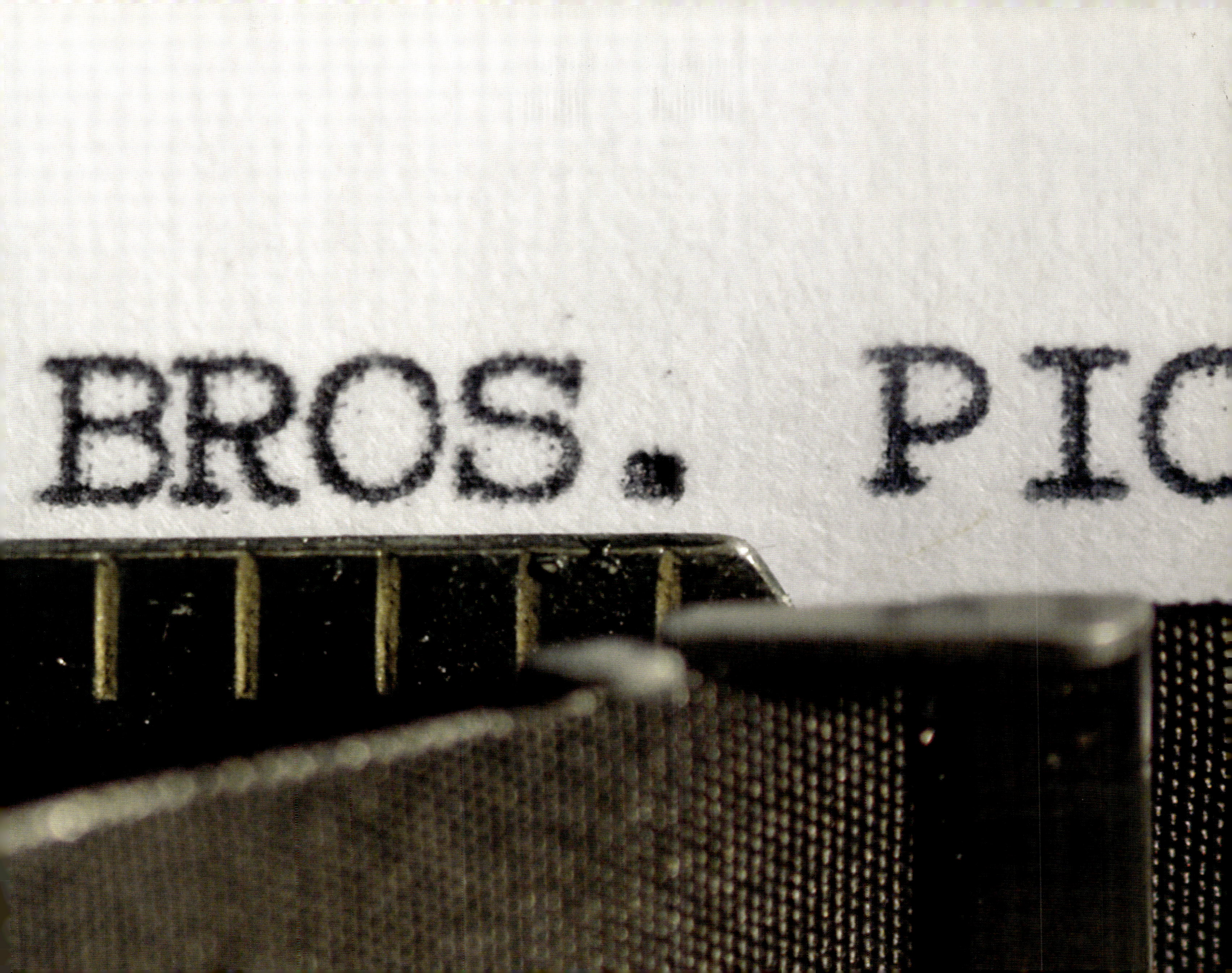
BROS. PIC

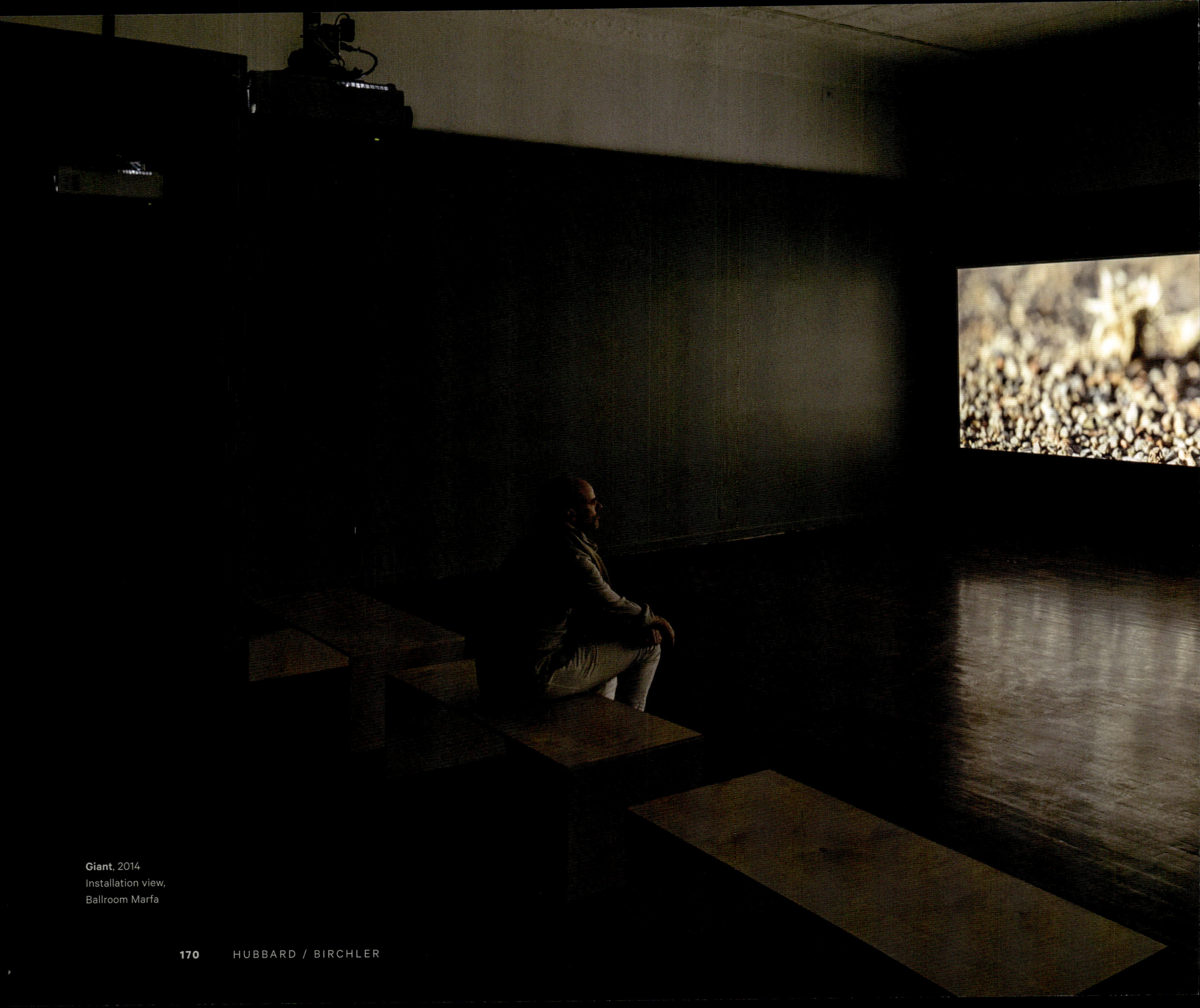

Giant, 2014
Installation view,
Ballroom Marfa

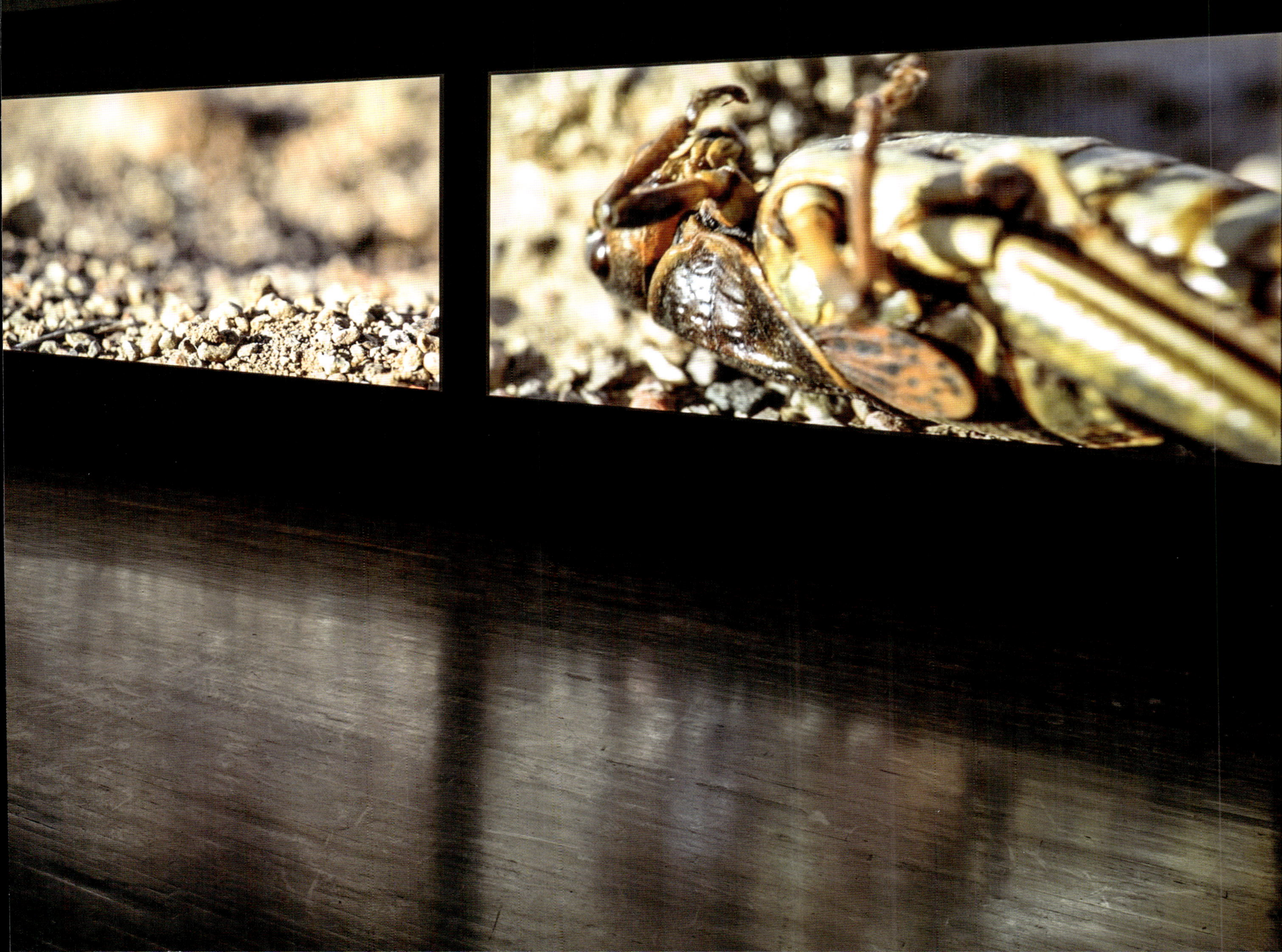

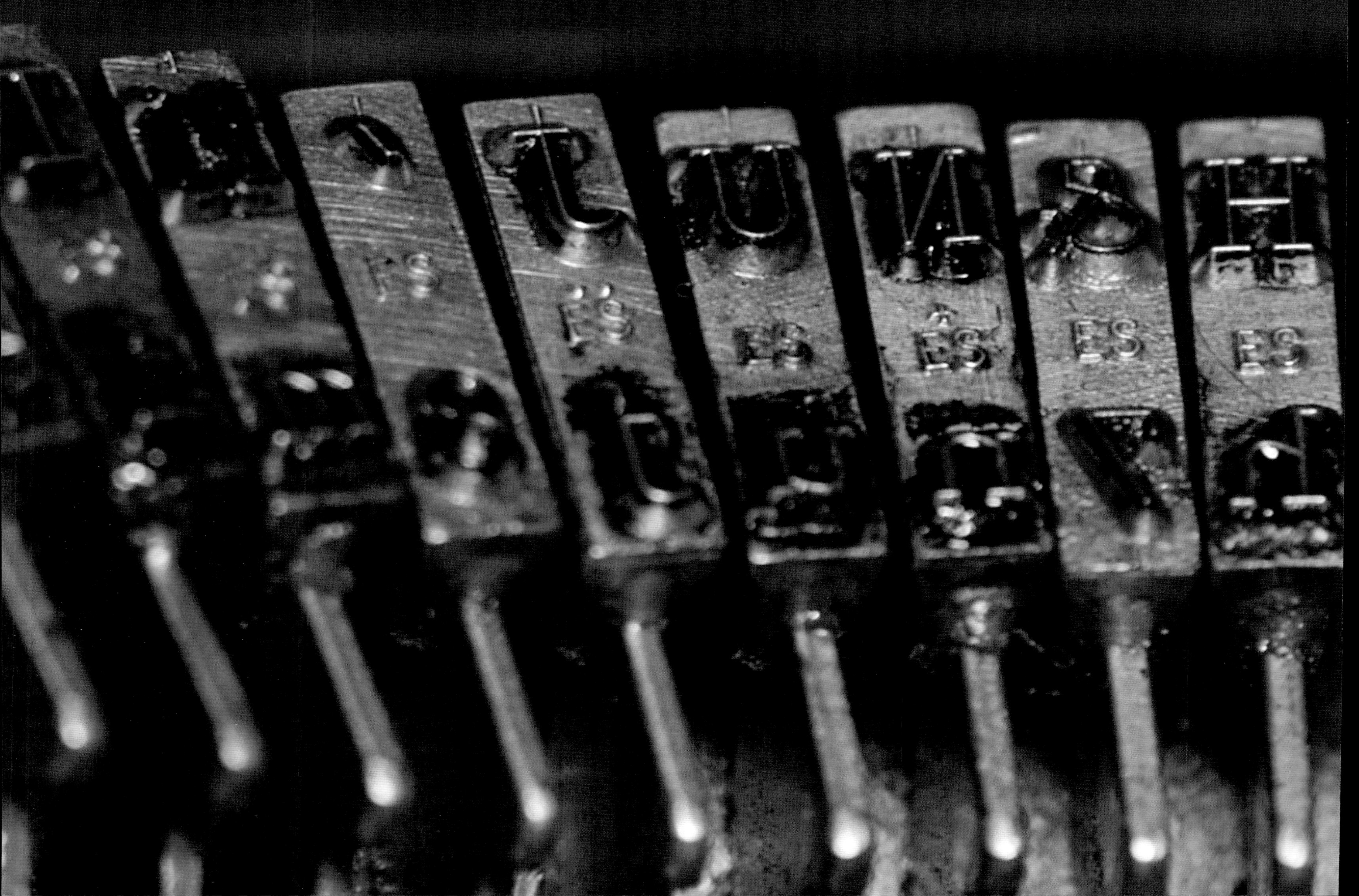

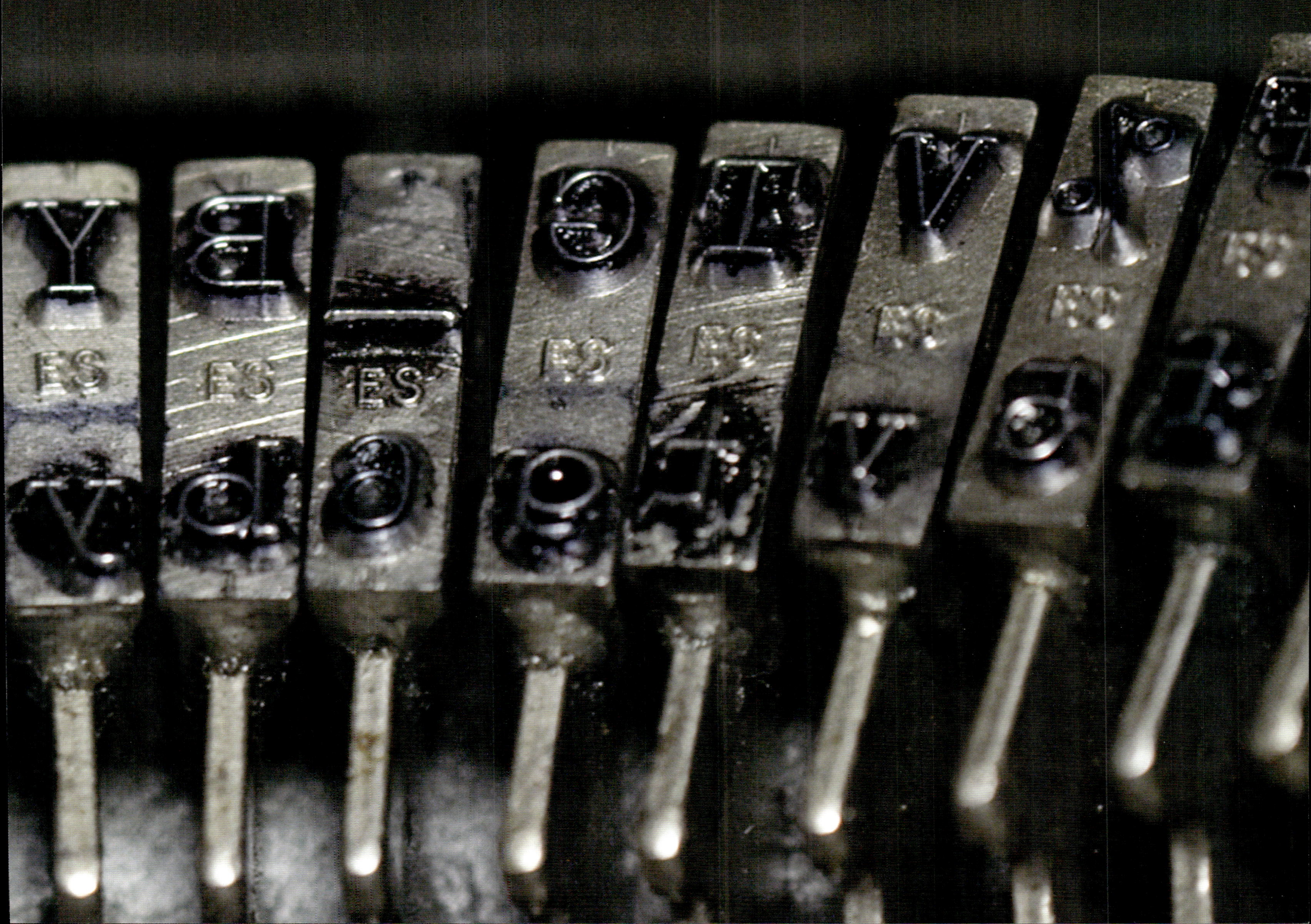

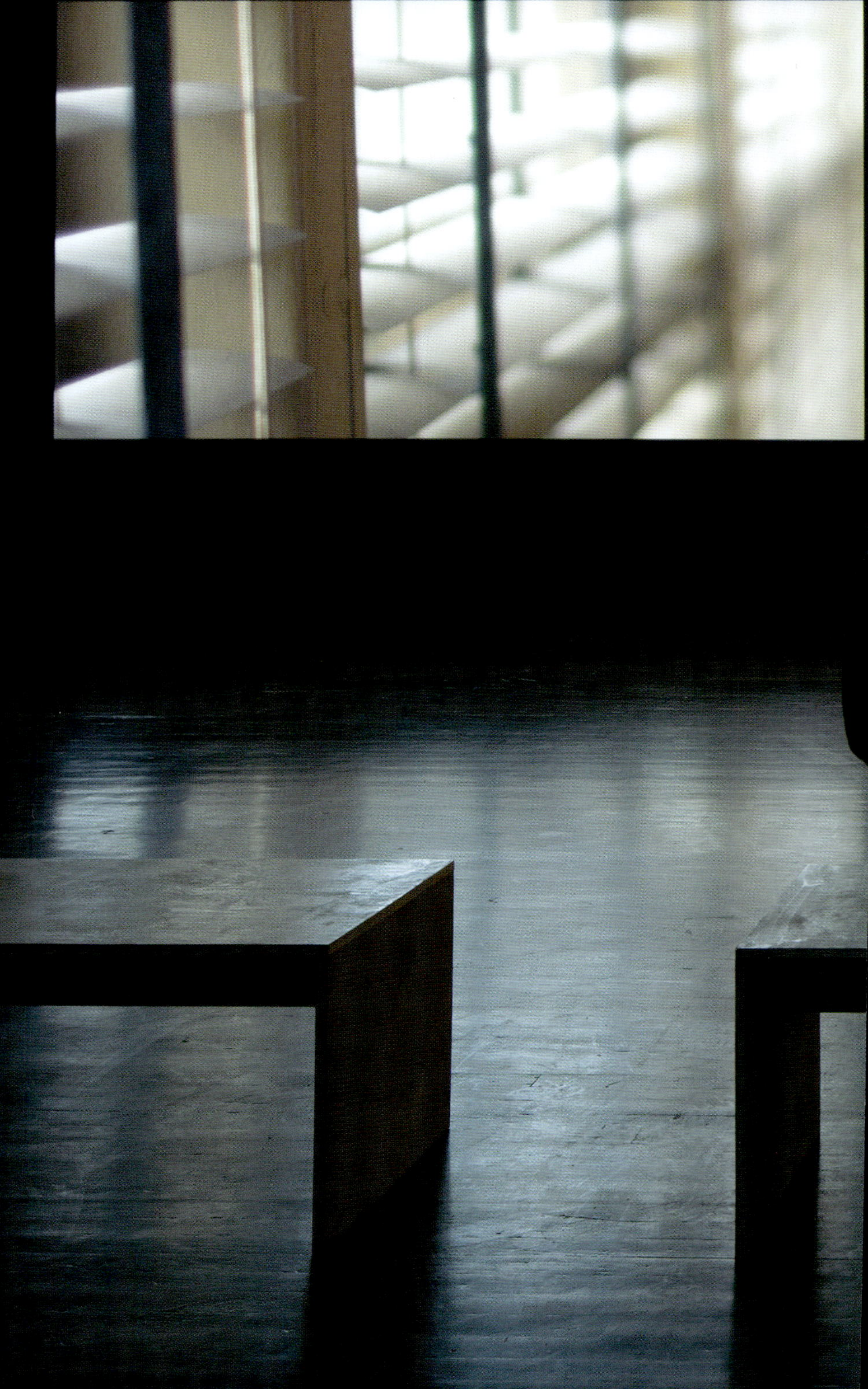

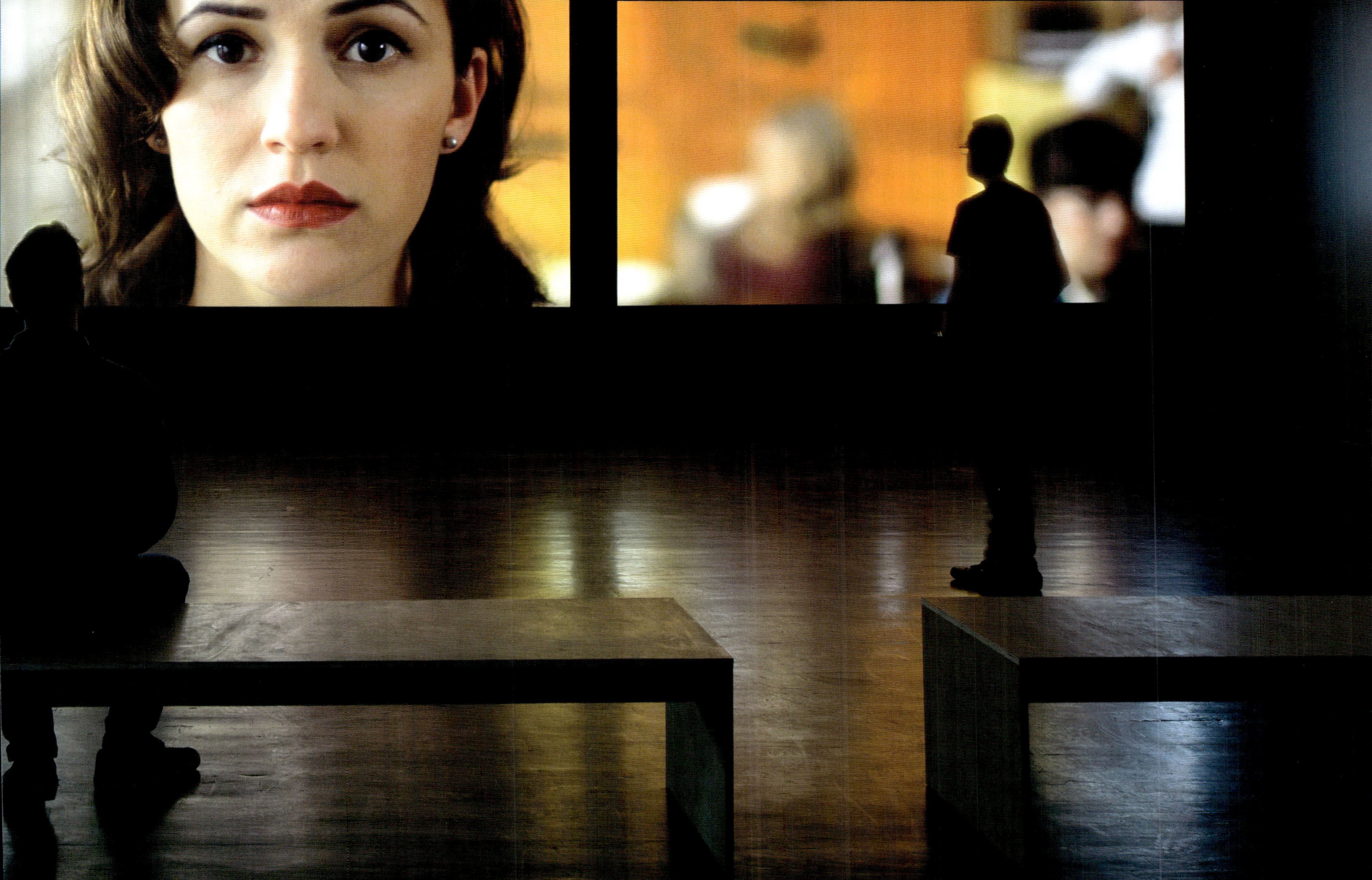

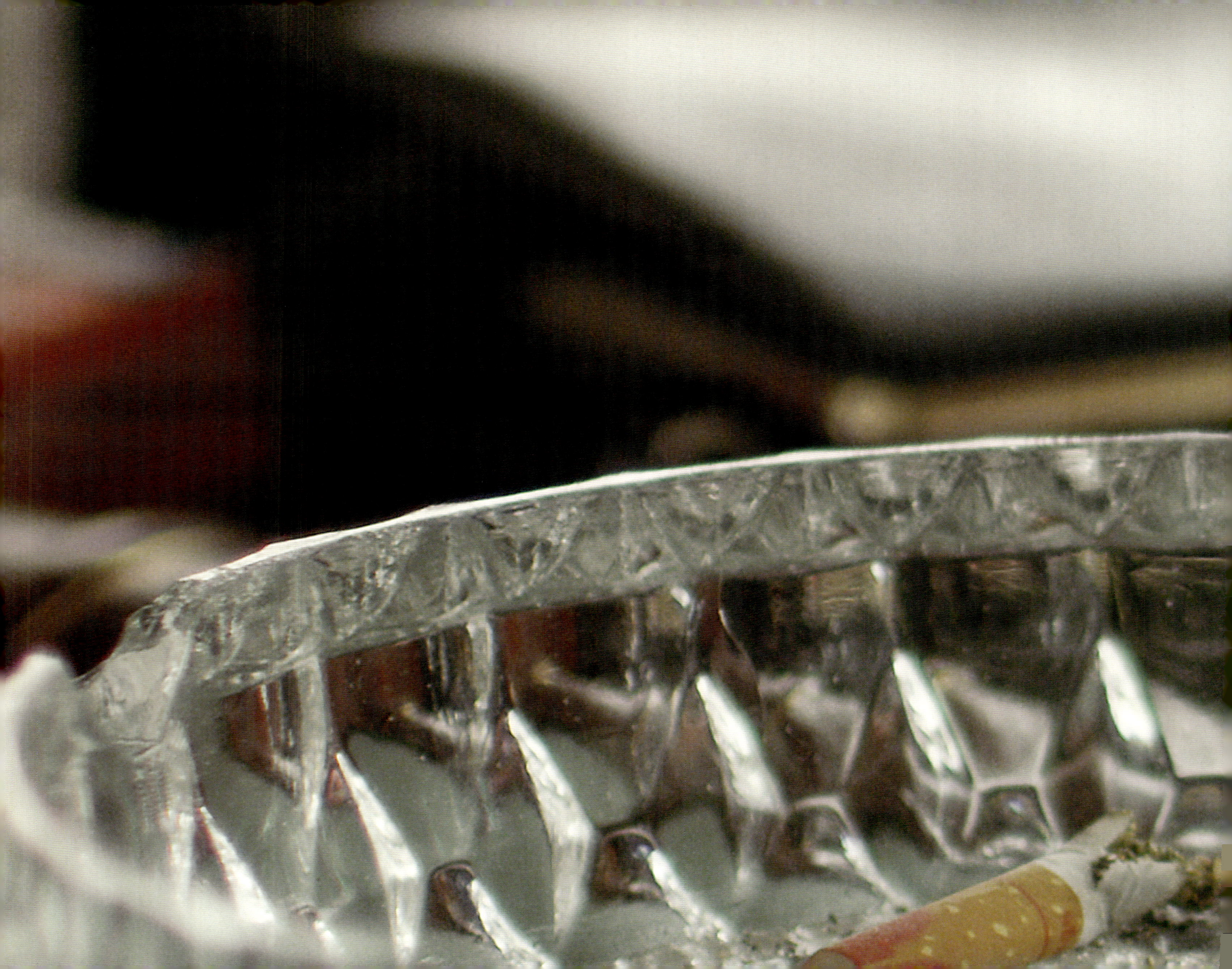

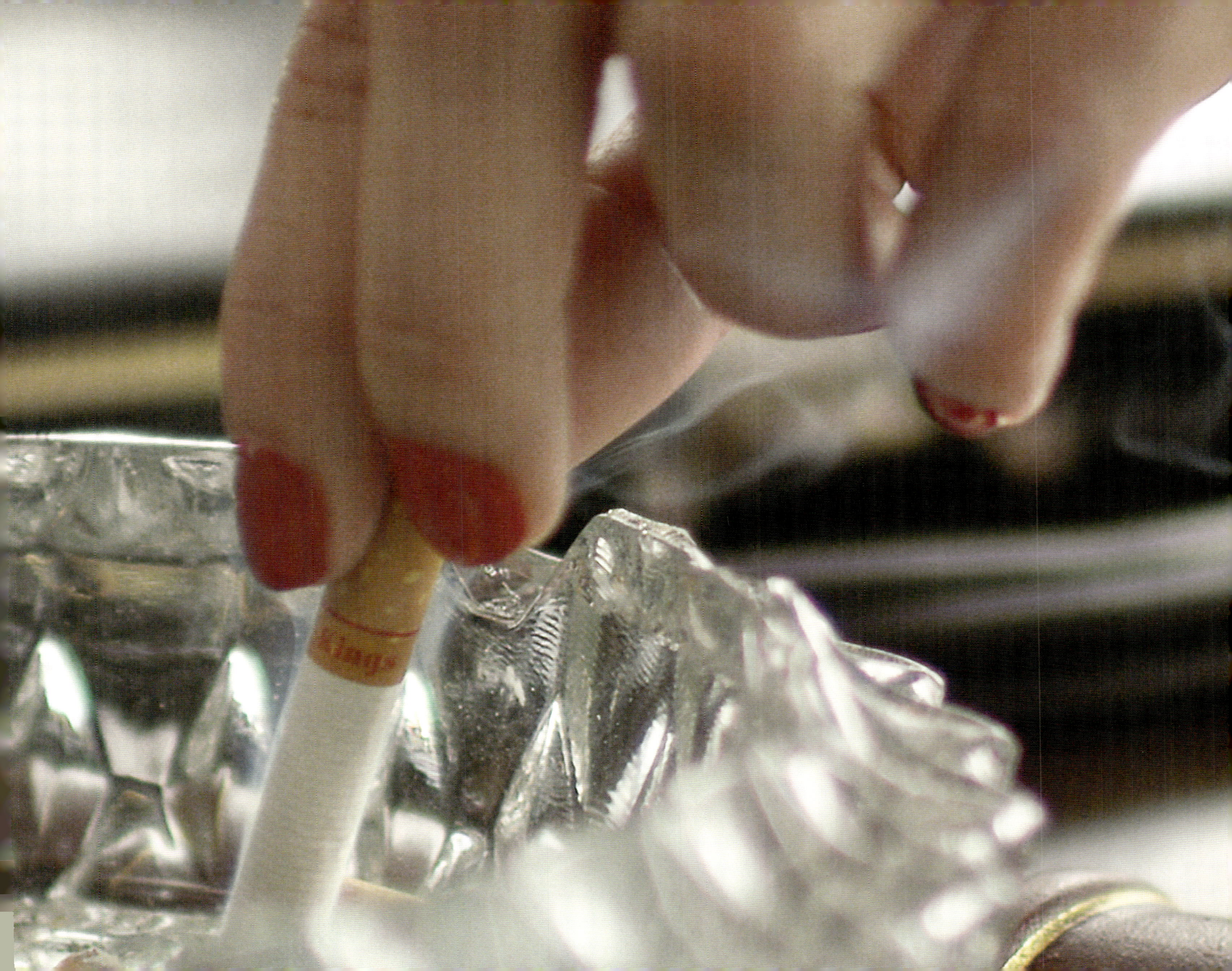
Kings

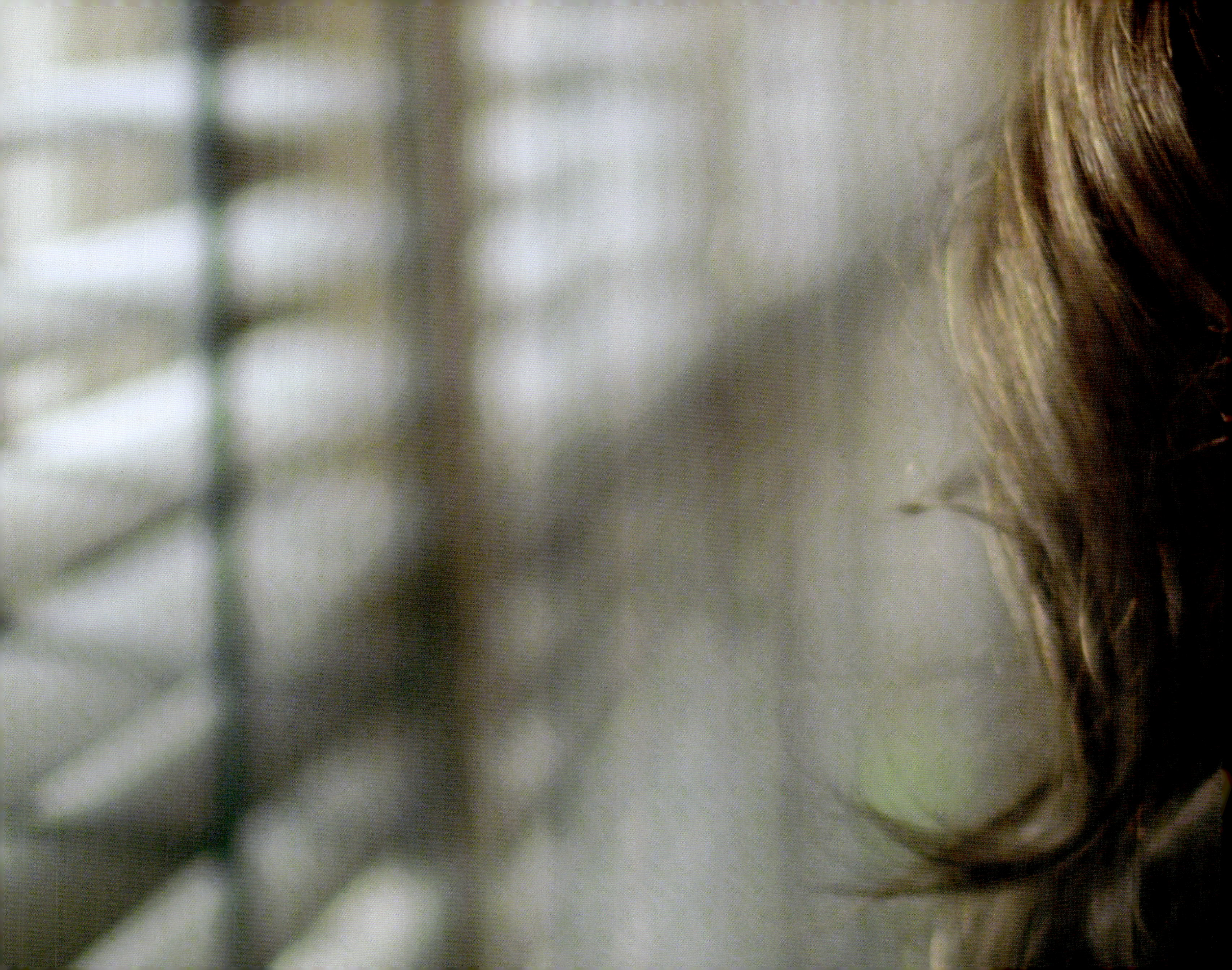

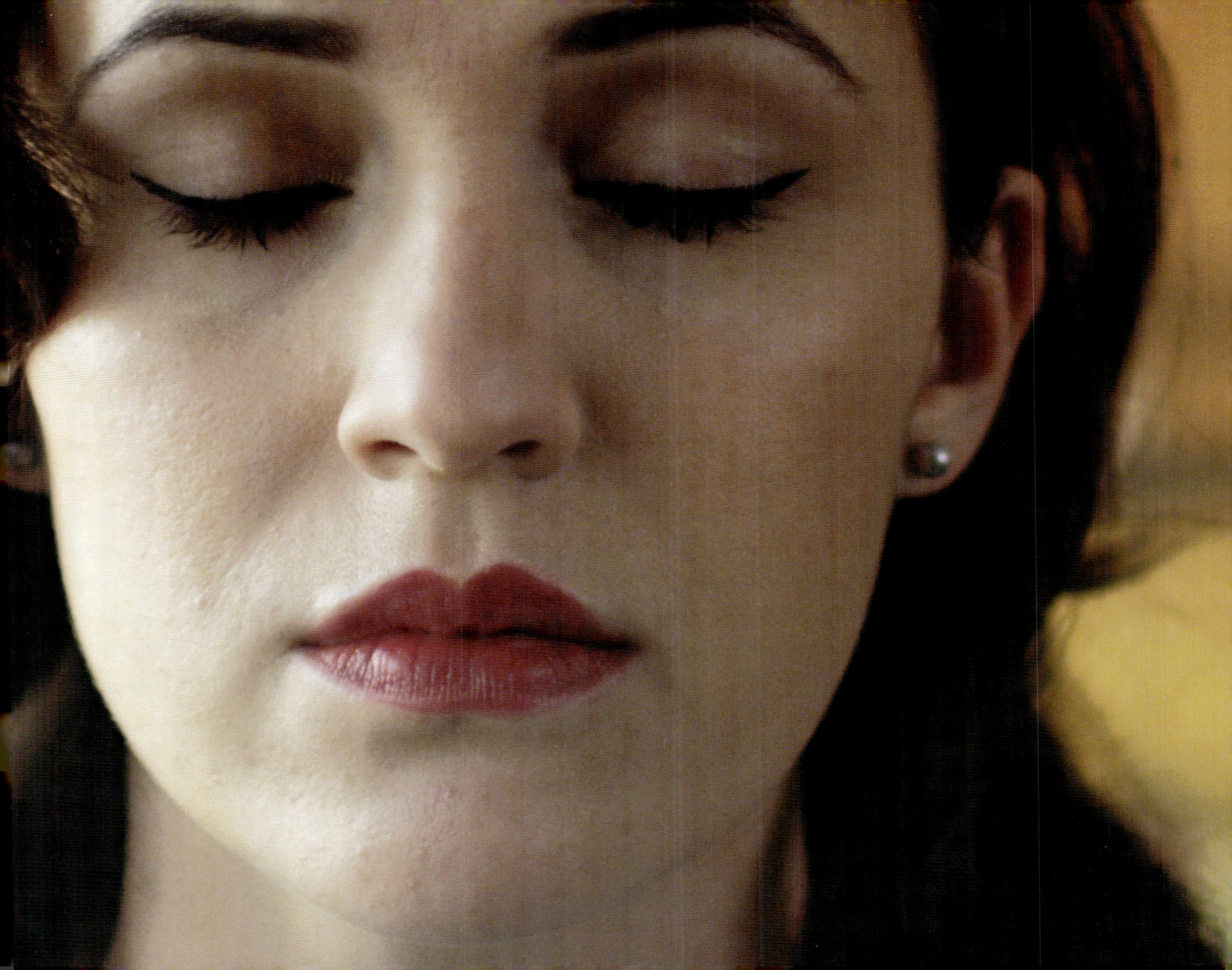

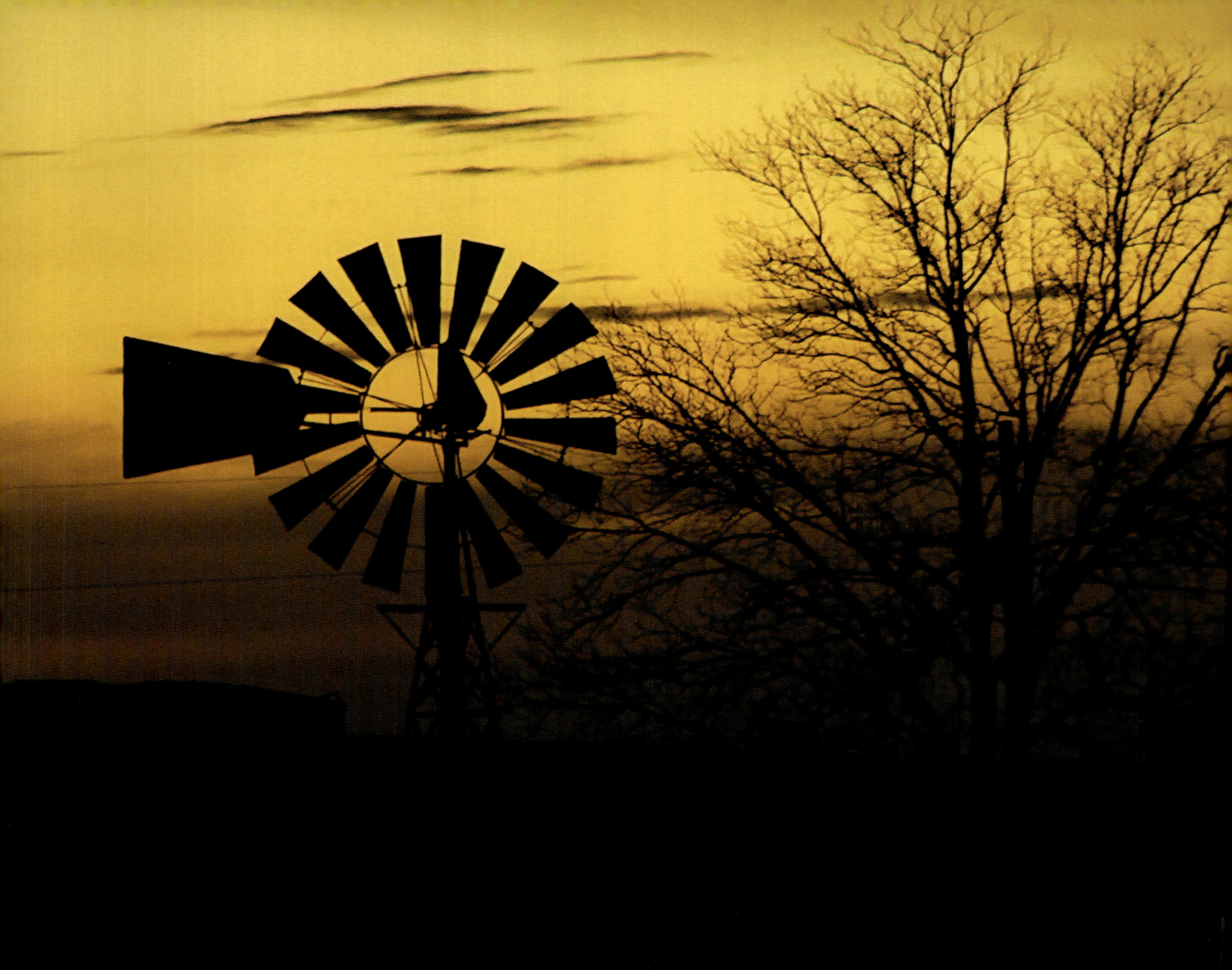

SOUND S

ANNE ELLEGOOD

The Cinema Effect[1]

We can never exactly present to ourselves, or to others. Thus we are not exactly real for one another, nor are we quite real even to ourselves. And this radical alterity is our best chance. ... Put simply, our chance at life.
—Jean Baudrillard, *The Vital Illusion* [2]

For fifteen years, Teresa Hubbard and Alexander Birchler have been using the moving image to mine the rich terrain where reality and fiction collapse in on one another—our understanding of each irrevocably altered and complicated in the process. Active participants in a generation of contemporary artists who turned to the medium of video to explore how the history of cinema has profoundly impacted numerous aspects of modern life—from our approach to storytelling to the formation of subjectivity—much of their work for more than a decade reveled in the seductive power of film to immerse us in a dreamscape where our willingness to suspend our disbelief allowed for experiences saturated with desire and a sense of wonderment. In 2001, Hubbard/Birchler completed one of their earliest videos composed as an infinite loop: *Eight*. With no beginning or end, the brief narrative, centered on a girl's eighth birthday party, is largely atmospheric. Its quiet yet steady rhythm is enacted by means of the widely used filmic technique of the panning (or tracking) shot whereby the camera slowly moves across a space, languorously taking in every detail like an attentive and patient lover.

Eight, 2001
High-Definition
Video with Sound,
Single Channel,
3:25 minutes, Loop
Collections, Kunsthaus
Zürich, Pinakothek der
Moderne, Munich,
and others

The camera in *Eight* scans the scene horizontally in a counter-clockwise direction. With very few edits, the only interruptions to the panning shot are moments when the camera pauses on the girl's face, who is as contemplative and pensive as the video itself, a kind of embodiment of the overarching mood of the piece. Without dialogue and featuring a single actor, *Eight* both invites a narrative reading by providing enough information for the viewer to piece together some of the action (the party has been interrupted by a storm) and resists the conventions of narrative by deliberately refusing resolution and, moreover, pulling the viewer into an anachronistic spatial black hole where the logic of time and space seems to be turned on its head. Rather than edit the footage so that the girl's progression from inside her house—where she stares at the unwelcome rain through a window—into the garden is unquestioned by the viewer, Hubbard/Birchler reveal the edge of the set of the interior space as they keep the camera moving steadily to the exterior scene, where the remains of her party are now utterly soaked. Incredibly, this maneuver resides in the realm of the real *and* the surreal, encompassing both so that our minds simultaneously accept them as equally valid and present. The artists deliberately pull back the curtain on the fabrication and artificiality so prevalent in filmmaking, jolting the viewer into the realization that what we are seeing is, after all, a replica of a house—a simulation, a set, a reproduction—rather than

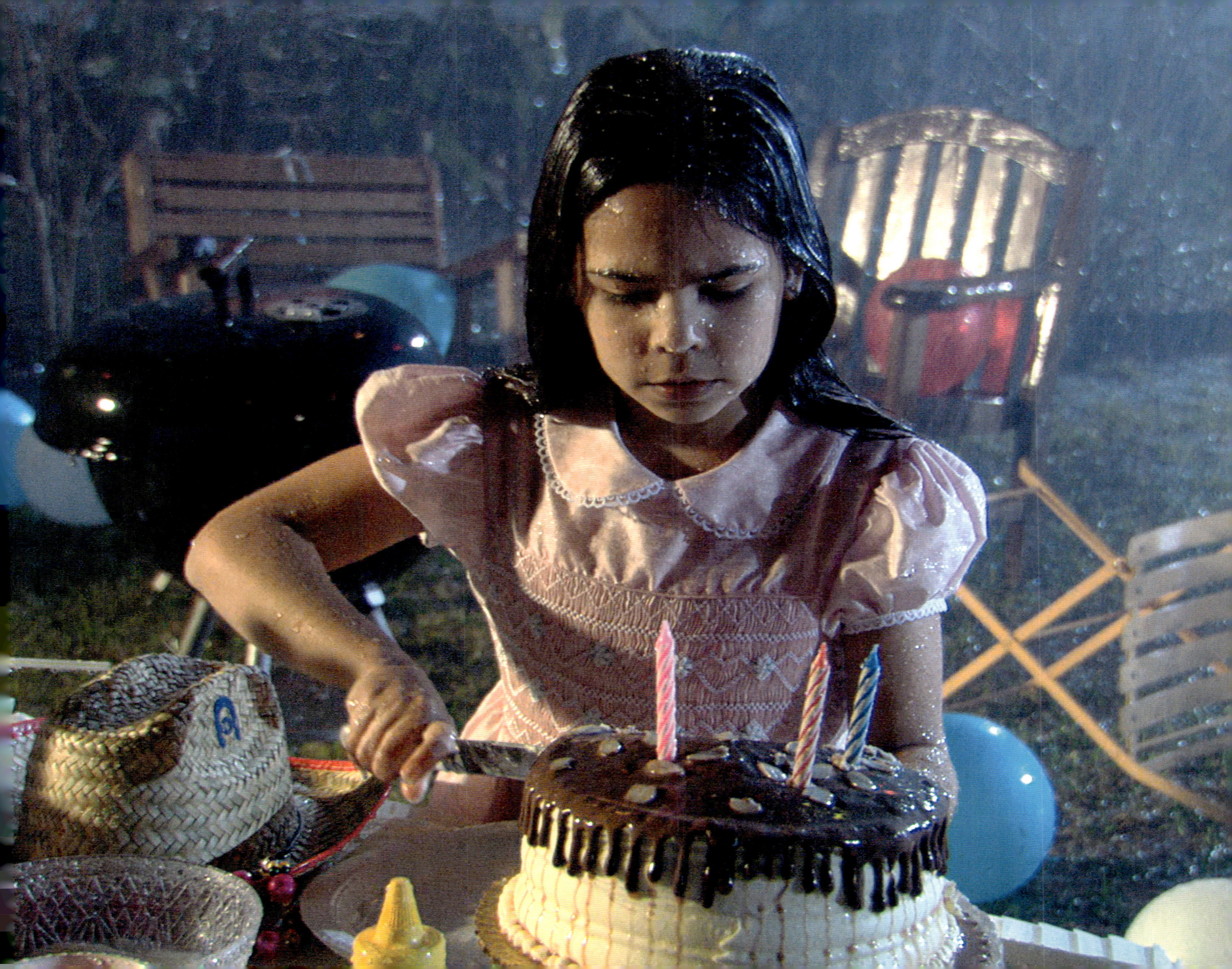

an actual home. Despite this, the experience of watching the endless loop of *Eight* still has the capacity to draw us into a kind of reverie, absorbed in the sheer visual splendor of the images yet also conscious of the artists' ability to manipulate.

Subsequent works like *Single Wide* (2002), *House with Pool* (2004) and *Eighteen* (2013), similarly keep the narrative structure both oblique and inconclusive, but highlight moments of deep conflict, pointing more overtly to the inevitable disappointments and difficulties of life. Events common to many—the end of a relationship, the tension between a mother and daughter—are examined with such intensity and heightened visuality that they become almost preternatural. The colors are lush, the lighting dramatic, the music affective. No detail is overlooked. The scenes seem to move toward a culimination, but the endless looping disallows the anticipated sequence of events from climax to finale. The ordinary is made extraordinary. By employing these cinematic techniques, the artists put the viewers into a trance-like state, one that masterfully entices both the intellect and the emotions by managing to be simultaneously rational and irrational. In these works, Hubbard/Birchler devise an approach that draws equally from reality and fiction. Realistic, even quotidian, events are made fictional through the widely recognized language of film. The cinematic space is understood to traffic in dramatization, fabrication and exaggeration. Moreover, this entwining of fact and fiction feels in some profound way perfectly reasonable to the viewer, for it is a reflection of contemporary culture where the distinctions between these previously cleanly demarcated categories have become increasingly unreliable.

Single Wide, 2002
High-Definition Video with Sound
Single Channel,
6:07 minutes, Loop
Collection, Museum of Contemporary Art, MOCA, Los Angeles, and others

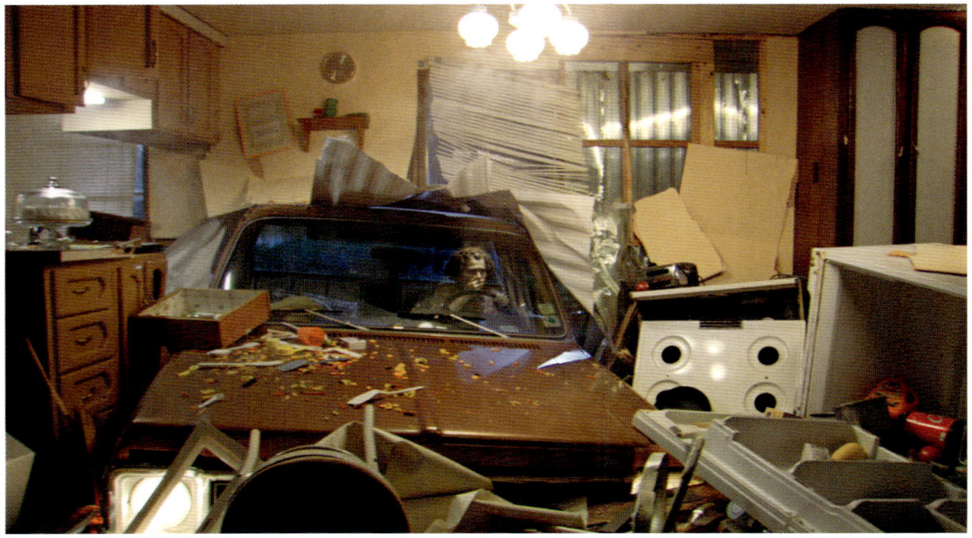

These works call attention to how our daily lives can take on the dramatic quality of cinema. The cinema effect here resides in the acknowledgement that film reflects our lives back to us, but writ large and in technicolor. In their newest work, the artists explore another aspect of the cinema effect: how the construction of subjectivity—our very sense of identity—has adapted to the age of cinema to fully integrate aspects of representation, reenactment and invention into our authentic notions of ourselves. As dramatic as this sounds, what is perhaps most compelling about how the artists reflect this new reality is that they do it *not* by engaging with spectacle but by looking to the everyday, the perfectly ordinary. Here, the ordinary does not become extraordinary, as in the earlier works, so much as the unremarkable becomes remarkable, for it reveals how deeply rooted the cinema effect has become.

In their recently completed trilogy, *Sound Speed Marker*, Hubbard/Birchler maintain their longstanding investigation into how reality and fiction inform one another, but rather than create works that borrow the seductive high-end production values from mainstream film for short videos that offer new temporal and spatial possibilities for the moving image, they

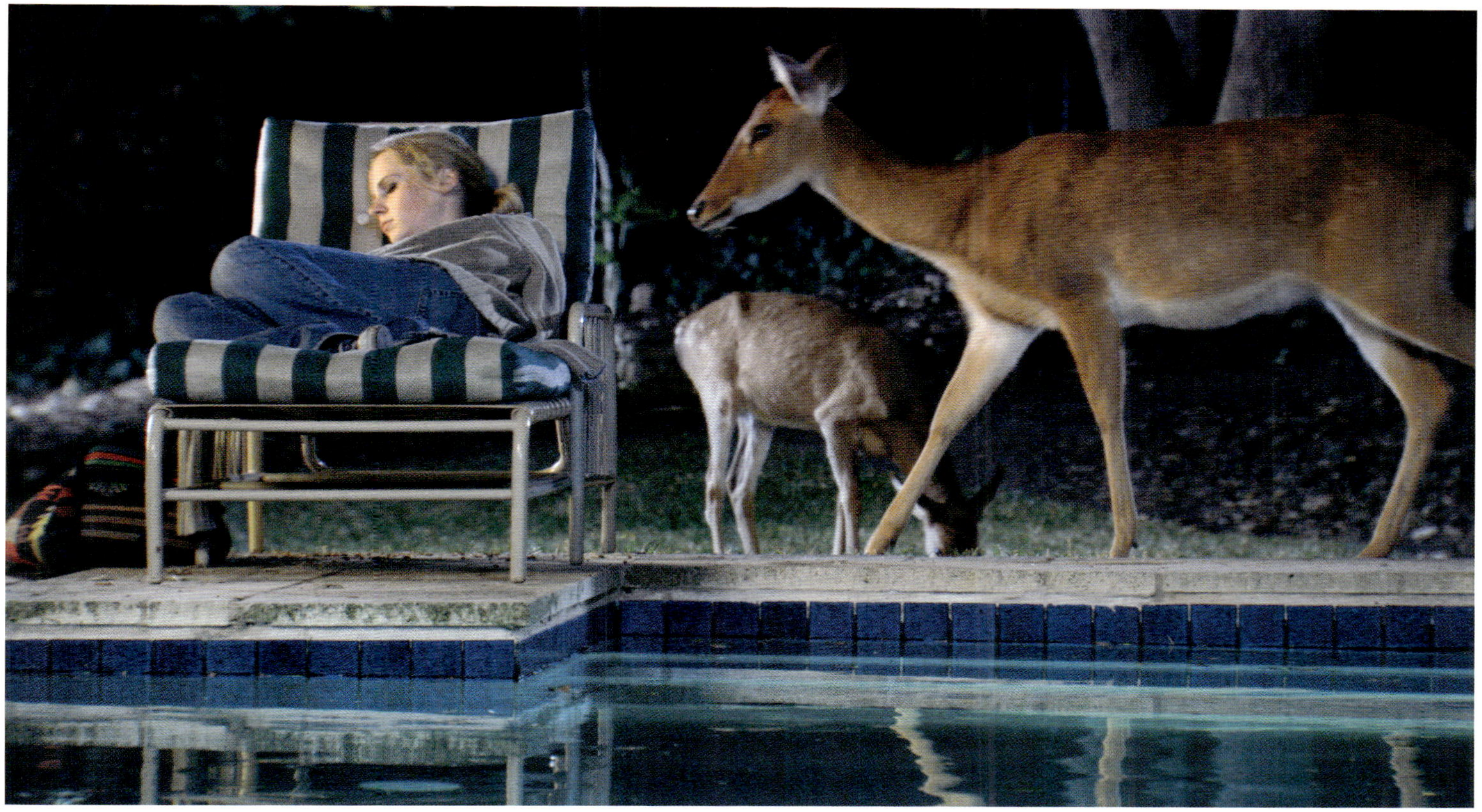

have chosen to take up the genre of the documentary. On the surface, these videos seem more conventional and less theatrical than their previous works. And to some degree this is true. And yet in the artists' insistent investigation into how cinema has, by the twenty-first century, seeped into nearly every aspect of our lives, the overall impact is in fact quite profound. The dreamscape has been replaced with something more subtle, yet perhaps more powerful: a profound awareness of the now constant presence of the camera (literally, historically, metaphorically) and the pervasive residue of cinema. Rather than borrow the visual language of the cinema to underscore its illusory nature, this trilogy of videos provides concrete examples of how cinema—and the film industry that produces it—has directly impacted people, their individual and shared identities, their personal histories, their memories and their sense of place. Each work in the trilogy—*Grand Paris Texas* (2009), *Movie Mountain (Méliès)* (2011) and *Giant* (2014)—takes up a different location in Texas and tells a distinct story. Yet the works almost seamlessly merge into one another to create an overarching argument: the cinema effect is ubiquitous, residing in even the most remote and unexpected places and touching the lives of innumerable people.

Each video takes as its starting place a particular subject and then moves out in a variety of directions, like the branches of

House with Pool, 2004
High-Definition
Video with Sound,
Single Channel,
20:39 minutes, Loop
Collection, Hirshhorn
Museum and Sculpture
Garden, Washington
D.C., and others

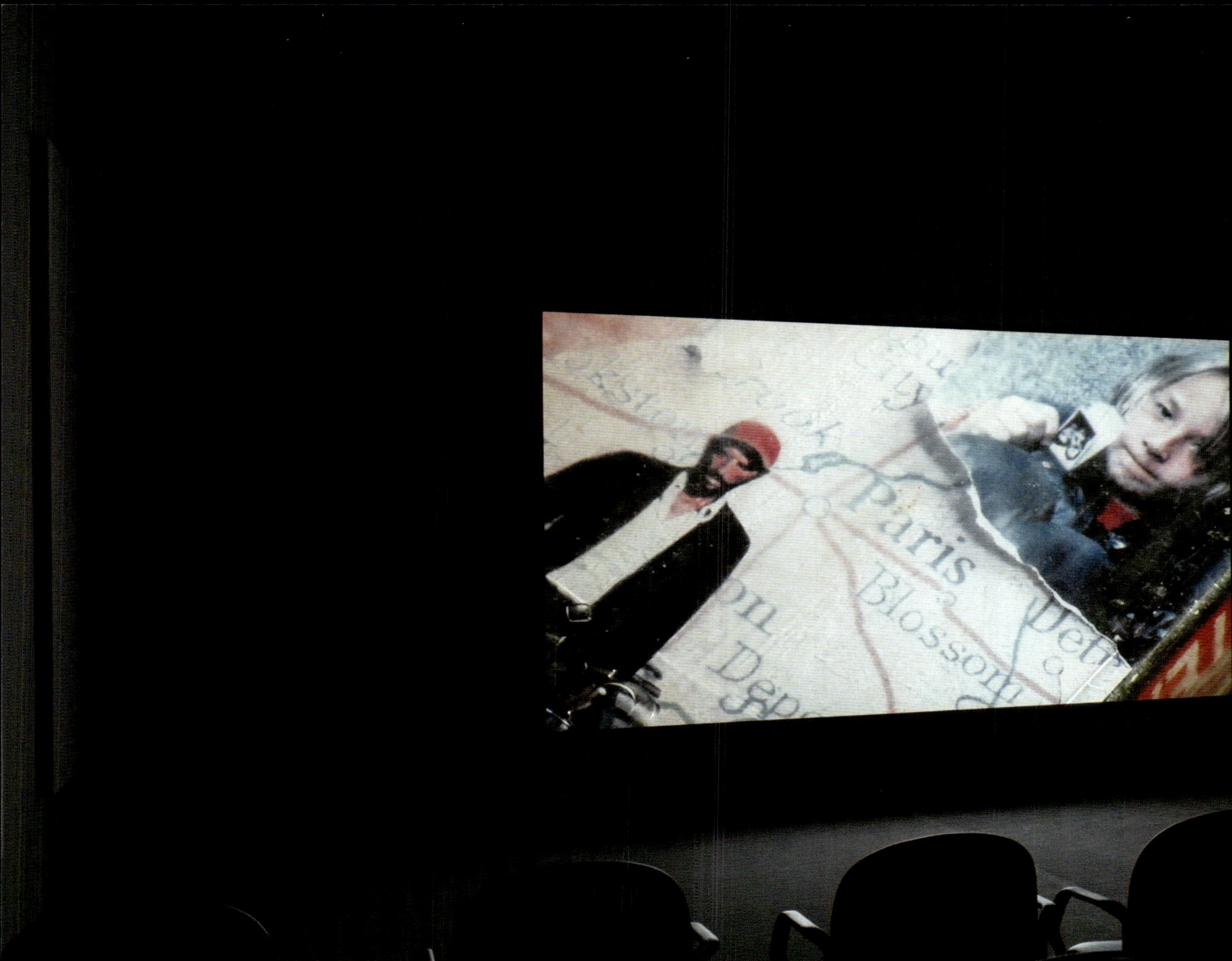
Paris
Blossom

a tree, as additional information is uncovered and further connections made. *Grand Paris Texas* begins as a visual meditation on a formerly central component of a small town's life: its single-screen movie theater, called the Grand. Long abandoned and left to decay, the theater has become a relic of the past. But rather than inflect their subject with wistfulness for the former glory of this once frequented site, Hubbard/Birchler examine the structure with a nearly forensic meticulousness. The theater is a compelling subject not just because it is located in the town that Wim Wenders adopted as the title for his 1984 film or because it represents the nationwide shift toward viewing films in the privacy of our homes on small screens, but because it functions as a time capsule of sorts. Presumably because the owners intended to close the theater only temporarily and re-open at a later date, it is filled with remnants of its former life—from movie posters to cups at the concession stand to empty film canisters that were never removed from the site. Decrepit but still regal, the theater's demise is hardly surprising given the economics of the current mainstream film industry. What is perhaps more surprising is the fact that a town of this size cannot seem to part with its theater, despite its condition. The residents would rather keep a ruin in the middle of town than tear it down because they recognize it as an integral part of their past—a container for shared memories—and perhaps want to keep alive the possibility that the past will be resurrected.

The other central protagonist in *Grand Paris Texas* is, of course, the Wenders film itself. Through a series of interviews with residents of Paris—including the local film critic, the longtime funeral director and a young woman who recounts renting the movie with a group of friends—we learn that despite its title, the Wenders film had very little to do with the actual place. *Paris, Texas,* was neither shot there nor are any of its characters from there. Rather the town comes to symbolize future possibilities, a

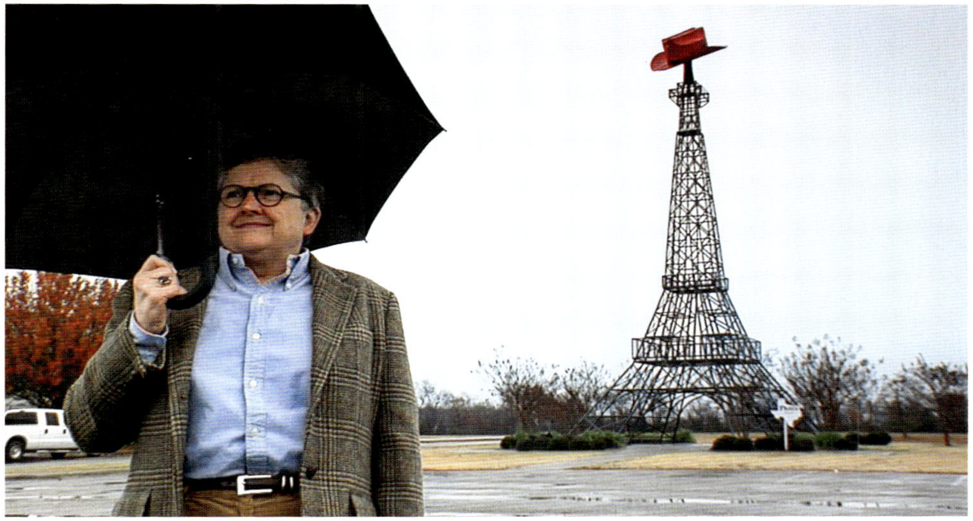

desire for change and new beginnings—something to strive for, a place to start over. And yet, the popularity of the film, not to mention the romanticism of the simple fact that a small town in Texas is named after the "city of light," has had the likely unanticipated effect of leaving a lasting imprint on this Texan community. *Paris, Texas,* the film, has become inextricably linked to the DNA of Paris, Texas, the place. Everyone who lives there knows about the film and those interviewed by Hubbard/Birchler share their experiences of watching it and attempt to interpret its convoluted meanings. Some have had a direct relationship to the film and the mechanisms that accompany Hollywood productions—the critic, for example, played a role in encouraging the production company to screen a premiere of the film at the Grand theater and later met Wenders at the town's miniature Eiffel Tower replica when he was brought to town to be in a commercial for a German newspaper. Mysterious occurrences unfold, such as the fact that the ending of the only available copy of the film—a VHS tape that can be rented from a nearby video store—has been taped over, leaving the conclusion an unanswered question for all those

ABOVE:
Grand Paris Texas, 2009
Video still

OPPOSITE:
Grand Paris Texas, 2009
Installation view,
Collection, Modern Art
Museum of Fort Worth

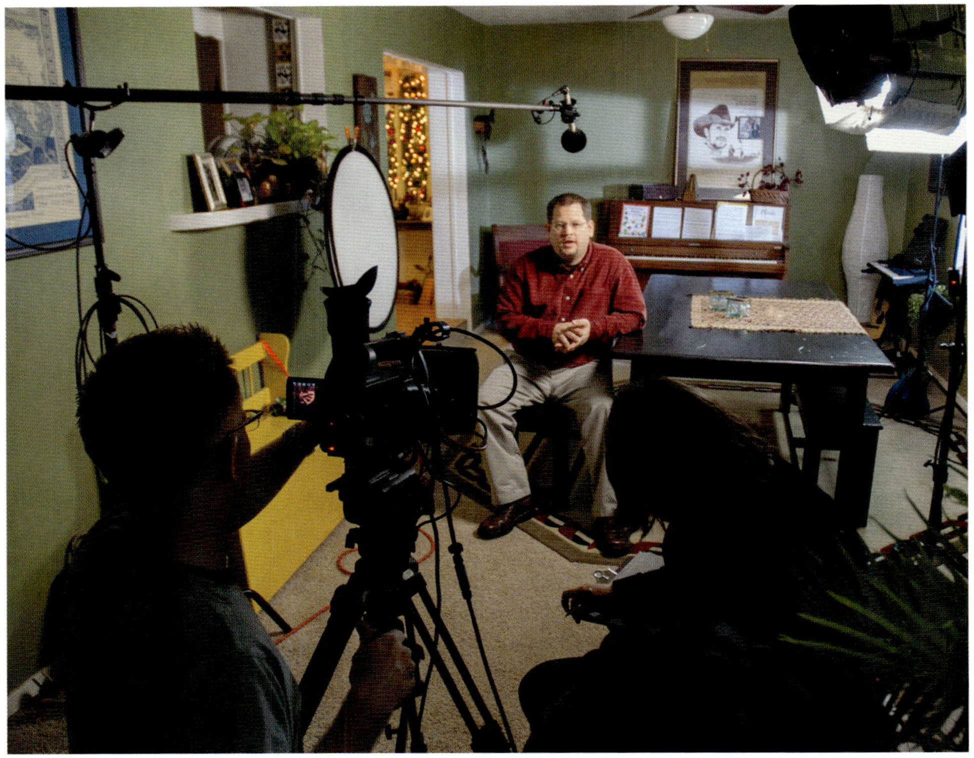

who rent it. In a strange coincidence, the footage that has been added by some unknown person to the VHS tape of *Paris, Texas,* is from *Tumbleweeds*, a silent film made in 1925. The search for a different silent film becomes the subject of another work in the trilogy—*Movie Mountain (Méliès).*

It turns out that yet a third film has directly impacted residents of Paris, Texas. The artists interview a man who at the age of nine starred with Robert Duvall in the 1983 film *Tender Mercies*. Widely acclaimed, the film was nominated for several Oscars, and following this early triumph the boy tried unsuccessfully to launch an acting career. But perhaps the most telling moments in *Grand Paris Texas* are the seemingly innocuous comments by subjects being interviewed that, in fact, reveal a great deal. When the local funeral director proclaims that his job is like that of a film director because it requires the orchestration of an event rather than mere observation, we see that movies are both the model used to understand other activities and the locus of deeply held desire. Similarly, in *Movie Mountain (Méliès)* an elderly gentleman describes his wife as "prettier than Elizabeth Taylor." This reference highlights once again how Hollywood, and specifically its widely admired celebrities, becomes both the fantasy and the point of reference understood as shared cultural knowledge (everyone knows who Elizabeth Taylor is!). But it also reveals the way affinities occur between the individual videos in the trilogy so that they seem to loop in on themselves at certain moments. Here the offhanded reference to Elizabeth Taylor connects perfectly with the third work in the trilogy, *Giant*, which takes up the famous film that starred Taylor alongside Rock Hudson and James Dean. *Movie Mountain (Méliès)* also features a cowboy who recounts moving to Los Angeles to try to be an actor and getting "shot down pretty quick." Back in Texas, where he runs cattle near Movie Mountain, the cowboy's dreams of being part of the Hollywood structure have not subsided despite the passing of many years, as he reads the opening lines from a screenplay he has written and still hopes to make into a movie.

The ostensible intention of *Movie Mountain (Méliès)* is to unravel the back story of how a low-slung butte near the Mexico border came to be given its name and whether, as rumor has it, the lesser-known brother of the famous French filmmaker Georges Méliès, Gaston, is indeed the one who came to the region in 1911 to make a silent film. Despite interviewing seven different people from Sierra Blanca—ranging

ABOVE:
Grand Paris Texas, 2009
Production still

OPPOSITE:
Movie Mountain (Méliès), 2011
Production still

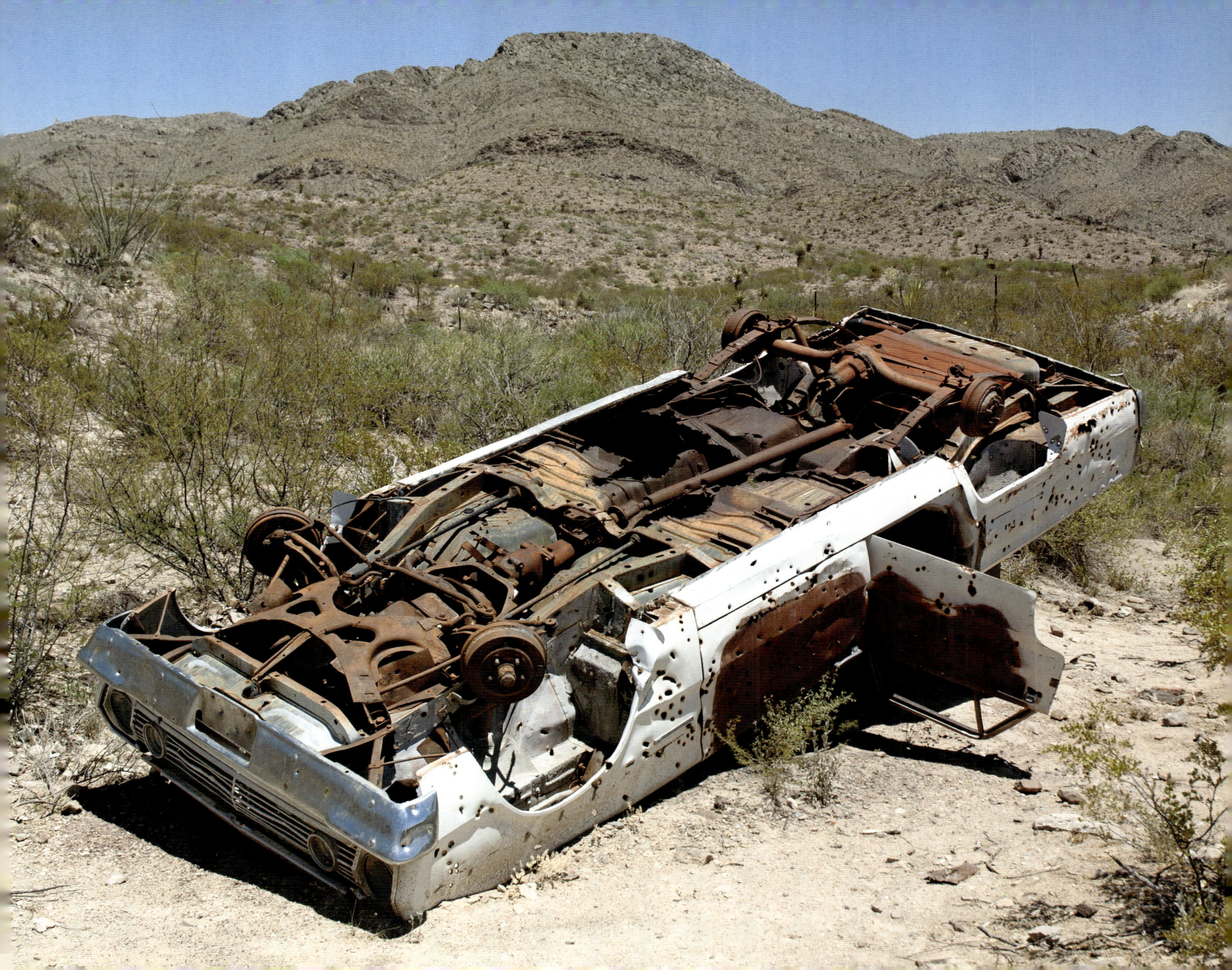

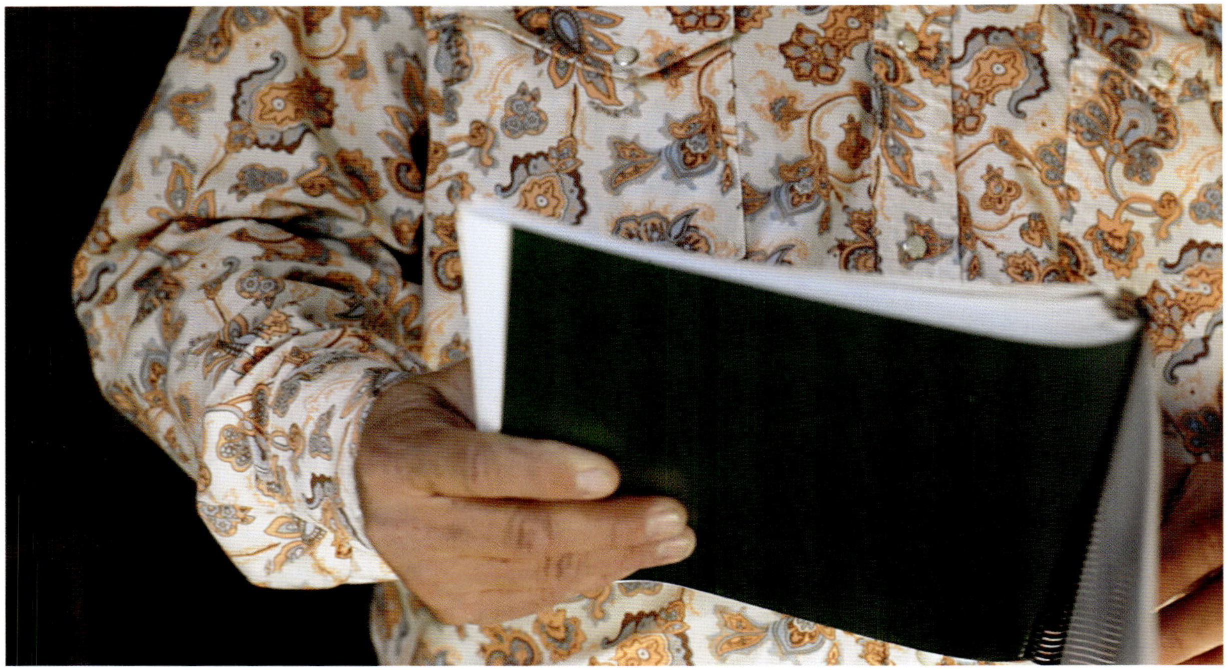

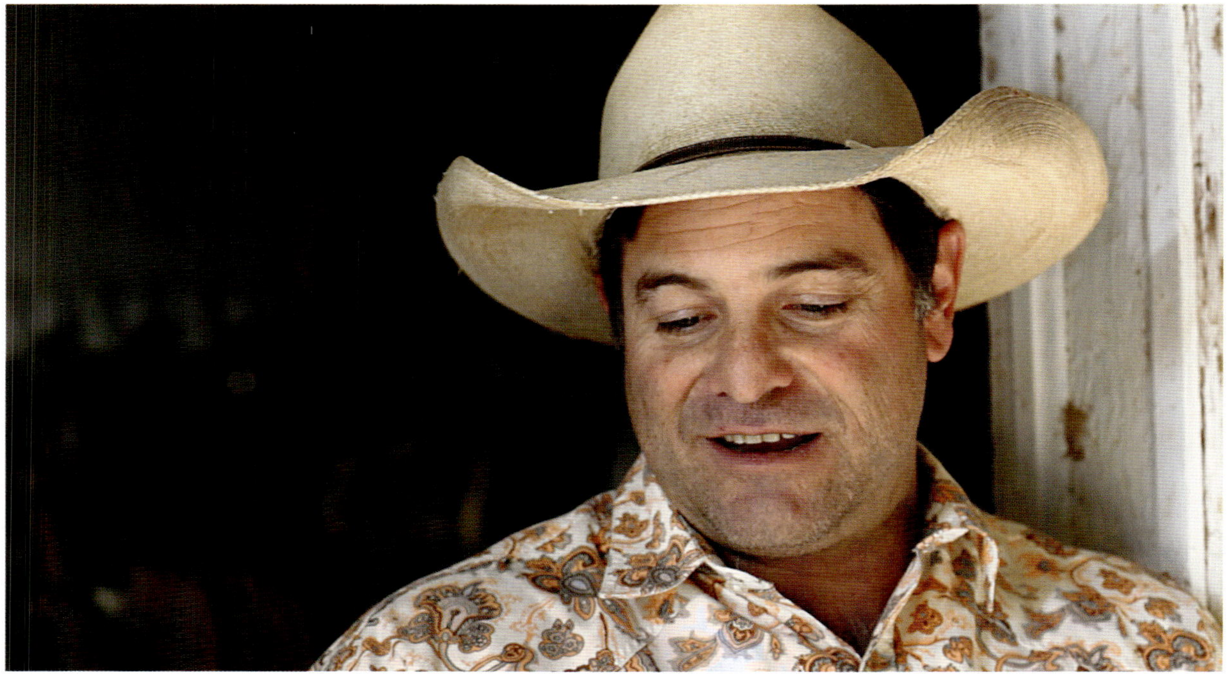

Movie Mountain (Méliès), 2011
Video stills

from a man who has been there several times but never knew it was called Movie Mountain to a woman whose family emigrated from Mexico during the revolution and whose uncle supposedly worked on the film—the mystery is never solved. The video ends with the voiceover of one of those interviewed saying "I have no idea why they chose that site to take a movie." We're left with the image of a landscape that bears the lasting trace of a brief encounter with the film industry, resulting in this unremarkable mountain range being officially named Movie Mountain. Ultimately, *Movie Mountain (Méliès)* becomes a view into small-town Texas life with its foundation in homesteading and ranching, its distinct ties to Mexico and its wonderfully compelling residents. Various people recall their tangential connections to the film and it is when one subject begins to speculate wildly about how a film crew in the early twentieth century might have gotten to the site and what they would have eaten along the way that we are reminded how tricky memory can be. Nothing expressed by these subjects is necessarily reliable information. Much of it is second hand, based in sketchy memories, or simply fabricated, and we're compelled by the knowledge that the evidence presented to audiences through the genre of the documentary can sometimes be circumstantial at best. The parts appear to add up to a whole, but in fact, when closely examined, they may be no more than mere speculation or even fantastical projection.

Movie Mountain (Méliès) both opens and closes with a scene of a sound technician setting up his large boom microphone outside. Throughout the video, we hear the sound of the wind, the passing traffic and the train's whistle as it runs through town without stopping. In this work, as in the others in the trilogy, the landscape is an important and wholly absorbing subject.

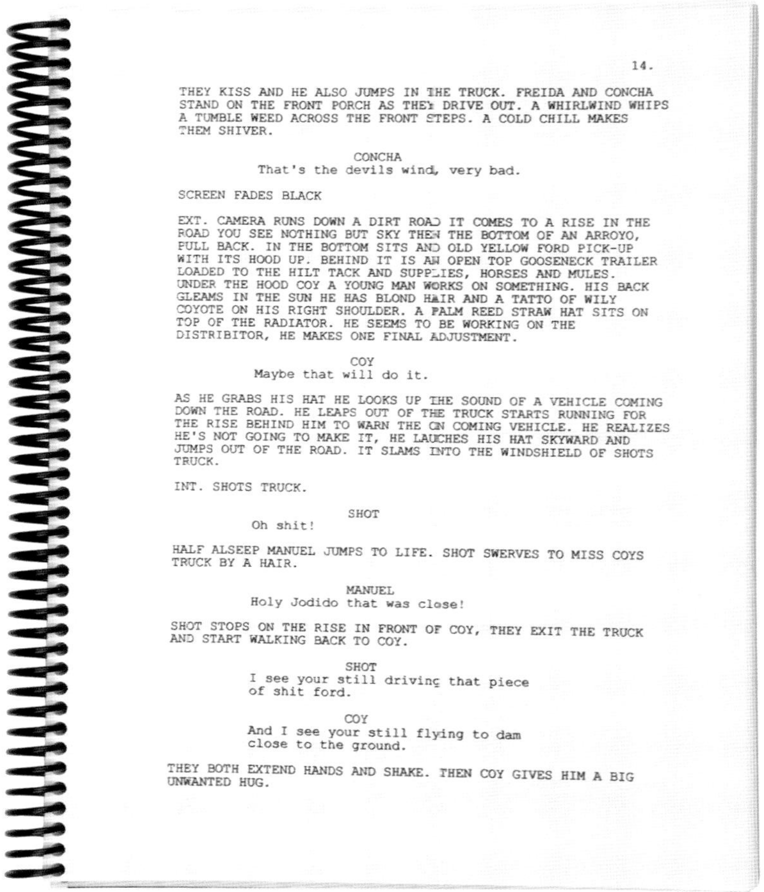
14.

THEY KISS AND HE ALSO JUMPS IN THE TRUCK. FREIDA AND CONCHA STAND ON THE FRONT PORCH AS THEY DRIVE OUT. A WHIRLWIND WHIPS A TUMBLE WEED ACROSS THE FRONT STEPS. A COLD CHILL MAKES THEM SHIVER.

CONCHA
That's the devils wind, very bad.

SCREEN FADES BLACK

EXT. CAMERA RUNS DOWN A DIRT ROAD IT COMES TO A RISE IN THE ROAD YOU SEE NOTHING BUT SKY THEN THE BOTTOM OF AN ARROYO, PULL BACK. IN THE BOTTOM SITS AND OLD YELLOW FORD PICK-UP WITH ITS HOOD UP. BEHIND IT IS AN OPEN TOP GOOSENECK TRAILER LOADED TO THE HILT TACK AND SUPPLIES, HORSES AND MULES. UNDER THE HOOD COY A YOUNG MAN WORKS ON SOMETHING. HIS BACK GLEAMS IN THE SUN HE HAS BLOND HAIR AND A TATTO OF WILY COYOTE ON HIS RIGHT SHOULDER. A PALM REED STRAW HAT SITS ON TOP OF THE RADIATOR. HE SEEMS TO BE WORKING ON THE DISTRIBITOR, HE MAKES ONE FINAL ADJUSTMENT.

COY
Maybe that will do it.

AS HE GRABS HIS HAT HE LOOKS UP THE SOUND OF A VEHICLE COMING DOWN THE ROAD. HE LEAPS OUT OF THE TRUCK STARTS RUNNING FOR THE RISE BEHIND HIM TO WARN THE ON COMING VEHICLE. HE REALIZES HE'S NOT GOING TO MAKE IT, HE LAUCHES HIS HAT SKYWARD AND JUMPS OUT OF THE ROAD. IT SLAMS INTO THE WINDSHIELD OF SHOTS TRUCK.

INT. SHOTS TRUCK.

SHOT
Oh shit!

HALF ALSEEP MANUEL JUMPS TO LIFE. SHOT SWERVES TO MISS COYS TRUCK BY A HAIR.

MANUEL
Holy Jodido that was close!

SHOT STOPS ON THE RISE IN FRONT OF COY, THEY EXIT THE TRUCK AND START WALKING BACK TO COY.

SHOT
I see your still driving that piece of shit ford.

COY
And I see your still flying to dam close to the ground.

THEY BOTH EXTEND HANDS AND SHAKE. THEN COY GIVES HIM A BIG UNWANTED HUG.

The recorded sound is an integral component of how time is portrayed by Hubbard/Birchler, one that is remarkably distinct from much of what we have become accustomed to seeing in contemporary culture. The quick pace of life and the abundance of stimulation that characterizes urban life today are often represented in moving-image mediums through chaotic scenes, saturated colors and rapid-fire editing. In what serves as an antidote or welcome relief to this approach, Hubbard/Birchler deliberately slow down time in

The screenplay *A Walk in the Park* by David Armstrong, registered in 2004 with The Writers Guild of America, West Inc.

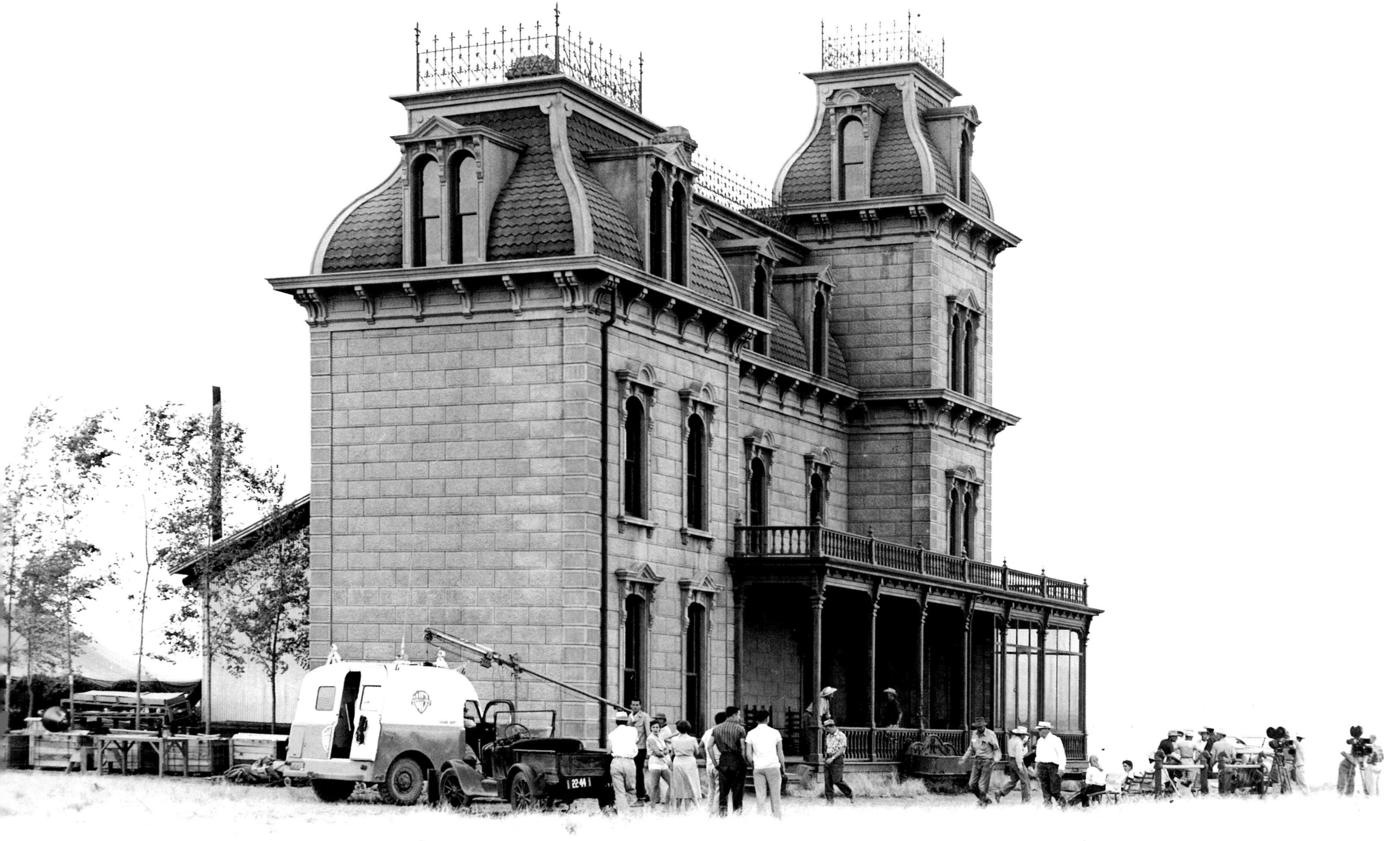

Sound Speed Marker. This is a kind of geologic time that is patient, meticulous and gradually unfolding. As with their earlier works employing the loop, the artists resist a sense of linear time by acknowledging the constant push and pull between the past and the present. The past will always inform the present, but the present is in a continual state of emerging. They are inextricably connected but each nonetheless has a distinct temporality.

Giant (2014), the final work in the trilogy, is a three-channel video projection that takes as its subject the 1956 Hollywood production of the same name and interweaves and overlaps two aspects of the now-iconic film: the lengthy contract that Warner Bros. made with property owners in Fort Davis, Texas, and the now dilapidated yet surprisingly still extant set of Reata, the ranch home that was built on that private property and sixty years later still sits amidst the landscape as a strange relic. Penetratingly contemplative and beautiful footage of the decaying set and its surrounding landscape as it changes throughout the seasons is juxtaposed with staged scenes of a secretary in the Warner Bros. Burbank offices in 1955 carefully typing up the contract that will later lead to the erection of the set. Although Hubbard/Birchler's trilogy never reverts to nostalgia, it does examine the inevitable obsolescence of technologies. *Giant* observes the typewriter upon which the secretary taps away with enormous care and scrutiny. It, too, is as much an historical artifact of a past event as the set itself. In *Grand Paris Texas*, the theater's former projectionist describes in great detail the process of showing film and switching the reels in order to maintain the image without interruption. The worn VHS tape of *Paris, Texas*, also figures prominently. Indeed, these technologies become metaphors for a meditation on time, memory and the changes that we witness throughout our lives.

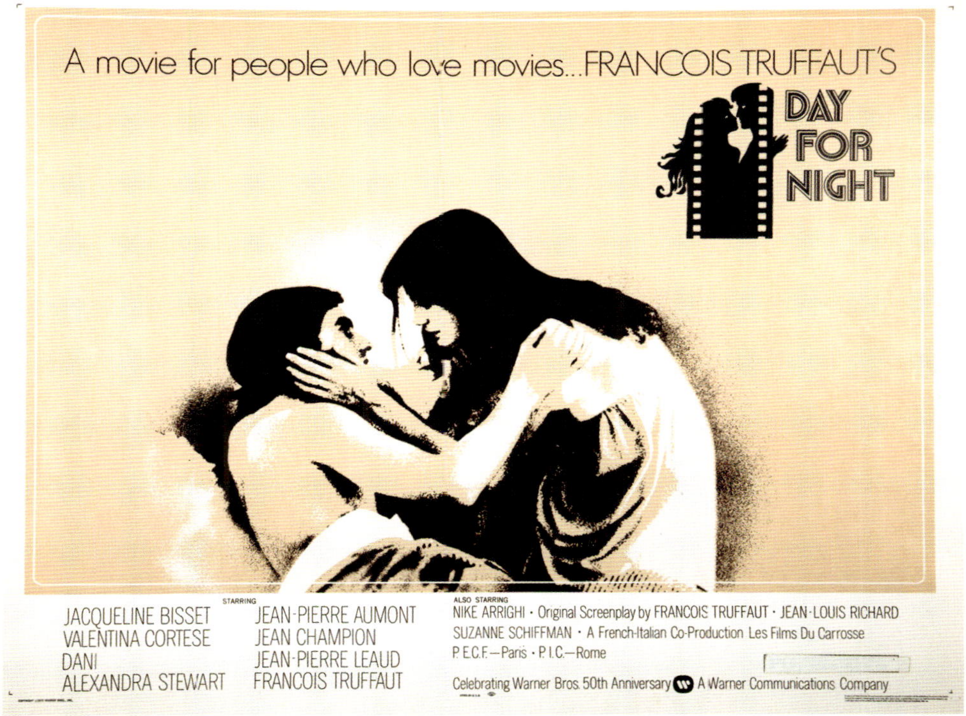

ABOVE:
Promotional movie poster for *Day for Night*, 1973

OPPOSITE:
Reata film set from the Warner Bros. production *Giant*, 1956, photographed in 1955

Despite the evidence of these changes, *Sound Speed Marker* makes abundantly clear that the language of cinema is here to stay.

In a rare sculptural work, Hubbard/Birchler take up film's integration into our everyday lives with both humor and poignancy. *Missing Truffaut* (2014) replicates a quotidian wooden lamppost and the type of handmade sign we sadly regularly find adhered to its surface announcing the loss of a pet. In bold black letters the sign broadcasts this unfortunate event and features a photo of the black-and-white "tuxedo" cat gone missing. Naming a cat after one of the French New Wave's most prolific and critically acclaimed filmmakers would seem to indicate a belief he had fully entered the mainstream, yet the cat's owners seem to have second thoughts about this, reflected in the addition of a parenthetical phonetic description of his name, reading "ANSWERS TO THE NAME TRUFFAUT (TRUE-FOE)," which seems to underscore the melancholy we feel when seeing these arguably futile attempts at communication. Captured in *Missing Truffaut*'s simple gesture is the range of effects the cinema has inscribed in our culture, from the enormous innovations of film's avant-garde in the 1950s and 1960s to the appropriation of the genre's noteworthy references into totally unrelated aspects of our daily lives.

No matter whether the specifics of its production or reception adapt and transform (film replaced with digital media, the movie theater less frequented than the individual screen, the VHS and the DVD set aside in favor of the download), the cinema—as an experience of narrative, space, time and memory—has irreversibly altered culture. It is a phenomenon so profoundly integrated into our society that we can map its innumerable points of contact even within a relatively specific geography. Hardly living in a post-cinema world, Hubbard/Birchler's trilogy seems to argue that we are living in a world saturated with the cinema effect.

1 In 2008, I was one of a team of curators at the Hirshhorn Museum & Sculpture Garden in Washington, DC, that organized a two-part exhibition entitled *The Cinema Effect: Illusion, Reality, and the Moving Image*. I borrow this title from the exhibition, in which Hubbard/Birchler participated, as it perfectly captures the desire to examine the impact of the cinema on society and culture in which the artists are engaged.

2 Jean Baudrillard, *The Vital Illusion* (New York: Columbia University Press, 2000), p. 71.

Giant, 2014
Production still

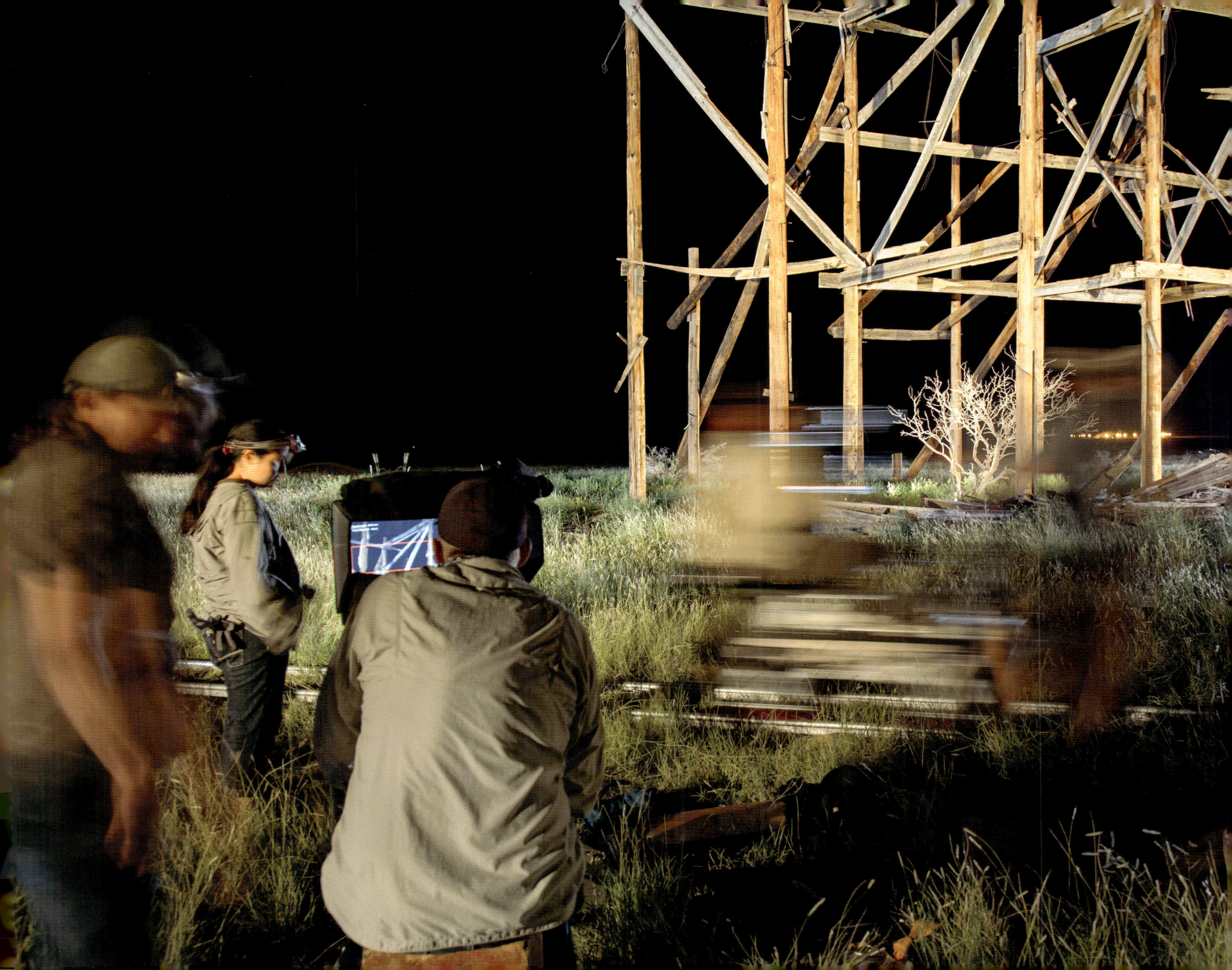

MISSING TRUFFAUT, 2014
Lamp, wooden pole, laser print on paper
Installation dimensions variable

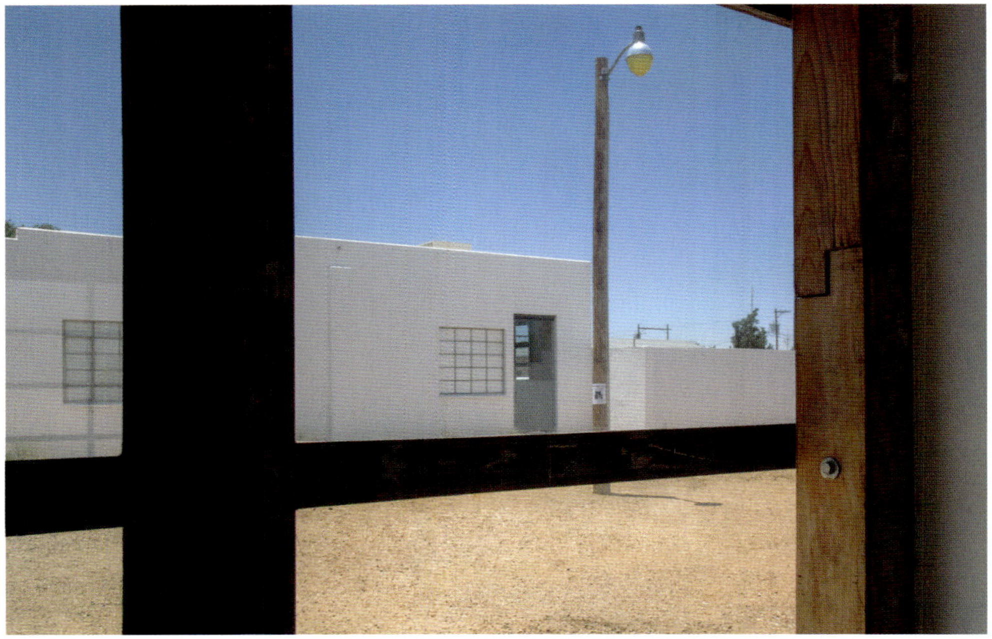

Missing Truffaut, 2014
Installation view,
Ballroom Marfa

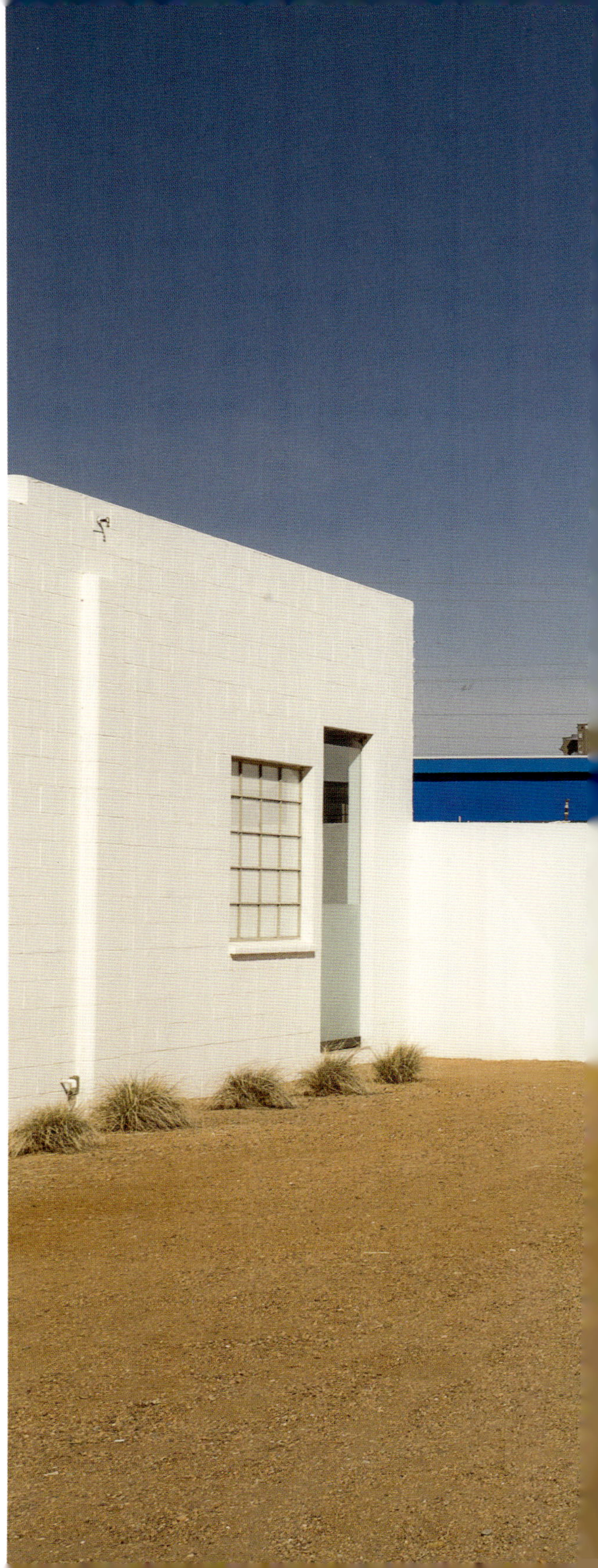

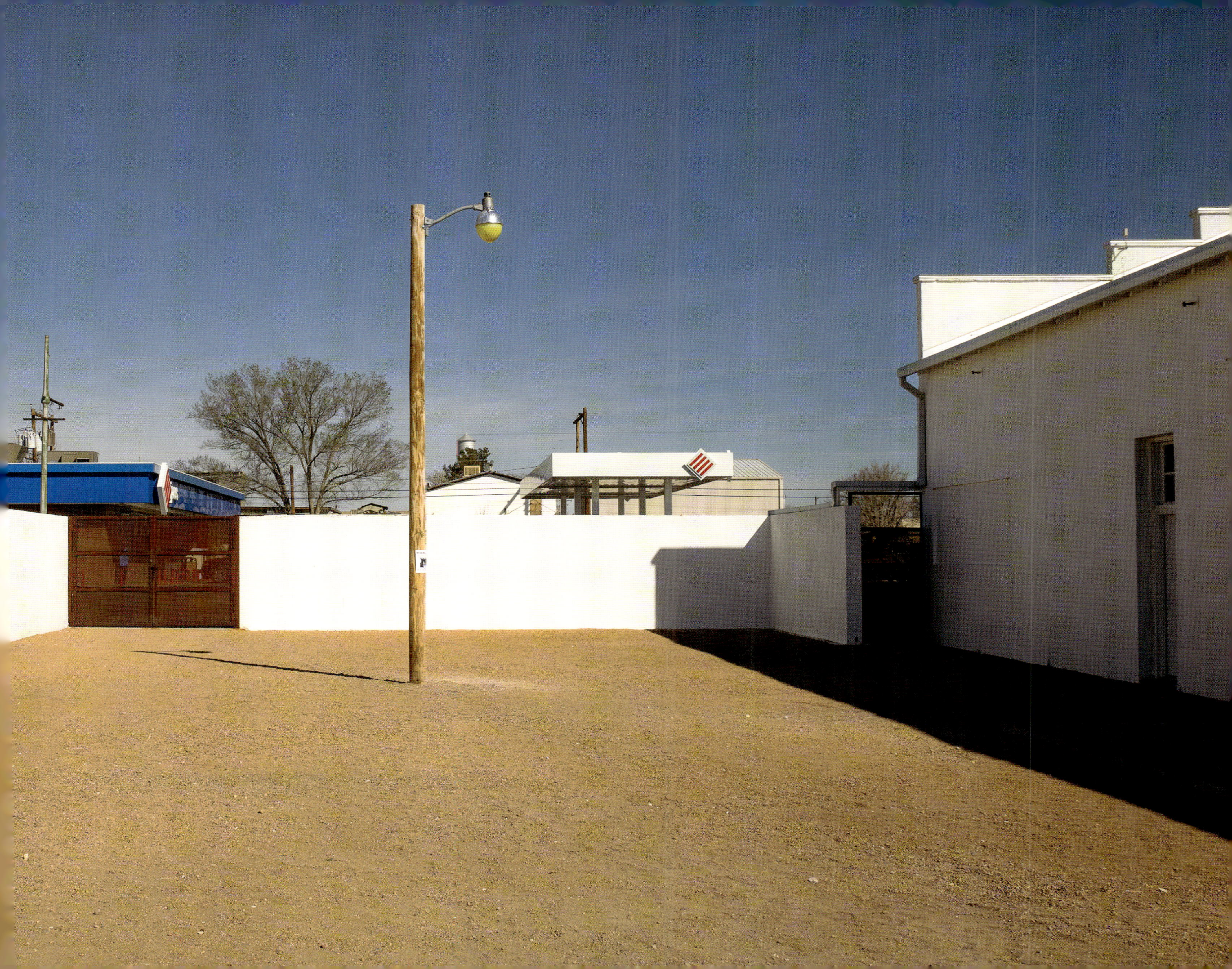

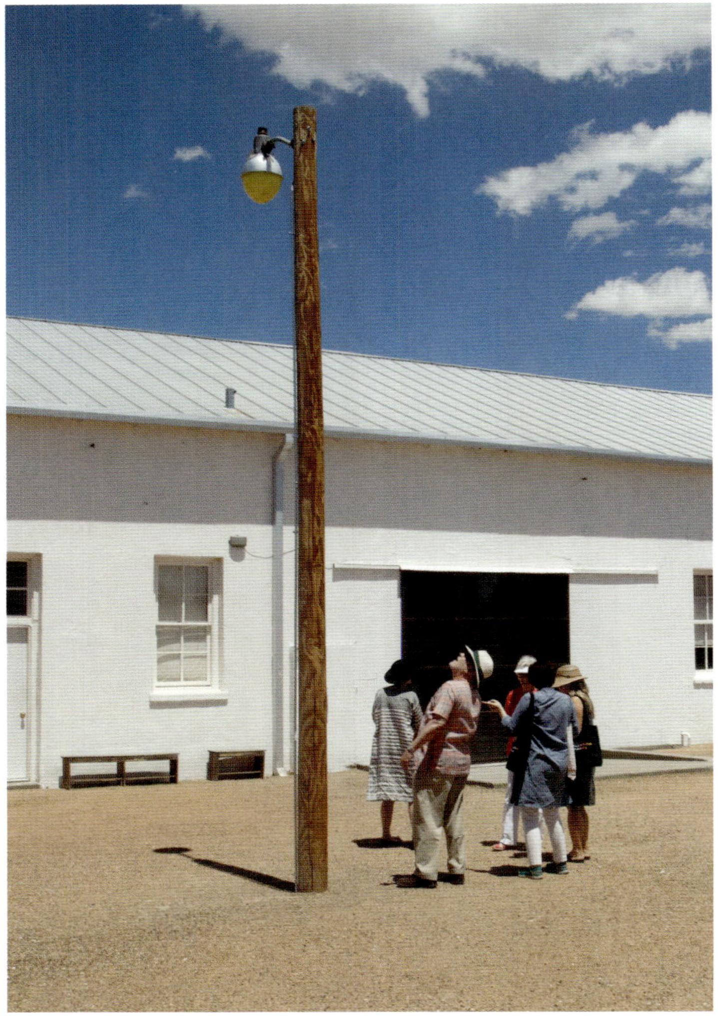

Missing Truffaut, 2014
Installation views,
Ballroom Marfa

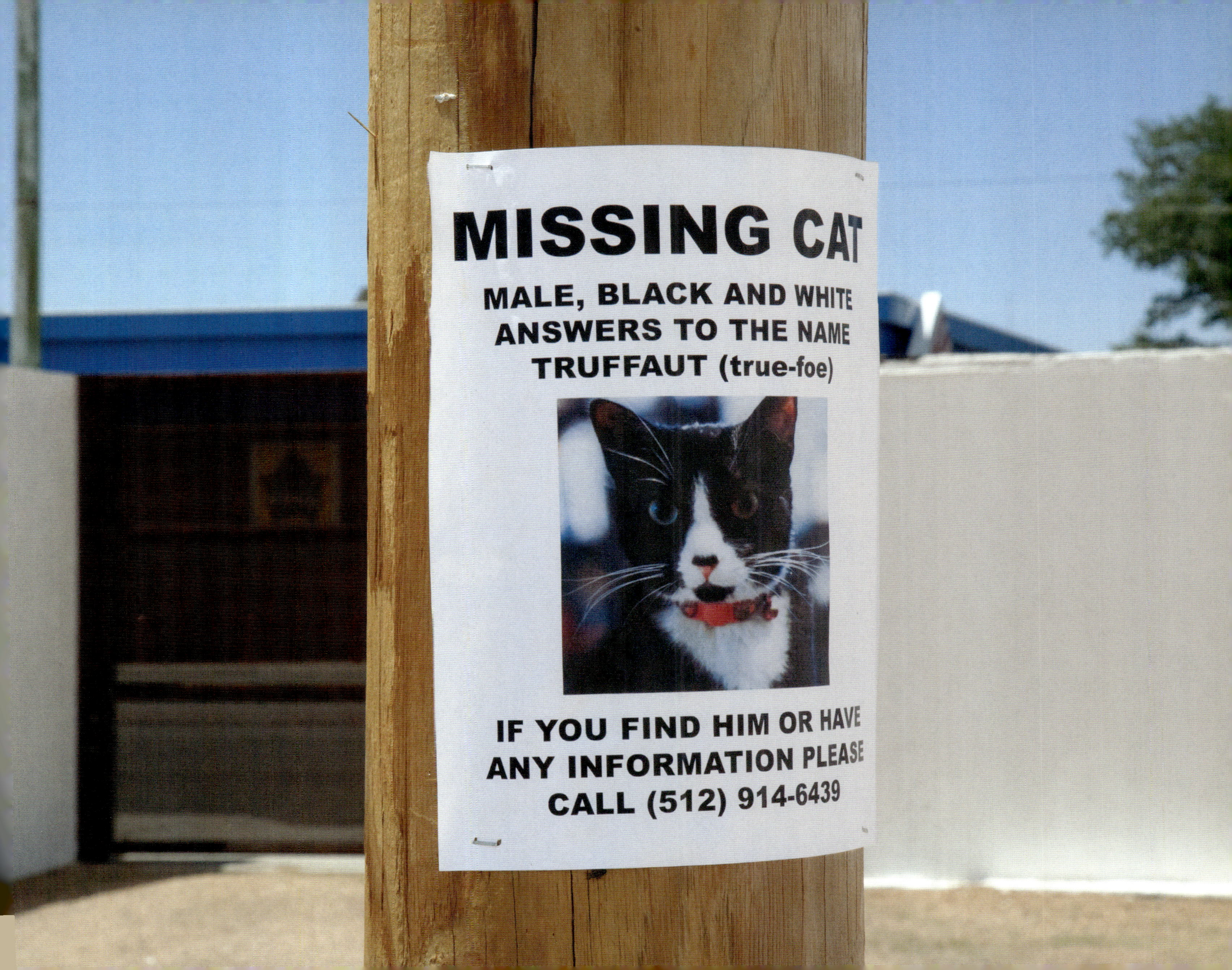
MISSING CAT
MALE, BLACK AND WHITE
ANSWERS TO THE NAME
TRUFFAUT (true-foe)
IF YOU FIND HIM OR HAVE
ANY INFORMATION PLEASE
CALL (512) 914-6439

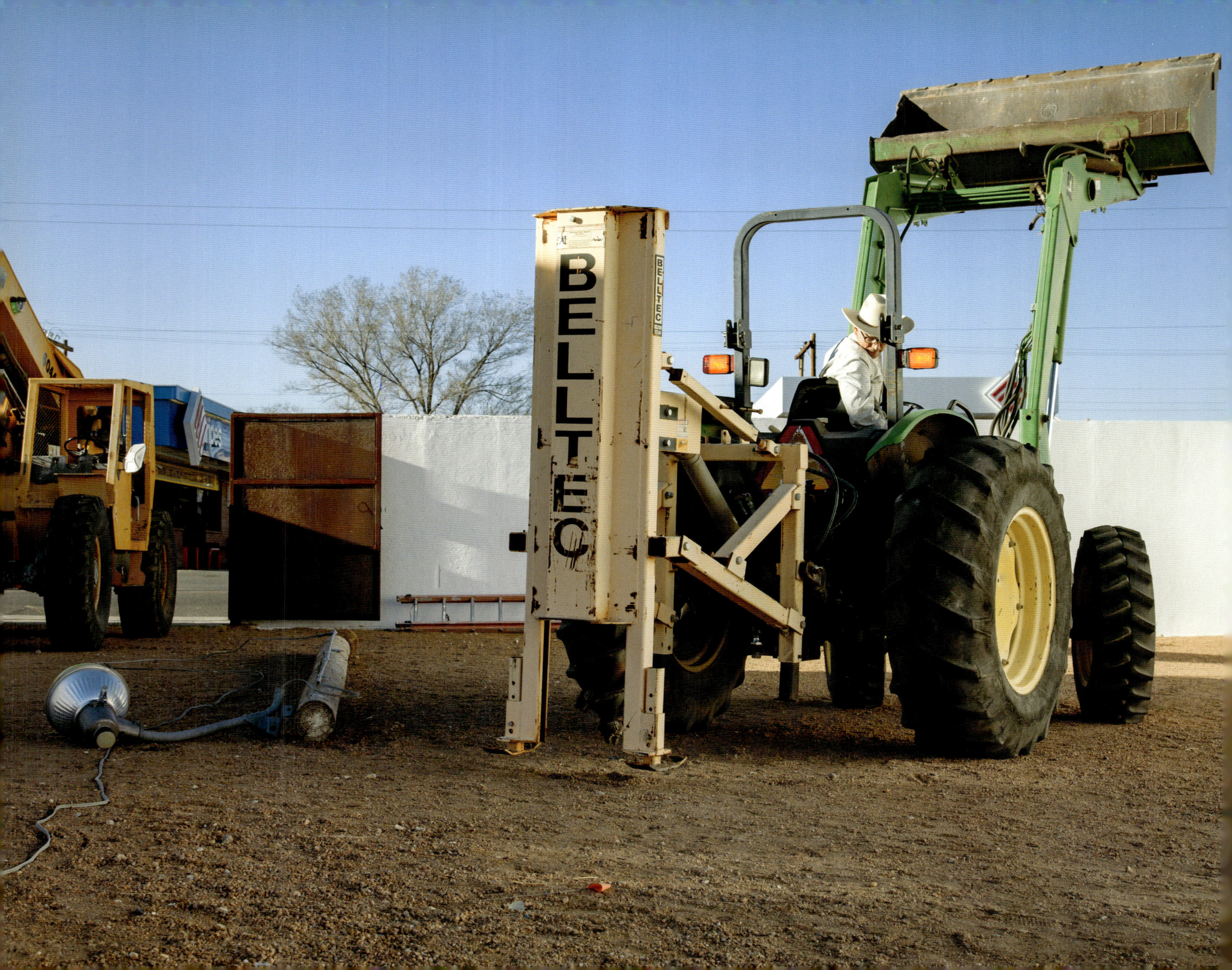
BELLTEC
BELLTEC

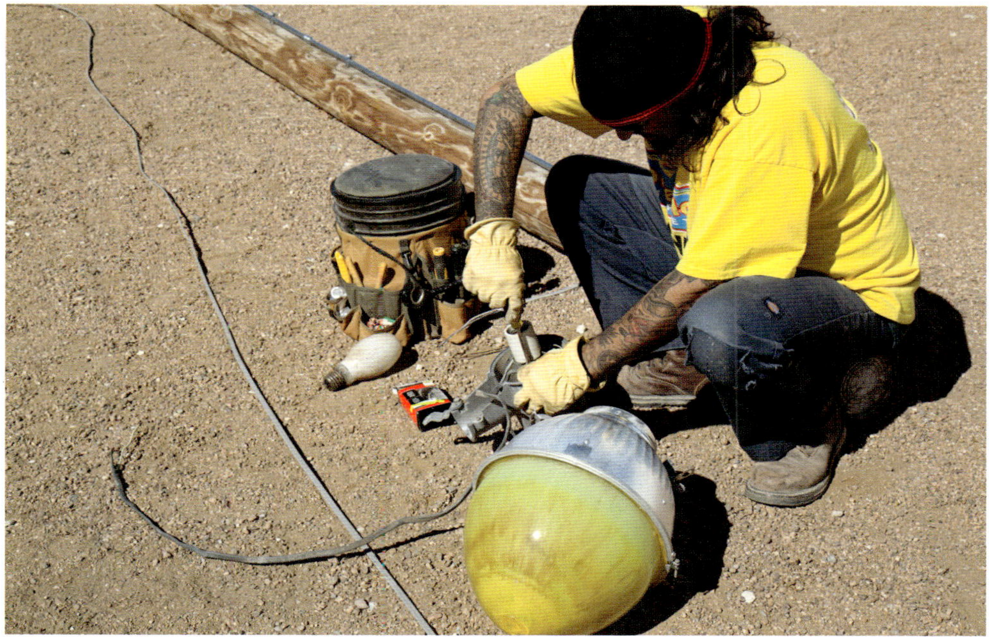

Missing Truffaut, 2014
Production stills

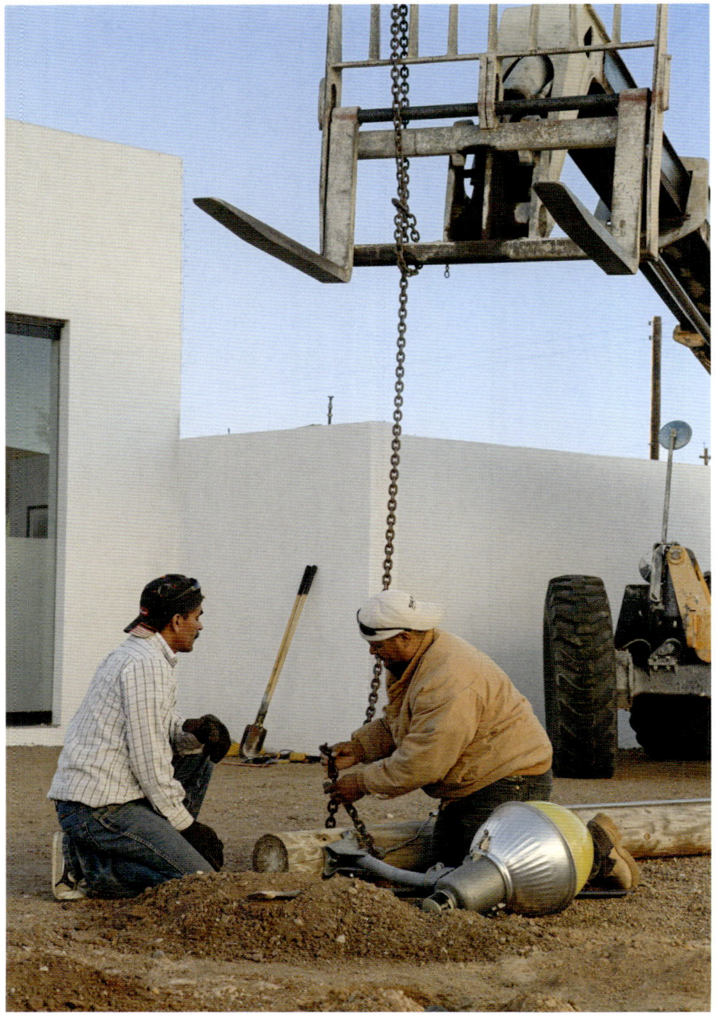

Missing Truffaut, 2014
Production stills

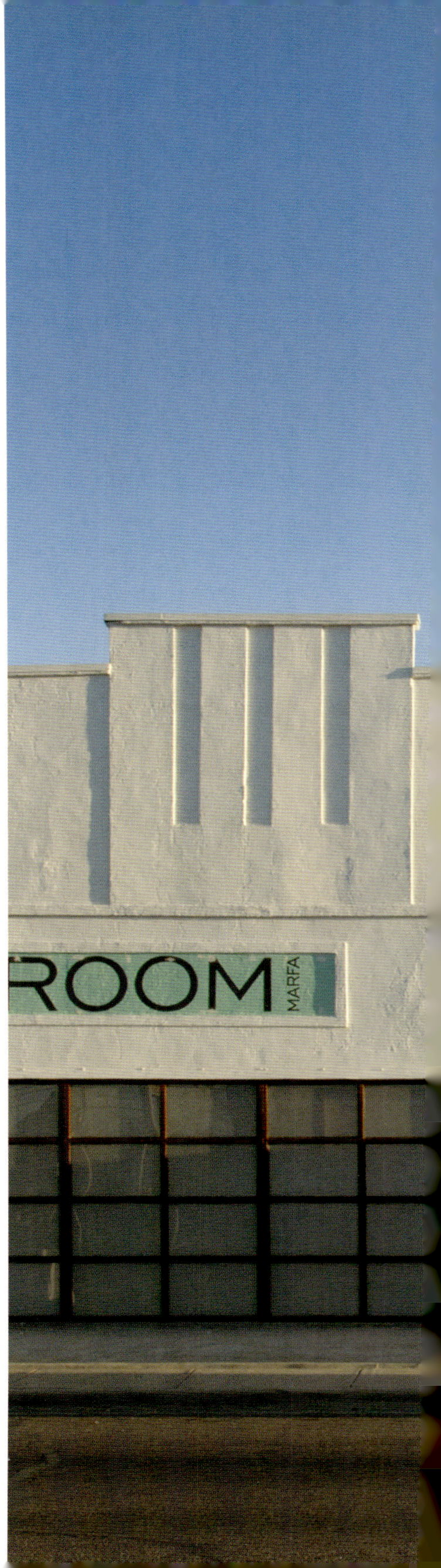

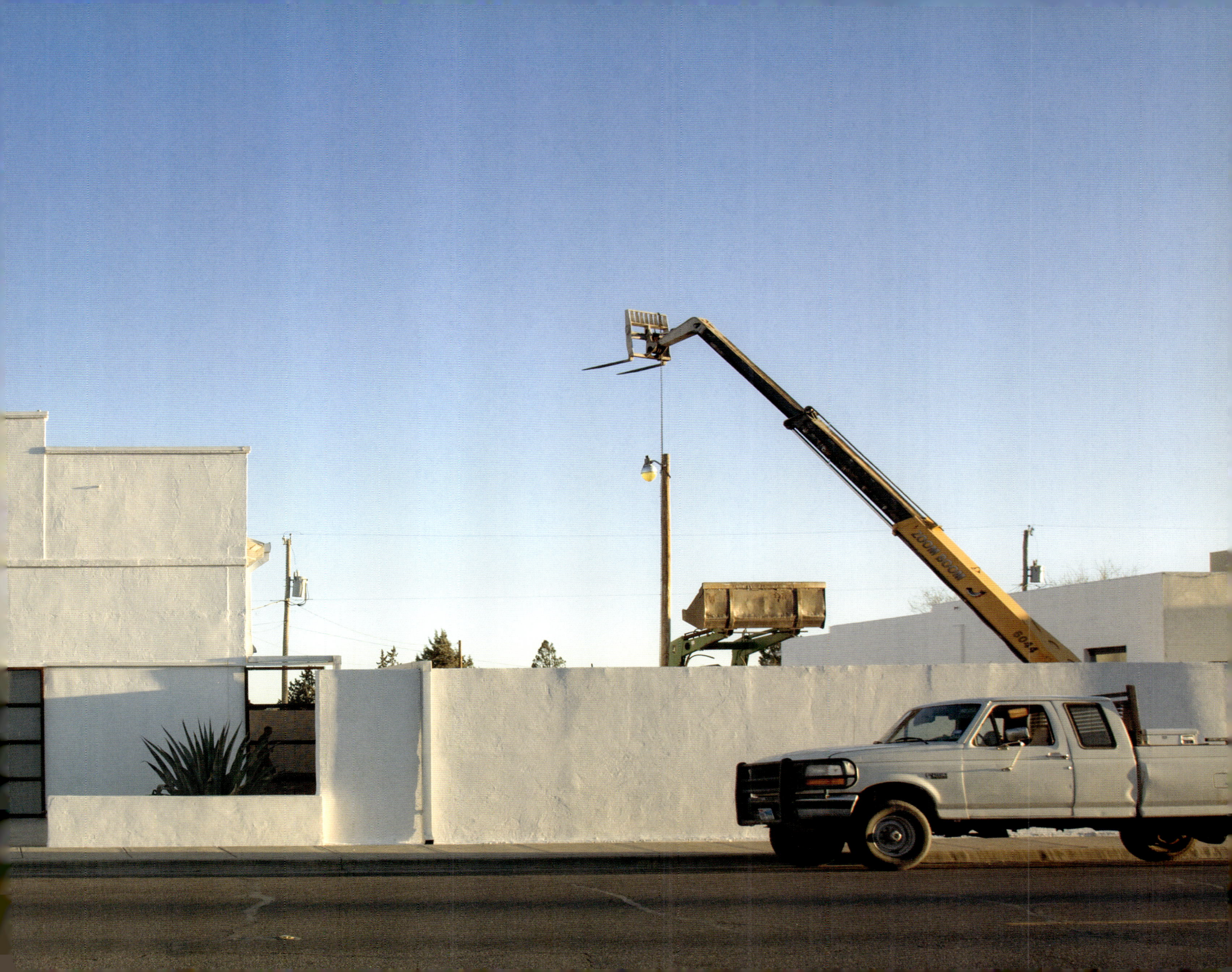
ZOOM BOOM
6044

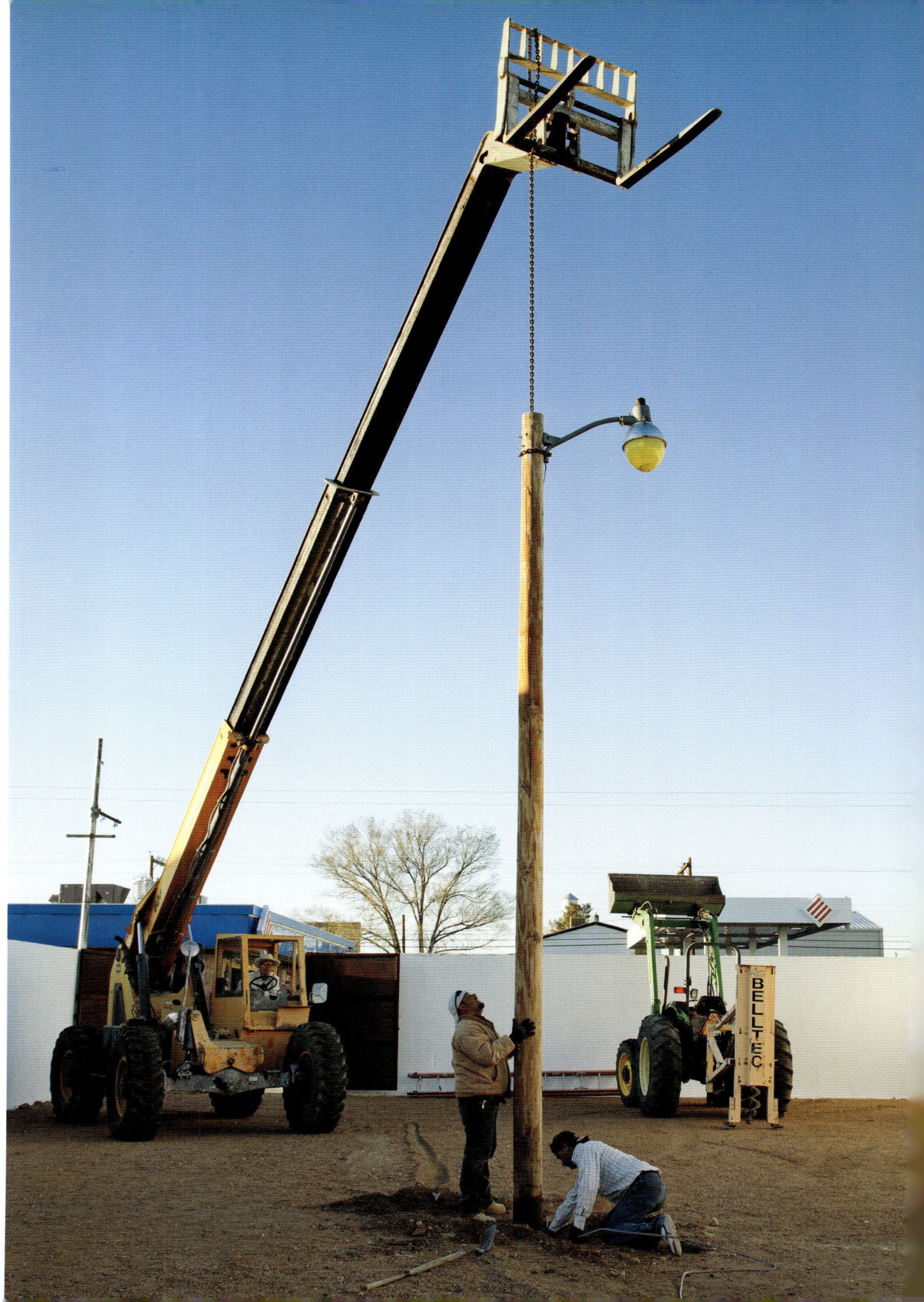

Missing Truffaut, 2014
Production stills

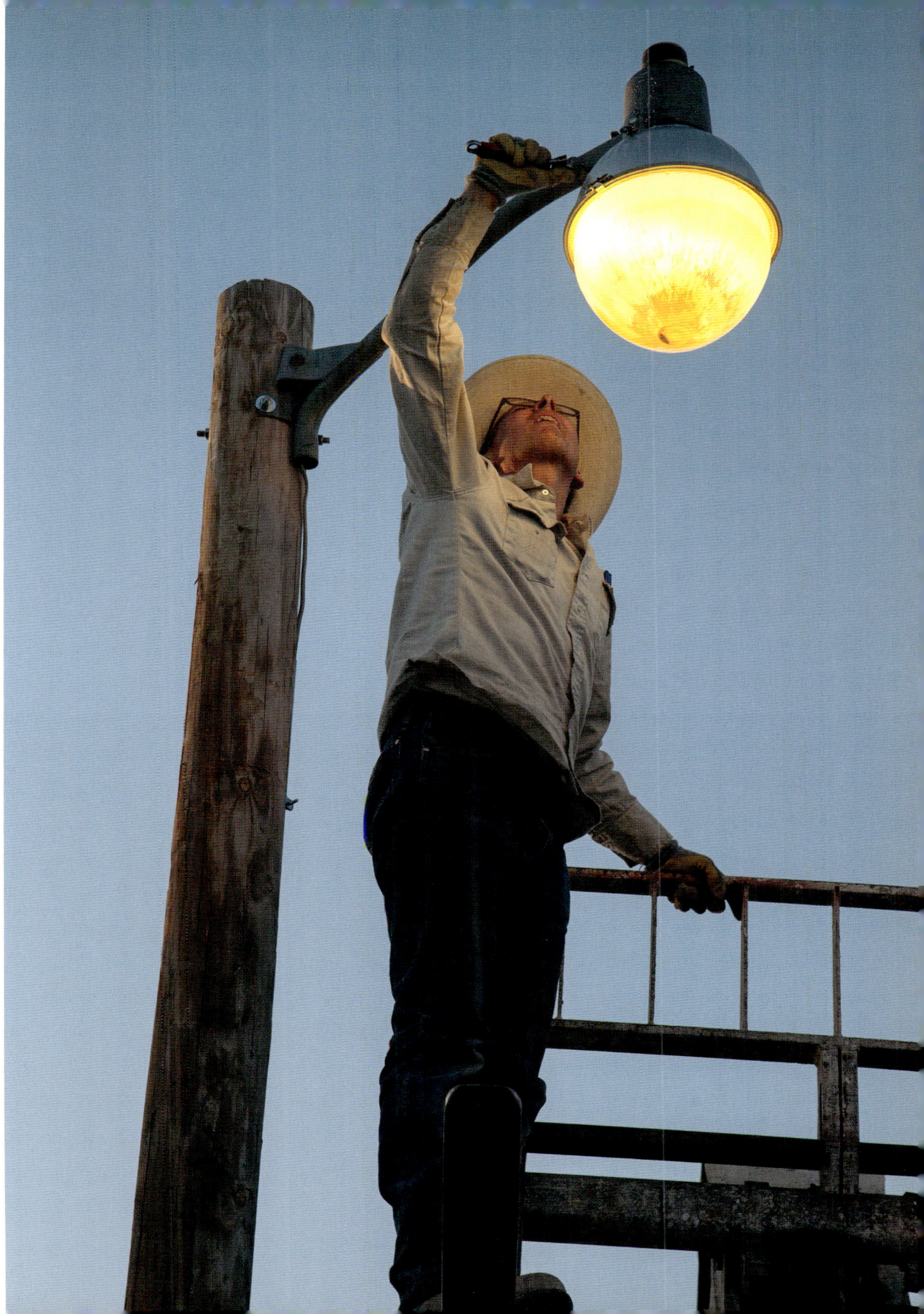

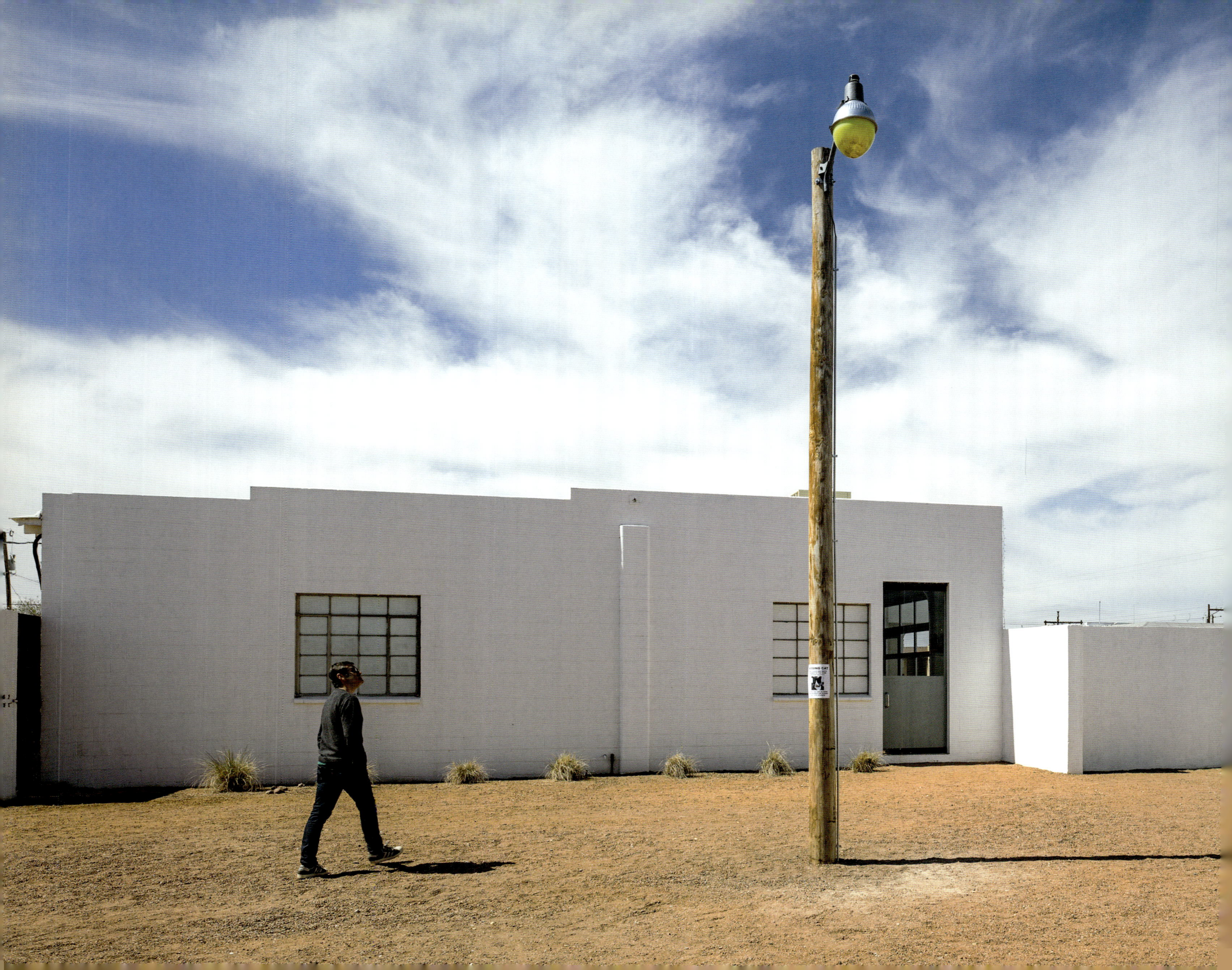

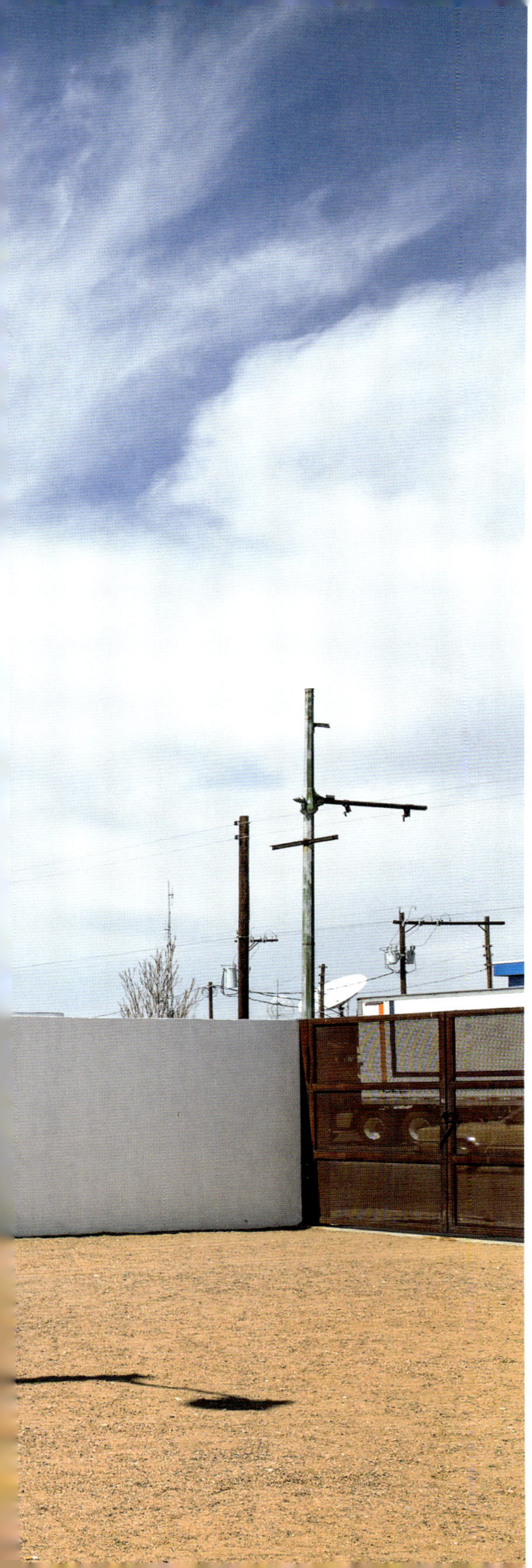

Missing Truffaut, 2014
Installation view,
Ballroom Marfa

INKA GRAEVE INGELMANN

Films and Funerals: A Conversation with Teresa Hubbard and Alexander Birchler

INKA GRAEVE INGELMANN: In the collection of the Pinakothek der Moderne in Munich there are two of your works produced around the turn of the millennium that seem to paradigmatically formulate your artistic concerns of that time. There is the four-part series *Filmstills,* made in 2000 in Berlin, an homage to the cinema as a social and urban site; and there is the video installation *Eight,* built around your protagonist's eighth birthday, in which you lay out the entire artistic grammar of your video works for those and subsequent years: a nonlinear narration that continually repeats and yet remains open, the apparently seamless sliding of the camera between exterior and interior space and the translation of the psychic processes and emotional conflicts of your mainly female protagonists into image and sound. The trilogy *Grand Paris Texas, Movie Mountain (Méliès)* and *Giant,* which you created over the past five years, represents a new stage of development within your artistic career. On the one hand, you pick up on central themes from your earlier works, while you simultaneously enter new terrain, especially formally—what I would refer to as a "shift toward the documentary." From different narrative perspectives and with various formal means, all three works comprise a kind of search for traces.

Grand Paris Texas, which seems the closest to a classic documentary film, pursues the present and history of the Grand Theater in the Texas town of Paris, and connects with the memories of various residents whose lives show a relationship to the theater as well as to Wim Wenders's masterpiece *Paris, Texas,* from 1984. As in a palimpsest, accounts and images are overlaid and bring the Grand, as well as Wenders's film, back to life from the perspective of the residents of Paris, Texas,

Eighteen, 2013
Production still

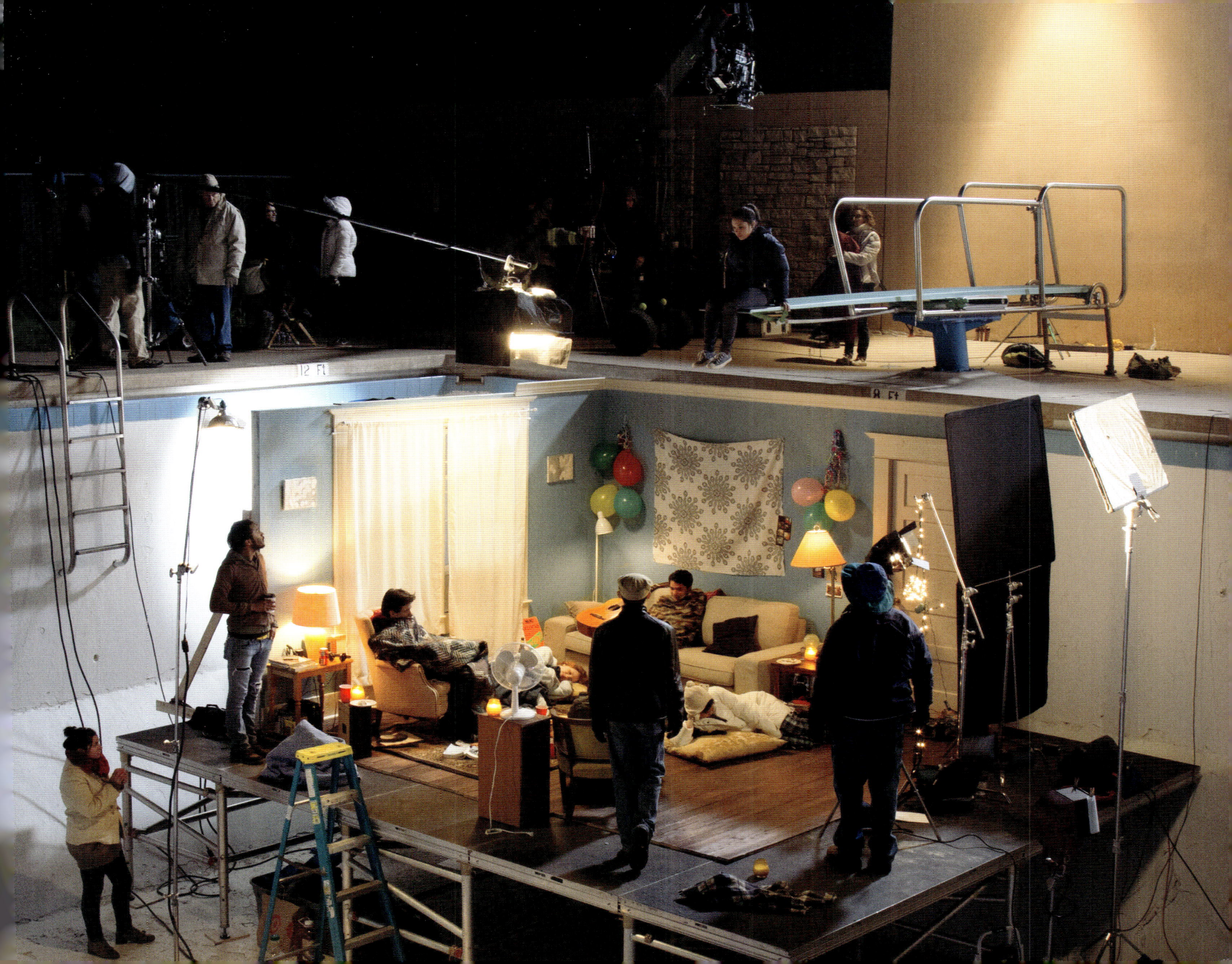
12 Ft
8 Ft

in the viewer's mind's eye. Seemingly less stringent is the account of *Movie Mountain (Méliès)*, a geographical feature known by this name near Sierra Blanca, where a silent Western was filmed in 1911, though none of the protagonists you interviewed themselves remembered it. Unlike *Grand Paris Texas*, *Movie Mountain (Méliès)* is a two-channel installation, in which the two projections at times show different pictorial and temporal levels, though occasionally also only a single shot, thus allowing a formally more multi-layered narrative. At the same time, however, the camera, in a manner similar to the vague second- and third-hand reports, remains at a distance to Movie Mountain, while in *Grand Paris Texas* it penetrates the innermost recesses of the theater like a probe. As the third and concluding part, *Giant* unfolds its narrative in three projections but eschews interviews or dialogue entirely. The real on-site explorations of a monumental relic from the eponymous film epic is coupled with the fictive account of the transcription of the original film contract, and as in a near-documentary film, its production design brings the viewer immediately back to the early days of the film. Thus, in contrast to your previous, unambiguously fictional works that denied linearity, this group of works makes immediate reference to real events in the present and the past. How should this turn to the documentary be understood?

TERESA HUBBARD: Considering the connections and differences between *Eight* and *Filmstills* and how these works stand in relation to the trilogy in *Sound Speed Marker* is an ideal place to start our conversation. In order to get closer to your question, I should begin a few years before *Eight* and *Filmstills* were realized. In the early 1990s, at the onset of our collaboration, Alexander and I were both working mostly in sculpture and thinking a lot about artifacts and the construction of their aura and narrativity as used in archaeology, ethnology and natural history museums. One of the works from that period that remains relevant is *Contestants in a Birdhouse Competition* (1991/96). From the beginning, photography was a part of our process and a few years into our practice we began to work almost exclusively with that medium—mostly in a closed studio setting, creating what people have described as staged narratives. These constructed settings were always sourced from actual locations and events or moments we experienced. The best way to describe these staged narratives would be using the idea of composite characters or composite locations. I think the practice of using a camera always contains an element of reportage—it's part of the nature of the tool.

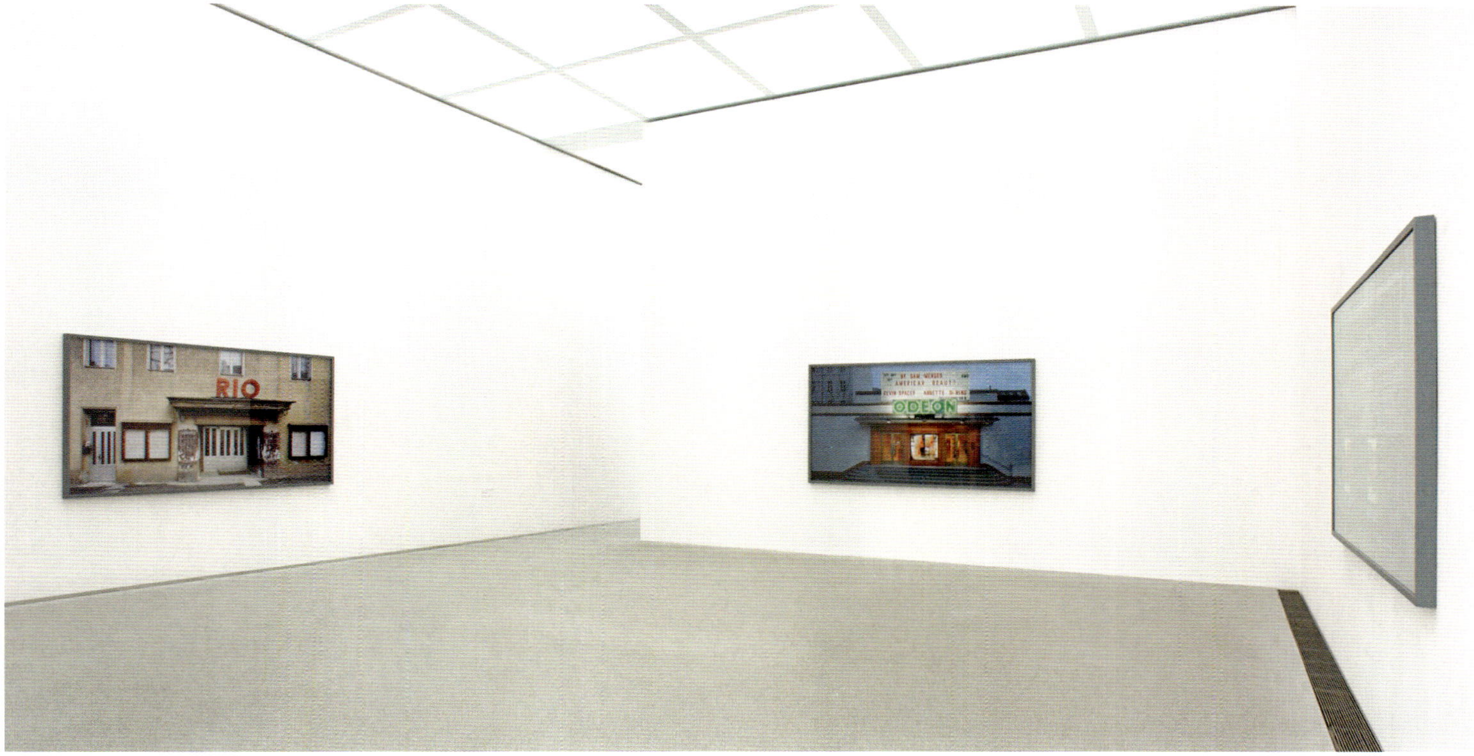

Since the beginning of our collaboration, our approach has always existed in relation to exploring an aspect of reportage in one way or another. Rather than considering genres of documentary or fiction from a binary, polarized sensibility, I don't think there's one way to come into that relationship.

ALEXANDER BIRCHLER: As Teresa says, we have been migrating between those two poles throughout our artistic practice. The series *Filmstills* followed a group of photographic works that we produced while still living in Berlin at the end of the 1990s. In the case of photographic works like *Stripping* (1998) and *Gregor's Room* (1999), we would photograph landscapes and buildings mostly on the outstkirts of Berlin and collect architectural debris that we would bring back to our studio, where we would create a composite environment filled with rear-screen projections, architectural fragments and actors. After having done this kind of work for a number of years, we decided to reverse the process by leaving the studio and shooting on actual locations. We would photograph cinema facades positioning ourselves frontally and parallel to the interior's

Filmstills (Berlin series), 2000
4 C-Print Photographs, each 55.2 x 102 inches
Installation view, Collection, Pinakothek der Moderne, Munich

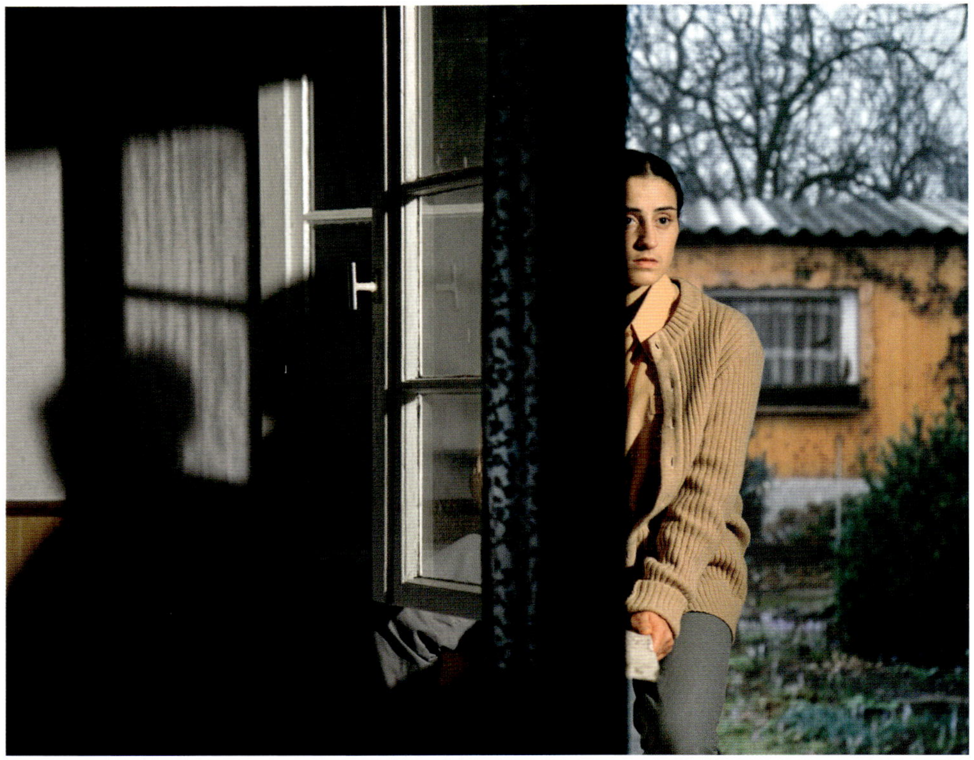

projection screen. There we would photograph from the same position for a period of time—sometimes for a few hours, other times over a period of several days. We then would go back to the studio and digitally create a composite environment. Thinking back over these two processes sheds a light on our migratory impulse.

I think what Teresa is describing in terms of the element of reportage comes from a sensibility that was informed by our graduate studies at the Nova Scotia College of Art and Design in Halifax, a program that has a noted history of conceptual practice. Within that context we felt strongly encouraged to always examine the medium we chose to work with as a means to generate strategies of production. As we started using a camera as a central medium in our practice, notions of reportage, documentary and essay were brought to the forefront. Reportage often deals with exposing what's hidden, what's left out, so to migrate toward the edge of the photographic frame—to what lies just outside of the edge of what can be seen—could be read as a documentary impulse. In *Stripping* we started employing Brechtian strategies by confusing the photographic frame with

Stripping, 1998
series of 5 C-Print Photographs, each 57.1 x 70.9 inches
Collection, Art Gallery of Western Australia, Perth, and others

architectural frames, an approach that we then employed in the video work *Eight*, the first component of a trilogy that includes *Detached Building* (2001) and *Single Wide* (2002). In the past we have often referred to those videos simply as "long photographs."

TH: For each of these videos we would search for a location and construct on-site architectural film sets, a process similar to what we developed when we were living in Berlin. While constructing these sets to be filmed, often a lengthy process taking several months, we would write a narrative script that was informed by the composite landscape we were in the process of building. For example, in *Single Wide* we were first searching for a specific location and then we acquired a defunct mobile home (also called a single wide), which was moved to the location. First we rebuilt the home and then we cut it open.

AB: The fragmentation, the gaps, the cutting, the frame and the edge all informed a narrative of a female protagonist, who in each of the three video works goes through a moment of passage, a moment of threshold. The camera appears to have no empathy: it continuously passes through the landscape, cutting through architecture, leaving and returning to the character in her unresolved state. As such, the camera could be described as an unblinking eye, a seemingly objective gaze that is detached, unemotional, documentary. This configuration of course clashes with the highly emotional fictional narrative that is unfolding.

IGI: Your current trilogy seems to explore different possibilities of documentary narration, but at the same time the fragmentary nature of memory always remains evident, in both content and form. Memory is another central motif within your work. You do not shy away from incorporating clear historical references. In the realm of film, you refer to works by Alfred Hitchcock, Michelangelo Antonioni, David Mamet and Terrence Malick. Literature also plays a formative role, with Kafka's *Metamorphosis* and Flaubert's *Madame Bovary* important influences, as well as Brecht's alienation effect and Walter Benjamin's concept of the aura. And in terms of visual art, you prominently cite Edward Hopper among your influences, as well as Jeff Wall. On the level of content, memory is an impulse that drives some of your protagonists, such as the two female characters in *House with Pool* (2004) and the young woman in *Single Wide*. How do you define the relationship of film and memory?

AB: Your question points to an interesting relationship between film and memory but also to a connection between motif and motivation. The characters we were creating for *House with Pool* and, similarly, *Eight, Detached Building* and *Single Wide*, are all in a state of struggle and are strongly motivated by events not depicted. In addition, the inherent looping narrative structure we developed for these works obscures the source of the character's motivation and the narrative never draws to a conclusion. With the *Sound Speed Marker* trilogy, our focus has continued to be directed on people's motivations and their relationship to absence, loss and events not depicted. In these works we have deliberately introduced a different aesthetic language—an artistic strategy that, when referring to the first two parts of the trilogy, has been sometimes described as a *Hinwendung zum Dokumentarischen*. In English, this could perhaps be described as exploring modes of documentality (versus modes of fictionality). The leitmotif connecting the narratives in the *Sound Speed Marker* trilogy and our earlier video works is that our protagonists are in a continuous search, constantly struggling to hold on and retrieve something that is implied but not revealed.

TH: The relationship of film to memory is incredibly expansive; they are tied to each other in a myriad of ways. One of film's most fundamental attributes—and I think this goes to the core of our interest—is that cinema always exists only in the head of the viewer; it's a direct result of our perceptual ability to memorize still images in fast succession and create an illusion of movement.

AB: One notable example of the complexities of memory, site and film is the story of Allan Hubbard (no relation to Teresa) in *Grand Paris Texas*. Allan, who grew up in Paris, Texas—a town that gained public recognition due to a famous movie that was *not* shot there—recounts how as a young boy he was cast in the Hollywood movie *Tender Mercies*, which starred Robert Duvall. In *Tender Mercies*, Allan played a character whose father had died in the Vietnam War. Allan describes in *Grand Paris Texas* that as an adult he came to the realization that he had gotten the role because he was able to convincingly relate to his character, since he had also lost his own father at an early age. In *Tender Mercies*, Robert Duvall's character becomes a surrogate father to Allan's character and teaches him to play the guitar. Shortly after filming the movie, which went on to win several Academy Awards, Duvall returned to Paris, Texas, and brought Allan a guitar as a birthday gift. As a young teenager, Allan learned to play guitar and as a grown man is seen playing it at the beginning and end of *Grand Paris Texas*.

IGI: While making *Sound Speed Marker* you also produced *Eighteen* (2013), a continuation of *Eight*, in which you once again incorporate the full breadth of characteristic stylistic devices of your earlier video pieces. To me, *Eighteen* represents a kind of memory work, not only with respect to the protagonist and her growing up, but also formally. Is it simultaneously a farewell?

AB: It's a great insight to consider *Eight, Eighteen* as a memory work. Since the time that *Eight* premiered in our 2001 exhibition *Wild Walls* at the Museum Haus Lange and Esters in Krefeld, it has been steadily exhibited in one institution or another. In part because *Eight* has maintained a presence in our lives, Teresa and I have been curious about what had happened to the young girl we cast back in 2001. Nine years later, we set about trying to find her. In *Eight*, the young girl constantly tries to retrieve a piece of her ruined

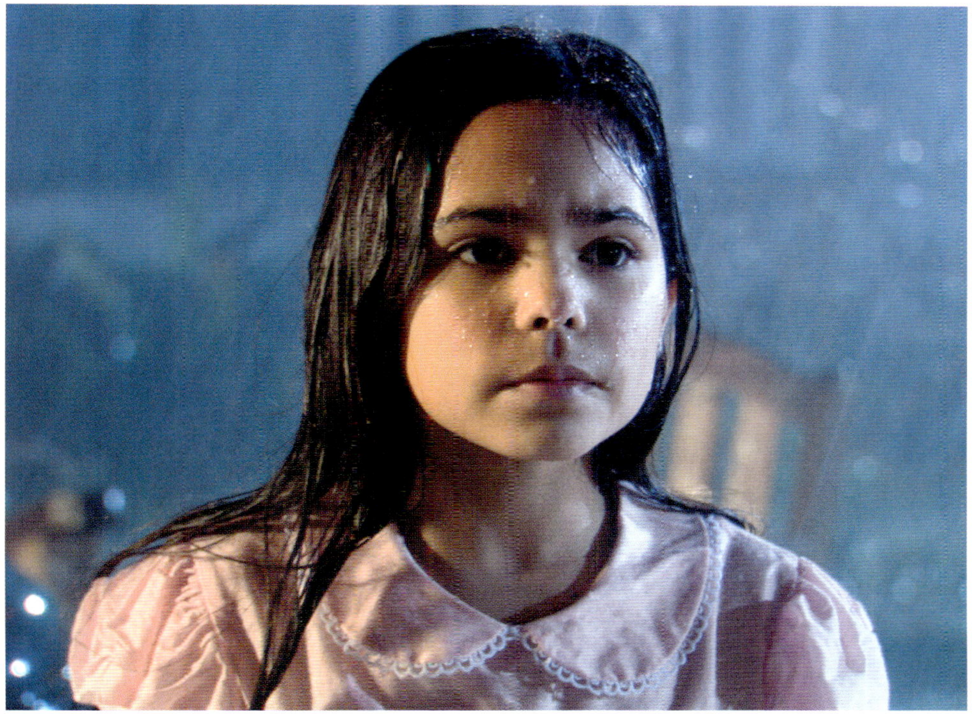

Eight, 2001
High-Definition
Video with Sound,
Single Channel,
3:25 minutes, Loop
Collections, Kunsthaus
Zürich, Pinakothek der
Moderne, Munich,
and others

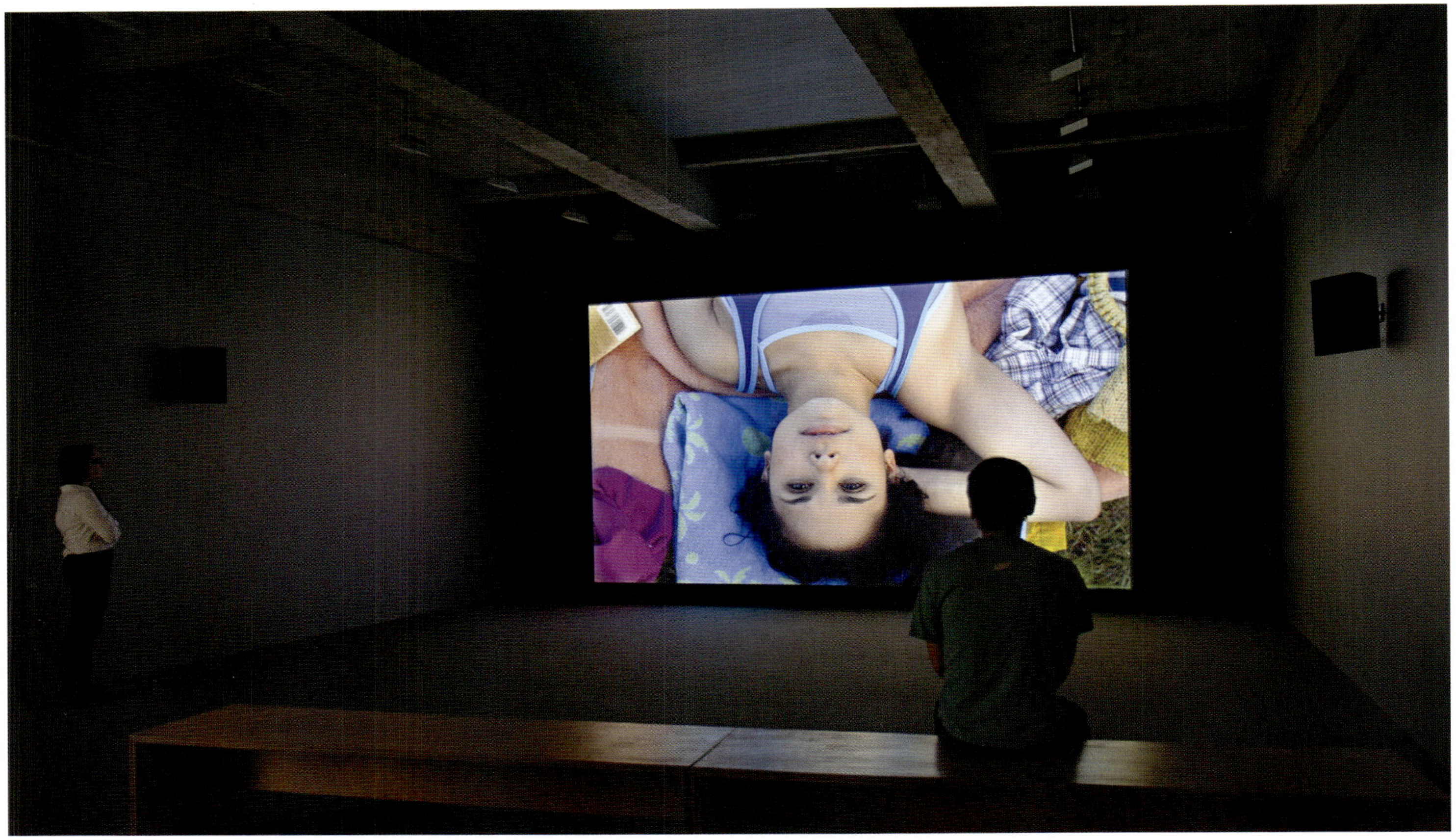

Eighteen, 2013
UHD Video with Sound
Single Channel,
18:30 minutes, Loop
Installation view, Tanya Bonakdar Gallery, New York, Collection, Linda Pace Foundation, San Antonio

birthday cake. The inherent loop that we built into the narrative structure of this piece has always been tied to ideas of forgetting and remembering. Over the years we've created different kinds of loops: inherent structural loops, spoken and gestural reiterative loops and historical loops.

TH: *Eighteen* was deeply influenced by the process of making the trilogy in *Sound Speed Marker*. The five-year period of time it took to make those works helped to bring about another kind of temporal consideration: of longitude and the role of lived duration and the gap between life lived and life as narrativized.

AB: There's a thematic thrust in both *Eight* and *Eighteen* that has to do with saying goodbye on a number of levels. Both of these ages share a critical transition of leaving something behind, whether childhood or adolescence. *Eight, Eighteen* is a narrative construct tethered to the perpetual ticking clock of experience—not only the character's but also our own.

IGI: In contrast to your early works, in which interior and exterior space was of central and psychological significance, your trilogy now features the Texas landscape, which acts like a parallel narrative to the accounts of your protagonists. That landscape is defined by its virtually endless expanse, its flora and fauna, its climatic and seasonal conditions, its use as both pasture and area of passage—but also by myths and clichés that have been transmitted over the past 100 years through cinema to those of us who do not live in Texas.

TH: The landscape can be read as a character. We use it as a construct that not only serves as a backdrop for our narratives but as a provocation that speaks to a condition of its inhabitants. Empty downtown areas once populated with economic activity; container trains filled with goods from China cutting through the landscape without stopping; fenced-off, shut-down industrial sites; over-grazed vast expanses of desert and the constant exposure to unrelenting weather: all chronicle a state of erosion and struggle. Dust, the enemy of any archive, is an ever-present element in all three films.

AB: In the *Sound Speed Marker* trilogy, we are setting out to search and revisit sites of cinema, traveling through landscapes informed by myth and clichés, in order to find another narrative that we never could have imagined in the first place.

IGI: You devote much attention to giving your works titles that always subtly encompass multiple levels of meaning. "Sound," "Speed," "Marker" are all terms used during filming. How do they relate to your trilogy?

AB: The terms are behind-the-scenes call outs between the director, the director of photography, the sound recordist and the camera assistant at the beginning of each take. We are interested in this vernacular, everyday and self-reflexive language in itself, as these words embody the history of cinema as well as describe its inherent qualities.

TH: "Dead Cat," another vernacular term from the film industry, has been incorporated into the title of one of our recent photographic works, *Dead Cat on Movie Mountain,* which depicts an audio microphone mounted on a stand and weighted down with sandbags on top of Movie Mountain. The microphone is covered with a blimp and a furry sock—both designed for minimizing wind noise when recording audio in high wind conditions. Two photographs of the microphone were made from the exact same location, one at sunrise and the other at sunset. Filmmakers often refer to the synthetic furry sock covering the microphone as a "Dead Cat." The origin of this name remains unclear: is it because historically this microphone cover used to be made of actual cat fur? Or is it because it simply looks that way?

IGI: More strongly than in earlier works, sound itself is a main character in the trilogy, both as a pictorial motif as well as an element that carries the action.

TH: In the early works, we used sound primarily to further define the interior and exterior spaces that allowed us, as you mentioned earlier, to create a psychological proximity and distance. As we've continued working with film over the past decade, we've focused on sound's potential to be a character itself. Futhermore in the trilogy, the sound recordist becomes an essential placeholder and can be seen as a symbolic figure.

IGI: What was the trilogy's genesis? What was the pivotal idea and how did the three works develop in relation to each other across five years?

AB: The trilogy leads back to the photographic series *Filmstills,* which we began in Berlin and have continued making over the years. One of the most recent photographic works coming out of the *Filmstills* series is called *Broken Screen* (2012), which was photographed over a period of about a week on the site of a long-abandoned drive-in cinema. Working with a large-format still camera in a place that is unfamiliar to us naturally draws out the attention and curiosity of all kinds of local people. It was on one of these kinds of trips that the genesis of the trilogy began, by both accident and incident—and of being curious about how one thing might lead to another.

TH: In the summer of 2007 we were driving across the United States, returning from teaching at Bard College in Upstate New York. We decided to take a detour on the way home and make a stop in the town of Paris, Texas. Both Alexander and I—growing up in Switzerland and Australia, respectively—had seen the Wim Wenders film and had admired it when it came out. When we arrived in Paris we went to find the local cinema in the hope that it might be another motif for the *Filmstills* series.

AB: The downtown movie theater, called the Grand, was dilapidated and surrounded by empty storefronts. The doors of the theater were chained up. After returning to Austin, we did some research and found out that the theater belonged to the city and had been closed for more than a decade. We organized getting permission to go inside. When we returned to Paris, city development officers met us outside the theater and gave us protective masks to wear. We stepped inside and realized that the officers would not follow us due to the hazardous conditions. With our flashlights, we continued on into the building alone. The interior was completely dark and I walked a few steps ahead of Teresa. When I entered the main auditorium I was startled by the sound of wings flapping, as dozens of nesting birds flew up, equally alarmed by our arrival. I turned back to Teresa and said, "This is it!"

TH: That was the start of a two-year period of making numerous research trips to Paris. The initial impetus of those trips—to find out what had happened to the Grand—led us on a journey uncovering a number of complex narrative strands. Early on, we recognized the city of Paris as an intriguing meta-location and we took a risk in allowing the circumstances of our research and the specificities of the location to shape the form of our film. This became the guiding principle for the other two works in the trilogy.

AB: We first heard about Movie Mountain by accident. We were driving in the desert with a rancher who mentioned it to us in passing. In our research we quickly realized that the name of the mountain was not just a vernacular term used by local residents, but an official geographical name. In *Movie Mountain (Méliès)*, our approach was grounded in absence and evidence. While we were finishing that work, we began looking for a third site, a location that could point to other kinds of traces that moviemaking has left behind. The town of Marfa, Texas—known as much for its connection to Donald Judd and the Chinati Foundation as it is for having been the town where the highly controversial movie

FOLLOWING TWO PAGES:
Broken Screen, 2012
2 Archival Pigment Inkjet Prints
each 43.5 x 54.5 inches
Private Collection

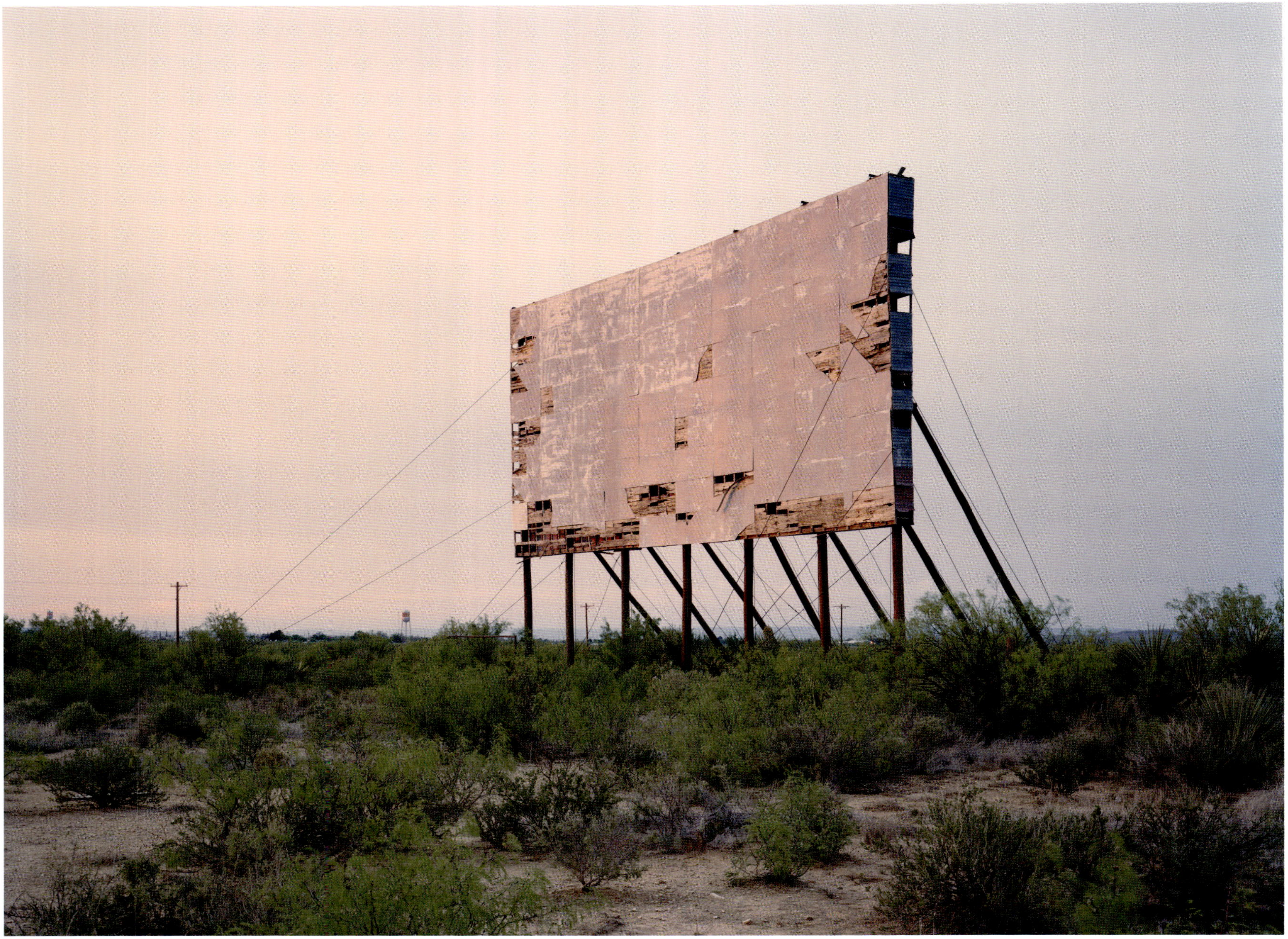

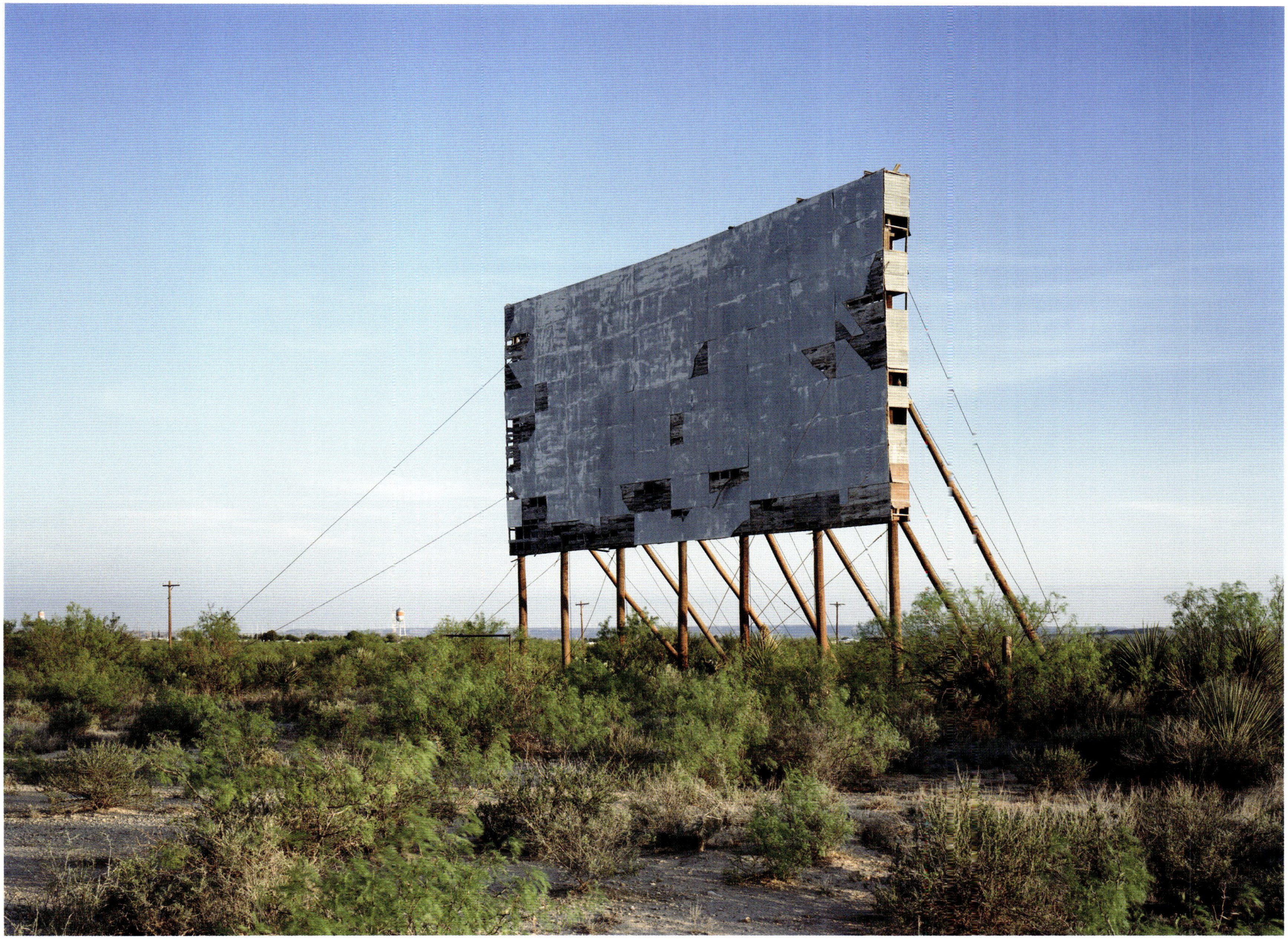

Giant was filmed—was from the onset an obvious choice. Across the trajectory of the trilogy, we imagined that each part would use a different framework of documentary and fiction—incorporating modes of reenactment, longitudinal study, interviews, observation, the performative and self-reflexivity.

IGI: In *Giant* you again take up a female main character whose appearance and actions form a central narrative strand. But unlike your female protagonists in *House with Pool* or *Single Wide,* for example, she does not seem to harbor a secret, but to a greater extent offers a projection screen. How can this character be read?

TH: The sound recordist working outdoors in a remote landscape in the "here and now" and the Warner Bros. secretary working in a distant office on February 9, 1955, in the "there and then" share an acknowledgement of each other. There are brief punctuated moments of exchange in which they seem to see or hear each other. The two women are also threaded together through the sentences of the location contract being typed out by the secretary. Each line of text, as a horizontal string of words, melds with the horizon of the landscape and becomes its own landscape like the long line of cargo trains passing in the distance. The sound recordist, on-site listening and recording, intersects with this text. There is a connection to how the female characters in *House with Pool* pass a sweater back and forth between each other, or in the way that the character Anna in *Eight* and *Eighteen* self-consciously maneuvers her way through her own narrative, back and forth between a zone of foreshadowing and hindsight. If there is a secret that is shared between the female characters in *Giant*, it's a secret that's generated through passage.

Edna Ferber's 1952 novel *Giant* and the subsequent 1956 film based on her book were controversial projects in their day. The Warner Bros. production is remembered, in part, as being one of the first major Hollywood blockbuster movies attempting to address issues of feminism and racism. Our research at the University of Southern California Warner Bros. Archive and the Margaret Herrick Library at the Academy of Motion Picture Arts and Sciences in Los Angeles led us to discover a surprisingly detailed range of pre-production "side notes" about *Giant* that became an important creative portal for us, and the roles occupied by women in filmmaking and filmmaking production

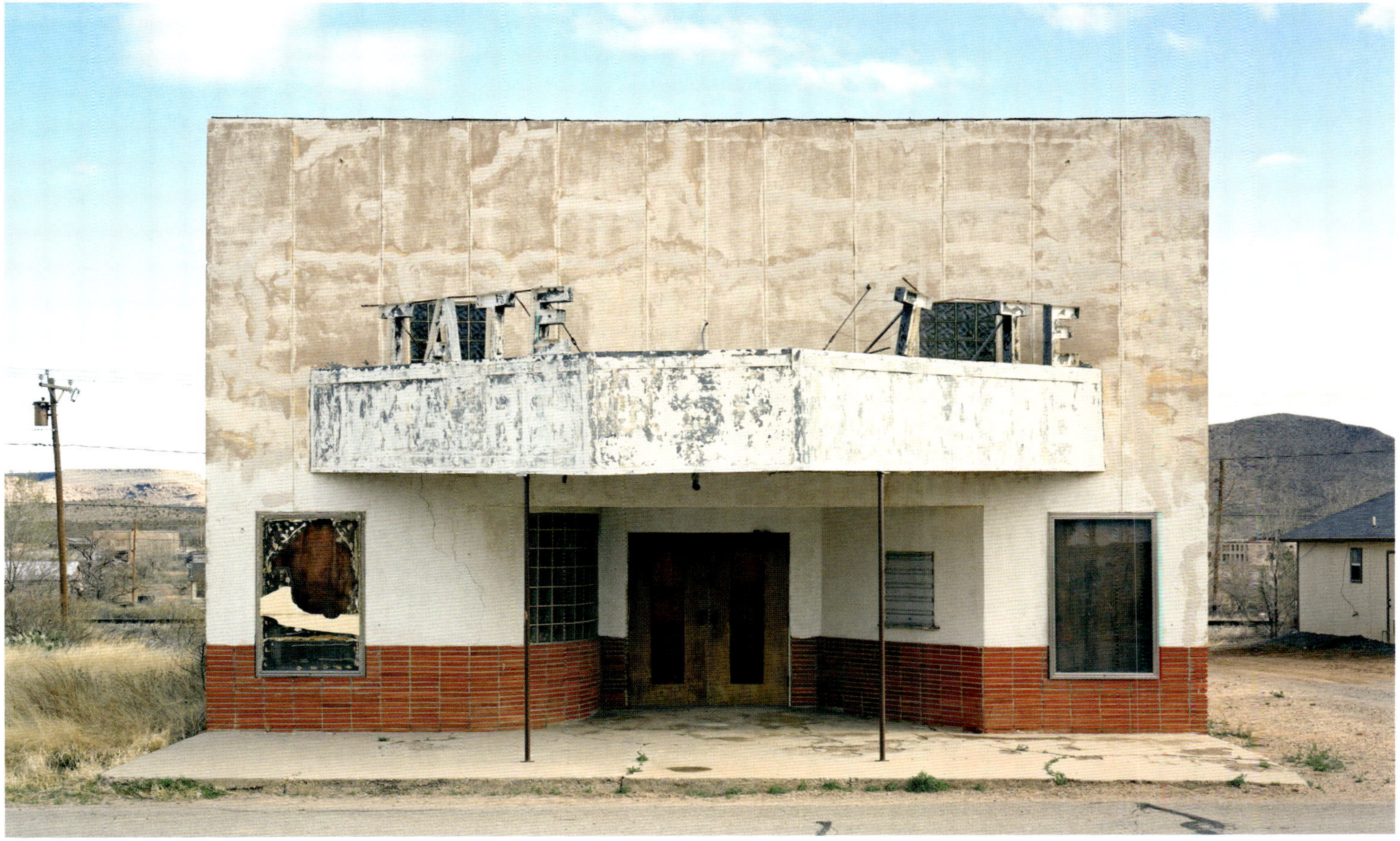

became a crucial link in interweaving the past and present. There is one scene in our work when the secretary, who has finished typing the location contract, stands at an office window and stares outside. She's watching something happening beyond the frame; we hear trucks pulling up and an indistinct conversation of male voices. Suddenly the secretary turns away from the window and directly faces the gaze of the camera. She stares directly at the viewer, long enough for us to become aware of it—a Brechtian moment—and as soon as we recognize the collapse of this immersive space, she closes her eyes and rejects our gaze.

IGI: Digitalization has changed photography, video and film to a great extent. Digital photography today follows different rules than analogue, and we have to reformulate our understanding of what photography is. This above all impacts the concept

Filmstills, Tate (The End series), 2011
Archival Pigment Inkjet Print, 43.5 x 67 inches
Private Collection

of the documentary, which was stylistically influential in the history of photography for a long time. What is your understanding of the documentary with respect to photography and film? What significance does it take on in the frame of your artistic reflections, and has your idea of it changed fundamentally in recent years?

TH: Early on in our work we sought out photography foremost for its narrative and analytical properties rather than for its evidentiary qualities. We've always considered photography as having a conflicted relationship to evidence and early works starting from *Small Town* (1990), our first collaborative piece, speak to that. As soon as digital technology became available to us we began to experiment and incorporate it into our work, although we've remained foremost interested in manipulation as it gives way to experience rather than evidence.

AB: Self-reflexivity, the performative, slowness and the longitudinal have become foregrounded concepts within our practice over the past years and can be read in direct relationship to the discourse surrounding the dramatic advancements of digital technology in photography and film within the past years.

IGI: In many of your works a melancholy is inscribed that above all seems to be characterized by the experience of loss and forgetting. The search for traces within your trilogy can also be read as a rebellion against collective forgetting—not only of places, people and events, but also of the history of the medium of film itself.

TH: Obsolescence in its many forms is a recurring motif in our work. In the *Sound Speed Marker* trilogy, we depict a procession of obsolescent technologies and the objects associated with them such as the VHS tape; the vinyl record; the medium of film; the film projector; silent movies and their orchestra accompaniment; the site of cinema itself; modes of transportation from the horse to the train to the automobile; the newspaper; stenography and the typewriter. The portrayal of these cultural artifacts could be seen as markers and placeholders for people's lives and experiences. The works explore the relationship between these objects, technologies and the people using them. In *Grand Paris Texas* our film crew is seen walking through a bird-infested, abandoned cinema, painstakingly filming tangled motion picture filmstrips, discarded projector lenses and film reels encrusted with layers of bird shit. They appear as archeologists, visitors from a different time, recording traces of the history of a cinema, the medium of film itself and subsequently a part of their own demise.

AB: The depiction of these forensic activities circle back and point to our role as artists. Marcus Roden, the funeral director in *Grand Paris Texas*, notes the desire of grieving family members to leave an object—a physical keepsake "such as a can of beer"—in the coffin of a loved one. We leave the viewer with Marcus's conclusion that directing a funeral has a lot in common with directing a film.

FOLLOWING TWO PAGES:
Sunrise, Filmset, Sunset, 2012
2 Archival Pigment Inkjet Prints
Collection, Blanton Museum of Art, Austin
Gift of Jeanne and Michael Klein, 2013

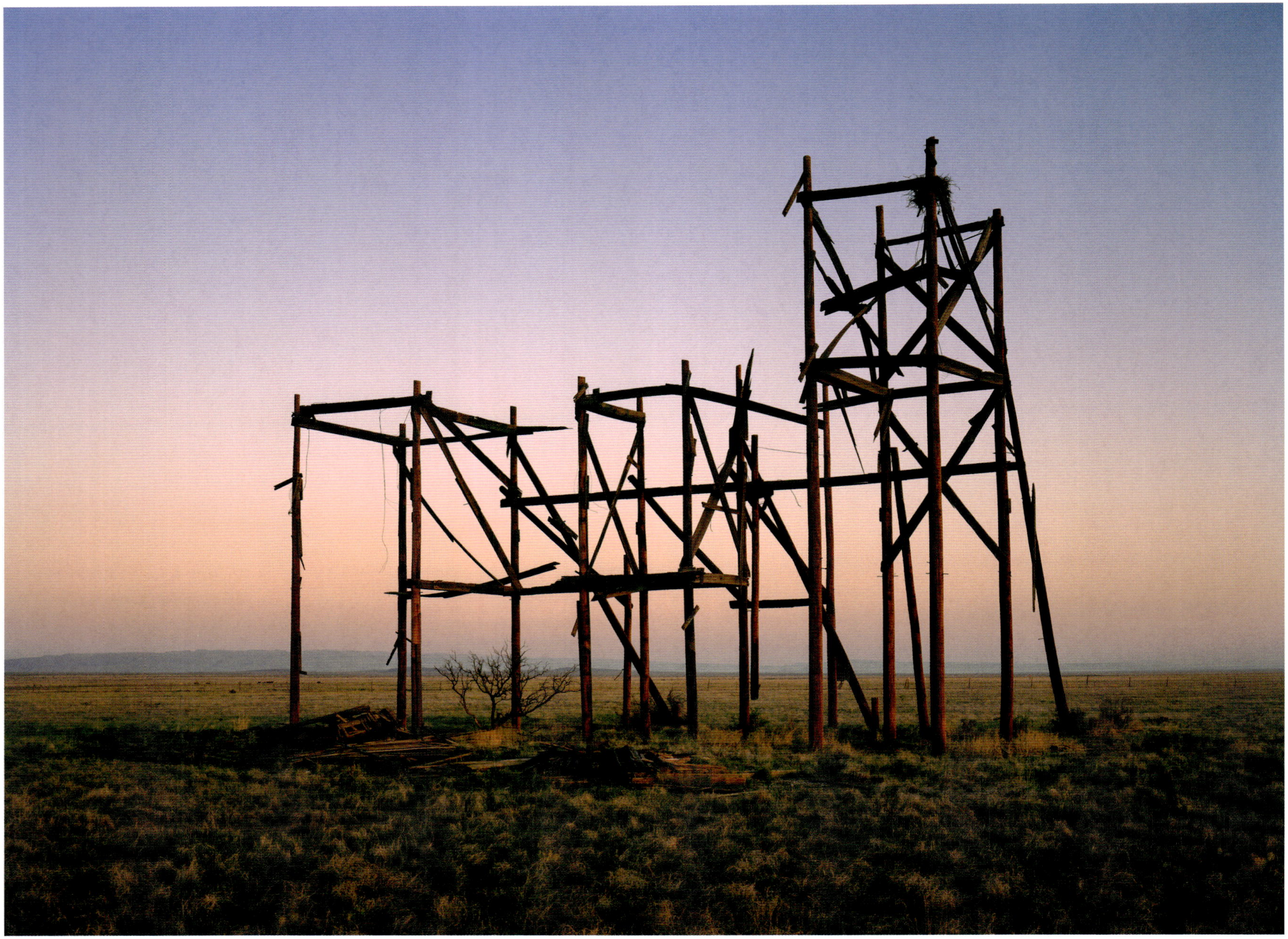

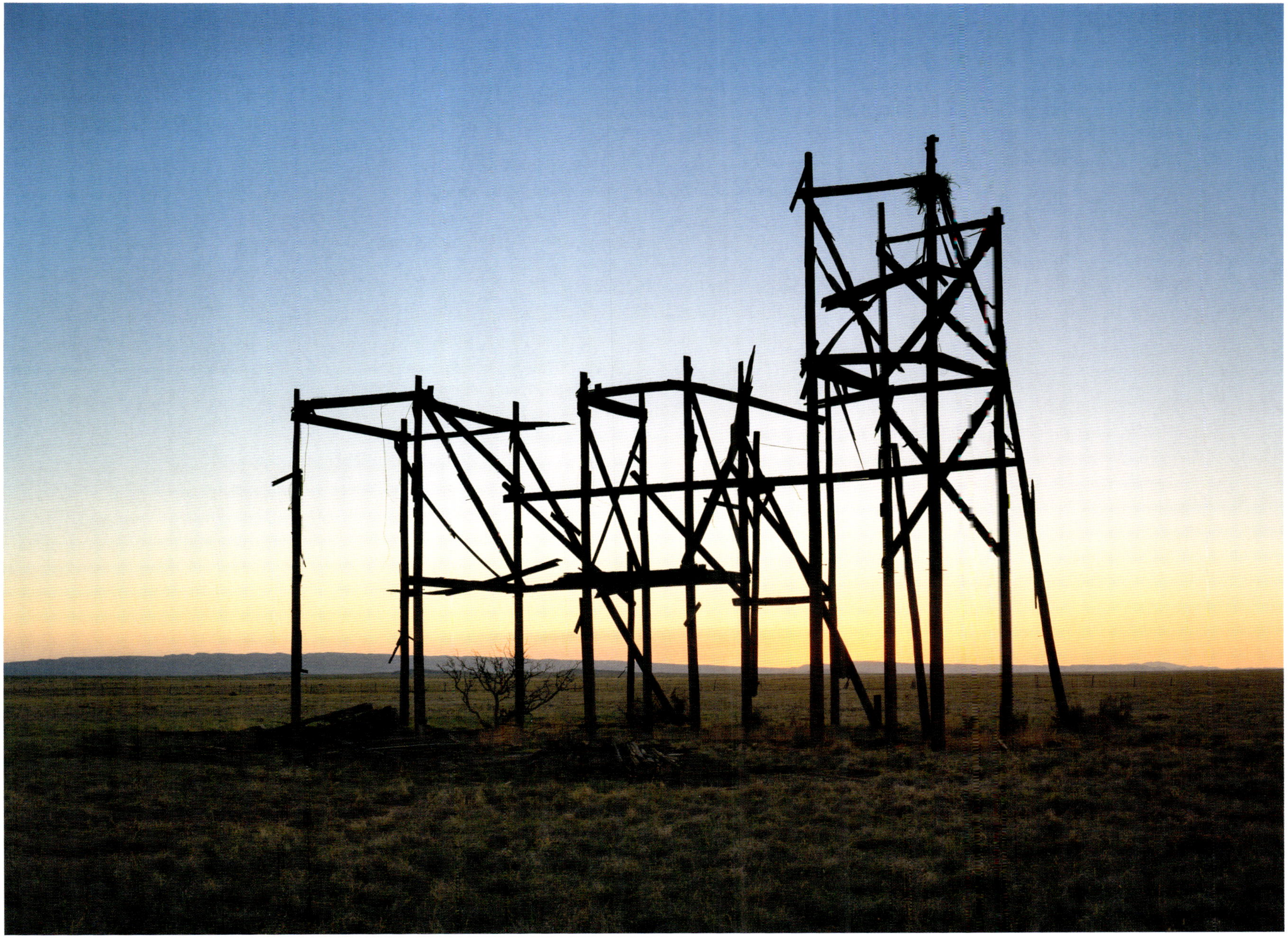

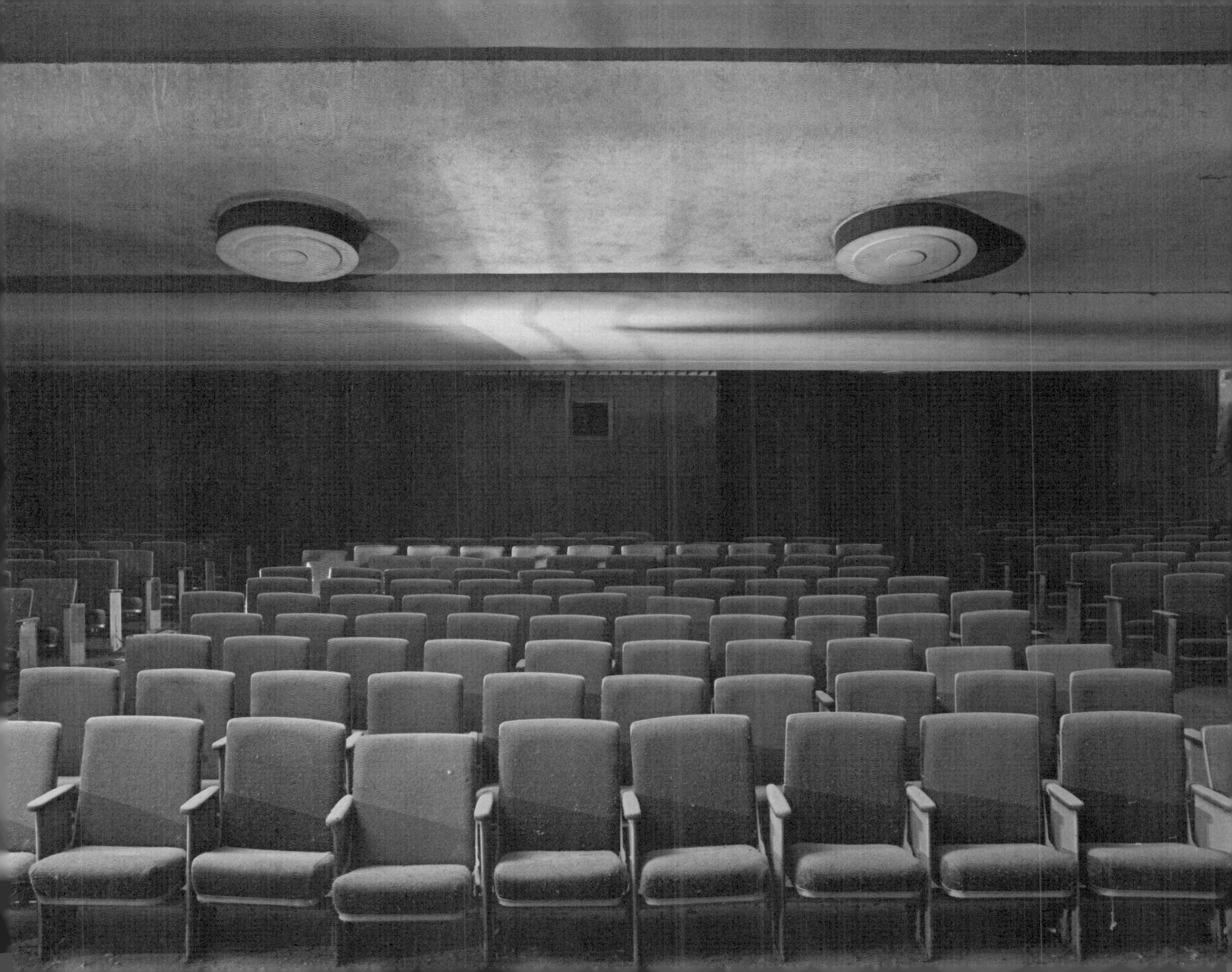

Works in the Exhibition

Grand Paris Texas, 2009
High-Definition Video with Sound
Single Channel, 54 minutes
Installation dimensions variable
Collection Modern Art Museum
of Fort Worth

Tape, 2009
4 Archival Pigment Inkjet Prints
Each image 24 x 30 inches
Courtesy of Tanya Bonakdar Gallery, New York,
and Lora Reynolds Gallery, Austin

Eiffel Tower Paris, Texas, 2009
Archival Pigment Inkjet Print
24 x 30 inches
Courtesy of Tanya Bonakdar Gallery, New York,
and Lora Reynolds Gallery, Austin

Movie Mountain (Méliès), 2011
High-Definition Video with Sound
2 Channel, 24 minutes, Loop
Installation dimensions variable
Collection Museum of Fine Arts, Houston

Dead Cat on Movie Mountain, Sunrise, 2011
Archival Pigment Inkjet Print
43.25 x 54.75 inches
Courtesy of Tanya Bonakdar Gallery, New York,
and Lora Reynolds Gallery, Austin

Dead Cat on Movie Mountain, Sunset, 2011
Archival Pigment Inkjet Print
43.25 x 54.75 inches
Collection Martin Riezebeek

Sunrise Filmset Sunset, 2012
2 Archival Pigment Inkjet Prints
Each image 43.5 x 54.5 inches
Courtesy of Tanya Bonakdar Gallery, New York,
and Lora Reynolds Gallery, Austin

Giant, 2014
High-Definition Video with Sound
3 Channel, 30 minutes, Loop
Installation dimensions variable
Collection Blanton Museum of Art, The University
of Texas at Austin, Gift of Jeanne and Michael Klein
and Suzanne Deal Booth, 2014

Missing Truffaut, 2014
Lamp, wooden pole, laser print on paper
Installation dimensions variable
Courtesy of Tanya Bonakdar Gallery, New York,
and Lora Reynolds Gallery, Austin

Film Sources

Giant is a 1956 film directed by George Stevens and starring Elizabeth Taylor, Rock Hudson and James Dean that portrays a powerful Texas ranching family and the challenges they face adjusting to the coming of big oil and changing societal mores. Adapted from a novel by the politically progressive writer Edna Ferber, *Giant* was one of the first mainstream Hollywood productions to express a critical attitude toward the myths of Texas history and its problematic treatment of women and Mexicans in the early decades of the twentieth century. Taylor's character, Leslie Benedict, is a socialite turned feminist and social reformer who serves as the conscience of the movie, while Dean plays Jett Rink, a one-time servant whose sudden rise to oil riches serves as a foil to Leslie's tradition-bound Texas husband, Bick (played by Hudson). *Giant* was a commercial and critical success, winning the Academy Award for Best Director and nine other nominations, including two for Best Actor in a Leading Role for Dean and Hudson's portrayals.

Méliès, Gaston (February 12, 1852–April 9, 1915) was the lesser-known brother of the famous French filmmaker Georges Méliès, who abandoned his first career as the head of the family shoe factory in Paris to move to the United States in 1902 to distribute Georges' films. Within a year of arriving in New York, he began directing his own one-reel westerns which led him to move to San Antonio, where he founded the Star Film Ranch movie studio. Only a year later, the director decided to move his struggling film company to a more moderate climate in Santa Paula, California. On April 22, 1911, he departed San Antonio with his family, film equipment, film crew and actors aboard the Sunset Express Train on a route that stopped in Sierra Blanca, Texas, the railroad's pivotal gateway junction to the West Coast.

Paris, Texas, is a 1984 drama directed by Wim Wenders that traces the quest of a homeless character named Travis Henderson (played by Harry Dean Stanton) to reunite with the son he abandoned and his wife Jane (Nastassja Kinski), who left them both years earlier. Wenders's distinctive version of the American road movie pairs the desolate longing of Henderson's broken character with the barren South Texas landscape and a haunting score composed by Ry Cooder that was influenced greatly by Blind Willie Johnson's 1927 blues song "Dark was the Night, Cold was the Ground." The film won numerous awards, most notably the Palme D'Or at the 1984 Cannes Film Festival.

Tender Mercies is a 1983 film written by Horton Foote and directed by Bruce Beresford that stars Robert Duvall as Mac Sledge, an alcoholic country singer who seeks redemption from his troubled past through a relationship with a young widow played by Tess Harper, her son and, ultimately, religious conversion. The landscape surrounding Waxahachie, Texas, provided Beresford with a fitting visual analogy to the emotionally stark story. Although the film had a limited box office run, *Tender Mercies* won two Academy Awards for Best Original Screenplay and Best Actor in a Leading Role (Duvall).

Truffaut, François Roland (February 6, 1932–October 21, 1984) was a French film director, screenwriter, producer, actor and film critic who first came to prominence in the mid-1950s as an iconoclastic film critic for *Cahiers du Cinéma,* the noted French film publication that became a locus of dialogue for Truffaut and his contemporaries Jean-Luc Godard, Claude Chabrol, Erich Rohmer and Jacques Rivette—all of whom were part of the cinematic movement known as the *Nouvelle Vague* (New Wave). With his semi-autobiographical storylines and nuanced shooting style, Truffaut became a prime example of the *auteur,* or director who closely controls all aspects of the film-making process. So completely did Truffaut associate himself with filmmaking that in his Oscar-winning *La nuit américaine (Day for Night,* 1973), he poses the question. "Are films more important than life?"

Tumbleweeds is a 1925 silent Western produced by and starring William S. Hart that depicts the exploits of a drifter (or "tumbleweed") caught up in the Oklahoma land rush of 1893. The film was remarkable for its epic scenes of Westward migration and the humane portrayal of Native Americans, who tended to be negatively characterized in the movies. In a 1939 rerelease of the film, Hart included an eight-minute introduction in which he waxes nostalgic about the Old West and "that mad rush of destiny" that characterized the mass expansion into new territory.

Wenders, Ernst Wilhelm "Wim" (born August 14, 1945) is a German filmmaker, playwright, author and photographer who played a critical role in the New German Cinema movement that spanned the late 1960s through the early '80s and included such celebrated directors as Rainer Werner Fassbinder, Werner Herzog and Volker Schlöndorff. Influenced in part by the work of the French *Nouvelle Vague* and sharing a concern with exploring the issues of the divided Germanys, this generation of German directors favored small-scale experimental productions that appealed to art-house audiences rather than the mainstream. Wenders is known to closely collaborate with writers such as Sam Shepard *(Paris, Texas)* and Peter Handke *(Wings of Desire).*

Production Credits

GRAND PARIS TEXAS 2009

High-Definition Video with Sound

Single Channel, 54 min

Installation dimensions variable

CAST

(in order of appearance)

Allan Hubbard

Toni Clem

Harold Wayne Adams

Marcus Roden

John I. (Jack) Norman

Dorothea Gillies

Elric De La Peña

Kristy Riffle

Harper and Rainer Hunt

CREW

Written and Directed
Teresa Hubbard / Alexander Birchler

Producer
Cara Carney, Teresa Hubbard

Production Company
HB Studio and Alpheus Media Inc.

Director of Photography
Wilson Waggoner

B Camera
David Dewitt

Editor and Sound Design
Alexander Birchler

Assistant Camera
Stuart McSpadden

Gaffer
Charles E. Seligman

Key Grip
Bobby Lewallen

Grip Electric
Chris Malloy

Best Boy/Swing
Scott Conn

Sound Recordists
Dennis Meehan, Ben Lowry

Crane Operator
Eric Young

Production Assistants
Taryn Hall, Kris Hernandez

Still Photographers
Adam Schreiber, Teresa Hubbard

Post Production Audio
Tom Hammond

Audio Studio
Soundcrafter, Austin

MUSIC

"Startled" by Allan Hubbard

"Special Angel" by Jimmy Duncan, performed by Bobby Helms, courtesy of Warner Chappell Music

SPECIAL THANKS

Lisa A. Wright, Director of Community Development, Paris, Texas; Carl Covert, Technical Services Librarian, Paris Junior College Library; Cathie Tyler, Art Professor, Paris Junior College; Hampton Hodges, Starrett Funeral Home; Skipper Steeley; Trenton Doyle Hancock; Holiday Inn; William & Bettye Nowlin Research Fellowship in Photography at the University of Texas at Austin

The production of **Grand Paris Texas** was commissioned by the Modern Art Museum of Fort Worth.

MOVIE MOUNTAIN (MÉLIÈS) 2011

High-Definition Video with Sound

2 Channel, 24 min, Loop

Installation dimensions variable

CAST

(in order of appearance)

Ben Lowry

Tom D. Ellison

David Armstrong

Sara Marta

Kit Bramblett

Tom Neely

John Elder

Julio Marta

James Rush

Christina Ramirez

Gary Jennings

CREW

Written and Directed
Teresa Hubbard / Alexander Birchler

Production Company
HB Studio

Director of Photography
Wilson M. Waggoner

Editor and Sound Design
Alexander Birchler

B Camera Operators
Teresa Hubbard, Adam Schreiber

Assistant Editor
María Clara García

Music Composed and Performed
Catherine Davis

Sound Recordist
Ben Lowry

Photography Assistants
Adam Schreiber, Santiago Forero
Alejandro Sánchez

AV Systems Design
Bill Haddad, Blue House Design

Production Assistant
Colin Doyle

Second Assistant Editor
Robert Melton

Recording Engineer
Jim Vollentine

Post Production Coordinator
Allison Turrell

Transcripts
Emily Ng

Re-Recording Mixer
Lyman Hardy

Colorist Consultant
Parke Gregg

Post Production Facility
StuckOnOn

SPECIAL THANKS

Paul Rascoe, University of Texas Libraries; Susan Dirks, Texas Archive of the Moving Image; Jared Case, George Eastman House, Rochester; Janet Staiger, College of Communication, University of Texas at Austin; Don Graham, College of Liberal Arts, University of Texas at Austin; Frank Thompson; Darleene Elder; Joe Elder; Bill Love; Mary J Joy; Angel Reyes; Carmen Hernandez; Jack Giacalone; Sandra Bean; Ona-Mae Bean; Lupe Ramirez; William & Bettye Nowlin Research Fellowship in Photography at the University of Texas at Austin

The Alturas Foundation supported the production of **Movie Mountain (Méliès)** as part of its Artist-in-Residence program.

GIANT 2014

High-Definition Video with Sound

3 Channel, 30 min, Loop

Installation dimensions variable

CAST

(in order of appearance)

Diane Zander Mason

Adriene Mishler

Briana McKeague

Jane Cowan

Aaron Leggett

CREW

Written and Directed

Teresa Hubbard / Alexander Birchler

Director of Photography

Wilson Waggoner

Editor and Sound Design

Alexander Birchler

Producers

Teresa Hubbard, Cara Carney, Jason Wehling

Assistant Editors

Maria Clara Garcia, Skye Ashbrook

Production Company

HB Studio

MARFA UNIT

Camera Operators

Wilson Waggoner, Alexander Birchler, Teresa Hubbard, Marco Naylor

Gaffer

Charles E. Seligman

1st Camera Assistant

Nathan Warren

Key Grip

Buzz Maloy

Best Boy Grip

Jason McKnight

Best Boy Electric

Rob Janecka

Boom Lift Operator

Wilson Waggoner

Still Photographer

Chris Austin

Location Sound Mixers

Alexander Birchler, Diane Zander Mason

Camera/Set PA

Esther Garcia

Production Assistants

Skye Ashbrook, Beau Rice

AV Systems Design

Bill Haddad, Blue House Design

Foley Artists

Susan Fitz-Simon, Glenn Eanes

BURBANK UNIT

Camera Operator

Wilson Waggoner

Gaffer

Bobby Lewallen

1st Camera Assistant

Wylie Earnhardt

Production Designer

Caroline Karlen

Set Dressers

Brad Mathis, Allen White, Skye Ashbrook

Makeup/Wardrobe

Lauren Gonzales

Location Scout

Kim LeBlanc, Texas Film Commission

Wardrobe Assistant

Andrea Day

Location Sound Mixer

Jason Wehling

Production Assistant

Skye Ashbrook

Post Production Facility

HB Studio

SPECIAL THANKS

Aargauer Kuratorium; Clay and Anne Evans; Fairfax Dorn; Charles Mary Kubricht; Ron Sommers; Lynda McKnight; Virginia Lebermann; University of Southern California Warner Bros. Archive, Los Angeles; Texas Film Commission; Margret Herrick Library, Academy of Motion Picture Arts and Sciences, Los Angeles; Lance Armstrong; Quality Quinn; Charles Attal; Suzanne Deal Booth; Travis Capo; Molly Kemp; Jeanne & Michael Klein; John Thornton; Melba & Ted Whatley; William & Bettye Nowlin Research Fellowship in Photography at the University of Texas at Austin

The production of **Giant** was commissioned by Ballroom Marfa.

Author Biographies

FAIRFAX DORN

Fairfax Dorn is the Co-Founder and Artistic Director of Ballroom Marfa, a nonprofit cultural arts space dedicated to exploring varied perspectives and issues through visual art, film, music and performance. Since 2003, she has been responsible for the artistic and programmatic vision of the organization and is also the Co-Founder of Marfa Dialogues, an inclusive public forum that utilizes art to address the critical issues of our time. In addition to her directorship of Ballroom Marfa, Dorn served as Guest Curator and Interim Program Director for the Linda Pace Foundation in San Antonio in 2012. She is currently a board member of the Judd Foundation, the Whitney Museum of American Art, the Centre Pompidou Foundation, *Triple Canopy* and Bunker259.

ANNE ELLEGOOD

Anne Ellegood is Senior Curator at the Hammer Museum at UCLA. Prior to joining the Hammer, she was Curator of Contemporary Art at the Hirshhorn Museum & Sculpture Garden in Washington, DC, since 2005. Previously, Ellegood was the New York–based Curator for Peter Norton's collection of more than 2,400 works of international contemporary art, and from 1998 to 2003 she was Associate Curator at the New Museum of Contemporary Art in New York. Ellegood's recent projects include *Take It or Leave It: Institution, Image, Ideology,* which explored the overlapping strategies of appropriation and institutional critique in American art (co-organized with Johanna Burton) and featured the work of 36 artists, and *Kelly Nipper: Black Forest*. Ellegood also co-organized the Hammer Invitational *All of this and nothing* (2011) and the Hammer's first biennial of Los Angeles–based artists, *Made in L.A.* 2012. She has organized Hammer Projects with Diana Al-Hadid, Eric Baudelaire, Claude Collins-Stracensky, Keren Cytter, Danica Dakic, Shannon Ebner, Latifa Echakhch, Dara Friedman, Rob Fischer, Mark Flores, Dara Friedman, Friedrich Kunath, Tom Marioni, Linn Meyers, My Barbarian and Sara VanDerBeek. Ellegood was selected by the Australian Council for the Arts to curate Sydney-based artist Hany Armanious's 2011 Venice Biennale exhibition. She is currently working on the first North American retrospective of the work of Jimmie Durham, a solo project with Laurie Anderson and Hammer Projects with Francis Upritchard, Pedro Reyes and Lily van der Stokker.

DR. INKA GRAEVE INGELMANN

Dr. Inka Graeve Ingelmann has been Director of the Sammlung für Fotografie und Neue Medien (Department of Photography and New Media) at the Pinakothek der Moderne in Munich since 2002. After beginning her career as an Assistant at the Metropolitan Museum of Art in New York in 1990, she earned her doctorate with a biography of the photographer Ellen Auerbach. In 1987, Graeve Ingelmann began working in Berlin as a freelance curator specializing in the history of photography, and realized exhibitions for such institutions as the Berliner Landesmuseum Berlinische Galerie, the Museum Folkwang Essen, the Sprengel Museum Hannover and the Fundacio la Caixa, Barcelona. In 2002 she took charge of the newly founded Sammlung für Fotografie und Neue Medien at the Pinakothek der Moderne in Munich, which was expanded by the Ann and Jürgen Wilde Foundation in 2010. Apart from the continual development and expansion of the collection in the areas of contemporary as well as historical photography, she has realized a large number of solo exhibitions on such artists as Karl Blossfeldt, August Sander, Moi Ver, Bernhard Wicki, William Eggleston Wolfgang Tillmans, Fiona Tan, Eva Leitolf, Zoe Leonard, David Claerbout, Pippilotti Rist and Jeff Wall, as well as comprehensive surveys of German and American photography and thematic shows such as *Female Trouble* (2008). Graeve Ingelmann is the author and editor of numerous publications on historical and contemporary photography, and a member of various national and international juries.

JEFFREY KASTNER

Jeffrey Kastner is a New York–based critic and journalist and the Senior Editor of *Cabinet* magazine. A regular contributor to *Artforum*, he has written on contemporary art and cultural issues for magazines and newspapers including *Afterall, Bookforum,* the *Economist, Frieze* and the *New York Times*. Kastner's monographic essays have appeared in exhibition publications for artists such as Doug Aitken, David Altmejd, Jeremy Blake, Michaël Borremans, Willie Doherty, Tomas Saraceno and Sarah Sze. A commissioning editor, with Sina Najafi, of the catalogue of the 55th Venice Biennale (2013), his most recent book is *Nature* (2012), a volume edited for the Documents of Contemporary Art series published by the MIT Press and Whitechapel Gallery, London.

SEÁN KISSANE

Seán Kissane is Curator of Exhibitions at the Irish Museum of Modern Art, Dublin. He has curated various shows bringing the work of international modern and contemporary artists to Ireland for the first time, including Frida Kahlo and Diego Rivera, Leonora Carrington, Isaac Julien, Carlos Garaicoa, Romuald Hazoumé, Rivane Neuenschwander and Shahzia Sikander. Solo exhibitions with Irish artists include Alice Maher, James McKenna, Cecil King, McDermott & McGough, Hughie O'Donoghue, Alan Phelan and Orla Barry as well as new commissions with Garrett Phelan, Alan Phelan, Alice Maher and Dennis McNulty.

At IMMA he has organized exhibitions with major figures such as Lucian Freud, Georgia O'Keeffe, Louise Bourgeois, Francesco Clemente, Howard Hodgkin, Rebecca Horn and Jasper Johns. A writer and award-winning editor, he has published on Carlos Garaioca, Romuald Hazoumé, Cecil King, McDermott & McGough, James McKenna, Shahzia Sikander, Marc Quinn, Isaac Julien, Orla Barry, Fiona Mulholland, Lu Chungsheng, Dorothy Cross, Sam Dargan, Suzy O'Mullane, Anita Groener, Michael Kane and contemporary Chinese art. He has edited a number of important monographs including books on Lucian Freud, Georgia O'Keeffe, Barry Flanagan, and the White Stag Group. He was co-editor of *Boulevard Magenta,* IMMA's biannual journal of the arts and letters. He has lectured widely including at the University of Ulster, the National Gallery of Ireland and the Peggy Guggenheim Foundation. He is a contributor to *Circa* and *Contexts* magazines as well as the *Shanghai Art Museum Review*. He has served as a judge and selector on panels including the Oriel Mostyn Open and the Central Bank of Ireland.

CLAUDIA SCHMUCKLI

Claudia Schmuckli is Director and Chief Curator of the Blaffer Art Museum at the University of Houston. Recent exhibitions and publications she has organized and authored include *Francesca DiMattio: Housewares* (2014), *Tony Feher* (2012), *Lynne McCabe: Room to be (Ms.)understood* (2012), *Johan Grimonprez: It's a Poor Sort of Memory That Only Works Backwards* (2011), *Okay Mountain* (2011), *Gabriel Kuri: Nobody Needs to Know the Price of Your Saab* (2010), *Jacco Olivier: Moving Paintings* (2010), *Jon Pylypchuk* (2009), *Existed: Leonardo Drew* (2009), *Chantal Akerman: Moving Through Time and Space* (2008), *Amy Sillman: Suitors & Strangers* (2007), *Katrina Moorhead: A Thing Called Early Blur* (2007) and *Urs Fischer: Mary Poppins* (2006). Before joining the Blaffer in 2004, Schmuckli served as Assistant Curator at the Museum of Modern Art, New York (2000–2003) and as Curatorial Assistant at the Solomon R. Guggenheim Museum, New York (1997–2000).

Artist Biographies

Teresa Hubbard

Swiss, Irish, American, born 1965 in Dublin, Ireland

1998	Fellow, Akademie Schloss Solitude, Stuttgart
1990–92	MFA, Nova Scotia College of Art and Design, Halifax
1988	Yale University School of Art, MFA Sculpture Program, New Haven, Connecticut
1987	Skowhegan School of Painting and Sculpture, Skowhegan, Maine
1985–88	BFA, University of Texas at Austin
Since 2000	Professor, Department of Art & Art History, University of Texas at Austin. Since 2014, holder of the William and Bettye Nowlin Endowed Professorship in Photography.
Since 2004	Graduate Faculty, Milton Avery Graduate School of the Arts, Bard College, New York

Alexander Birchler

Swiss, born 1962 in Baden, Switzerland

1998	Fellow, Akademie Schloss Solitude, Stuttgart
1990–92	MFA, Nova Scotia College of Art and Design, Halifax
1985	University of Art and Design, Helsinki
1983–87	Schule für Gestaltung, Basel
Since 2004	Graduate Faculty, Milton Avery Graduate School of the Arts, Bard College, New York
1993–95	Lecturer, Philosophische Fakultät I, University of Zürich

Selected Solo Exhibitions

2014 *Sound Speed Marker*, Irish Museum of Modern Art, Dublin
Sound Speed Marker, Ballroom Marfa
Eight, Eighteen, Tanya Bonakdar Gallery, New York
2013 *Eight, Eighteen*. Linda Pace Foundation, San Antonio
Hubbard / Birchler—Eight. Neu im Museum, Museum Brandhorst, Munich
2012 *Hubbard / Birchler*. New Media Exhibition Series, Saint Louis Art Museum, Saint Louis
2011 *Hubbard / Birchler*. Tanya Bonakdar Gallery, New York
Hubbard / Birchler. Lora Reynolds Gallery, Austin
2010 *Grand Paris Texas* at the Paramount Theater. Film Screening, in association with Lora Reynolds Gallery, Arthouse at the Jones Center and the Austin Film Society
2009 *No Room to Answer*. Aargauer Kunsthaus, Aarau
No Room to Answer—Projections. Württembergischer Kunstverein Stuttgart
Grand Paris Texas. Gallery Barbara Thumm, Berlin
2008 *No Room to Answer*. Modern Art Museum of Fort Worth
Hello Darkness. K21 Kunstsammlung Nordrhein-Westfalen, Düsseldorf
2006 *House with Pool*. Gallery Barbara Thumm, Berlin
House with Pool. Perez Art Museum Miami
2005 *Teresa Hubbard / Alexander Birchler*. Museum Sammlung Goetz, Munich
Little Pictures at Mrs. Owen's House. Centro Galego de Arte Contemporánea, Santiago de Compostela
Troop. Gallery Bob van Orsouw, Zürich
Editing the Dark. Kemper Museum of Contemporary Art, Kansas City
Single Wide. Kaiser Wilhelm Museum, Krefeld
New Spaces: Hubbard / Birchler and Fischli / Weiss. Pinakothek der Moderne, Munich
Single Wide. Herzliya Museum of Contemporary Art, Herzliya
2004 *Single Wide*. Whitney Museum of American Art at Altria, New York
House with Pool. Tanya Bonakdar Gallery, New York
House with Pool. Museum für Gegenwartskunst, Basel
2003 *Eight*. Centro Galego de Arte Contemporánea, Santiago de Compostela
Teresa Hubbard / Alexander Birchler. Vera Munro Gallery, Hamburg
County Line Road. Gallery Barbara Thumm, Berlin
2002 ArtPace Foundation for Contemporary Art, San Antonio
Wild Walls. Kunsthalle zu Kiel
Wild Walls. Kunstmuseum St. Gallen
Tanya Bonakdar Gallery, New York
2001 *Wild Walls*. Museum Haus Lange and Museum Haus Esters, Krefeld
Wild Walls. Huis Marseille. Foundation for Photography, Amsterdam
Gallery Bob van Orsouw, Zürich
2000 *Arsenal*. Bonakdar Jancou Gallery, New York
Werk Raum 1. National Gallery in the Hamburger Bahnhof, Museum of Contemporary Art, Berlin (with Sophie Calle and Remy Markowitsch)
1999 *Motion Pictures*. Gallery Barbara Thumm, Berlin
National Gallery, Collection of Modern and Contemporary Art, Prague
Gregor's Room. Gallery Bob van Orsouw, Zürich
1998 Akademie Schloss Solitude, Stuttgart
Stripping. Künstlerhaus Bethanien, Berlin
1997 *Slow Place*. Museum für Gegenwartskunst, Basel
Hubbard / Birchler. Gallery Bob van Orsouw, Zürich

Selected Group Exhibitions

2014 *Bad Thoughts: Collection Martijn and Jeanette Sanders*. Stedelijk Museum, Amsterdam

Manifesta 10: Unlooped Kino. Works from the Goetz Collection. St. Petersburg

Summerstage. Gallery Barbara Thumm, Berlin

The Bigger Picture. Tanya Bonakdar Gallery, New York

Go-Betweens: The World Seen through Children. Mori Museum, Tokyo / Nagoya City Museum / Okinawa Prefectural Museum / The Museum of Art, Kochi

Zugaben—Sammlung Freunde der Kunstmuseen Krefeld. Krefeld

2013 *Sanft entrückt—Kinder wie im Traum*. Kunsthaus Zürich

Forever Young. Kunsthalle Nürnberg

Cut! Video Art from the Collection. Aargauer Kunsthaus, Aarau

Kino der Kunst. Pinakothek der Moderne / Schaustelle, Munich

Selections from the Permanent Collection. Modern Art Museum of Fort Worth

Open Spaces | Secret Places. Museum der Moderne, Salzburg

Open End—works from the Goetz Collection. Haus der Kunst, Munich

Reality is not a Common Place: Photographs and Videos from the Julius Baer Art Collection. Museo Cantonale d'Arte Lugano

Kunst fürs Kunsthaus. Editionen des Aargauischen Kunstvereins 1991–2013. Aargauer Kunsthaus, Aarau

2012 *A Window on the World. From Dürer to Mondrian*. Museo d'Arte, Lugano

Eröffnung des Städel Erweiterungsbaus mit dem Sammlungbereich Gegenwartskunst. Städel Museum, Frankfurt am Main

Viewpoint / A Closer Look at Showing. Huis Marseille Museum of Photography, Amsterdam

Resonance and Silence: Synaesthetic aspects in film and video. Sammlung Goetz at the Haus der Kunst, Munich

Lichtsensibel: Fotokunst aus der Sammlung. Aargauer Kunsthaus, Aarau

An Orchestrated Vision: The Theater of Contemporary Photography. Saint Louis Art Museum, Saint Louis

Performing for the Camera. Arizona State University Art Museum, Herberger Institute for Design and the Arts, Tempe

The Undercurrent of Boredom. Lothringer Halle 13, Munich

Reverberations: Cinema Regained. Official Selection, International Film Festival Rotterdam

2011 *The Cinema Effect: Illusion, Reality, and the Moving Image*. Organized by the Hirshhorn Museum and Sculpture Garden, CaixaForum, Barcelona

Videonale 13. Kunstmuseum Bonn

The Heinz and Marianne Ebers Foundation Collection. Museum Haus Lange, Krefeld

2010 *The Night Pleases Us*. 51st Edition October International Salon, Belgrade

4x2. Four premiers: 2 screenings. Museo Nacional Centro de Arte, Reina Sofia Museum, Madrid

Berger + Berger, A Prefabricated Movie Theater, Works from the Thyssen-Bornemisza Collection, Venice Biennial, 12th International Architecture Exhibition, Venice

Unsichtbare Schatten/Invisible Shadows. Museum Marta Herford

Projections. Bonniers Konsthall, Stockholm

Everyday Ideologies—Zeitläufe, Lebenswege. Kunstmuseum Magdeburg

2009 *Anabasis: Rituals of Homecoming*. Villa Grohman, Festival of Dialogue of Four Cultures, Lodz

Art, Media and Material Witness. Harn Museum, Gainesville, Florida

Conflicting Tales: Subjectivity Quadrilogy, Part 1. Burger Collection, Berlin

Götenborg International Biennial. Götenborg

Parades & Processions. Here comes everybody. Parasol Unit, Foundation for Contemporary Art, London

Filmes e vídeos da Coleção Goetz. Itaú Cultural, Sao Paulo

Three leap seconds later, 1998 ... 2008. Ankäufe aus der Bundeskunstsammlung. Kunsthaus Grenchen

Dialog der Generationen. Kunsthalle Palazzo, Liestal

Held Together with Water: Art from the Sammlung Verbund. Modern Art Museum Istanbul

2008 *Interior / Exterior*. Kunstmuseum Wolfsburg

Expenditure. Busan Biennial, Busan

Made Up. Liverpool Biennial, Tate Liverpool

The Morning After. Weserburg Museum für Moderne Kunst, Bremen

Atelier 2008. Blanton Museum of Art, Austin

The Cinema Effect: Illusion, Reality, and the Moving Image. Hirshhorn Museum and Sculpture Garden, Washington D.C.

Existencias. MUSAC Collection, Museo de Arte Contemporáneo de Castilla y Leon

2007 *Big Picture*. Norton Museum of Art, West Palm Beach

12th Biennial of Moving Images. Center for Contemporary Images, Geneva

Unidentified Emotions. Art Statements Gallery, Hong Kong

Seduction—A Theory-Fiction between the Real and the Possible. Borderline—Moving Images, Beijing Centre for Creativity, Beijing

Novelle (not yet another story). Halle für Kunst Lüneburg

Replaying Narrative. Le Mois de la photo 2007, VOX Centre de l'image contemporaine, Montreal

Dialogues and Attitudes. Works from the DZ Bank Collection, Museum of Contemporary Art, Budapest

Kunst aus der Sammlung Verbund. MAK, Museum für angewandte Kunst / Gegenwartskunst, Vienna

L'oeil écran ou la nouvelle image / The Screen Eye or The New Image. Casino Luxembourg, Forum d'art Contemporain, Luxembourg

Une Question de Génération. Museum of Contemporary Art, Lyon

Raised by Wolves. Art Gallery of Western Australia, Perth
Imagination Becomes Reality. Werke aus der Sammlung Goetz. ZKM, Museum für Neue Kunst, Karlsruhe

2006 *Gefrorene Augenblicke. Von Vallotton bis Hubbard / Birchler.* Kunsthaus Zürich
Touch My Shadows. New Media Works from the Goetz Collection. The Centre for Contemporary Art, Ujazdowski Castle, Warsaw
Auflösung III—Entgrenzung. NGBK Neue Gesellschaft für Bildende Kunst, Berlin
Upsetting the Balance—Irritation des Gleichgewichts. Paul Klee Museum, Bern
La Vie, La Ville. La Bienniale du Havre
No Peak No View. Viper International Festival for Video and Media Art, Kunsthalle Basel
Kunst Lebt!. Landesmuseen Baden-Württemberg Stuttgart
Melancholy. Nationalgalerie Berlin

2005 *Contenance.* Württembergischer Kunstverein Stuttgart
Vertiges. Les Abbatoirs Museum, Toulouse
Johnny. ArtUnlimited, Basel. Gallery Bob van Orsouw, Zürich
Esprit es-tu lá?. Fondation Claude Verdan, Musée de la Main, Lausanne
Swiss Video Landscape Today—Looped Sensations. Park Tower Hall, Tokyo / Goethe Institute, Kyoto / Fukuoka City Public Library, Fukuoka / Aichi Arts Center, Nagoya / 21st Century Museum of Contemporary Art, Kanazawa / Yokohama Museum of Art, Yokohama
Geschichtenerzähler. Kunsthalle Hamburg
The World is a Stage. Mori Art Museum, Tokyo
Vanishing Point. Wexner Center for the Arts, Columbus
Roaming Memories. Ludwig Forum, Aachen
Me Myself I. Kunstmuseum St. Gallen
Contained. Tanya Bonakdar Gallery, New York
Les Grands Spectacles. 120 Jahre Kunst und Massenkultur. Museum der Moderne, Salzburg

2004 *3': Condensed Information.* Schirn Kunsthalle, Frankfurt am Main
Take 5 jaar Huis Marseille. Huis Marseille Foundation for Photography, Amsterdam
Video dreams: between the cinematic and theatrical. Kunsthaus Graz
The Cobweb. Centro Galego de Arte Contemporánea, Santiago de Compostela
Einleuchten—Works from the Thyssen-Bornemisza Contemporary Art Foundation. Museum der Moderne, Salzburg
StadtRäume. Kunstforum Baloise, Basel
Yet Untitled: Works from the Bernd F. Künne Collection. Kunsthalle Nürnberg / National Museum of Photography, Copenhagen
Reordering Reality: Collecting Contemporary Art. Columbus Museum of Art, Ohio
Plus ou Moines Jeunes. Centre Culturel Suisse, Paris
Sammlung Plum. Museum Kurhaus Kleve
So Wie Die Dinge Liegen. Hartware Medien Kunstverein, Phoenixhalle Dortmund
Short Stories. Fotomuseum Antwerp, Antwerp

2003 *Festival Video.* Vira Gambarogno, Ticino
Fast Forward—Works from the Goetz Collection. ZKM/Zentrum für Kunst und Medientechnologie, Karlsruhe
Eight. Hordaland Art Center, Bergen
10th Biennial of Moving Images. Centre for Contemporary Images, Geneva
Child in Time. Views on Contemporary Artists on Youth and Adolescence. Gemeente Museum, Helmond
Brightness—Works from the Thyssen-Bornemisza Contemporary Art Foundation. Museum of Modern Art Dubrovnik
Looking in—Looking out, Positions in Contemporary Photography. Oeffentliche Kunstsammlung Basel, Kunstmuseum Basel
Single Wide. ArtUnlimited, Basel. Gallery Bob van Orsouw, Zürich and Vera Munro Gallery, Hamburg
Adolescence. Reina Sofia Museum, Madrid
Suiza en ARCO. La Casa Encendida, Madrid
Neuerwerbungen. Museum für Gegenwartskunst, Kunstmuseum Basel,
Yet Untitled: Works from the Bernd F. Künne Collection. Städtische Galerie Wolfsburg / Suermondt-Ludwig-Museum, Aachen

2002 *The Starting Line.* Pinakothek der Moderne, Munich
On Stage. Kunstverein Hannover / Villa Merkel, Esslingen
Wallflowers, Grosse Fotografien. Kunsthaus Zürich
Out of Place: Contemporary Art and the Architectural Uncanny. Museum of Contemporary Art, Chicago
Eight. ArtUnlimited, Basel. Gallery Bob van Orsouw, Zürich
Im Sucher. Zeitgenoessiche Fotografie in Solothurner Sammlungen. Kunstmuseum Solothurn
22 to Watch. New Art in Austin. Austin Museum of Art
Say Hello to Peace and Tranquility. Netherlands Media Art Institute, Amsterdam / Nikolaj Contemporary Art Museum, Copenhagen
Das Weiss Dahinter. Spurensuche in der Aargauischen Kunstsammlung. Kunsthalle Palazzo, Liestal

2001 *New Work.* Tanya Bonakdar Gallery, New York
I Like Theater & Theater Likes Me. Deutsches Schauspielhaus, Hamburg
Dialogues & Stories. Museum Sammlung Grothe, Duisburg
Das Versprechen der Fotografie. Schirn Kunsthalle, Frankfurt
Prospekt! Zu einer Sammlung für Gegenwartskunst. Aargauer Kunsthaus, Aarau
Photography from the KPN. Huis Marseille. Foundation for Photography, Amsterdam
Missing Link. Kunst Haus Dresden / Ujazdowski Castle, Center for Contemporary Arts, Warsaw
Crossover Theater & Art. Offenes Kulturhaus Center for Contemporary Art, Linz
9th Biennial of Moving Images. Centre for Contemporary Images, Geneva
6 Artists—6 positions. Museum Sammlung Goetz, Munich
Julius Bär Art zu Gast im Helmhaus. Helmhaus, Zürich

2000 *Scène de la Vie Conjugale.* Villa Arson, Nice
Anti-Memory. Yokohama Museum of Art, Yokohama
U.T. Faculty. Blanton Museum of Art, Austin

Every Time. La Biennale de Montréal
No Vacancies. Gallery Barbara Thumm, Berlin
Solitude im Museum. Staatsgalerie, Stuttgart / Musèe d'Art Moderne de St. Etienne
Mnemosyne, Encontros de Fotografia 2000. Coimbra / Lisbon
Imago. Center for Photography, University of Salamanca
Staged. Bonakdar Jancou Gallery, New York
Nachbilder, Neue Fotografien in der Sammlung, Kunsthaus Zürich

1999 *dAPERTutto*. 48th Venice Biennial, Venice
Tomorrow For Ever. Museum Sammlung Grothe, Duisburg / Kunsthalle Krems
Signs of Life. Melbourne International Biennial, Melbourne
Solitude in Budapest. Kunsthalle Budapest
Skulpturen Biennale. Westfälisches Landesmuseum, Münster
DACH.AT. Gallery Krinzinger, Vienna
Dislocation. hARTware Projekte, Dortmund
40 Jahre Schweizer Kunst. Aargauer Kunsthaus, Aarau
Missing Link. Kunstmuseum Bern
Galerie Christine König, Vienna
Le Sommeil. Musèe cantonal des Beaux-Arts, Lausanne
Eidgenössischer Preis für Freie Kunst. Kunsthalle Zürich
NB. Centre d'Art Neuchâtel

1998 Ausstellungsraum Mezzanin, Vienna
L'Art du Monde 98. Passage de Retz, Paris
Freie Sicht aufs Mittelmeer. Kunsthaus Zürich / Schirn Kunsthalle, Frankfurt a.M.
Photography as Concept. Triennale der Fotografie, Villa Merkel, Esslingen
Nonchalance revisited. Akademie der Künste, Berlin
Anticipation. Centre Pour l'Image Contemporaine, Geneva
Im Kontext. Kunstmuseum St. Gallen
Positionen der 90er Jahre aus der Sammlung Künne. Städtische Galerie Wolfsburg

1997 *Alice hinter den Spiegeln*. Kunstverein Baselland, Sissach
Extended Objects. Art Gallery, Mount Saint Vincent University, Halifax
Eidgenössischer Preis für Freie Kunst. Musèe cantonal des Beaux-Arts, Lausanne
P.O. Box. Museum für Gegenwartskunst, Basel / Portikus Frankfurt / Kunstmuseum Bonn / Museum van Hedendaagse Kunst, Ghent
Nonchalance. Centre Pasquart, Biel
Check in! Museum of Contemporary Art, Basel

1996 *Young Art*. Kunsthalle Bern / Museé d'art et d'histoire, Geneva / Kunsthalle Zürich
Cabines de Bain. Projekt Attitudes, Fribourg

1995 Kunsthalle Palazzo, Liestal
East. Sainsbury Centre for Visual Arts, Norwich

1994 *Körper, Fragment, Wirklichkeit. Schweizer Kunst des 20. Jahrhunderts*. Kunstmuseum Solothurn *Small Histories*. Southern Alberta Art Gallery, Lethbridge

1993 *Speicher, Versuche zur Darstellbarkeit von Geschichte/n*. Offenes Kulturhaus, Linz
Exchange 2. Shedhalle, Zürich

Selected Public Collections

Aargauer Kunsthaus, Aarau, Switzerland
Art Gallery of Western Australia, Perth, Australia
Walter A. Bechtler Stiftung, Switzerland
Blanton Museum of Art, University of Texas, Austin, USA
Centre for Photography, University of Salamanca, Spain
Centro Galego de Arte Contemporánea, Santiago de Compostela, Spain
Columbus Museum of Art, Ohio, USA
Daros Collection, Zürich, Switzerland
Hirshhorn Museum and Sculpture Garden, Washington D.C, USA
Huis Marseille Museum for Photography, Amsterdam, Netherlands
International Centre for Photography, New York, USA
Israel Museum, Jerusalem, Israel
Kaiser-Wilhelm Museum, Krefeld, Germany
Kunsthaus Zürich, Switzerland
Kunsthalle zu Kiel, Germany
Kunstmuseum Luzern, Depositum Kanton Luzern, Switzerland
Kunstmuseum St. Gallen, Switzerland
Linda Pace Foundation, San Antonio, USA
Museum of Contemporary Art, MOCA Los Angeles, USA
Museum of Fine Arts Houston, USA
Museum für Gegenwartskunst, Basel, Kunstmuseum Basel, Switzerland
Modern Art Museum of Fort Worth, Fort Worth, USA
Museo de Arte Contemporáneo de Castilla y León, Spain
Museum Sammlung Goetz, Munich, Germany
Neues Museum Nuremberg, Germany
Norton Museum of Art, West Palm Beach, USA
Städel Museum Frankfurt, Germany
Staatsgalerie Stuttgart, Germany
Pinakothek der Moderne, Munich, Germany
Swiss Federal Office of Culture, Bern, Switzerland
Thyssen-Bornemisza Contemporary Art Foundation, Vienna, Austria
Ulrich Museum of Art, Wichita, Kansas, USA
University of St. Gallen, Switzerland
Yokohama Museum of Art, Yokohama, Japan

Bibliography

Selected Exhibition Catalogues and Books

2014 Araki, Natsumi, Sasaki Hitomi et al. *In-Betweens: The World Seen through Children.* Exh. cat. Tokyo: Mori Museum, 2014.

Ruf, Beatrix, and Martijn van Nieuwenhuyzen et al. *Bad Thoughts: Collection Martijn and Jeannette Sanders.* Exh. cat. Amsterdam: Stedelijk Museum, 2014.

Terranova, Charissa N. *Automotive Prosthetic: Technological Mediation and the Car in Conceptual Art.* Austin: University of Texas Press, 2014.

2013 Enwezor, Okwui, and Ingvild Goetz. *Open End: Goetz Collection at Haus der Kunst.* Exh. cat. Munich: Haus der Kunst, 2013.

Franciolli, Marco, Elio Schenini et al. *Reality is not a Common Place.* Exh. cat. Lugano: Museo Cantonale d'Arte, 2013.

Graeve Ingelmann, Inka, Philip Ursprung et al. *Open Spaces Secret Places.* Exh. cat. Salzburg: Museum der Moderne, Cologne: Walther König, 2013.

Hentschel, Martin, and Sabine Röder et al. *Zugaben: Sammlung Freunde der Kunstmuseen Krefeld.* Exh. cat. Krefeld: Kunstmuseen Krefeld / Museum Haus Lange, 2013.

Krauss, Rosalind, Daniela Ferrari, Marco Franciolli et al. *A Window on the World: From Dürer to Mondrian and Beyond.* Exh. cat. Lugano: Museum d'Arte Lugano, 2013.

Seifermann, Ellen, and Harriet Zilch et al. *Forever Young.* Exh. cat. Cologne: Walther König, 2013.

2012 Hollein, Max, Martin Engler et al. *Gegenwartskunst: 1945–Heute im Städel Museum.* Ostfildern-Ruit: Hatje Cantz, 2012.

Laabs, Annegret, and Uwe Gellner. *Everyday Ideologies: Zeitläufe, Lebenswege.* Exh. cat. Magdeburg: Kunstmuseum Kloster Unser Lieben Frauen, 2012.

Sayre, Henry M. *A World of Art, Sixth Edition.* New Jersey: Prentice Hall Publishers, 2012.

2011 Elben, Georg, and Dirk Rustemeyer. *Videonale 13 Contemporary Video Art.* Exh. cat., Kunstmuseum Bonn. Bielefeld: Kerber Verlag, 2011.

Heynen, Julian, and Martin Hentschel. *Heinz and Marianne Ebers Foundation: A Collection with Stature.* Exh. cat., Kunstmuseum Krefeld. Bielefeld: Kerber Verlag, 2011.

2010 Fast, Friederike, Michael Kröger, Thomas Niemeyer et al. *Unsichtbare Schatten / Invisible Shadows.* Exh. cat. Herford: Marta Herford, 2010.

Günzel, Wolfgang. *Kunst in der Helaba.* Frankfurt am Main: Landesbank Hessen-Thüringen Collection, 2010.

Pousette, Johan, and Celia Prado. *The Night Pleases Us.* Exh. cat., 51st Octobers Salon. Belgrade: Cultural Center of Belgrade, 2010.

2009 Kaiser, Philipp. *"Erzählung und Stillstand: Zu den Arbeiten von Teresa Hubbard und Alexander Birchler / Narration and Stillstand: About the Work of Teresa Hubbard and Alexander Birchler."* PhD Diss, University of Basel, 2009.

Kaiser, Philipp, Rosa Olivares, David A. Ross et al. *100 Video Artists.* Madrid: Exit Publications, 2009.

Krasny, Elke, Mark Wigley et al. *Thyssen-Bornemisza Art Contemporary: The Collection Book.* Cologne: Walther König, 2009.

Kurjaković, Daniel, Beate Söntgen et al. *Conflicting Tales: Subjectivity.* Exh. cat. Zürich: The Burger Collection and JRP Ringier, 2009.

Schuppli, Madeline, Andrea Karnes, Iris Dressler, Sara Arrhenius. *No Room to Answer: Extended Version.* Exh. cat. Aarau: Aargauer Kunsthaus, 2009.

Schwarz, Dieter, and Ziba Ardalan de Weck. *Parades and Processions: Here Comes Everybody.* Exh. cat. Parasol Unit Foundation for Contemporary Art. Cologne: Walther Koenig, 2009.

Scorzin, Pamela C., et al. *Künstler: Kritisches Lexikon der Gegenwartskunst.* Munich: Weltkunst Verlag, 2009.

2008 Beck, Hubert, Günter Engelhard et al. *Index: Fotographie. DZ BANK Sammlung im Städel Museum.* Osterfildern-Ruit: Hatje Cantz, 2008.

Breuer, Gerda, Annelie Lütgens et al. *Interieur Exterieur: Wohnen in der Kunst.* Exh. cat., Kunstmuseum Wolfsburg. Osterfildern-Ruit: Hatje Cantz, 2008.

Biggs, Lewis, Laurence Sillars et al. *Liverpool International Biennial.* Exh. cat. Liverpool: Liverpool University Press, 2008.

Brougher, Kerry, Kelly Gordon et al. *The Cinema Effect: Illusion, Reality, and the Moving Image.* Exh. cat., Hirshhorn Museum and Sculpture Garden. New York: Distributed Art Publishers, 2008.

Geha, Katie. *Atelier 2008: Selections from the Department of Art and Art History Faculty at the University of Texas at Austin: Teresa Hubbard / Alexander Birchler.* Exh. cat. Austin: Blanton Museum of Art, 2008.

Karnes, Andrea, Iris Dressler, Sara Arrhenius. *No Room to Answer.* Exh. cat. Osterfildern-Ruit: Hatje Cantz, 2008.

Park, Son Ju, Jeon Hyo Gwan, Kim Chang Jo et al. *Busan Biennial.* Exh. cat. Busan, 2008.

Weinberg, Adam D., and Shamim M. Momin. *Whitney Museum of American Art at Altria 25 Years.* New Haven: Yale University Press, 2008.

Friese, Peter, Ingo Clauß, Ingvild Goetz et. al. *The Morning After.* Exh. cat. Bremen: Weserberg Museum für Moderne Kunst, 2008.

2007 Ammann, Jean-Christophe. *Bei näherer Betrachtung: Zeitgenössische Kunst verstehen und deuten.* Frankfurt am Main: Westend Publishing, 2007.

Becher, Jörg. *Die 50 wichtigsten Künstler der Schweiz.* Basel: Echtzeit Verlag, 2007.

Cameron, Dan, Toni Morrison et al. *Artworks: The Progressive Collection.* New York: Distributed Art Publishers, 2007.

Cook, Robert. *Raised by Wolves.* Exh. cat. Perth: Art Gallery of Western Australia, 2007.

Gisbourne, Mark. *Double Act: Two Artists One Expression.* New York: Prestel Publishing, 2007.

Graeve Ingelmann, Inka, et al. *Held Together With Water: Art from the Sammlung Verbund.* Exh. cat. ed. Gabriele Schor. Osterfildern-Ruit: Hatje Cantz, 2007.

Gruithuijsen, Krist, and Bettina Steinbrügge. *Novella (not yet another story).* Exh. cat. Lüneburg: Halle für Kunst, 2007.

Herzogenrath, Wulf, Veronika Baksa-Sóos et al. *Dialogues & Attitudes*. Exh. cat. Osterfidern-Ruit: Hatje Cantz, 2007.

Michel, Régis, et al. *L'oeil-écran: ou la nouvelle image*. Exh. cat. Luxembourg City: Casino Luxembourg, 2007.

Pauli, Lori, Jean-Christophe Royoux et al. *Replaying Narrative*. Exh. cat. Montreal: National Library of Canada, 2007.

Sayre, Henry. *The World of Art, 5th Edition*. New Jersey: Perarson Education / Prentice Hall, 2007.

2006 Bolter, Angélique, Peter Rummel. *Tif: Einflüsse Neuer Medien auf Zeitgenössische Fotokunst*. Stuttgart: Merz Akademie Hochschule für Gestaltung, 2006.

Gosselin, Claude, Linda Morren et al. Arts: *Le Havre 2006: biennale d'art contemporain*. Exh. cat. Cologne: Snoeck, 2006.

Gosselin, Claude, et al. *La Vie, La Ville*, Biennale d'art Contemporain. Cologne: Snoeck, 2006.

Graeve Ingelmann, Inka, Bernhart Schwenk et al. *Pinakothek der Moderne: Malerei, Skulptur, Fotografie, Neue Medien*. Pinakothek der Moderne, Munich. Cologne: DuMont, 2006.

Osterwold, Tim, et al. *Irritation des Gleichgewichts*. Exh. cat., Zentrum Paul Klee Bern. Cologne: Snoeck, 2006.

Osterwold, Tim, Nicole Fritz et al. *Kunst Lebt!*. Exh. cat., Grosse Landesausstellung Baden-Württemberg, Stuttgart. Cologne: Snoeck, 2006.

Sollins, Susan, et al. *Art: 21. Art in the Twenty-First Century*. New York: Harry N. Abrams, Inc., 2006.

Urbaschek, Stephan, et al. *Imagination Becomes Reality*. Exh. cat. Munich: Museum Sammlung Goetz, 2006.

2005 Araki, Natsumi. *The World is a Stage: Stories Behind Pictures*. Exh. cat. Tokyo: Mori Museum, 2005.

Bustamante, Jean-Marc, et al. *Printemps de Septembre*. Exh. cat. Toulouse: Les Abbatoirs Museum, 2005.

Dunbar, Elizabeth. *Editing the Dark*. Exh. cat. Kansas City: Kemper Museum of Contemporary Art, 2005.

Groys, Boris, Juri Steiner et al. *Before the Sun Rises*. Zürich: JRP / Ringier, 2005.

Ise, Claudine. *Vanishing Point*. Exh. cat. Columbus: Wexner Center for the Arts, Ohio State University, 2005.

Brehm, Magrit, Roberto Ohrt, Klaus Theweleit. *Les Grands Spectacles: 120 Jahre Kunst und Massenkultur*. Exh. cat., Museum der Moderne Salzburg. Osterfildern-Ruit: Hatje Cantz, 2005.

2004 Bal, Mieke, Adam Budak, Laura Mulvey, Kaja Silverman et al. *Videodreams: Between the Cinematic and the Theatrical*. Exh. cat., Kunsthaus Graz. Cologne: Walther Koenig, 2004.

Barents, Els. *Take Five! Vijf Jaar Huis Marseille*. Exh. cat. Amsterdam: Huis Marseille Foundation for Photography, 2004.

Dressler, Iris, Hans. D. Christ. *So Wie Die Dinge Liegen*. Exh. cat., Hartware Medien Kunstverein. Frankfurt am Main: Revolver Publishers, 2004.

Kaiser, Philipp, Dominic Molon, Maya Naef. *House with Pool*. Exh. cat., Museum für Gegenwartskunst, Basel. Basel: Christoph Merian, 2004.

Moenig, Roland, et al. *Sammlung Plum*. Exh. cat. Kleve: Museum Kurhaus Kleve, 2004.

Momin, Shamim M. *Single Wide*. Exh. cat. New York: Whitney Museum of American Art at Altria, 2004.

Nill, Annegreth T. *Reordering Reality*. Exh. cat. Columbus: Columbus Museum of Art, 2004.

Weibel, Peter, Daniela Zyman et al. *Ein-Leuchten*. Exh. cat. Salzburg: Museum der Moderne Salzburg, 2004.

Weinhart, Martina, Hans Ulrich Obrist et al. *3': Condensed Information*. Exh. cat. Frankfurt am Main: Kunsthalle Schirn, 2004.

2003 Dressler, Iris, and Hans D. Christ. *Hartware 2001*. Exh. cat. Dortmund: Hartware Medien Kunst Verein, 2003.

Farquharson, Alex, and Soraya Rodriguez. *Brightness: Works from the Thyssen-Bornemisza Contemporary Art Foundation*. Exh. cat. Dubrovnik: MW Projects, Museum of Modern Art Dubrovnik, 2003.

Fernández-Cid, Miguel, Martin Hentschel et al. *A revista do CGAC*. Exh. cat. Santiago de Compostela: Centro Galego de Arte Contemporánea, 2003.

Fernández-Cid, Miguel. *Ten Years*. Exh. cat. Santiago de Compostela: Centro Galego de Arte Contemporánea, 2003.

Seelig, Thomas, Brigitte Weneburg, Christoph Ribbat. *Yet Untitled: Works from the Bernd F. Künne Collection*. Exh. cat. Ostfildern-Ruit: Hatje Cantz, 2003

Smith, Roberta, et al. *Charley*. The Deste Foundation for Contemporary Art. Dijon: Les Presses du Réel, 2003.

Weibel, Peter, Sabine Himmelsbach et al. *Fast Forward*. Exh. cat. Karlsruhe: Zentrum für Kunst und Medientechnologie, 2003..

2002 Baumstark, Reinhold, Carla Schulz-Hoffman, Winfried Nerdinger et al. *Pinakothek der Moderne: Kunst, Grafik, Architektur, Design*. *Pinakothek* der Moderne. Cologne: DuMont, 2002.

Berg, Stephan, Martin Engler et al. *On Stage*. Exh. cat. Hannover: Kunstverein Hannover / Villa Merkel, 2002.

Bezzola, Tobia. *Wallflowers*. Exh. cat. Zürich: Kunsthaus Zürich, 2002.

Dressler, Iris. *Say Hello to Peace and Tranquility*. Exh. cat. Amsterdam: Hartware Projekte, 2002.

Friis-Hansen, Dana. *22 to Watch: New Art in Austin*. Exh. cat. Austin: Austin Museum of Art, 2002.

Molon, Dominic. *Out of Place: Contemporary Art and the Architectural Uncanny*. Exh. cat. Chicago: Museum of Contemporary Art, 2002.

Pinakothek der Moderne: Malerei, Skulptur, Neue Medien. Ed. Carla Schulz-Hoffman. Pinakothek der Moderne. Cologne: DuMont, 2002.

Schwenk, Bernhard. *Futur Drei*. Exh. cat. Hannover: Pinakothek der Moderne, 2002.

2001 Barents, Els, et al. *KPN Collectie Fotografie*. Exh. cat. Amsterdam: Huis Marseille, Foundation for Photography, 2001.

Gale, Peggy, Claude Gosselin et al. *Every Time: La Biennale de Montréal*. Exh. cat. Montreal: Centre international d'art contemporain, 2001.

Gateau, Laurence, Jean-Christophe Royoux et al. *Action, On Tourne / Action, We're Filming*. Exh. cat. Nice: Villa Arson, 2001.

Hentschel, Martin, Philipp Kaiser, Konrad Bitterli. *Wild Walls*. Exh. cat. Bielefeld: Kerber, 2001.

2000 Amano, Taro, et al. *Anti-Memory*. Exh. cat. Yokohama: Yokohama Museum of Art, 2000.

Beauffet, Jacques, Martine Dancer, Ulrike Gauss, Gudrun Inboden, Jean-Baptiste Joly, Philipp Kaiser et al. *Solitude im Museum*. Exh. cat. Stuttgart: Staatsgalerie Stuttgart, Edition Solitude, 2000.
Blume, Eugen and Jörg Makarinus. *Werk Raum: Sophie Calle, Teresa Hubbard / Alexander Birchler, Rémy Markowitch*. Exh. cat. Berlin: Nationalgalerie im Hamburger Bahnhof, Museum der Gegenwart, 2000.
Kaiser, Philipp, Lilian Pfaff et al. *Imago*. Exh. cat. Salamanca: Junta de Castilla y León y Ediciones Universidad de Salamanca, 2000.
Sardo, Delfim, et al. *Mnemosyne. Encontros de Fotografia*. Exh. cat. Coimbra: Encontros de Fotografia de Coimbra, 2000.

1999 Aigner, Carl, Hubertus von Amelunxen et al. *Tomorrow For Ever*. Exh. cat., Kunsthalle Krems, Museum Sammlung Grothe, Duisburg. Cologne: Dumont, 1999.
Blaser, Christophe, Pierre-André Lienhard and Marc-Olivier Wahler. *NB: Ateliers de la Confédération 1997–1998*. Exh. cat., Centre d'Art Neuchâtel. Bern: Bundesamt für Kultur, 1999.
Doswald, Christoph, Gerrit Gohlke et al. *Missing Link*. Exh. cat., Kunstmuseum Bern. Thalwil / Zürich: Edition Stemmle, 1999.
Engberg, Juliana. *Melbourne International Biennial: Signs of Life*. Exh. cat. Melbourne: City of Melbourne, 1999.
Engelbach, Barbara, Florian Matzner, Teresa Hubbard, Alexander Birchler et al. *Skulpturen Biennale*. Exh. cat., Westfälisches Landesmuseum Münsterland. Munster: Laumann, 1999.
Sànchez, Yvette. *Coleccionismo y Literatura*. Madrid: Ediciones Cátedra, 1999.
Schwander, Martin. *Kunstforum Baloise*. Exh. brochure. Basel: 1999.
Schwander, Martin, Harald Szeeman et al. *La Biennale di Venezia, dAPERTutto*. Exh. cat. Venice: Marsilio Editions, 1999.

1998 Curiger, Bice, Michelle Nicol, Juri Steiner et al. *Freie Sichtaufs Mittelmeer*. Exh. cat., Kunsthaus Zürich. Zürich: Scalo Publisher, 1998.
Gohlke, Gerrit. *In Wirklichkeit*. Exh. brochure. Berlin: Künstlerhaus Bethanien, 1998
Gohlke, Gerrit. *Stripping*. Exh. cat. Prague: National Gallery, Collection of Modern and Contemporary Art, 1998.
Von Amelunxen, Hubertus, and Philip Ursprung. *Scene*. Zürich: Codax, 1998.
Wiehager, Renate, Teresa Hubbard, Alexander Birchler et al. *Fotografie als Handlung / Photography as Concept, 4. Internationale Foto-Triennale Esslingen*. Exh. cat, Villa Merkel. Ostfildern-Ruit: Hatje Cantz, 1998.

1997 Doswald, Christoph, Andreas Meier, Jean Baptiste Joli et al. *Nonchalance*. Exh. cat., Centre Pasquart, Biel. Wabern: Benteli, 1997.
Doswald, Christoph, Theodora Vischer, Teresa Hubbard and Alexander Birchler. *Slow Place*. Exh. cat. Basel: Museum für Gegenwartskunst, 1997.
Vischer, Theodora, et al. *Check in!* Exh. cat. Basel: Museum für Gegenwartskunst, 1997.

1996 Armleder, John, Lionel Bovier et al. *Never Say Never*. Exh. cat. Zürich: Offizin, 1996.
Burkhardt, Barbara. *Small Histories*. Exh. cat. Lethbridge: Southern Alberta Art Gallery, 1996.
Morris, Linda, et al. *East*. Exh. cat. Norwich: Sainsbury Centre for Visual Arts, University of East Anglia, 1995.
Sanchez, Yvette. *Ein Baum ist ein Baum ist ein Baum*. Exh. brochure. Basel: 1995.
Sturm, Eva. *Im Engpass der Worte: Sprechen über Moderne und Zeitgenössische Kunst*. Berlin: Dietrich Reimer Publisher, 1996.

1994 Graber, Hedy, Philip Ursprung. Andrea Fisher, Gery de Smet, *Teresa Hubbard / Alexander Birchler*. Exh. cat., Kunsthalle Palazzo. Basel: Schwabe, 1994.

1993 Horisberger, Christina, et al. *Körper—Fragment—Wirklichkeit: Beispiele aus der Schweizer Kunst des 20. Jahrhunderts*. Exh. cat. Solothurn: Kunstmuseum Solothurn, 1993.
Lux, Harm, Philip Ursprung, Teresa Hubbard, Alexander Birchler et al. *Exchange 2*. Exh. cat. Zürich: Verein Shedhalle, 1993.
Sturm, Eva, et al. *Speicher: Versuche zur Darstellbarkeit von Geschichte/n*. Exh. cat. Linz: Offenes Kulturhaus, 1993.

Selected Articles

2014 Arnaut, Irina. "Where cinema and video overlap: the filmmakers on their subjects, process, and recent exhibitions." *Bomb Magazine*, July 3, 2014. http://bombmagazine.org.
Johnson, Grant. "Teresa Hubbard and Alexander Birchler." *Artforum*, October 2014. http://artforum.com.
Volk, Gregory. "Hubbard and Birchler." Art in America, October 2014.

2013 Matzner, Alexandra. "Louise Lawler, Teresa Hubbard / Alexander Birchler, Räume neu gesehen." *Texte zur Kunst*, 2012

2012 Lutz, Eric. "An Orchestrated Vision: The Theater of Contemporary Photography." Saint Louis Art Museum, 2012.

2011 Hang, Patricia. "Crumbling Picture Palaces." *Icon International*, October 2011.
Johnson, Ken. "Teresa Hubbard and Alexander Birchler at Tanya Bonakdar Gallery." *New York Times*, January 14, 2011.
Kastner, Jeffrey. "Teresa Hubbard / Alexander Birchler." *Artforum*, March 2011.
Lima, Benjamin. "Teresa Hubbard / Alexander Birchler." *Artforum*, April 21, 2011. http://artforum.com.
Stevens, Rachel. "Cinematic Time Replayed." *Millenium Film Journal*, no. 54, Fall 2011.
Von Taube, Annika. "Paris Texas." *Sleek*, Spring 2011.

2010 Zucker, Stefan. "Teresa Hubbard and Alexander Birchler—Aargauer Kunsthaus." *Artforum*, March 1, 2010.

2009 Aicher, Annik. "Zuhause im Leben der Anderen: No Room to Answer—Projections im Württembergischen Kunstverein Stuttgart." *Kultur*, April 2009.
Blättner, Martin. "Teresa Hubbard / Alexander Birchler: No Room to Answer—Projections." *Kunstforum International*, no. 197, 2009.
Braun, Adrienne. "Rätselhafte Bilderschleifen." *Art*, no. 3, March 2009.

Braun, Adrienne: Alles Bleibt Anders—Geschichten, die Sich im Kreis Drehen: Die Surrealen Video-Loops von Teresa Hubbard und Alexander Birchler in Stuttgart." *Süddeutsche Zeitung*, March 24, 2009.

Forstbauer, Nicolaus B. "Teresa Hubbard und Alexander Birchler zeigen No Room to Answer—Projections: Die Stadt, das Haus und die Stadt." *Stuttgarter Nachrichten*, February 3, 2009.

Hasenmeyer, Valérie. "Nicht von dieser Welt." *Kunstmagazine*, no. 4, 2009.

Leisten, Georg. "Den entscheidenden Moment verpassen—Filme von Teresa Hubbard und Alexander Birchler im Württembergischen Kunstverein." *Stuttgarter Zeitung*, February 3, 2009.

Morgenthaler, Daniel. "Das Leben ist ein Loop." *Basler Zeitung*, October 28, 2009.

Mutti, Sylvia. "Suspense in Endlosschleife." *Artensuite Kunstmagazin*, October 3, 2009.

Olonetzky, Nadine. "Das Bild als Parasit." *NZZ*, August 30, 2009.

Schindler, Feli. "Das Vorher und Nachher der Augenblicke." *Tage-Anzeiger*, September 19, 2009.

Schindler, Feli. "Der Entscheidende Augenblick." *Der Bund*, September 25, 2009.

Speidel, Klaus. "Hubbard & Birchler: Espaces de Doute." *Art21*, no. 21, 2009.

Tobler, Konrad. "Und das Schweben Packt." *Aargauer Zeitung*, September 5, 2009.

Von Burg, Dominique. "Teresa Hubbard und Alexander Birchler: Loops Zwischen Amnesie und Wiederholung." *Kunstbulletin*, November 2009.

2008 Bourbon, Matthew. "Hubbard / Birchler: No Room to Answer." *Artforum*, November 2008. http://artforum.com.

Büsing, Nicole. "Das Traute Heim als Höhle und Hölle." *Nürnberger Nachrichten*, June 12, 2008.

Czöppan, Gabi. "Wohnen wie von Sinnen." *Focus Magazin*, November 11, 2008.

Dee Mitchell, Charles. "Question Time." *Dallas Morning News*, September 23, 2008.

Klaas, Heiko. "Die Ausenwelt der Innenwelt." *Kieler Nachrichten*, December 30, 2008.

Koon, Yee-wan. "Eyes Wide Open." *Muse*, January 2008.

Leung, Janice. "Unidentified Emotions." *South China Morning Post*, January 1, 2008.

McNatt, Glenn. "Hirshhorn Exhibit Examines Reel vs. Real." *Baltimore Sun*, February 17, 2008.

Simblist, Noah. "Teresa Hubbard / Alexander Birchler." *Artlies*, issue 60, Winter 2008.

Robinson, Gaile. "Moving Pictures." *Star-Telegram*, September 14, 2008.

Terranova, Charissa N. "Hubbard / Birchler: No Room to Answer at the Modern." *Glasstire*, October, 2008.

2007 Heard, Lisa. "Gregor's Room: Recent Acquisitions." *Norton Museum of Art Magazine*, May 2007.

Obrist, Hans Ulrich. "Ever 3/3 Ever." *ARTiT*, Summer/Fall 2007.

Schwan, Gary. "Seeing Big Pictures." *Palm Beach Post*, August 10, 2007.

2006 Hubbard, Teresa. "Notes on House with Pool." *Artlies*, Spring 2006.

Kuni, Verena. "Verschiebungen in der Nachtschicht." *Kunstmagazin: Zeitgenössiche Kunst im Raum Basel*, May 11, 2006.

Morales, Réne. "Teresa Hubbard and Alexander Birchler." *MAM Portrait: Miami Art Museum*, July–September 2006.

Müller, Katrin Bettina. "House with Pool von Teresa Hubbard and Alexander Birchler." *Berliner Morgenpost*, May 7, 2006.

2005 Armetta, Amoreen. "Teresa Hubbard / Alexander Birchler." *Flash Art*, January 2005.

Bitterli, Konrad. "Profile: Teresa Hubbard / Alexander Birchler." *Contemporary*, issue 71, February/March 2005.

Butler, Robert. "Stretch Your Movie-Going Mind at Kemper." *Kansas City Star*, March 17, 2005.

DiPietro, Monty. "From Zen to Story: A Tale of Artists East and West." *The Japan Times*, April 7, 2005.

Hess, Ewa. "Johnnys Heimkehr." *Sonntags Zeitung*, November 27, 2005.

Iorg, Emily. "Kemper's Editing the Dark." University News, *University of Missouri*, April 3, 2005.

Jones, Kristin. "Teresa Hubbard / Alexander Birchler." *Frieze*, issue 89, 2005.

Mctavish, Brian. "'Dark' Recesses." *Kansas City Star*, March 22, 2005.

2004 Baur, Simon. "Teresa Hubbard und Alexander Birchler im Museum für Gegenwartskunst." *Kunstbulletin*, February 2004.

Imhof, Dora. "Teresa Hubbard und Alexander Birchler: 'House with Pool.'" *Kunstforum* 161, March/April 2004.

Johnson, Ken. "The Dark Night of a Woman, the Tragic Victim of... What?" *New York Times*, September 3, 2004.

Kuni, Verena. "3' in der Kunsthalle Schirn." *Kunstbulletin*, December 2004.

Marzahn, Alexander. "Vorgestellte Räume: Echte Rolle." *Basler Zeitung*, February 2, 2004.

Yates, Christopher. "Contemporary View." *Columbus Dispatch*, May 2, 2004.

Schwendener, Martha. "House with Pool." *Time Out New York*, November 4, 2004.

Spiegler, Almuth. "Das Kunsthaus Graz im Land der "Videodreams": Eine dunkle Versuchung ohne Orientierung." *Die Presse*, July 23, 2004.

Starker, Melissa. "Reality, What a Concept." *Alive*, April 28, 2004.

2003 Ammann, Jean-Christophe. "Endlosschlaufe." *Kunstzeitung*, no. 86, October 2003.

Ammann, Jean-Christophe. "Magistral: Single Wide by Teresa Hubbard and Alexander Birchler." *UBS AG Art Banking News*, no. 3/4, September 2003.

Asthoff, Jens. "Teresa Hubbard und Alexander Birchler in der Galerie Vera Munro." *Kunstbulletin*, December 2003.

Berg, Roland. "Crash! Surrealismus der Amerikanischen Seele: Künstler duo Teresa Hubbard und Alexander Birchler bei Barbara Thumm." *Der Tagespiegel*, July 6, 2003.

Koerner von Gustorf, Oliver, und Brigitte Werneburg. "Teresa Hubbard / Alexander Birchler: 'Hard Boiled Wonderland' at Galerie Barbara Thumm." *Neue Review Art in Berlin*, no. 3, October 2003.

Peschke, Marc. "Gefangen in Gedächtnis." *Szene Hamburg*, October 2003.

Mack, Gerhard. "Der Augenblick, der ein Leben Verändert." *Art das Kunstmagazin*, September 2003.
Müller, Katrin Bettina. "Zukunft ist Vergangenheit." *Tip Magazine*, no. 13, 2003.
Hoffmann, Justin. "The Starting Line der Pinakothek der Moderne." *Kunstbulletin*, Jan/Feb 2003.
Stange, Raimar. "On Stage im Kunstverein und in der Villa Merkel." *Kunstbulletin*, Jan/Feb 2003.

2002 Bitterli, Konrad. "Schwebenden Bilder: Rätselhafte Narrationen Zu den Aktuellen Videoarbeiten von Hubbard / Birchler." *Parkett*, no. 65, September 2002.
Cabello, Helena, and Ana Carceller. "At Short Distances: Notes on Collaborative Artistic Creation." *Exit*, no. 7, 2002.
Goldie, Kaelen Wilson. "Wild Walls." *Dutch*, no. 38, March/April 2002.
Puvogel, Renate. "Rätselhafte Szenen ohne Anfang und Ende." *Frame*, no. 10, January/March 2002.
Rauterberg, Hanno. "Eine Tiefgekühlte Sehnsucht." *Die Zeit*, December 2002.
Sailer, Alexia. "Vom Gefühl zur Meta-Reflexion." *Südkurier*, June 6, 2002.
Schoch, Ursula Badrutt. "Zwischenraum zur Wildnis." St. Galler *Tagblatt*, June 4, 2002.
Smith, Roberta. "Teresa Hubbard and Alexander Birchler." *New York Times*, February 15, 2002.
Spiegler, Marc. "Teresa Hubbard and Alexander Birchler." *ARTnews*, vol. 101/no. 1, January 2002.
Valdez, Sarah. "Teresa Hubbard and Alexander Birchler at Tanya Bonakdar." *Art in America*, no. 10, October 2002.
Wisse, Jan. "Na de Angst: De Jongste Richting in de Beeldende Kunst Volgens Basel 2002." *Pulchri*, no. 4, 2002.

2001 Macchi de Vilhena, Catherine. "Scène de la Vie Conjugale." *Art Press*, no. 266, March 2001.
Puvogel, Renate. "Rätselhafte Szenen ohne Anfang und Ende." *Frame*, December 2001.
Robinson, Joel. "Anti-Memory: Contemporary Photography II at the Yokohama Museum of Art." *Asian Art News*, vol. 11, no. 2, March/April 2001.
Sommer, Tim. "Mit den Waffen des Kinos." *Art das Kunstmagazin*, no. 9, September 2001.

2000 Blume, Eugen. "Narziss hat das Kino Erfunden." *Museums Journal*, no. 111, July, 2000.
Braun, Adrienne. "Nervöse Bilderschau." *Stuttgarter Zeitung*, October 4, 2000.
Braun, Adrienne. "Schnitzelljagd der Einsamen." *Süddeutsche Zeitung*, October 25, 2000.
Brunold, Georg. "Dein Bild ist Dir Nicht Ähnlich: ein Realistisches Ammenmärchen." *Du Magazin*, no. 708, July/August, 2000.
Forstbauer, Nikolai B. "Die Kunst Findet Doch im Saale Statt." *Stuttgarter Nachrichten*, September 30, 2000.
Heueiux, Guy. "The Montreal Biennale." *Canadian Art Magazine*, vol. 17, no. 3, Fall 2000.
Hoffmann, Gabriele. "18 Monate Einsamkeit." *Frankfurter Rundschau*, October 12, 2000.
Hunt, David. "Teresa Hubbard and Alexander Birchler: Arsenal." *Time Out New York*, October 12–19, 2000.
Maurer, Ruth. "The Unique Encounter Between the Ordinary and the Alien." *BE Magazine*, no. 6, October, 2000.
Ulmer, Brigitte. "Shooting Stars." *Bolero Magazin*, no. 4, April, 2000.

1999 Böker, Carmen. "In Kafkas Raum." *Berliner Zeitung*, July 24, 1999.
Kaiser, Philipp. "Gregor's Room." *Camera Austria*, no. 65, 1999.
Krienke, Mary. "Building Pictures." *Swiss News*, June 1999.
Meier, Philipp. "Ein Menschenzimmer." *Neue Zürcher Zeitung*, June 3, 1999.
Müller, Katrin Bettina. "Neue Videoarbeiten von Teresa Hubbard und Alexander Birchler." *Der Tagesspiegel*, July 24, 1999.
Nicholson, Tom. "Signs of Life: Melbourne International Biennial 1999." *Art and Australia*, vol. 36, no. 4, 1999.
Reust, Hans Rudolph. "Teresa Hubbard and Alexander Birchler at Gallery Bob van Orsouw." *Artforum*, October 1999
Schenk-Sorge, Jutta. "Teresa Hubbard und Alexander Birchler: Motion Pictures." *Kunstforum*, no. 147 September/November, 1999.
Ursprung, Philip. "Viewmaster: New Photographs by Teresa Hubbard and Alexander Birchler." *Camera Austria*, no. 65, 1999.

1998 Kaiser, Philipp. "Freie Sicht aufs Mittelmeer: Junge Schweizer Kunst." *Eikon Internationale Zeitschrift für Photographie & Medienkunst*, no. 25, 1998.
Krienke, Mary. "Teresa Hubbard and Alexander Birchler." *ART News*, May 1998.
Mack, Gerhard. "Junge Kunst Soll Berge Versetzen." *Cash Zeitung*, no. 23, May 6, 1998.
Spinelli, Claudia. ":Nonchalance Revisited." *Kunstforum*, no. 142, October–December 1998.

1997 Beil, Ralf. "Kleine Gesten Ganz Gross: Hubbard und Birchler in Basel." *Neue Zürcher Zeitung*, March 29–30, 1997.
Müller, Hans-Joachim. "Die Pause, der Patzer oder Was die Lücke Lehrt." *Basler Zeitung*, March 13, 1997.
Spinnelli, Claudia. "Slow Place: zu den Arbeiten von Hubbard und Birchler." *Kunstbulletin*, March 1997.

1996 His, Claudia. "Schnittstellen des Alltäglichen: Teresa Hubbard und Alexander Birchler." *Neue Bildende Kunst*, no. 3, June/July, 1996.

1994 Reck, Hans Ulrich. "Konstruktionen des Erinnerns." *Kunstforum*, no. 127, July 1994.

Acknowledgments

Sound Speed Marker
Ballroom Marfa
February 28–October 26, 2014

Sound Speed Marker and its programs have been made possible by the generous support of the Andy Warhol Foundation for the Visual Arts; L & M Charitable Foundation, Inc.; National Endowment for the Arts; Texas Commission on the Arts; The Moody Foundation; the Aargauer Kuratorium, Switzerland; and The Brown Foundation, Inc., Houston.

With underwriting support provided by Charles Attal, Suzanne Deal Booth, J. Travis Capps, Jr., Molly Kemp, Jeanne & Mickey Klein, John Thornton, Melba & Ted Whatley and Ballroom Marfa members.

In-kind support provided by Lance Armstrong, Big Bend Brewing Company, Rob Crowley, Quality Quinn, Charles Mary Kubricht & Ron Sommers, and the Marfa Visitor Center. Additional support provided by the Blaffer Art Museum at the University of Houston, Irish Museum of Modern Art, Lora Reynolds Gallery, Tanya Bonakdar Gallery and William & Bettye Nowlin Research Fellowship in Photography at the University of Texas at Austin.

Special thanks to AEP Texas, Francesca Altamura, Skye Ashbrook, Lalo Baeza, Brice Beasley, Jennifer Bell, the *Big Bend Sentinel*, Michael Camacho, Joe Cashiola, Ross Cashiola, Rob Crowley, JD DiFabbio, Dan Dunlap, Hilary duPont, Boyd Elder, the Evans family, Fat Lyle's, Cuca Flores, Frama, Mahala Guevara, Bill Haddad, Nicki Ittner, Erin Kimmel, Gerry Luján, Melissa McDonnell Luján, Marfa Public Radio, Rosa McElheny, Nicolas Miller, Minerva Lopez, William Parrott, Francisco Rosas, Gory Smelley, Jennifer Trammell, Junie Villareal, Sam Winks and WNP Industries.

Ballroom Marfa Staff

Fairfax Dorn Artistic Director
Susan Sutton Executive Director
Katherine Shaughnessy Deputy Director
Daniel Chamberlin Communications Director
Rebecca McGivney Gallery Manager
Irma Salgado Bookkeeper

Sound Speed Marker
Irish Museum of Modern Art, Dublin
December 5, 2014–May 4, 2015

The presentation of *Sound Speed Marker* at the Irish Museum of Modern Art, Dublin is made possible, in part, by Pro Helvetia; the Swiss Embassy in Ireland; the Department of Arts, Heritage and the Gaeltacht; the Irish Film Institute; and the Dylan Hotel, Dublin.

Special thanks to Gerard Byrne, Maeve Connolly and Sarah Pierce.

Irish Museum of Modern Art Exhibition Team

Sarah Glennie Director
Rachael Thomas Senior Curator
Seán Kissane Curator, Exhibitions
Cillian Hayes Technical Crew Supervisor
Edmond Kiely Lead Technician
Paul Hallahan Exhibitions Assistant
Sophie Byrne Assistant Curator, Talks and Lectures

Irish Museum of Modern Art Patrons

Emma Goltz, Brian Murray, Jonathan Ellis-King, Gearoid O'Faherty, John & Catherine Field, Maurice G. Collins, David Barniville, Denis Mortell, Bank of America, Mason, Hayes & Curran

Sound Speed Marker
Blaffer Art Museum, University of Houston
May 31–September 5, 2015

The presentation of *Sound Speed Marker* at the Blaffer Art Museum, University of Houston is made possible, in part, by the Cecil Amelia Blaffer von Furstenberg Endowment for Exhibitions and Programs and the Houston Endowment, with additional support from Major Exhibition Fund sponsors Leslie and Brad Bucher, William J. Hill and Jane Dale Owen. Additional support comes from the City of Houston through the Houston Arts Alliance, Texas Commission on the Arts, the Jo and Jim Furr Exhibition Endowment at Blaffer Art Museum and the George and Mary Josephine Hamman Foundation.

Blaffer Art Museum Staff

Claudia Schmuckli Director and Chief Curator
Youngmin Chung Chief Registrar and Exhibition Manager
Emily Church Director of Development, College of Liberal Arts and Social Sciences
Michael Guidry Curator of University Art Collection
Teresa Munisteri Assistant Registrar and Installation Manager
Tabitha Peters Security Coordinator
James Rosengren Deputy Director
Tracy E. Smith Director of Development and Membership
Katherine Veneman Curator of Education
Karen Zicterman Museum Administrator
Devon Britt-Darby Director of External Affairs

Blaffer Art Museum Advisory Board

Ex-Officio Members

Lifetime Members

Reproduction Credits

All photographs are by Hubbard/Birchler Studio unless otherwise noted.

Frontispiece, Contents, Pages 125, 231: Adam Schreiber
Introduction, Page 195: Chris Austin
Pages 4–9, 34–35, 74–75, 88–89, 104–105, 130–131, 140–141, 158–159, 170–171, 174–175, 199, 208-209: Fredrik Nilsen Studio
Page 16: Courtesy Vocalion, Decca Records, New York
Page 17, top: Courtesy Universal City Studios, Los Angeles
Pages 19, 70: David Aebi, Courtesy Aargauer Kunsthaus, Aarau
Pages 20, 29: Courtesy Margaret Herrick Library, Academy of Motion Picture Arts and Sciences, Los Angeles
Page 21, bottom: Santiago Forero
Page 22, left: Courtesy United Artists Picture
Pages 22, right, 30, bottom, 193: Courtesy Warner Bros. Inc.
Page 24: Courtesy the Evans Family, Ryan, Texas
Page 30, top: © 2014 Wim Wenders Foundation
Page 31: Jack Lewis, Courtesy Texas Department of Transportation, Media Production Library, Austin
Page 68, top: Museum Boijmans Van Beuningen, Rotterdam. Photographer: Studio Tromp, Rotterdam
Page 68, bottom: © 2000 Isaac Julien, Courtesy ArtPace, San Antonio
Page 113: Martin Bühler, Courtesy Museum für Gegenwartskunst Basel
Pages 114, 115, 218: Jean Vong, Courtesy Tanya Bonakdar Gallery, New York
Page 119: Courtesy Hudspeth County Courthouse, Sierra Blanca
Pages 122, 123: Courtesy Perry-Castañeda Library Map Collection, University of Texas at Austin
Page 122: Estate of Robert Smithson, Courtesy James Cohan Gallery, New York. © Estate of Robert Smithson/Licensed by VAGA, New York, NY
Page 127: Courtesy, Tulsa Library, Chapman Research Center, Oklahoma
Page 191: © 2004 David Armstrong
Page 192: Courtesy Warner Bros. Archives, University of Southern California, School of Cinematic Arts, Los Angeles
Page 211: Colin Doyle
Page 213: Courtesy Pinakothek der Moderne, Munich

We would like to thank all those who gave their kind permission to reproduce material. All reasonable efforts have been made to obtain copyright permission for the images in this book. The publishers apologize for any inadvertent errors or ommissions.

Thank You Note

It is essential that artists have the opportunity to create new work. The Aargauer Kuratorium, Alturas Foundation, Ballroom Marfa and the Modern Art Museum of Fort Worth are institutions embodying this fundamental premise and we are extremely grateful for their unwavering support in the creation of works that make up *Sound Speed Marker*. We also want to express our deep gratitude to Fairfax Dorn at Ballroom Marfa, Seán Kissane at the Irish Museum of Modern Art, Dublin, and Claudia Schmuckli at the Blaffer Art Museum, University of Houston, for their dedication in bringing this exhibition to their respective institutions. We deeply appreciate their thoughtful contributions to this book, as well as the astute questions and essays contributed by Anne Ellegood, Jeffrey Kastner and Inka Graeve Ingelmann.

Creating our video work involves the dedication and creative resources of a number of individuals. We are grateful to all the people who have helped along the way. Specific mention goes out to Skye Ashbrook, our Studio Manager, for his tenacity, late nights and deep caring in overseeing every aspect of the productions in this exhibition project. Bill Haddad contributed invaluable technical expertise, making the video and audio presentation of *Sound Speed Marker* possible. Wilson Waggoner, our Director of Photography, worked tirelessly alongside us on this trilogy over a period of five years. We appreciate his perceptive eye and the relationship we've developed by working together for more than a decade. We are grateful to María Clara García, our former Assistant Editor, for her attention to detail and tireless sense of humor.

We wish to thank Julie Savasky and DJ Stout from Pentagram, for their creative input and expertise in the catalogue design as well as Andrea Codrington Lippke for her close reading and editorial attention to detail.

We value our long-standing, special relationship with Tanya Bonakdar and Lora Reynolds and we are deeply grateful to them and their wonderful staff at their respective galleries for the support of this exhibition and publication.

Finally, we extend a special thanks to Sara Arrhenius, Suzanne Deal Booth, Adam Budak, Hans D. Christ, Francesca Consagra, Iris Dressler, Louis Grachos, Alison de Lima Green, Philipp Kaiser, Andrea Karnes, Jeanne and Michael Klein, Lutz Koepnik, Benjamin Lima, Ralph McKay, Vera Munro, Yasufumi Nakamori, Bob van Orsouw, Heather Pesanti, Veronica Roberts, Madeleine Schuppli and Barbara Thumm, for their support, ongoing dialogue and critical feedback during the process of completing the works in *Sound Speed Marker* and this publication.

Teresa Hubbard and Alexander Birchler

Colophon

Published by

Ballroom Marfa
PO Box 1661
108 E San Antonio Street
Marfa, Texas 79843
www.ballroommarfa.org

Blaffer Art Museum, University of Houston
3401 Cullen Blvd
Houston, TX 77004
www.blafferartmuseum.org

Irish Museum of Modern Art, Dublin
Royal Hospital, Military Road, Kilmainham
Dublin 8, Ireland
www.imma.ie

Distributed by

D.A.P. Distributed Art Publishers
155 Sixth Avenue
New York, NY 10013
www.artbook.com
Tel. 212 627 1999

Translation by Elizabeth Tucker

Library of Congress Control Number: 2014957059
ISBN 978-1-938922-82-4

Printed in China through Asia Pacific

Text set in Calibre

Exhibition concept by Fairfax Dorn, Seán Kissane, Claudia Schmuckli and Hubbard / Birchler Studio

Book concept by Hubbard / Birchler Studio
Book design by Julie Savasky and DJ Stout, Pentagram, Austin, Texas

BALLROOM MARFA

Irish Museum of Modern Art
Áras Nua-Ealaíne na hÉireann

BLAFFER ART MUSEUM
UNIVERSITY of HOUSTON

AARGAUER KURATORIUM

swiss arts council
prohelvetia

Texas Commission on the Arts

MOODY FOUNDATION

The Andy Warhol Foundation for the Visual Arts

HOUSTON ENDOWMENT
A PHILANTHROPY ENDOWED BY JESSE H. AND MARY GIBBS JONES

dylan

haa houstonartsalliance

THE BROWN FOUNDATION, INC.

ART WORKS.
National Endowment for the Arts
arts.gov

DATE DUE
